A Thematic Guide to Optimality Theory

This book describes Optimality Theory from the top down, explaining and exploring the central premises of OT and the results that follow from them. Examples are drawn from phonology, morphology, and syntax, but the emphasis throughout is on the theory rather than the examples, on understanding what is special about OT and on equipping readers to apply it, extend it, and critique it in their own areas of interest. To enhance the book's usefulness for researchers in allied disciplines, the top-down view of OT extends to work on first- and second-language acquisition, phonetics and functional phonology, computational linguistics, historical linguistics, and sociolinguistics. Furthermore, to situate OT for those coming from other traditions, this book also contains much discussion of OT's intellectual origins, its predecessors, and its contemporary competitors.

Each chapter concludes with extensive suggestions for further reading, classified by topics and supplemented by a massive bibliography (more than 800 items). The book ends with a list of frequently asked questions about Optimality Theory, with brief answers and pointers to a fuller treatment in the text.

John J. McCarthy began his work on Optimality Theory in 1992, when he received a Guggenheim Fellowship to support his research on prosodic morphology. He is the author of *Formal Problems in Semitic Phonology and Morphology* (1985) and has coedited three books, including *The Logical Problem of Language Acquisition* (1981). Dr. McCarthy has served on the editorial boards of *Language, Linguistic Inquiry, Natural Language and Linguistic Theory*, and *Phonology*.

Research Surveys in Linguistics

In large domains of theoretical and empirical linguistics, scholarly communication needs are directly comparable to those in analytical and natural sciences. Conspicuously lacking in the inventory of publications for linguists, compared to those in the sciences, are concise, single-authored, non-textbook reviews of rapidly evolving areas of inquiry. Research Surveys in Linguistics is intended to fill this gap. It consists of well-indexed volumes that survey topics of significant theoretical interest on which there has been a proliferation of research in the last two decades. The goal is to provide an efficient overview and entry into the primary literature for linguists – both advanced students and researchers – who wish to move into, or stay literate in, the areas covered. Series authors are recognized authorities on the subject matter as well as clear, highly organized writers. Each book offers the reader relatively tight structuring in sections and subsections and a detailed index for ease of orientation.

A Thematic Guide to Optimality Theory

JOHN J. McCARTHY

University of Massachusetts, Amherst

CAMBRIDGE
UNIVERSITY PRESS

PUBLISHED BY THE PRESS SYNDICATE OF THE UNIVERSITY OF CAMBRIDGE
The Pitt Building, Trumpington Street, Cambridge, United Kingdom

CAMBRIDGE UNIVERSITY PRESS
The Edinburgh Building, Cambridge CB2 2RU, UK
40 West 20th Street, New York, NY 10011-4211, USA
10 Stamford Road, Oakleigh, VIC 3166, Australia
Ruiz de Alarcón 13, 28014 Madrid, Spain
Dock House, The Waterfront, Cape Town 8001, South Africa

http://www.cambridge.org

First published 2002

Printed in the United Kingdom at the University Press, Cambridge

Typefaces Times Roman 10/12 pt. and Franklin Gothic   *System* QuarkXPress [BTS]

A catalog record for this book is available from the British Library.

Library of Congress Cataloging in Publication Data
McCarthy, John J., 1953–
A thematic guide to optimality theory / John J. McCarthy.
p.   cm. – (Research surveys in linguistics)
Includes bibliographical references and index.
ISBN 0-521-79194-4 (hb) – ISBN 0-521-79644-X (pb)
1. Optimality theory (Linguistics)   I. Title.   II. Series.
P158.42 .M43   2001
410′.1–dc21
00–069655

ISBN   0 521 79194 4   hardback
ISBN   0 521 79644 X   paperback

Contents

How to Use This Book

This book is one of a series called Research Surveys in Linguistics, the goal of which is to provide compact overviews of the background to and current state of the art in an area of linguistics. The series is addressed to graduate students and professionals in linguistics and allied fields.

In this book, I am trying to explain Optimality Theory in a way that is both accurate and accessible. I want to be faithful to the preciseness that is one of OT's attributes, but at the same time I want to avoid letting the details of particular analyses distract from the main message. And in keeping with the plan for the series Research Surveys, I also have to be concise. For these reasons, this book is organized thematically, focusing on concepts and general results rather than phenomena.

To make this book more useful, I have given it a lot of structure. Because some readers might want to use it as a reference or as an adjunct to a textbook, it is divided into relatively small sections. These can be read on their own because there are literally hundreds of cross-references of the form §x.y, where x is the chapter and y the section. To make room for ample bibliography without overburdening the text, I have kept in-text citations to a bare minimum. Instead, the text frequently contains the annotation 📖$_{§x.y¶n}$. This directs readers to paragraph n in section y, which is the last section of chapter x. There they will find extensive suggestions for further reading, organized by topic. And because these suggestions are useless unless the readings are readily available, they are limited to publications, technical reports and working papers, doctoral dissertations, and materials downloadable from the Rutgers Optimality Archive or other Internet sites. (There are a few exceptions, when there is no other way to acknowledge a seminal contribution.)

Readers who are interested in a specific topic can use the table of contents or the index to head straight for the relevant section and then work outward from there using the cross-references and the suggested readings. Readers who have been puzzled or put off by certain aspects of OT might want to start with the list of frequently asked questions (the FAQs) at the back of the book. These questions were compiled from various sources over the years: my own doubts and misunderstandings from the 1991 course where I first encountered OT; University of Massachusetts students taking my courses since 1992; suggestions from colleagues and from the reviewers of my book proposal; audiences at lectures I've given; publications; and the Optimal List discussion forum (optimal@ucsd.edu). The FAQs give short answers to the questions and refer to more detailed discussion in the text.

Introductory graduate linguistics courses are organized around fields like phonology or syntax rather than theories like OT. For that reason, publishers provide textbooks focused on phonology or syntax. This book is different, which is why it would not be suitable as the sole textbook in one of those courses. But I hope this book would be helpful as an adjunct to the traditional textbook or as a supplement to materials prepared by the instructor. A particular reader I have kept in mind while writing is the graduate student who has finished a semester or two of coursework, has seen some applications of OT, and is looking for help in putting it all together.

Here is some advice about how to negotiate one's way through this book. Begin by reading §1.1 and §1.2 very lightly, getting the general idea but not sweating the details. (In fact, it is best to skip §1.2.3 entirely at this stage.) Then read §1.3 and §1.4 more attentively, trying to work through and understand the basic results and techniques. After that, it might help to reread §1.1 and §1.2, but more closely. (It is probably best to skip §1.2.3 once again.) After this introduction, readers are prepared to forage throughout the rest of the book. If the goal is an understanding in depth of OT, then §3 should get the most attention, since it presents and illustrates the broad consequences of the theory. (And §3.1.5.4 says when it's best to read §1.2.3!)

I have written this book for readers who understand the goals of linguistic theory and the nature of linguistic argumentation but are not necessarily specialized in a field like phonology or syntax. I have tried to get a balance of examples from phonology, morphology, and syntax. The examples are always there to illustrate some point about OT as a theory; they are never intended to show how to analyze some particular phenomenon and should not be read or used as such. The examples and the associated constraints are nearly always simplified, so readers interested in the phenomenon itself and the unexpurgated analysis need to consult the original source (always cited nearby) and the related readings at the end of the chapter.

Improvements and additions will be made available on the author's webpage, http://www.umass.edu/linguist/faculty/mccarthy.html. Comments and suggestions are welcome – e-mail me at jmccarthy@linguist.umass.edu.

Acknowledgments

I have been fortunate to receive much help during the past year and a half. I owe a lot to Christine Bartels, formerly of Cambridge University Press, for first suggesting this project to me, for her guidance, and for supplying me with seven often wise and always helpful anonymous reviews. In addition, Jane Grimshaw, Alan Prince, Paul Smolensky, and Ellen Woolford gave valuable feedback about the original proposal. Later on, the following persons read portions of the manuscript and gave me extensive advice about how to improve it: John Alderete, Eric Bakovic, Jill Beckman, Andries Coetzee, Stuart Davis, Paul de Lacy, Jane Grimshaw, René Kager, Ed Keer, John Kingston, Linda Lombardi, Elliott Moreton, Scott Myers, Jaye Padgett, Steve Parker, Joe Pater, Alan Prince, Vieri Samek-Lodovici, Jen Smith, Shin-ichi Tanaka, Bruce Tesar, Suzanne Urbanczyk, and Ellen Woolford. Linda Lombardi and Jane Grimshaw deserve special mention; Linda read the manuscript twice, giving me extensive comments both times, and Jane generously shared many of her ideas. Della Chambless, Paul de Lacy, Maria Gouskova, Ania Lubowicz, and Monica Sieh helped with the proofreading and indexing. Merely listing their names is an inadequate indication of my gratitude to all of these colleagues and students; it doesn't begin to do justice to the quantity and quality of the criticisms I received from them. Of course, I alone am responsible for everything here.

The initial planning of this book was done under a National Science Foundation grant (BNS-9420424) and the writing was made possible by a sabbatical from the University of Massachusetts, Amherst. I am in addition grateful to Dean Lee R. Edwards of the College of Humanities and Fine Arts for indispensable research support.

This book is dedicated to the memory of my father, John J. McCarthy (July 17, 1925–February 13, 1997). "They will rise up on wings like eagles; they will run and not grow weary; and they will walk and not be faint."

Prologue

Optimality Theory (OT) was first described in depth by its creators, Alan Prince and Paul Smolensky, in a course presented at the University of California, Santa Cruz, in 1991 (Prince and Smolensky 1991). The first detailed exposition of the theory appears in Prince and Smolensky (1993). Since 1993, there has been a great deal of interest in this emerging theory; it has been the subject of a large and growing literature, an extensive electronic archive (http://roa.rutgers.edu), many courses and conference papers, and several textbooks. Although it was originally applied to phonology, the relevance of OT to topics in morphology, syntax, sociolinguistics, psycholinguistics, and semantics has become increasingly apparent.

One of the most compelling features of OT, in my view, is the way that it unites description of individual languages with explanation of language typology. As a phonologist, I have always been impressed and sometimes overwhelmed by how the complexity and idiosyncrasy of each language's phonology is juxtaposed with the clarity and abundance of solid typological generalizations. Even though this is arguably the central research problem of phonology and of linguistic theory in general, progress in consolidating description and explanation has at best been halting and occasionally retrograde.

OT, though, is inherently typological: the grammar of one language inevitably incorporates claims about the grammars of all languages. This joining of the individual and the universal, which OT accomplishes through ranking permutation, is probably the most important insight of the theory. It comes up again and again throughout this book, as a core premise of the theory, as a discipline for practitioners, and as the source of many empirical results in phonology, syntax, and allied fields.

1

The Core of Optimality Theory

This chapter introduces the central premises of Optimality Theory. The chapter begins (§1.1) with the overall structure of OT, as proposed by Prince and Smolensky (1993).📖§1.5¶1 It continues with some general remarks about the nature of constraints (§1.2) and their modes of interaction through ranking (§1.3). These threads are joined to some practical suggestions for doing OT in §1.4. Readers encountering OT for the first time are advised not to read this chapter straight through; see "How to Use This Book" for a better plan of attack.

1.1 Basic Architecture

1.1.1 Candidate Comparison

Many theories of language can best be described as operational, rule based, or transformational: they take an input and apply some procedure that changes it into an output. But the primary action in OT is *comparative*: the actual output is the optimal member of a set of *candidate* output forms. Interesting analytic and theoretical results in OT come from understanding the details of how candidates are compared.

Candidates are compared by applying a hierarchy of violable constraints. The constraints assess the form of a candidate and its relationship to the input. Candidates inevitably differ in performance on various constraints. Of two candidates, the more *harmonic* is the one that performs better on the highest-ranking constraint that distinguishes between them. The actual output – the most harmonic or *optimal* candidate – is the one that is more harmonic in all its pairwise competitions with other candidates.[1]

Because constraints are violable, the output typically disobeys at least some of the lower-ranking constraints. To draw an analogy from ethics, optimality is more like moral relativism or the Three Laws of Robotics[2] than the Ten Commandments; it is about being the best among a choice of options, not about being objectively perfect. In the simplest situation, two candidates are under evaluation by a single constraint C. The optimal candidate is the one that incurs fewer violations of C. When there is more than one constraint, the ranking is strictly respected in comparing candidates; there is no global assessment of candidates based on their performance on the whole constraint gestalt. In fact, the optimal candidate may actually perform worse than its competitor on some constraint(s) ranked below the decisive one. So, if constraint C1 is ranked above C2 and C3 (that is, C1 *dominates* C2 and C3), then the output may perform worse than its competitor on both C2 and C3, as long as it performs better on C1. To cite an example from Prince and Smolensky (1993), "azzzzz" is alphabetized before "baaaaa" because alphabetical order is based on the leftmost distinguishing letter, regardless of how much the letters farther to the right might seem to encourage a different order.

This property, which Prince and Smolensky dub the *strictness of strict domination*, is somewhat counterintuitive, since it is quite unlike the more flexible system of priorities we apply in our everyday lives. For example, given a primary career goal of making lots of money and a secondary goal of living in an exciting city, few among us would stubbornly persist with these priorities when faced with offers of a job paying $61,000 in Paris, Texas, and a job paying $60,000 in Paris, France. Yet constraint ranking in OT has exactly that stubborn persistence. (Strict domination is the main difference between OT and connectionist models. See §2.4.)

Candidate comparison is often shown in a *tableau*, where an optimal candidate is compared with one or more of its competitors with respect to their performance on two or more constraints. A tableau therefore gives a perspicuous view of some of the constraints and rankings that are crucial in selecting a candidate as optimal. As in (1), constraints are given in domination order from left to right, and the rows contain the different candidates, one of which is optimal. The individual cells show the violation-marks (*) incurred by each candidate relative to each constraint. The optimal candidate is called out by the pointing hand.[3]

(1) A ranking argument

		C1	C2
a.	☞ Cand$_{Opt}$		*
b.	Cand$_{Comp}$	*	

Readers wanting to see real tableaux now can take a look at §1.3, and in §1.4.1 I discuss the practical aspects of ranking constraints, introducing another tableau format that is particularly useful for discovering rankings.

In (1), C1 and C2 conflict in their evaluation of two candidates. C1 prefers Cand$_{Opt}$, but C2 prefers the competitor Cand$_{Comp}$. Since Cand$_{Opt}$ is the observed output form, the conflict is resolved by ranking C1 above C2. A situation like this is a necessary condition for a valid *ranking argument*, a kind of proof that C1 dominates C2 in the hierarchy (written $[\![C1 \gg C2]\!]$). To ensure sufficient conditions for the validity of a ranking argument, it is also necessary to check that there is no constraint C3 with both of the following properties: C3 is ranked above C2, and C3 concurs with C1 by preferring $Cand_{Opt}$. In that situation, C3 invalidates the argument for $[\![C1 \gg C2]\!]$ because C3 can also produce the effect of the ranking being argued for.[4]

Conflict is not the only possible relation between two constraints, but it is the only relation that can serve as the basis for a valid ranking argument. In the situations shown in (2a–c), there is no conflict between the constraints and so there is no basis for ranking them.

(2) a. C1 and C2 agree

		C1	C2
i.	☞ $Cand_{Opt}$		
ii.	$Cand_{Comp}$	*	*

b. C1 does not distinguish the candidates (both obey it)

		C1	C2
i.	☞ $Cand_{Opt}$		
ii.	$Cand_{Comp}$		*

c. C1 does not distinguish the candidates (both violate it)

		C1	C2
i.	☞ $Cand_{Opt}$	*	
ii.	$Cand_{Comp}$	*	*

These tableaux separate the constraint columns with a dotted line to show that neither constraint provably dominates the other. These tableaux will not support a ranking argument because C1 and C2 concur in eliminating $Cand_{Comp}$ (2a) or one of them assesses both candidates as equally good or bad (2b–c).

A constraint may assign more than one violation-mark to a candidate in one of two situations: either the constraint is violated at several different spots in the candidate under evaluation (e.g., the constraint assesses some aspect of syllable form, and a polysyllabic word contains several offenders, as in (14d)), or the constraint is violated gradiently, distinguishing noncompliant candidates by extent of violation (as is the case with edge Alignment constraints (§1.2.3)). As

OT is presently understood, multiple violations from either source are usually treated the same; they are just lumped together in the pile of violation-marks assigned to a candidate.

Candidate comparison is no different when there are multiple violations, and there is no need to count violation-marks, since better or worse performance is all that matters. Driving this point home, Prince and Smolensky introduce the *method of mark cancellation.*⊞§1.5¶2 If and only if a tableau compares exactly two candidates, violation-marks that the two candidates share can be ignored or *canceled*, since those violation-marks contribute nothing to that particular comparison. For example, both candidates in (2c) share a violation-mark in the C1 column. These shared marks can be canceled, reducing (2c) to (2b). By reducing (2c) in this way, we can readily see that C1 contributes nothing to selecting the optimal candidate. Though this example involves single violations, mark cancellation is also useful when candidates incur multiple violations: if one candidate has three violation-marks from some constraint and another candidate has five, mark cancellation reduces this to zero and two, respectively. Comparison, rather than counting, is what matters.

Mark cancellation cannot be meaningfully applied to tableaux with more than two candidates since its purpose is to bring out the better and the worse in a pairwise comparison. With several candidates in play, it is better to use the comparative tableau format described in §1.4.1.

1.1.2 Ranked Constraints and EVAL

Winning isn't everything. It's the only thing.
– Attributed to Vince Lombardi

The grammar of a language is a specific constraint ranking. Language-particular ranking is the most important and perhaps only method in OT for explaining how and why languages differ from one another (§3.1.5). The ranking in a particular language is, in theory, a total ordering of a set of universal constraints.

In practice, though, it is not usually possible to discover a total ordering, and so the analyst must be satisfied with a partial ordering. There are just two legitimate ways of showing that C1 dominates C2: by a valid direct ranking argument like (1) or by a legitimate inference from valid direct ranking arguments. An example of the latter is a ranking argument based on transitivity of constraint domination, such as showing that C1 dominates C3 by establishing that C1 dominates C2 and that C2 dominates C3.[5] When direct and inferred arguments for ranking are both present, they have to agree. Otherwise the analysis or the theory is just plain wrong. But when there is no evidence or inference available for ranking certain constraints, it is good analytic practice to report a partial order, as in (11) in §1.3.2. Partial ordering in the absence of constraint conflict is not the same thing as deliberate *ties* between conflicting constraints.

Tied rankings are a proposed extension of standard OT to account for within-language variation (§4.5).

Under the assumption that all constraints are universal (§1.2.1), the ranking is all that the learner must discover, and learning some workable ranking turns to be a surprisingly easy task (§4.2.1). The analyst's job is much harder than the learner's: ranking arguments need to be discovered and their validity checked in a context where all hypotheses about universal constraints are necessarily tentative and mutable. Still, there are some useful heuristics to follow when positing or assessing proposed constraints (§1.4.4).

Suppose H is the constraint hierarchy for some language. To use H to select the most harmonic member of some candidate set, OT calls on the function EVAL, which gives meaning to the domination relation "≫," generalizing pairwise comparison to larger (possibly infinite) sets of candidates. The function EVAL returns the candidate set as a partial order, with its most harmonic member, the actual output form, standing at the top.📖 §1.5¶1

In theory, there is no guarantee that EVAL will always return a single most harmonic member of the candidate set. Suppose two candidates incur identical violation-marks from all constraints. EVAL will be unable to decide between them, and if no other candidate is more harmonic, both will be optimal. In this case, within-language variation ought to be observed. In practice, though, this possibility might not be easy to realize; the universal constraint set is rich enough that EVAL usually returns a unique winner for any real-life H applied to any real-life candidate set. For this reason, within-language variation has usually been analyzed in other ways (§4.1.3, §4.5).[6]

Although EVAL imposes a harmonic ordering on all the candidates, the standard approach assigns no interpretation to the details of the ordering below the topmost candidate. Suppose EVAL returns the harmonic ordering $[\![Cand_{Opt} \succ Cand_{Comp1} \succ Cand_{Comp2}]\!]$, where $\succ$ denotes the relation "is more harmonic than." From this, we know that $Cand_{Opt}$ is the actual output form, but nothing can be concluded from the relative harmony of $Cand_{Comp1}$ and $Cand_{Comp2}$ – only the optimum is given a linguistic interpretation. This is an important methodological point: valid ranking arguments like (1) must always involve an actual output form as one of the candidates being compared.

Samek-Lodovici and Prince (1999: 18) have a particularly clear and insightful way of describing EVAL.[7] Think of a constraint as a function from sets of candidates to sets of candidates. Each constraint takes a set of candidates and returns the subset consisting of those candidates that perform best on that constraint. EVAL can then be understood in terms of *function composition*: a lower-ranking constraint takes as input the set of best performers on the higher-ranking constraint. For instance, if the set of candidates {Cands} and the hierarchy $[\![C1 \gg C2]\!]$ are handed to EVAL, then the set of winners will be given by $(C2 \circ C1)(\{Cands\})$ or equivalently $C2(C1(\{Cands\}))$. Since a constraint can never return less than one best performer, this formalization of EVAL correctly guarantees at least one winner. It also allows for the theoretical possibility of more than one winner when the outermost constraint returns a set containing two or more candidates. This formalization conforms rather well to the usual intuitive sense of how EVAL works: first it applies the highest-ranking (or inner-most) constraint, then the next highest, and then the next, downward through the hierarchy (or outward through the composed functions) until there are no constraints left.

1.1.3 GEN

Thus far I have described two of the main components of OT, the language-particular constraint hierarchy H and the universal function EVAL, which applies H to a set of candidates. There are two others: a putatively universal set of con-straints CON, discussed in §1.2, and the universal candidate generator GEN. The latter has two closely related functions: it constructs candidate output forms, such as words or sentences, and it specifies a relation between the candidate output forms and the input. Though details of the internal structure of GEN are still under development, the general principles underlying the theory of GEN are clear.📖 §1.5¶1

GEN is universal, meaning that the candidate forms emitted by GEN for a given input are the same in every language. These candidates are also very diverse. This property of GEN has been called *inclusivity* or *freedom of analysis*. Precisely because GEN is universal, it must at a minimum supply candidates varied enough to fit all of the ways in which languages can differ. For example, languages disagree in how they syllabify a consonant cluster like *br* (cf. English *alge.bra* vs. Arabic *jab.rī* 'algebraic'), so GEN will offer competing candidates that differ along this dimension, leaving the choice of the right one to the language-particular rankings in H. This freedom is limited only by primitive structural principles essential in every language, perhaps restricting GEN to a specific alphabet of distinctive features (in phonology) or to some version of X-bar theory (in syntax). Beyond this, the details of GEN are a matter for empirical investigation in the context of specific hypotheses about the nature of the input and the constraints. In phonology, there is a rough con-sensus about the properties of GEN (§1.1.3), but in syntax it is still more of an open question (§4.1).

Since GEN is the same in every language, it initially seems like a good place to deposit a wide variety of "hard" universals, beyond the bare structural prin-ciples just mentioned. For example, no known language syllabifies intervocalic *br* as *algebr.a*, so why not incorporate this observation into the statement of GEN? This strategy is a natural continuation of several decades of linguistic the-orizing that has sought to document various universal constraints and refine the statement of them. There is a flaw here, though. Hardwiring universals into GEN is inevitably a matter of brute-force stipulation, with no hope of explanation or connection to other matters – it is the end of discussion rather than the beginning. The right way to look at most universals in OT is in terms of the core idea of the theory: constraint interaction through ranking. By deriving universals and typology from constraint interaction, we ensure that there are connections between the universal properties of language and between-language variation, since both follow from the properties of constraint ranking. Interesting universals and successful explanations for them can indeed be obtained from constraint interaction (§3.1.5).[8]

GEN is also *input dependent*. The candidates emitted by GEN bear a determinate relation to some sort of input form, which might be a phonological underlying representation, a syntactic D-structure, or a morphosyntactic feature specification. The candidates record, by some means, how they differ from the input. This record is used by constraints that evaluate candidates for their faithfulness to the input (§1.2.2). Various implementations of this basic idea can be imagined and have been explored: candidates distinguish derived properties structurally, as in trace theory (Chomsky 1973); each candidate brings with it a function describing how it differs from the input; or each candidate brings with it a description of the operations that produced it from the input. Except for the need to maintain this record in some form, the theory of GEN, and of OT generally, has no special representational or operational commitments.

If GEN incorporates any recursive or iterative operations, as it surely must, then there is no bound on the size of a candidate and every candidate set, from every input, is infinite. This is perhaps not too surprising in syntax, where the infinity of sentences has long been accepted, but it is also true in phonology. Epenthesis is an iterative procedure of candidate-generation, so the set of candidates derived from input /ba/ must include *bati, batiti, batititi,* . . . No GEN-imposed bound on the number of epenthesis operations is appropriate. Rather, the economy of epenthesis should and does follow from constraint interaction (§3.2.3).

In this context, it is appropriate to point out that OT shares with the rest of generative grammar a commitment to *well-definition* but not to *efficient computation*. Here is how Chomsky has characterized that distinction:

> To avoid what has been a continuing misunderstanding, it is perhaps worth while to reiterate that a generative grammar is not a model for a speaker or a hearer. . . . When we say that a sentence has a certain derivation with respect to a particular generative grammar, we say nothing about how the speaker or hearer might proceed, in some practical or efficient way, to construct such a derivation. (Chomsky 1965: 9)
>
> [A]lthough we may describe the grammar *G* as a system of processes and rules that apply in a certain order to relate sound and meaning, we are not entitled to take this as a description of the successive acts of a performance model such as *PM* – in fact, it would be quite absurd to do so. (Chomsky 1968: 117)

> Recall that the ordering of operations is abstract, expressing postulated properties of the language faculty of the brain, with no temporal interpretation implied. (Chomsky 1995: 380 n. 3)

In short, a grammar is a function from some kind of input to some kind of output. A grammar is not an algorithm for computing that function nor is it a description of how speakers actually go about computing that function. Chomsky (1968: 117) sums up with "If these simple distinctions are overlooked, great confusion must result."

That confusion has sometimes led to skepticism about OT: how can EVAL sort an infinite set of candidates in finite time (cf. Bromberger and Halle 1997)? The error lies in asking how long EVAL takes to execute. It is entirely appropriate to ask whether EVAL, like Chomsky's *G*, is well defined, captures linguistically significant generalizations, and so on. But questions about execution time or other aspects of (neural) computation are properly part of the performance model *PM* and must be addressed as such. And, not too surprisingly, there are computational models for OT that do not require infinite time to execute (see §4.3 and the references in §4.6 ¶11).

1.1.4 Summary, with Possible Variations

The core universal elements of the OT architecture are summarized in (3).

(3) Basic OT architecture

GEN receives an input and emits a set of candidates that, in some precise way, depend upon the input. (There are also important things to say about the input itself – see §3.1.2.4.) EVAL applies the language-particular constraint hierarchy H to this candidate set, locating its most harmonic member. The most harmonic candidate is the output; it may be a phonological surface form, a syntactic S-Structure, or some other linguistic object.

The model in (3) is the simplest architecture compatible with OT's basic assumptions. It maximally exploits OT's capacity for *global, parallel* evaluation (§3.3). The output of an entire linguistic component, such as the phonology, is obtained from the input in a single pass through GEN and EVAL, which means that the candidates offered by GEN may show the effects of several notionally distinct processes simultaneously. The constraints applied by EVAL then rank these candidates for their global fitness, evaluating the effects of all of those processes in parallel. To see why it is described as global and parallel, compare this model to a theory like standard generative phonology (§2.1), where each rule applies in serial order and in isolation from all other rules coexisting in the grammar.

Some variations on this basic architecture reduce or eliminate the effects of global, parallel evaluation. Suppose that the output in (3) becomes the input for another pass through GEN, yielding a new set of candidates for evaluation. The most familiar version of this approach imposes a kind of modular or componential structure, treating the whole grammar of a language as a composite entity, as in Lexical Phonology or various instantiations of the Principles and Parameters (P&P) approach. Each module has its own distinct constraint hierarchy H_i and perhaps even its own set of universal constraints CON. The output of the final module in the series is the observed surface form of the language (§3.3.3.4).

Another version of this approach is called *harmonic serialism*. It applies the same constraint hierarchy at each pass through EVAL, continuing until there is convergence, when the output of one pass is identical to the output of the immediately preceding pass. Harmonic serialism unpacks some of the effects of globality and parallelism by imposing restrictions on GEN's freedom of analysis. See §3.3.2.8 and §3.3.3.2 for further discussion.

Refinements or extensions like these still have the essential elements of OT: EVAL-mediated comparison of candidates by a hierarchy of violable constraints. No matter how the details are executed or in what overall context it is embedded, any model with these indispensable characteristics will express the central claim and insight of OT.

1.2   The Theory of Constraints

1.2.1   The Universality of Constraints

Apart from the bare structural primitives embedded in GEN, all constraints in OT are in principle and in fact violable. This statement follows from the basic architecture of the theory: constraints have nowhere else to reside except in the language-particular hierarchy H, which means that any constraint could, in some language, be ranked below another constraint that compels it to be violated.

The null hypothesis is that all constraints are universal and universally present in the grammars of all languages (Prince and Smolensky 1993), and so UG incorporates a constraint component CON. What makes this the null hypothesis is a kind of Occamite reasoning: since language-particular ranking is in general able to account for languages where a putatively universal constraint does not hold true, it does not seem necessary to recognize a special class of language-particular constraints. (See §1.2.3 for some possible qualifications.) Differences between languages are no barrier to constraint universality when constraints are violable.

Constraint violability is a very different thing from parametrization. A parameter describes a requirement that is either reliably enforced or completely ignored: syllables must have onsets (yes/no); heads must precede/follow their complements. A constraint, no matter where it is ranked, always asserts its preference: ONSET is violated by any syllable that lacks an onset in any language, *tout court*. Whether it *visibly* asserts that preference depends on details of the language-particular ranking and the candidates under evaluation.

Suppose we say that a constraint is *active* if and only if it is the highest-ranking constraint that distinguishes some losing candidate from the winner. What we are talking about, then, is visible activity: every constraint, no matter where it is ranked, evaluates every candidate, but not every constraint will be visibly active. Whether a constraint is visibly active depends on the constraints that dominate it and the candidates that it evaluates. Even within a language, when different candidate sets from different inputs are considered, a constraint might be active sometimes and inactive otherwise. This middle ground of partial activity follows from the interactional nature of OT (§1.3, §3.1, §3.2), but it is difficult or impossible to achieve in parametric models. (See the FAQ about parameters for a list of places in the text where this important difference between ranking and parameters is discussed.)

Universal constraints and language-particular ranking yield a *factorial typology*, another key notion from Prince and Smolensky (1993). Every permutation of the constraints in CON is predicted to be a possible human language, and the grammar of every observed human language must be one of those permutations. There are, however, some minor qualifications. There is no guarantee that every permutation will yield an observably distinct human language. For example, if two constraints in CON happen never to conflict on any candidate, then switching their ranking will have no effect. CON may also include universally fixed constraint hierarchies related to natural linguistic scales (§1.2.3). These fixed hierarchies limit the typological consequences of ranking permutation – in fact, they are themselves supported by typological considerations. In deference to this, the term "permutation" is implicitly qualified by "licit" throughout this book.

Here is an analogy to help clarify the notion of a factorial typology. Imagine a mode of psychotherapy based on the hypothesis that each type of human personality reflects a different prioritization of four universal desires (such as love, wealth, progeny, and power). Since these desires are universal and there are $4! = 24$ different ways to rank them, there will be 24 distinct personality types. The goal of this psychotherapeutic modality is to determine how the analysand fits into this factorial typology. The "ranking arguments" consist of simple scenarios that involve clear choices between maximizing one desire or another – for instance, would you consider running for mayor if it meant giving up a better-paying but much less powerful job as a piano tuner, supposing that the choice had no effect either way on love or progeny?

Factorial typology makes a strong claim with important implications. It means, as a matter of simple methodological competence, that analysts must test every proposed constraint for its typological consequences under ranking permutation, and no phenomenon can be definitively analyzed in a particular language without considering cross-linguistic variation. OT's inherently typological character thus places severe conditions on the adequacy of proposed analyses.

1.2.2 Constraint Typology

Two basic types of constraints are distinguished in OT, *faithfulness* and *markedness*. Faithfulness constraints require identity between the input and the output candidate under evaluation, using the record of input/output disparity supplied by GEN (§1.1.3). Markedness constraints evaluate the form of the output candidate, favoring certain structural configurations (e.g., syllables with onsets, accusative objects) over others (e.g., syllables without onsets, dative objects). Constraints of both types are undoubtedly necessary. Without faithfulness constraints, all distinctions made by input forms would be reduced to some least-marked output (see the FAQ about unmarked form and *ba*). And without markedness constraints, there would be no way to account for languages differing systematically in the structures they permit (their *inventories* – §3.1.2). Interaction between faithfulness and markedness constraints is a key element of any OT analysis (§1.3).

In the earliest work on OT, markedness and faithfulness constraints were formally rather similar though notionally distinct. Faithfulness constraints were made to resemble markedness constraints by strictly limiting the kinds of mappings that GEN could perform. As in trace theory (Chomsky 1973) and some versions of autosegmental phonology (e.g., Selkirk 1981; Steriade 1982), surface forms were enriched to include covert structural indications of the unfaithful mappings that produced them. Phonological epenthesis involved a kind of overparsing: surface forms contained present-but-incomplete syllabic structures, as in Spanish /skwela/ → [Δskwela] for *escuela* 'school'. Phonological deletion involved underparsing: surface forms contained segments that were present but not syllabified, as in English /bamb/ → [bam⟨b⟩] *bomb* (cf. *bombard, bombardier*). These assumptions about GEN allowed the faithfulness constraints, like the markedness constraints, to evaluate surface structures alone. The faithfulness constraint FILL militated against empty segments like the [Δ] in [Δskwela], and its counterpart PARSE was violated by unsyllabified segments like the final [⟨b⟩] in *bomb*. (See §3.3.3.5 for further developments along these lines.)

These simplifying assumptions about faithfulness are obviously not necessary elements of OT, and when it proved difficult to extend the early PARSE/FILL model to the full range of phonological generalizations, alternatives were sought. The correspondence theory of faithfulness posits a correspondence relation ℜ from the input to each of its output candidates.📖§1.5¶3 For example, in the mapping /bat/ → *bati*, the candidate *bati* includes the information that *b*, *a*, and *t* correspond to segments of the input, but *i* does not. This is a violation of the constraint DEP, which says that ℜ must be surjective (onto), so every element of the output stands in correspondence with the input. Analogously, MAX militates against deletion, requiring that the inverse relation ℜ⁻¹ be surjective, so every element of the input is in correspondence with the output. (The names of these constraints allude mnemonically to their functions: the output

*dep*ends upon the input; the input is *max*imally expressed in the output.) Other
constraints of correspondence theory prohibit one-to-many mappings, many-to-
one mappings, and various other imaginable derangements of perfect identity
between input and output. (On further extensions of faithfulness, see §3.2.1.2,
and §3.3.3.5, and the references in §1.5 ¶3.)

Correspondence theory provides a general framework for stating constraints
that demand faithfulness to linguistic objects. A candidate is unfaithful whenever its associated correspondence relation describes anything other than an
order- and structure-preserving mapping that is one-to-one and onto. Research
continues on the details of what the faithfulness constraints are, but the general
outlines of the theory are fairly clear – in phonology at least.

In syntax, there is as yet no consensus on the form of faithfulness constraints: they might prohibit movement and other syntactic operations or require
accurate surface spell-out of underlying distinctions (such as morphosyntactic
features). A prohibition on movement is, of course, reminiscent of the Economy
principles of the Minimalist Program. For example, any metric that prefers
shorter derivations (as in Chomsky 1995: 138ff.) will roughly approximate the
effects of faithfulness constraints. There are differences though: this Economy
principle evaluates derivations, while faithfulness evaluates input → output
mappings; faithfulness constraints are typically a good deal more specific than
most proposed Economy principles; and Economy, unlike faithfulness, is seen
as having a functional basis in minimization of effort. See §4.1 for more about
faithfulness in syntax, §3.2.3 for some comparison of OT with Economy principles, and §4.4.2 for a proposed relation between minimization of effort and
markedness constraints in OT.

Markedness constraints evaluate output structures. Like the phrase "faithfulness constraint," the phrase "markedness constraint" is a term of art in OT:
it refers to any constraint that assigns violation-marks to a candidate based
solely on its output structure, without regard to its similarity to the input. A candidate is marked by or with respect to that constraint if it receives at least one
violation-mark from it.[9] For example, ONSET and SUBJECT are two markedness
constraints that have been proposed in the OT literature (§1.3.1, §3.1.4.8).
ONSET assigns a candidate one violation-mark for each vowel-initial syllable
that it contains, demanding instead that syllables begin with a consonant (called
the *onset*); SUBJECT assigns a candidate one violation-mark for each Spec-less
IP (= subjectless sentence) that it contains. These are typical markedness
constraints.

When they first encounter OT, many people share certain concerns about
constraints. Most of these concerns have a common source: the projection of
ideas about familiar constraints in other linguistic theories onto OT. Since faithfulness constraints are unique to OT, they do not bring this baggage with them;
the problem mostly involves markedness constraints. Here are some possible
misunderstandings and clarifications of the differences between OT constraints
and the constraints of other theories.

The technical sense of markedness, as used in OT, is distinct from and a good deal more specific than the more familiar usage of this word in linguistics, dating back to the Prague School of the 1930s: "The concept of markedness in its most general characterization is concerned with the distinction between what is neutral, natural, or most expected (UNMARKED), and what departs from the neutral (MARKED) along some designated parameter" (Kean 1992: 390). A markedness constraint in OT may produce results related to this descriptive or typological sense of markedness (§3.1), but the formal constraint and the typological observation are two different things.

This terminological ambiguity can be a source of considerable confusion. I once received the following advice from an anonymous referee for a prominent journal:

> My first comment addresses the discussion of segmental markedness: the primary evidence for markedness is implicational statements of the form: "If language L has structure *A*, it also has structure *B*". . . . In the absence of such implicational relations between *A* and *B*, there is no consensus on what should count as marked and why.

This reviewer is assuming that OT markedness is exactly the same thing as Praguian markedness, leading to confusion of OT as a *theory* with a Prague-inspired *methodology*. In OT, because constraints are violable and one markedness constraint can conflict with another (see the next two paragraphs), an observed implicational relation "*A* only if *B*" is a sufficient but not a necessary condition for positing a markedness constraint that *A* violates and *B* does not (see §3.1.1 and §3.1.5.4). Implicational relations, then, are not the "primary evidence" for markedness constraints; they are just one clue.[10] The real primary evidence for markedness constraints is the correctness of the typologies they predict under permuted ranking of the constraints in CON.

Mixing up these two different senses of markedness is also the source of another objection to OT: how is it possible for two markedness constraints to conflict with one another? The idea of markedness/faithfulness conflict is intuitively clear, but conflict among markedness constraints does not make sense from the Prague School perspective. Praguian markedness is married to implicational relations like "*A* only if *B*," so it is inherently unidimensional and non-conflicting: *A* is more marked than *B* in all languages under all circumstances. In OT, though, markedness is multidimensional – different constraints favor or disfavor different properties, and it would be astonishing if there were no conflicts. So, while CON may supply a constraint that *A* violates and *B* obeys, this by itself does not entail the implicational relation "*A* only if *B*," since there may be another markedness constraint in CON favoring *B* over *A* – perhaps under other conditions or even under exactly the same conditions. For examples of conflicting markedness constraints, see (13) and Chapter 3 passim.[11] For "opposite" constraints, see §3.2.1.3.

At the other extreme is the occasionally voiced a priori insistence that every constraint in OT should conflict with every other constraint. This is of course not true. The source of this idea is harder to figure out, but it may stem from an assumption that OT constraints are really an elaborated system of parameters. There are basic differences between parameters and OT constraints and between parameter setting and constraint ranking. See the parameters FAQ for brief treatment of these differences and exhaustive references to discussion elsewhere in this book.

The word "constraint" itself is another source of terminological ambiguity. The constraints of more familiar theories are inviolable, whereas OT constraints can be violated under duress. It is tempting to import the inviolable constraints of other theories into CON, but this temptation should be resisted. The inviolable constraints of other theories are intended to state universals of human language; the violable constraints of OT do *not* state universals of human language, precisely because they are violable. Rather, OT requires that universals be derived from constraint interaction (§3.1.5).

There is another, more specific problem with importing constraints from other theories, where they are often surrounded by an apparatus of codicils necessary simply to assure inviolability.[12] It is also common to find constraints in other theories that explicitly refer to other constraints in ways that mimic constraint domination in OT. Here are some examples (emphasis added throughout):

- In phonology, the Obligatory Contour Principle prohibits adjacent identical elements *except* across morpheme boundaries (McCarthy 1986).
- Hayes's (1995: 95) Priority Clause involves implicit comparison of alternative outputs and explicit reference to another constraint prohibiting degenerate (e.g., monosyllabic) feet: "If at any stage in foot parsing the portion of the string being scanned would yield a degenerate foot, the parse scans further along the string to construct a proper foot *where possible.*"
- Halle and Vergnaud's (1987: 10, 15) theory of metrical parsing implements several interdependent constraints. The Exhaustivity Condition says that parsing is exhaustive "*subject to*" a Recoverability Condition. And the Maximality Condition says that parsing constructs constituents that are as large as possible, "*provided that* other requirements on constituent structure are satisfied."
- In syntax, "[m]ovement must be done after SPELL-OUT *whenever* it is possible to converge by doing so" (Poole 1998: 385 after Chomsky 1995: 398).
- From Roberts (1997: 426):
    a. Head movement is copying.
    b. *[x^0 W$_1$ W$_2$], where W$_n$ are morphological words.
    c. A head is spelled out in the highest position of its chain, *subject to* (b).

These hedges are descriptive necessities when constraints are inviolable and when there is no general theory of constraint interaction, but in OT they ought to follow from principled interaction of simple, violable constraints (§1.3). Constraints with hedges or codicils are not ready-made for importation into OT; they are research problems.

A final remark. First exposure to OT sometimes leads to insistence on a shortcut: "Just tell me what the constraints are." This request is unreasonable. OT is a general framework for constraint interaction, and as such it does not entail a particular set of constraints in Con.[13] Indeed, if OT is the right framework, and if all the constraints in Con were somehow known, then the profession of linguistics would be at an end. The constraints will be discovered gradually by time-honored methods of analysis, theorizing, further analysis, improved theorizing, and so on (see §1.4.4 for some research strategies). Constraints are specific empirical hypotheses about Universal Grammar (UG), and so it is inappropriate to demand a full accounting of them in advance of empirical research.

1.2.3 Constraint Schemata and Fixed Hierarchies

Certain ideas about the form of constraints have proven useful in both phonology and syntax. This section gives a brief overview of three of these ideas, leaving more detailed explanation and exemplification for Chapter 3. If this material seems unfamiliar, it might be better to skip it for now and return to it when alerted in Chapter 3.

There is considerable internal structure to Con, making it much more than a mere deuteronomic list of what is forbidden and what is required. One source of structure is the *constraint schema*, an abstract formula for constructing all constraints of a certain type. The constraint schema that has been most extensively studied is edge *Alignment*, which supplies a template for constraints that refer to the edges of constituents. *Local constraint conjunction* is another, more controversial source of internal structure to Con. Local conjunction is a way of combining two constraints to get the force of both simultaneously. *Harmonic alignment* goes from substantive universal scales, like sonority or animacy, to universally fixed constraint rankings. It is the basis of many implicational universals. These three ideas are discussed in turn.

Edge Alignment constraints are subsumed under the schema shown in (4). 📖 §1.5¶4

> (4) ALIGN(Cat$_1$, Cat$_2$, Edge)
>   The element standing at the *Edge* of any *Cat$_1$* also stands at the *Edge* of some *Cat$_2$* (where *Cat$_1$* and *Cat$_2$* are grammatical or prosodic constituents and *Edge* is left or right).

Alignment constraints demand that constituent-edges coincide. They quantify universally over their first argument and existentially over their second. For example, the constraint ALIGN (Foot, Word, Right) (often abbreviated ALIGN-R(Ft, Wd)) says that every stress foot is final in some word, while

ALIGN-L(Accusative, S) says that every instance of the morphosyntactic feature accusative must be realized initially in some clause. For examples and applications, see §3.1.2.4 (13), §3.1.4.6 (37), §3.1.5.3, §3.2.1.2 (59) and (61), §3.2.1.3, §3.2.3, §3.3.2.5, and §3.3.3.3.

Alignment constraints are usually construed gradiently. Suppose some high-ranking constraint rules out the perfectly aligned candidate, and two candidates, neither of which is perfectly aligned, remain. The Alignment constraint favors the one that is closer to perfect alignment than the other. In such situations, it is of course necessary to be precise about how the extent of violation is to be translated into violation-marks. But no literal counting of violations is required, since it is enough for EVAL to distinguish better from worse performance (§1.1.2).[14]

Local constraint conjunction is another source of internal structure in CON, originally proposed by Smolensky (1995b). 📖$_{\S1.5\P5}$ The local conjunction of constraints C1 and C2 in domain D, written [C1&C2]$_D$, is violated if an only if both C1 and C2 are violated by the same instance of D. Suppose C1 and C2 are markedness constraints, each expressing some simple prohibition. The intuition behind local conjunction is to combine C1 and C2 to express some more complex prohibition, singling out "the worst of the worst" for special attention. For example, if first person objects are marked and null exponence of a morphological distinction is marked, then a fortiori null exponence of a first person object is marked (see §3.1.2.5, §3.1.5.4, and Aissen 1999). This basic idea has been extended to include the rather different notion of *local self-conjunction*, defining [C1&C1]$_D$ to prohibit two distinct instances of C1 violation in D. This is one possible approach to dissimilation and similar processes.[15] 📖$_{\S1.5\P5}$

Local conjunction is a powerful idea, but in the long run we also will need limits on which constraints can be combined in this way. The possibility of conjoining constraints somewhat mitigates the effects of the strictness of strict domination (§1.1). Suppose the ranking [[C1 ≫ C2, C3]] has previously been established. Ranked above C1, the conjoined constraint [C2&C3]$_D$ would allow the two otherwise low-ranking constraints to collude against the high-ranking one, approximately as in a connectionist model (§2.4). Nevertheless, there are important differences between local conjunction and numerical weighting: conjunction is categorical in its effects, locality is enforced by the domain argument D, and there is some potential for placing limitations on what constraints can be conjoined and in what domains (see the next paragraph). For further discussion and exemplification, see §3.1.2.5, §3.3.2.8 (95), §3.3.3.5 (103), and §4.4.2.

Because the Alignment schema and local conjunction are general techniques for constraint construction, they inevitably raise questions about the universal versus the language-particular.[16] On the formal/substantive side, the main question is whether the Alignment and local conjunction schemata are enough, or whether there are also substantive limitations. Concretely, does UG contain constraints aligning either edge of every constituent with every other constituent, and does it contain the local conjunction of every pairing of simple constraints on every possible domain? Or are there substantive limitations on these schemata, so that UG contains only certain natural Alignment constraints or constraint conjunctions? It seems likely that there are indeed substantive limitations and hence that the space of imaginable Alignment or conjoined constraints is rather sparsely populated. Research on the interface between prosodic constituency and syntactic or morphological constituency has turned up certain specific natural pairings – for instance, the edges of phonological words are naturally aligned with the edges of lexical roots – and some bias toward a particular edge as well. Relatedly, there is evidence that Alignment constraints may be relativized to particular affixes, to allow prefix ~ infix ~ suffix alternations to be obtained through constraint interaction (§3.1.5.3, §3.2.2.1). Here again, the schema is narrowly limited (affixes are aligned at the left or right periphery of the stem), though its argument – the affected morpheme(s) – is obviously free. Substantive or formal limitations on constraint conjunction have also received some attention, though research is less far along.📖 §1.5¶5

The issue of universal versus language-particular applications of constraint schemata has, as yet, not received as much attention (though see the references in §4.6 ¶14). Because they provide ways of constructing constraints from simpler elements, the Alignment and local conjunction schemata might seem to hark back to the rule-writing theories of early generative grammar (Chapter 2). Could learners, armed only with the schema (4), use their early experience to discover all of the Alignment constraints operative in their native language? Do learners have an innate but modest set of simple constraints, with part of learning being devoted to the discovery of how the universal constraints are conjoined in their native language?

The answer to both these questions could, in principle, be "no." The schemata could play a purely passive role, giving structure to universal CON without being involved in learning. Since universal constraints must be supported by factorial typology, it might seem that there is an easy strategy for finding language-particular constraints and thereby falsifying the null hypothesis: check every dubious constraint for its typological consequences under ranking permutation. This strategy is not quite complete, though. A constraint for which there is no typological support cannot be universal, but this does not mean a language-particular constraint is required instead. Another possibility is to look more closely at the interaction of known constraints as the source of the phenomena that seem to motivate the dubious constraint. Because ranking is language particular and because interaction comes from ranking, interaction is by far the most common source of language-particular patterns and must always be considered as an alternative to a language-particular constraint (or a universal one, for that matter). Of course, interactional solutions will not always be self-evident.

The last organizing principle for CON to be discussed here bears on the analysis of multi-tiered implicational universals. These are observed universal patterns of the form "... *A* only if *B* only if *C* ...," where some kind of scale of relative markedness is involved. Two techniques have been developed for analyzing implicational universals in OT; both involve imparting some internal structure to CON.

One idea is to define two constraints standing in a *stringency* relation, as in (5): if the violations of C1 are always a proper subset of the violations of C2, then C2 imposes a more stringent test than C1 does.$\square$$_{§1.5¶6}$

(5) A stringency relation

	C1	C2
Struc$_a$		
Struc$_b$		*
Struc$_c$	*	*

The constraints in (5) give the harmonic ordering $[\![$Struc$_a$ ≻ Struc$_b$ ≻ Struc$_c$ $]\!]$. That ordering holds regardless of how C1 and C2 are ranked with respect to one another. Through interaction with faithfulness constraints (§3.1.5.4), C1 and C2 define a system of implicational universals: any language that includes Struc$_c$ in its inventory of output forms must also include Struc$_b$, but not vice versa; and any language that includes Struc$_b$ in its inventory must also include Struc$_a$, but not vice versa – as long as no other constraints in CON favor Struc$_b$ over Struc$_a$ or Struc$_c$ over Struc$_a$ or Struc$_b$ (§1.2.2). Typical applications of the stringency idea involve a contextually restricted constraint as C1 and its context-free counterpart as C2. Some examples: be faithful to lexical forms versus be faithful to all forms, lexical or functional (§3.1.4.3); or, nasals are prohibited before voiceless consonants versus nasals are prohibited everywhere (cf. §3.1.4.2).

Another approach to multi-tiered implicational universals involves universally fixed constraint rankings. Though the discussion so far has rightly emphasized the permutability of constraints, there are certain situations where a fixed universal hierarchy, as in (6), can prove useful.

(6) A fixed universal hierarchy

	C1	≫	C2
Struc$_a$			
Struc$_b$			*
Struc$_c$	*		

Like (5), (6) yields the harmonic ordering $[\![$Struc$_a$ ≻ Struc$_b$ ≻ Struc$_c$$]\!]$ and thus would account for the same implicational universal under the same assumptions about the rest of CON. Observe that if the ranking were (wrongly) permutable, the same results would not be obtained, since if C2 dominates C1, the harmonic ordering is $[\![\text{Struc}_a \succ \text{Struc}_c \succ \text{Struc}_b]\!]$.[17]

Allowing free stipulation of fixed universal hierarchies involving arbitrary sets of constraints would greatly limit the interest and attractiveness of factorial typology. But there is some reason to think that all such hierarchies are derived by *harmonic alignment of prominence scales.*📖§1.5¶7 (Despite the terminological overlap, harmonic alignment and edge Alignment have nothing to do with one another.) Language is replete with natural scales, with one end more prominent, in an abstract sense, than the other: on the sonority scale, vowels are more prominent than liquids, which are more prominent than nasals, and so on; persons are numbered first, second, and third, in order of prominence; subject is more prominent than object, accusative more prominent than dative, and so on. Prominence scales are inferred orderings of linguistic objects; they are not the same thing as constraint hierarchies. Prominence scales, though, can be combined by harmonic alignment to form constraint hierarchies.

Harmonic alignment is defined as in (7) (after Prince and Smolensky 1993: 136).

(7) Harmonic alignment

   Given a binary dimension D_1 with a scale X > Y and another dimension D_2 with a scale a > b > ... > z, the *harmonic* alignment of D_1 and D_2 is the following pair of harmony scales:

   $H_X = X/a \succ X/b \succ \ldots \succ X/z$
   $H_Y = Y/z \succ \ldots \succ Y/b \succ Y/a$

   The *constraint* alignment is the following pair of constraint hierarchies:

   $C_X = {}^*X/z \gg \ldots \gg {}^*X/b \gg {}^*X/a$
   $C_Y = {}^*Y/a \gg {}^*Y/b \gg \ldots \gg {}^*Y/z$

The notation *X/d* describes a linguistic element that combines the properties *d* and *X*, such as a *d* that occurs in position or context *X*. The notation *X/d denotes a constraint that *X/d* violates.

Three different relations are symbolized in (7). As usual, "$\gg$" means "dominates." It is a relation between constraints. The other two relations, ">" and "$\succ$," are relations between linguistic objects. The first, ">," means "is more prominent than" on some natural linguistic scale. The relation "$\succ$" means "is more harmonic than" on a harmony scale derived by aligning two natural linguistic scales.

The idea in (7) is that two natural linguistic scales, one of which is binary, can be combined to form two harmony scales by aligning their most and least prominent elements. In one harmony scale, H_X, the more prominent member of the binary scale D_1 is mapped onto the other scale D_2 in D_2's order. Hence, a prominent element on one scale combines most felicitously with a prominent element on the other scale, and so on down the line. The prominent *X* combines least felicitously with *z*, which is least prominent on D_2. Conversely, in H_Y, the less prominent member of the binary scale D_1 is mapped onto D_2 in the opposite of D_2's order. The least prominent element on one scale combines most felicitously with the least prominent element on the other scale, and so on *up the line*. The constraint alignment, derived from the harmony scales, consists of two fixed universal hierarchies. They are, in effect, the contrapositive of the corresponding harmony scales. If, as in H_X, $[\![X/a \succ X/b]\!]$, then, as in C_X, $[\![*X/b \gg *X/a]\!]$. In other words, for a to be a better instance of X than b is, the constraint against X/b must dominate the constraint against X/a.

Harmonic alignment of prominence scales establishes a preferred correlation between two distinct but related dimensions; it is something like the height-weight tables in diet books. For example, the syllable-position prominence scale $[\![\text{Nucleus} > \text{Onset}]\!]$ can be combined with the sonority scale $[\![\text{vowel} > \text{liquid} > \text{nasal} > \text{fricative} > \text{stop}]\!]$ to form two harmony scales, $[\![\text{Nucleus/vowel} \succ \text{Nucleus/liquid} \succ \ldots]\!]$ and $[\![\text{Onset/stop} \succ \text{Onset/fricative} \succ \ldots]\!]$. By quasicontraposition, these harmony scales are transformed into universally fixed constraint hierarchies, $[\![\ldots \gg *\text{Nucleus/Liquid} \gg *\text{Nucleus/Vowel}]\!]$ and $[\![\ldots \gg *\text{Onset/Fricative} \gg *\text{Onset/Stop}]\!]$. Both hierarchies have important empirical consequences: the nucleus hierarchy accounts for the implicational universal that some languages have only vowel nuclei (Italian) and some have both liquid and vowel nuclei (English *bottle*), but no language has only liquid nuclei; the effect of the onset hierarchy can be observed in early acquisition, when many children avoid nasal or liquid onsets (§4.2.2). For further discussion and exemplification, see §3.1.5.4.[18]

1.3   Constraint Interaction

Constraint interaction through ranking is the basis of description and explanation in OT. The interaction of simple constraints can produce patterns of surprising complexity. Permuting the ranking yields an array of typological predictions. The discussion in this section, based on Prince and Smolensky (1993: Chapter 3–4), gives a summary of the main kinds of interaction. 📖 §1.5¶8 The material in Chapter 3 shows how these simple interactions fit into the larger picture.

1.3.1   Faithful and Unfaithful Mappings

In theory, the interaction of a few constraints should always be studied in the broader context of the full constraint hierarchy. In practice, and in the current expositional context, it is useful to look at a small number of constraints in isolation. We begin with a constraint set that consists of one markedness constraint M and one faithfulness constraint F. (Here and throughout this section, I assume that the constraints under discussion *can* interact – that is, that they deal with sufficiently similar matters as to make interaction possible.) Two rankings are possible: if F dominates M, then nothing happens, because violations of M are

tolerated in the output if necessary to remain faithful to the input; if M dominates F, then some inputs will be unfaithfully mapped to M-obeying outputs
instead of faithful M-violating ones.

Suppose concretely that M is ONSET, which prohibits vowel-initial syllables, and that F is DEP, which prohibits epenthesis. In a language with the
ranking ⟦DEP ≫ ONSET⟧, and assuming for now that there are no other constraints or candidates, all inputs will be mapped to faithful output candidates,
as shown in (8a–b).[19]

(8) a. Input /pata/ → Output *pata*

/pata/	DEP	ONSET	Remarks
i. ☞ pa.ta			Faithful
ii. a.pa.ta	*	*	Gratuitous epenthesis
iii. ʔa.pa.ta	**		Ever more gratuitous epenthesis

b. Input /apata/ → Output *apata*

/apata/	DEP	ONSET	Remarks
i. ☞ a.pa.ta		*	Faithful
ii. ʔa.pa.ta	*		Epenthesis

In (8a), there is no real competition for the faithful candidate. Since *pa.ta*
violates no constraints, it *harmonically bounds* any candidate like *a.pa.ta* or
ʔa.pa.ta that incurs violations of DEP and/or ONSET. Harmonic bounding is
defined as in (9) (§3.1.5.3).

(9) Harmonic bounding 📖 §1.5¶9

The mapping /A/ → B harmonically bounds the mapping /A/ → C if and
only if the /A/ → B mapping incurs a proper subset of the constraint violations incurred by the /A/ → C mapping. (In other words, no constraint assigns
more violation-marks to the /A/ → B mapping than to the /A/ → C mapping,
and at least one constraint assigns more violation-marks to the /A/ → C
mapping.)

In tableau (8a), given just the constraints and candidates shown, no language
can map /pata/ onto anything except *pa.ta*, since *pa.ta* is fully faithful and has
no markedness violations, harmonically bounding its competitors. This situation evidences a kind of economy of derivation that follows from the definition
of EVAL in OT (§3.1.5.2, §3.2.3): the "economy" constraint DEP is violable, but
violation is never gratuitous; it must always be compelled.

In tableau (8b), however, there is an interesting competing candidate – interesting precisely because it is not harmonically bounded. In *a.pa.ta*, faithful

analysis leads to ONSET violation, while in *ʔa.pa.ta*, unfaithful analysis yields a candidate that obeys ONSET. This sort of competition forms the basis of a valid ranking argument (§1.1.1) showing that DEP dominates ONSET. With input /apata/ and with only the candidates shown, either DEP or ONSET must be violated by the output form. The ranking ⟦DEP ≫ ONSET⟧ ensures that DEP is obeyed and ONSET violated precisely in situations where obedience to both is impossible.[20]

In a different language, with the ranking ⟦ONSET ≫ DEP⟧, input /pata/ is still faithfully analyzed as *pata* because *pata* harmonically bounds all its competitors. (By definition, harmonic bounding depends on what constraints are in CON but not on how they are ranked.) But the treatment of input /apata/ is different, as evidenced in (10).

(10) Different ranking: Input /apata/ → Output *ʔapata*

/apata/		DEP	ONSET	Remarks
i.	☞ ʔapata		*	Epenthesis
ii.	apata	*		Faithful

Because the markedness constraint ONSET is top ranked, violation of the faithfulness constraint DEP is compelled. The result is an unfaithful mapping.

An ⟦M ≫ F⟧ ranking like ⟦ONSET ≫ DEP⟧ is how OT approximates the effects of processes, rules, transformations, or operations in other linguistic theories (see §3.1.1 for the details). When faithful analysis of some input would violate M, a candidate that obeys M by violating F is chosen instead. In fact, there is no other reason why F would be violated: an unfaithful mapping is never possible unless it achieves improved performance on the markedness constraints of UG as they are ranked in some language-particular hierarchy (see Moreton 1996/1999 and §3.1.4.5). For this reason, OT can be described as a *teleological* or *output-oriented* theory. The motivation for a process is always to be found in the output configuration that it achieves or avoids.

Even when F is crucially dominated, violation of F is minimal because of the way that EVAL selects the most harmonic candidate. If M dominates F, no candidate that violates F more than is necessary to obey M will ever be optimal. For this reason, mappings like /pata/ → *ʔapata* or /apata/ → *ʔaʔapata* are sure losers if CON consists of just these two constraints. In short, EVAL entails that mappings are unfaithful only when necessary and only to the extent necessary (another economy effect).

Sometimes, as in the previous paragraphs, the workings of OT constraints are described in teleological or functional language: "epenthesis is triggered by the need to satisfy ONSET" or "the faithfulness constraint is violated no more than necessary to obey the markedness constraint." Do not be misled by these external descriptions of the work that EVAL accomplishes. Despite the expository usefulness of these paraphrases, OT has no literal triggering or blocking of constraints or processes, nor is there any directed progress toward the goal of satisfying some constraint. All EVAL does is apply a constraint hierarchy to a set of candidates, proceeding in the same unintelligent, localistic way as function composition (§1.1.2). Triggering, blocking, and overall teleology are ways to understand the effects that EVAL produces, but they are not overt or covert properties of EVAL itself.

1.3.2 Homogeneity of Target/Heterogeneity of Process

The next level of interactional complexity involves a markedness constraint M in a hierarchy with two faithfulness constraints, F1 and F2. If both F1 and F2 dominate M, then all mappings are faithful, as in (8). But if at least one of F1 or F2 is ranked below M, then M compels violation of the lower-ranked one. Concretely, suppose M and F1 are ONSET and DEP, as before, and F2 is MAX, which prohibits deletion. Four permuted rankings, shown in (11), have ONSET dominating at least one of the faithfulness constraints.

(11) Permuted rankings where ONSET dominates DEP and/or MAX

    a. ONSET ≫ DEP ≫ MAX

       DEP ≫ ONSET ≫ MAX   } ONSET, DEP ≫ MAX

    b. ONSET ≫ MAX ≫ DEP

       MAX ≫ ONSET ≫ DEP   } ONSET, MAX ≫ DEP

The rankings in (11a) with MAX at the bottom favor the mapping /apata/ → *pata*, as shown in (12).

(12) a. Input /apata/ → Output *pata*

/apata/	ONSET	DEP	MAX	Remarks
i. ☞ pata			*	Deletion
ii. apata	*			Faithful
iii. ʔapata		*		Epenthesis

    b. Input /apata/ → Output *pata*

/apata/	ONSET	DEP	MAX	Remarks
i. ☞ pata			*	Deletion
ii. apata		*		Faithful
iii. ʔapata	*			Epenthesis

The output is the same in (12a) and (12b), showing that the ranking of ONSET with respect to DEP is irrelevant to determining the outcome. (It is good analytic practice in such situations to report only those rankings for which there is evidence, using the format on the right in (11).) So, with the rankings ⟦ONSET ≫ MAX⟧ and ⟦DEP ≫ MAX⟧, inputs like /apata/ map to unfaithful candidates with deletion of the offending initial vowel. But if DEP is at the bottom of the hierarchy, as in (11b), then /apata/ maps to *Ɂapata*.

The partial factorial typology in (11) exemplifies OT's explanation for *homogeneity of target/heterogeneity of process* (§2.1, §3.1.4.2). There are many cases in phonology where the same target is reached in different ways in different languages. (The term "target," in the sense I am employing, is a loose metaphor for required or prohibited output configurations.) For example, certain consonant clusters are avoided by deletion in Diola Fogny (Niger-Congo, Senegal) but by vowel epenthesis in Ponapean (Austronesian, Micronesia).[21] In OT, the markedness/faithfulness dichotomy, combined with factorial typology, predicts exactly this cross-linguistic variation. In contrast, rule-based theories typically do not (§2.1).

Homogeneity of target/heterogeneity of process is not a very familiar problem in syntactic typology, but the Romance clitics provide a striking example.[22] The target is avoidance of clitic duplication. Three dispositions are observed: in some dialects of Spanish, one of the offending clitics is deleted (*Se lava* for **Se se lava* 'one washes oneself'); in standard Italian, one of the clitics is changed to a non-duplicative form (*Ci si lava* for **Si si lava*); and in the Conegliano Italian dialect, duplication is simply tolerated (*Si si lava*). This typology is typical of the effects of ranking permutation, where a single markedness constraint can be satisfied in diverse ways or even not at all, depending on its ranking with respect to faithfulness and other markedness constraints.

1.3.3 Blocking Effects

Because constraints are violable, a language may allow outputs that violate some markedness constraint M. Nevertheless, M may also be active in that same language under other conditions (§3.1, §3.2.2). For example, the basic ⟦M ≫ F⟧ ranking can be modified by deploying a third constraint, C, that dominates M and sometimes compels violation of it. In this situation, C can be said to "block" the process characterized by the ⟦M ≫ F⟧ ranking. There are two ways for this to happen, depending on whether C is another markedness constraint or another faithfulness constraint.

Suppose C is a markedness constraint, C_M. To produce a blocking pattern where M is only partially active, C_M must be violated by some, but not all, of the otherwise favored M-obeying candidates. Dutch supplies a concrete example.[23] This language has the ranking ⟦ONSET, MAX ≫ DEP⟧, with glottal-stop epenthesis to relieve onsetless syllables after *a*: *pa[Ɂ]élla* 'paella'; *a[Ɂ]órta* 'aorta'. But there is no epenthesis, and consequently there is surface violation of ONSET, when the offending syllable is unstressed: *chá.os* 'chaos'; *fára.o* 'Pharaoh'. The responsible markedness constraint C_M prohibits the weakest consonant, glottal stop, from serving as the onset to a weak (unstressed) syllable, as illustrated in (13a–b).

(13) a. Input /fárao/ → Output *fa.ra.o*

/fárao/	C_M	MAX	ONSET	DEP	Remarks
i. ☞ fá.ra.o			*		Faithful
ii. fá.ra.ʔo	*			*	Epenthesis
iii. fá.ra		*			Deletion

b. cf. Input /aórta/ → Output *.a.ʔ ór.ta*

/aórta/	C_M	MAX	ONSET	DEP	Remarks
i. a.ór.ta		*		Faithful	
ii. ☞ a.ʔór.ta				*	Epenthesis
iii. ór.ta		*			Deletion

We know that ONSET is active in Dutch and that it crucially dominates DEP, because of forms like *a[ʔ]órta*. Nevertheless, the actual output in (13a.i) violates ONSET. Violation is required because the otherwise attractive alternative, (13a.ii), violates a higher-ranking markedness constraint, C_M. Alternative paths of unfaithfulness, as in (13a.iii), are ruled out by high-ranking MAX, leaving (13a.i) as optimal. (Other constraints militate against epenthesizing some consonant besides ʔ.)

This is a blocking interaction. By dominating ONSET, C_M blocks the process of glottal-stop epenthesis. In other words, ʔ is epenthesized into empty onsets *except when* it would produce a prohibited ʔv̆ syllable. Interactions like these are abundant throughout grammar: mark the plural with -*s* except when there is a lexical plural form; *wh* must move except when movement is prohibited (say, because [Spec, CP] is already filled). Blocking indicates crucial domination, and hence partial activity, of a markedness constraint. Though the effect of ⟦M ≫ F⟧ can be observed from some mappings, there are nonetheless M-violating surface forms. The precise conditions where M is violated are defined by its interaction with C_M.

Through factorial typology, the analysis proposed for Dutch also leads to predictions about other languages. Suppose that ONSET dominates C_M: ʔ will be epenthesized into all onsetless syllables, whether stressed or unstressed (as in Arabic). Or consider the ranking ⟦ONSET, C_M ≫ MAX ≫ DEP⟧. This hierarchy will produce a language where all syllables have onsets, with stress determining whether epenthesis or deletion is used to achieve it: /aorta/ → *a[ʔ]órta*

versus /fárao/ → *fára* or *fáro*. (Situations like this are known in the phonological literature as conspiracies – see §2.1 and §3.1.4.3 for examples). These
observations emphasize the intrinsically typological nature of OT. It is simply
impossible to analyze a single language without considering the broader
typological context.

Another way to get the blocking pattern is to deploy a high-ranking faithfulness constraint, C_F, above M in the ⟦M ≫ F⟧ ranking. To produce a blocking pattern where M is only partially active, C_F must rule out some, but not all,
of the unfaithful mappings that ⟦M ≫ F⟧ would otherwise compel. One way for
that to happen is if C_F is a *positional faithfulness* constraint, standing in a stringency relation (cf. (5)) to F. Positional faithfulness constraints are identical to
general faithfulness constraints, except that they only have force over the elements of some restricted domain: in phonology, some of the loci of positional
faithfulness are roots or lexical items, word-initial syllables, and stressed syllables (§3.1.3.5). Suppose C_F is a positionally restricted version of DEP, limited
to word-initial syllables. Ranked above ONSET, C_F will bar epenthesis into initial
syllables but will say nothing about epenthesis elsewhere. The resulting pattern
is frequently encountered in the world's languages: onsetless syllables are permitted initially but prohibited everywhere else. Tableau (14) illustrates this with
data from Axininca Campa (Arawakan, Peru).[24]

(14) Input /iŋ-koma-i/ → Output *iŋ.ko.ma.ti*

/iŋ-koma-i/	C_F	MAX	ONSET	DEP	Remarks
a. ☞ iŋ.ko.ma.ti			*	*	Medial epenthesis only
b. tiŋ.ko.ma.ti	*			**	Medial & initial epenthesis
c. ko.ma.ti		**		*	Deletion
d. iŋ.ko.ma.i			**		Faithful

This example shows both activity by and blocking of ONSET. It is visibly active
on the medial /a-i/ vowel sequence, forcing epenthesis of *t* in preference to the
faithful form in (14d). Now compare (14a) and (14b). The latter has two
epenthetic consonants so it incurs two DEP violations, but that should not matter
because ONSET dominates DEP and (14a) has an ONSET violation that (14b)
lacks. But ONSET is inactive on initial syllables, where it conflicts with the
positional faithfulness constraint C_F. In that position, then, the force of ONSET
is blocked by this higher-ranking constraint.

The competition between (14a) and (14b) nicely illustrates Prince and
Smolensky's (1993: 130, 148, 221) *Cancellation/Domination Lemma.* 📖$_{§1.5¶1}$
This lemma (see (15)) follows from the definition of constraint domination and
hence from the nature of EVAL, so it is not unfamiliar. It succinctly states what
is necessary for one candidate to be more harmonic than another.

(15) Cancellation/Domination Lemma (C/D Lemma) (paraphrased)
    Suppose two candidates *A* and *B* do not incur identical sets of violation-marks. Then *A* is more harmonic than *B* iff every uncanceled mark incurred by *A* is dominated by an uncanceled mark incurred by *B*.

For *A* to beat *B*, *every* constraint favoring *B* over *A* must be dominated by *some* constraint favoring *A* over *B*. That's it.

Recall from §1.1.1 how mark cancellation works. In a tableau that compares exactly two candidates, shared violation-marks can be safely deleted, since they make no contribution to the comparison. Suppose (14a) is compared with (14b), ignoring all other candidates.

(16) Mark cancellation

/iŋ-koma-i/	C$_F$	MAX	ONSET	DEP
a. ☞ iŋkomati			*	X̶
b. tiŋkomati	*			X̶*

In (16), the canceled marks are overstruck with ×. Now, according to the C/D Lemma, any (uncanceled) mark incurred by the winner must be dominated by some uncanceled mark incurred by the loser. After mark cancellation, the winner has just one violation-mark, located in the ONSET column. Because C$_F$ dominates ONSET, this mark is indeed dominated, and so (16a) is more harmonic. As always, the choice between candidates is made by the highest-ranking constraint on which they differ (§1.1.1), and in (16) that constraint is C$_F$.

Factorial typology must also be considered. With the ranking ⟦M ≫ C$_F$, F⟧, M is active on the whole language, but with the ranking ⟦C$_F$ ≫ M ≫ F⟧ (as in Axininca Campa), M's activity is limited to contexts not targeted by C$_F$. The result is a well-documented difference in inventories (§3.1.2): the inventory of permitted linguistic objects may be richer in certain contexts than in others (§3.1.3.5). For example, Axininca Campa permits syllables with and without onsets in word-initial position, but only syllables with onsets elsewhere; Hindi allows verbs to select ergative-nominative or nominative-accusative case marking in perfective clauses, but only nominative-accusative case marking is permitted elsewhere.[25]

1.3.4 Summary

Permuted ranking supplies various ways to control the activity of markedness constraints and thereby to limit the unfaithful mappings they can compel. With the ranking ⟦F ≫ M⟧, all mappings are faithful, even if the output violates M. The opposite ranking, ⟦M ≫ F⟧, yields unfaithful mappings and outputs that consistently obey M. Adding a third constraint, markedness or faithfulness, that is crucially ranked above $[\![M \gg F]\!]$ restricts the unfaithful mappings to certain conditions, producing a bifurcation or nonuniformity in observed output forms (§3.2.1). Remarkably, even the $[\![F \gg M]\!]$ ranking cannot guarantee that M is entirely inactive; it can only say that M will not compel unfaithful mappings. Even low-ranking M can have visible activity in situations where faithfulness is not at issue (§3.2.2).

This range of interactional possibilities is essential to explanation and analysis in OT. With it, the goal of positing a set of simple, universal constraints may be attainable. Through ranking permutation, interaction predicts a typology that follows directly from the hypothesized constraint set. As we will see in Chapter 3, interaction of simple constraints can produce complex surface patterns. Interaction also sharply distinguishes OT from parametric theories, since through interaction a constraint can be active but not always obeyed (§3.2.2).

1.4 How to Do OT

In the previous sections we have looked at OT from the top down: what are its basic premises, and how do they apply to language? Here we look at OT from the bottom up: how should an analyst informed about OT's premises apply it to data, construct novel hypotheses, and generally proceed to explore the theory, critique it, and seek to improve it? This section is less about theory, then, and more about practice; the dicta here are not assumptions or deductions but rules of thumb derived from experience. Readers wondering when it starts to get easy can safely assume that everything that seems hard really *is* hard and that every potential mistake hinted at in this section is one that I have made, sometimes more than once, and not just when I was first learning about OT.

1.4.1 Ranking Known Constraints

A ranking argument (§1.1.1) uses exactly two candidates to rank two constraints. For the argument to be valid, certain conditions must be met:

- The constraints must conflict; they must assess different members of the candidate pair as superior. Conflict is the only basis for a direct ranking argument.
- One of the candidates must be a winner and the other must be a loser. The whole point of constraint ranking is to select the right candidate as the winner. There is nothing to be learned by comparing one nonoptimal candidate with another.
- The ranking argument must be checked in the context of the full analysis. Suppose there is a tentative argument for $[\![C1 \gg C2]\!]$ based on comparing $Cand_{Winner}$ with $Cand_{Loser}$. This argument is not solid until we have checked for the existence of a third constraint, C3, that meets the following condi-

tions: it is ranked above C2, and it concurs with C1 by assigning fewer violation-marks to Cand$_{\text{Winner}}$ than Cand$_{\text{Loser}}$. If C3 with these properties exists, then the ranking argument for [[C1 ≫ C2]] is not valid.

In real life, the first two conditions for a valid ranking argument are of constant applicability, whereas the third turns out to be a problem only once in a while.

The tableaux in (17a–h) schematize various situations that can arise in practice. Ask yourself whether each tableau presents a valid argument for [[B ≫ C]], then check your answers in the footnote.[26]

(17) Practice tableaux

a.

/in/		B	C
i.	☞ out1	*	
ii.	out2	*	*

b.

/in/		B	C
i.	☞ out1		
ii.	out2	*	*

c.

/in/		B	C
i.	☞ out1		*
ii.	out2	*	*

d.

/in/		B	C
i.	☞ out1	**********	*******
ii.	out2	************	******

e.

/in/		B	C
i.	☞ out1		
ii.	out2		*

f.

/in/		A	B	C
i.	☞ out1			*
ii.	out2	*	*	

g.

/in/		A	B	C
i.	☞ out1	*		*
ii.	out2	*	*	

h.

/in/		B	C	A
i.	☞ out1		*	
ii.	out2	*		*

Ranking arguments are often easier to develop and understand using the comparative tableau format introduced by Prince (2000). In a comparative tableau, each row shows the results of a direct comparison between the optimal candidate and one of its competitors. The cells show how each individual constraint evaluates that comparison: Does it favor the optimal candidate, in which case "W" (for winner) appears in the cell? Or does it favor the competitor, in which case "L" (for loser) appears in the cell? Or does it favor neither, in which case the cell is left blank? For an illustration, look at the tableau in (18), which translates the traditional violation tableau (14) into comparative format.[27]

(18) Tableau (14) in comparative format

/iŋ-koma-i/	DEP$_{INIT-\sigma}$	MAX	ONSET	DEP
a. iŋ.ko.ma.ti ~ tiŋ.ko.ma.ti	W		L	W
b. iŋ.ko.ma.ti ~ ko.ma.ti		W	L	
c. iŋ.ko.ma.ti ~ iŋ.ko.ma.i			W	L

Remember: the rows compare the winner *iŋ.ko.ma.ti* with each of the losing candidates, indicating whether *iŋ.ko.ma.ti* (W) or a loser (L) fares better on each constraint. Look at row (18a) for an example. The winner *iŋ.ko.ma.ti* fares worse than the loser *tiŋ.ko.ma.ti* on ONSET, so there is an L in the cell referring to this comparison. Neither *iŋ.ko.ma.ti* nor **iŋ.ko.ma.ti* violates MAX, so that cell is left blank. And because **tiŋ.ko.ma.ti* has initial epenthesis but *iŋ.ko.ma.ti* does not, the winner *iŋ.ko.ma.ti* is favored by $\text{DEP}_{\text{INIT-}\sigma}$.

Because the comparative tableau eponymously shifts the emphasis from accumulated violation-marks to direct candidate comparison, it eliminates the technical difficulties of mark cancellation and shows directly why a particular candidate is optimal. Succinctly, in any proper comparative tableau, the left-most filled cell of any row must contain a W.[28] This follows from the C/D Lemma (15), which says that any constraint favoring a loser must be dominated by some constraint favoring the winner. That is what we see in (18): every L, which indicates a loser-favoring comparison, is dominated by some W, which indicates a winner-favoring comparison.

Comparative tableaux make OT's inherently comparative nature particularly apparent. They can also considerably simplify the problem of determining constraint rankings in situations where there are several failed candidates and several relevant constraints to juggle. Imagine that we are in the middle of analyzing Axininca Campa, with some hypotheses about what constraints are involved but little understanding of their ranking. The as-yet unranked comparative tableau in (19) illustrates that situation. (This tableau is like (18), but the columns have been deliberately scrambled to simulate ignorance of the correct ranking.)

(19) Comparative format prior to ranking

/iŋ-koma-i/		ONSET	MAX	DEP	$\text{DEP}_{\text{INIT-}\sigma}$
a.	iŋkomati ~ tiŋkomati	L		W	W
b.	iŋkomati ~ komati	L	W		
c.	iŋkomati ~ iŋkoma.i	W		L	

From the C/D Lemma, we know that every constraint favoring the loser must be dominated by some constraint favoring the winner. This is equivalent to requiring, typographically, that every cell containing an L be preceded in the same row by a cell containing a W. So row (19a) is relatively uninformative: it tells us that DEP and/or $\text{DEP}_{\text{INIT-}\sigma}$ dominates ONSET but not which one. Row (19b) is more helpful: as long as all relevant constraints are on the table, we can be certain that MAX dominates ONSET, because MAX supplies the only W in that row to dominate ONSET's L. Row (19c) offers equal certainty that ONSET dominates DEP. Together, rows (19b) and (19c) yield the ranking ⟦MAX ≫ ONSET ≫ DEP⟧, resolving the disjunction in (19a): since DEP is ranked below ONSET, only $\text{DEP}_{\text{INIT-}\sigma}$ can supply the W that overrules ONSET's L in (19a). The final ranking, then, is ⟦MAX, $\text{DEP}_{\text{INIT-}\sigma}$ ≫ ONSET ≫ DEP⟧. (In §4.2.1, this same example is used to illustrate a learning algorithm that bypasses the rather tricky disjunction of (19a).)

When it comes to figuring out constraint rankings, comparative tableaux have a big advantage over the traditional violation tableaux. In the traditional format, ranking arguments must be done with 2×2 tableaux to avoid massive confusion, but they also need to be checked with the full set of constraints and additional candidates to avoid potential invalidity. In the comparative format, it is possible to combine these two steps and get a much better picture of how several constraints assess a set of candidates.

Simple 2×2 ranking arguments are nonetheless essential for developing analyses and especially for presenting them in articles or lectures. It is a big mistake to take shortcuts. For instance, when I first drafted the Emai analysis in §3.1.4.3, I skipped the ranking arguments, wrote down some tableaux with the ranking that I thought was right, and proceeded from there. Fortunately, I discovered my blunder before circulating the draft. It is also wise not to lay down a giant constraint hierarchy at the beginning of a paper and then try to justify it retrospectively. Giant hierarchies are usually incomprehensible to everyone, the author no less than the reader, and even if they contain no outright errors, they often overspecify the rankings that can be proven with proper arguments.[29]

1.4.2   Selecting Informative Candidates

Everyone who has ever presented a lecture about OT has had the unpleasant experience of suddenly hearing about a problematic candidate from an irritatingly astute member of the audience. Finding the right candidates to study may be the hardest but also the most useful practical skill in doing OT. This section includes some strategies for finding the right candidates to worry about and for eliminating uninformative candidates from further consideration. The next section describes the encounter with a problematic candidate and how to proceed from there.

For the analyst, figuring out which candidates *not* to worry about is the easiest task. If all the forms or mappings in a language obey some known constraint C, then it is safe to say that C is undominated in that language. And if C is undominated, then candidates violating C will not be instructive. For example, a first encounter with the Axininca Campa example in (18) might lead to concerns about the failed candidate *ŋikomati, where the initial ONSET violation is relieved by metathesis. But if metathesis is never observed in the language, then the faithfulness constraint militating against it (LINEARITY in correspondence theory) must be undominated. Under these circumstances, *ŋikomati is just a distraction from the real business at hand – it deserves a footnote at best, and it definitely should not claim space in every tableau when the analysis is written up.

Incremental progress in developing an analysis can also help narrow the candidate set under active investigation. For instance, once it has been established that MAX dominates ONSET in Axininca Campa, there is nothing to be gained by incorporating MAX-violating candidates in subsequent tableaux, and there can be a price to pay as readers' attention flags.

Candidates that are harmonically bounded (§1.3.1) by other candidates can never win, and so they should not detain the analyst or the reader. Cand1 harmonically bounds Cand2 if and only if Cand1 incurs a proper subset of Cand2's violation-marks, as in tableau (8a). In a comparative tableau (§1.4.1), candidates that are harmonically bounded by the winner are those that have a W but no L in their row.

The harder task is figuring out which candidates one *should* worry about. There is no certain procedure here, because OT's highly interactive character can challenge the best analyst's skills. But there are three basic strategies: one to use at the beginning of analysis, one in the middle, and one at the end.

At the outset of analysis, start with the fully faithful candidate, since it is guaranteed to be a member of every candidate set and to obey many constraints (all of the faithfulness constraints, at least). It is never harmonically bounded and so must always be dealt with by constraint ranking, if an unfaithful mapping is the intended outcome. Then proceed to deform the faithful candidate systematically, introducing individual unfaithful mappings and combinations of them to construct additional candidates. It is helpful to have a more or less explicit theory of GEN to aid in this systematic exploration of the candidate space. It is also helpful to have an overall sense of what the undominated constraints are to limit the task by setting aside hopeless candidates. Do not neglect to construct candidates that vary in properties not normally thought of as matters of faithfulness, such as differences in syllabification or perhaps other structural properties.

For example, suppose we are analyzing the Axininca mapping /iŋ-koma-i/ → [iŋ.ko.ma.ti]. We start with the fully faithful candidate but take note of differences in syllabification that can distinguish otherwise identical candidates: [iŋ.ko.ma.i] and [iŋ.ko.mai] are different candidates. We then systematically deform the faithful candidate, perhaps starting with deletion – [iŋ.ko.ma], [iŋ.ko.mi], [ŋko.ma.i], [ko.ma], and so forth. Some of these candidates are readily disposed of. For example, [ŋko.ma.i] starts with a consonant cluster, unlike any actual word of Axininca. This suggests that [ŋko.ma.i] violates an undominated markedness constraint, so it and other candidates like it can be safely set aside as footnote material at best. Similarly, once it has been established that MAX dominates ONSET on the basis of candidates like [iŋ.ko.ma], candidates with even more deletion, such as [ko.ma], do not merit further attention. Once we have learned what we can from candidates with deletion, we can proceed in the same fashion to candidates with epenthesis and other, less familiar unfaithful mappings.

The suite of candidates produced by the procedure just described will make a good starting point. Subsequent development of the analysis will target in on candidates showing particular properties. One important strategy in the middle of the analysis is to think logically about how the as-yet unranked constraints (such as MAX and DEP$_{\text{INIT-}\sigma}$ in (19)) can be brought into conflict, so as to get a fuller picture of the constraint hierarchy. The results of this deduction can then be brought to bear on the search for input-candidate pairs that can supply ranking arguments for these constraints. Another strategy is to seek confirmation for transitive rankings from direct arguments. If ranking arguments for ⟦A ≫ B⟧ and ⟦B ≫ C⟧ have already been established, it is wise to look for an input-candidate pair that brings A and C into direct conflict. Unwelcome proof of ⟦C ≫ A⟧ would call the whole analysis into question. Failure to take this necessary step "invites theoretical disaster, public embarrassment, and unintended enrichment of other people's careers" (McCarthy and Prince 1993b: 12).

When the work seems more or less done, the *method of mark eliminability* (Prince and Smolensky 1993: Chapter 7) can be used to check whether all potentially problematic candidates are under the control of the analysis. Start with the traditional violation tableau, like (20) from Axininca Campa.

(20) Violation tableau based on (14)

/iŋ-koma-i/	DEP$_{\text{INIT-}\sigma}$	MAX	ONSET	DEP
a. ☞ iŋkomati			*	*
b. tiŋkomati	*			**
c. komati		**		*
d. iŋkoma.i			**	

Now look at each violation-mark incurred by the winning candidate and consider a competitor that eliminates it, keeping all else equal. Has the analysis successfully disposed of that competitor, as it must? Well, *iŋkomati* violates ONSET, and that mark could be avoided by deleting the initial syllable (**komati*), epenthesizing a consonant (**tiŋkomati*), metathesizing (**ŋikomati*), devocalizing (**ykomati*), and so on. Using these candidates, determine whether *iŋkomati*'s ONSET mark is eliminable by violating some constraint ranked below ONSET or, worse yet, no constraint at all. If it is, the analysis has a problem and further study is needed.

None of these methods is perfect, since all rely on the analyst's ingenuity. Perhaps the hardest thing is realizing the diversity of ways that a constraint could in principle be satisfied, so that this diversity can be placed under analytic control. The space of what is logically possible is very broad, because GEN affords so many options. There is no easy way around this.

1.4.3 Diagnosing Problems

The analyst usually explores some empirical domain, attempting to gain insight by studying the interactional capabilities of some small set of simple constraints against some inputs and candidates. In this situation, it is not unusual to run up against problems of *stinginess*. For some inputs, the wrong candidate is selected by the hierarchy, and further ranking is impossible or unhelpful. The only possible conclusion (short of changing one's underlying assumptions about GEN or the input) is that the constraint set being studied is too stingy and must be expanded.

The next section describes some heuristics for positing new constraints, but even without looking at an actual example, it is possible to draw some inferences about what the new constraint must do and how it must be ranked. There are three possible situations, simplified down to the bare bones in (21a–c). All three assume that the ranking $[\![A \gg B]\!]$ has been established independently and that *out1* is the intended output form.

(21) Situations requiring an additional constraint

a.

/in/		A	B
i.	☞ out1	*	*anything*
ii.	out2		*anything*

b.

/in/		A	B
i.	☞ out1		*
ii.	out2		

c.

/in/		A	B
i.	☞ out1		*
ii.	out2		*

In (21a) and (21b), the wrong candidate wins because the higher-ranking constraint favors *out2* or both candidates tie on the higher-ranking constraint and the lower-ranking one favors *out2*. And in (21c), the candidates tie on both constraints, so there is insufficient discrimination between them.

The logic of the C/D Lemma (15) provides clues about the new constraint needed to solve these problems. The revised tableaux in (22a–c) illustrate.

(22) Like (21), but with additional constraint supplied

a.

/in/		C	A	B
i.	☞ out1		*	*anything*
ii.	out2	*		*anything*

b.

/in/		A	C	B
i.	☞ out1			*
ii.	out2		*	

c.

/in/		A	B	C
i.	☞ out1		*	
ii.	out2		*	*

To ensure that *out1* wins in (21a), a constraint is needed that assigns fewer
marks to *out1* than to *out2* and that dominates A. This constraint, C, has
been added to (22a). Likewise, to select *out1* as optimal in (21b), we require
a constraint that assigns fewer marks to *out1* than to *out2* and that dominates
B, as shown in (22b). For (21c), a constraint is likewise necessary that
assigns fewer marks to *out1* than to *out2*, but its ranking cannot be determined
on the basis of this evidence. (In general, constraints that only break ties
between two candidates are unrankable, since they will correctly break the tie
no matter where they appear in the hierarchy.) Once this bit of reasoning is out
of the way, the search for the needed constraint is a lot simpler.

The process of inference just sketched allows the analyst to deduce some
desiderata for a new constraint before that constraint has been formulated.
This logic also allows the analyst to determine the indesiderata for any new
constraints when a result derived from factorial typology is at stake. Many
universals of language can be derived from factorial typology under specific assumptions about CON (§3.1.5.3): if CON contains only the constraints A,
B, and C, then the only possible languages are those with grammars chosen
from the six permutations of these constraints. In real life, of course, CON is not
so small, but the logic of constraint interaction can help determine what constraints, if they existed, would invalidate results obtained from permuting a
small set of constraints. For a concrete example, see the discussion of (51) in
§3.1.5.3.

Factorial typology is also at stake when an existing constraint set is
guilty of *profligacy*, that is, if it yields nonoccurring languages under ranking permutation. Analysis and theorizing in OT combine the study of language-
particular patterns with universal typology. A constraint set may be too rich
in the typology it yields, even if it works for a particular language. Suppose
study of some language has produced the tableau in (23), with the constraints
ranked as shown.

(23) Profligacy illustrated

/in/	A	B	C	D
i. ☞ out1			*	*
ii. out2	*	*		
iii. out3		*	*	

If this tableau includes all of the relevant candidates and constraints, there are certain inferences that can be drawn with certainty:

(i) There is a language (the one shown in the tableau) where /in/ is mapped most harmonically to *out1*.
(ii) There is a language where /in/ is mapped most harmonically to *out2* (if C dominates A and B).
(iii) There is a language where /in/ is mapped most harmonically to *out3* (if D dominates B and A dominates C).

Suppose, though, that diligent research in Harvard's Widener Library has failed to uncover any languages of the predicted type (iii), where /in/ maps to *out3*. The overgenerating constraint set needs to be reined in, and the only way to do that is to eliminate constraints or change their definitions so they assign different violations. In (23), the solution is to eliminate constraint D. Once that constraint is gone, *out1* harmonically bounds *out3*, and so the /in/ → *out3* mapping can never be optimal.

1.4.4 Positing New Constraints

Positing a new constraint is not to be undertaken lightly. Constraints in OT are not merely solutions to language-particular problems; they are claims about UG with rich typological consequences. Moreover, the need for a new constraint has to be established securely. The first and best place to look for the solutions to analytic problems is in interaction of known constraints, because that is where the most interesting results and explanations are to be found. The next place to look is in modification of a known constraint. Perhaps a subtle change in the formulation of a preexisting constraint will produce the desired result without adversely affecting other results attributed to that constraint. New constraints may seem to offer an easier solution, but they can bring a cost in typology, especially if the new constraint cannot eliminate an old one.

Suppose, though, that the need for a new constraint has been established conclusively. How does one proceed to formulate it? The learner is arguably supplied with an innate, universal constraint component CON.[30] But the analyst is in the more difficult position of attempting to determine the contents of CON from indirect clues in the form of linguistic generalizations. The remarks in §1.2, while not providing a comprehensive theory of possible constraints, suggest several heuristics to follow.

Descriptive universals rarely make good constraints, but descriptive *tendencies* often do. Indeed, the success of OT in incorporating phonetic or functional generalizations is largely a consequence of its ability to give a fully formal status to the otherwise fuzzy notion of a cross-linguistic tendency (§4.4). Tendencies, then, are a good place to start in theorizing about constraints, but they are not a good place to end up. Constraints need to apply in fully determinate ways; a constraint like "syllables tend to have onsets" is simply unintelligible as an instruction for how candidates are to be evaluated. Think of a constraint as a function that assigns a set of violation-marks to a candidate, and make sure that the function is well defined. Constraints formulated as "assign one violation-mark for every . . ." might seem wordy, but they are admirably explicit.

Another heuristic is to avoid slipping bits and pieces of EVAL into constraint definitions. For example, constraints should not make overt comparisons, since EVAL already has that job well in hand. A constraint like "*l* is a better (*or* less marked) syllable nucleus than *n*" is therefore inappropriate, as is "minimize the duration of a short vowel in an open syllable." For the same reason, it is not necessary for constraint formulations to contain "should" or equivalent expressions, as in "syllable weight should not exceed two moras" or "avoid Pronoun." Constraints prohibit or demand; they do not urge, cajole, or suggest. As a general strategy, constraint definitions requiring "except if" or "only if" clauses, such as "the head or specifier of a CP may be deleted only if that CP is a complement," should be split into two constraints, leaving the contingency up to EVAL.[31] Likewise, constraints should not paraphrase rewrite rules or transformations, like "form perfect iambs" or "move *wh*," because OT attributes rewrite or transformational effects to markedness/faithfulness interaction (§1.3).

Constraints that merely describe a required or forbidden state of affairs are probably too superficial. Analyses, including some in this book, will occasionally invoke ad hoc state-of-affairs constraints, but this should always be seen as a temporary expedient to avoid a long diversion. State-of-affairs constraints typically have several problems. Since they derive from specific observations about a single language, they are unlikely to lead to a successful typology under ranking permutation. In addition, because OT explains things by constraint interaction, a complex descriptive constraint pretty much explains nothing. And taking the long view, state-of-affairs constraints are antithetical to developing an underlying theory of constraints along the lines of §1.2.3.[32]

The final heuristic is to proceed cautiously, or at least consciously, when importing background assumptions from other theories. For example, research in phonology since the days of Trubetzkoy has often equated being more marked with having more structure. Contemporary versions of this representational theory of markedness include radical underspecification (Archangeli 1984; Kiparsky 1981, etc.) and privative features (Avery and Rice 1989; Steriade

1995, etc.). Representational markedness might make sense in OT, or it might not.[33] This is an empirical question to be decided by the usual methods and not aprioristically. (See §3.2.1.4 for related discussion.)

Here is an example to illustrate many of the points made in this section.[34] An analysis of the null pronoun *Pro* must account for contrasts like those given in (24).

(24) Distribution of *Pro*
    a.   Mary$_i$ hopes *Pro$_i$* to see Bill.
       * Mary$_i$ hopes she$_i$/her$_i$ to see Bill.
    b. * Mary$_i$ hopes *Pro$_i$* will see Bill.
         Mary$_i$ hopes she$_i$ will see Bill.

Though there is much more to the problem than (24) lets on, I will as usual simplify the example and discussion down to just this contrast: a null pronoun in infinitival clauses versus an overt pronoun in finite clauses.

Observationally, *Pro* must be coindexed with an antecedent in the smallest XP that contains *Pro* and Tns (tense), which is why *Pro* subjects are not possible in tensed clauses like *Pro will see Bill* in (24b). This observation, though it accurately describes a state of affairs, would not make a good constraint. It has a composite structure that looks like several constraints rolled into one. Above all, the putative constraint makes an overt comparison, "smallest XP," that is best left up to EVAL. Extremes like smallest or largest should be obtained by EVAL using simple constraints that describe prohibited or required configurations. (See Legendre, Smolensky, and Wilson 1998: 251–52 for an application of this reasoning in similar circumstances and §3.2.3 for related discussion.) What we want, then, is something more like the two constraints in (25) to characterize the observed state of affairs.

(25) Some tentative constraints for *Pro*
    a. CONTROL
        Pro is coindexed with something. Assign one violation-mark * for every
        Pro that is not coindexed.
    b. DOMAIN
        If *Pro$_i$* is coindexed with A$_i$, assign one violation-mark * for every XP$_k$ that
        contains *Pro$_i$* and Tns and does not contain A$_i$.

These constraints are not things of beauty (nor are they a complete analysis of (24)), but they have certain virtues. They decompose the observed state of affairs into smaller constraints whose interaction through factorial typology can be studied. They rely on EVAL itself to obtain the notion "smallest XP." And, not inconsequentially, they are defined clearly enough to be usable without ambiguity.

To sum up, here is a research strategy that has often proven to be productive. Take an intuition or observation about language and restate it as a constraint; that is, formulate it as a simple, unadorned demand or prohibition. Resist temptations toward complication, and take care to avoid the pitfalls described here. Even at the earliest stages of theorizing, it is very important that the constraint be precise, so that violations can be determined exactly for any candidate. Details of formalization or representation are not as important at this point as preciseness and can probably be safely set aside for later.

Now begin studying the typological and interactional capacities of the hypothesized constraint. Permute its ranking relative to other constraints previously hypothesized, considering how each permutation applies to a wide range of inputs and of candidates derived from them. There is no way to know in advance which inputs or candidates will be most instructive, but systematic rather than random exploration of the input and candidate spaces is obviously the better strategy. This investigation of typology and interaction under permuted ranking is the crucial test of any proposed constraint in OT. It can lead in just three directions: the proposed constraint contributes new insight; the proposed constraint leads to an implausible and irremediable typology; or an additional constraint is required that, through interaction, produces a typology that is more plausible.

Beyond these considerations that are special to OT, a proposed constraint needs to be evaluated by the same criteria as any other scientific hypothesis: Is it simple? Is it aesthetically pleasing? Does it account for the observations? Does it yield interesting and accurate predictions? And, as in any scientific field, errors are sometimes made and dubious constraints postulated. But factorial typology provides a strong corrective influence (§3.1.5, §3.2.2): it is a discipline for testing constraints since all must produce plausible effects through ranking permutation; and it may even supply a way to use interaction of other constraints to eliminate the need for the dubious constraint.

1.5   For Further Reading

¶1   *The Basics*

The locus classicus of OT is Prince and Smolensky (1993). Their Chapter 5 would be appropriate (though challenging) reading at this stage. Other treatments of the fundamentals, in varying degrees of technical detail, include Archangeli and Langendoen (1997b), Kager (1999a), McCarthy and Prince (1993b: Chapter 2), Prince and Smolensky (1997), and Tesar, Grimshaw, and Prince (1999). Legendre's (to appear-a) introduction to OT focuses on syntax. Beckman, Walsh Dickey, and Urbanczyk (1995) is a useful compilation of papers on a variety of phonological and syntactic topics. The Rutgers Optimality Archive (http://roa.rutgers.edu) is indispensable.

¶2   *Mark Cancellation*

The method of mark cancellation is introduced by Prince and Smolensky (1993) and applied in Prince (2000) and Tesar and Smolensky (1998).

¶3   Correspondence Theory and Faithfulness

Correspondence theory is introduced by McCarthy and Prince (1995a, 1999). Works containing significant applications or extensions of this theory include (but are by no means limited to) Alderete (1998), Benua (1997), Bresnan (to appear-b), Burzio (1997), Causley (1997, 1999b), Crosswhite (1998), Hume (1998), Ito, Kitagawa, and Mester (1996), Ito and Mester (1997a, 1999a), Keer (1999a), Lamontagne and Rice (1995), Orgun (1996a), Spaelti (1997), Struijke (1998, 2000a), and Urbanczyk (1996). Also see the references in §3.4 ¶7 and ¶9.

¶4   Alignment Constraints

The original idea of Alignment constraints comes from Prince and Smolensky (1991), while the formalization and applications are developed in McCarthy and Prince (1993a). Further applications and refinements in phonology are too numerous to mention, but Kager (1999a: 117–24) provides a useful and accessible overview. Alignment has also been applied to the phonology/syntax interface (Selkirk 1995; Truckenbrodt 1995), to focus (Choi 1996, to appear; Costa 1998, to appear; Grimshaw and Samek-Lodovici 1995; Samek-Lodovici 1996, 1998), and to various syntactic phenomena, especially clitics (see §3.2.1.2 and the references in §3.4 ¶19).

¶5   Local Constraint Conjunction

The idea of local constraint conjunction first appears in Smolensky (1995b, 1997), where it is used to decompose complex markedness constraints into the conjunction of two simple markedness constraints (cf. Fukazawa and Lombardi to appear for a different view). Smolensky also develops a related notion of constraint self-conjunction, which produces a power hierarchy of constraints $[\![\ldots \gg C^2 \gg C^1]\!]$, where C^n is violated if and only if there are at least n distinct instances of C-violation in the domain of evaluation.

Alderete (1997) and Ito and Mester (1998) apply conjunction of a markedness constraint with itself to the phenomenon of phonological dissimilation, and Legendre, Smolensky, and Wilson (1998) propose self-conjunction as a theory of barriers. Kirchner (1996) uses conjunction of two faithfulness constraints to account for chain shifts, Lubowicz (1999) conjoins markedness and faithfulness constraints to deal with derived environment or strict cycle effects, and Fukazawa (1999) and Fukazawa and Miglio (1998) propose limits on conjoinability, for which also see Ito and Mester (1998, to appear). Aissen (1999), Artstein (1998), Baertsch (1998), and Gafos and Lombardi (1999) extend local conjunction to encompass combinations of a constraint and a hierarchy and of two hierarchies, applying their results to syntactic agentivity and animacy/person hierarchies (Aissen, Artstein), to sonority relations in onsets (Baertsch), and to featural co-occurrence restrictions (Gafos and Lombardi). Another sense of constraint conjunction is discussed by Crowhurst and Hewitt (1997) and Hewitt and Crowhurst (1996).

¶6 *Stringency Relations among Constraints*

Prince (1997b) undertakes a thorough study of stringency relations, and Prince (1996) makes contact with the Elsewhere Condition (v., inter alios, Anderson 1974; Halle and Idsardi 1997; Hastings 1974; Janda and Sandoval 1984 [which includes an extensive bibliography]; Kiparsky 1973b; Koutsoudas, Sanders, and Noll 1974; Sanders 1974), as does the discussion of *Pāṇini's Theorem* in Prince and Smolensky (1993: Chapter 5, 7). Implications for learning are studied by Hayes (to appear), Prince and Tesar (1999), and Smith (2000b).

¶7 *Harmonic Alignment of Prominence Scales*

Harmonic alignment of prominence scales is introduced in Prince and Smolensky (1993: Chapter 6, 8). Discussion and applications in phonology include Anttila (1997a), de Lacy (1999), Gnanadesikan (1997), Green (1993), Kenstowicz (1994b), and Lombardi (to appear). Aissen (1999), Artstein (1998), Grimshaw (to appear), and Lee (2000) discuss extensions and applications to morphosyntactic hierarchies (animacy, person/number/gender), and Burzio (1998) uses similar notions. Also see the references in §3.4¶17.

¶8 *Basic Effects of Constraint Interaction*

The treatment of constraint interaction in Prince and Smolensky (1993: Chapter 3, 4) is lucid. Some representative applications of permuted ranking to (morpho)syntactic typology include Bresnan (to appear-b), Grimshaw (to appear), Keer (1999b), Samek-Lodovici (1998), and Woolford (to appear). On homogeneity of target/heterogeneity of process and positional faithfulness, see the references in §3.4 ¶8 and ¶7.

¶9 *Harmonic Bounding*

Harmonic bounding was introduced by Samek-Lodovici (1992) and figures prominently in works like Keer (1999a), Morelli (to appear), Prince and Smolensky (1993: Chapter 9), and Samek-Lodovici and Prince (1999).

Notes

1. This formulation is based on Grimshaw (1997b), Prince (2000), and, ultimately, the Cancellation/Domination Lemma of Prince and Smolensky (1993: 130, 148, 221) (see (15)). See Samek-Lodovici and Prince (1999: Appendix A) for further formal development.
2. The Three Laws of Robotics are
   1. A robot may not injure a human being, or, through inaction, allow a human being to come to harm.
   2. A robot must obey the orders given to it by human beings except where such orders would conflict with the First Law.
   3. A robot must protect its own existence as long as such protection does not conflict with the First or Second Law.

From *Handbook of Robotics* (56th Edition, published 2058), as cited by Asimov (1950). (I am indebted to Elliott Moreton for bringing these laws to my attention.)

3. Additional helpful annotations are often used in tableaux, including an exclamation point to mark fatal violations (such as Cand$_{Comp}$'s violation of C1 in (1)) and shading of cells that are irrelevant because higher-ranking constraints have been decisive. For typographic clarity, I do not use these annotations.

4. What if C3 concurs with C1 and there is no evidence that either one is ranked below C2? We are then stuck with a disjunction: we know that C1 or C3 dominates C2, but we do not know which one. Disjunctions like this are particularly problematic for learning theories, though an important idea in the learning of OT grammars avoids this difficulty (see §4.2.1).

5. Vieri Samek-Lodovici suggests the following as an example of a logical inference about ranking. Suppose there is a ranking argument establishing that A *or* B dominates C. (This can happen when the losing candidate violates both A and B, so it is unclear which is the fatal violation. See note 4.) Suppose another, independent ranking argument establishes that A or C dominates B. It is now legitimate to infer that A is top ranked, dominating both B and C, since that is the only way to combine the results of the two ranking arguments into a consistent constraint hierarchy. See Hayes (1997) for discussion of this and other situations where ranking inferences can be drawn.

6. Grimshaw (1997b: 411) exploits the possibility of multiple optimal outputs to account for syntactic optionality (§4.1.3). Hammond (2000) also discusses this point.

7. Also see Karttunen (1998) for a similar approach.

8. For the same reason, it is wrong to see GEN as somehow equivalent in its explanatory responsibilities to other theories' generative components, such as Chomsky's (1995) computational system for human language, C$_{HL}$. For example, the dialogist "L" in Uriagereka (1998: 168) insists that "an optimality approach isn't particularly useful for combinatorial systems: what we want to understand is why Gen gives the structures it does. . . . the bottom line is that something has to give us those structures, whether it's called C$_{HL}$, Gen, or God. Personally, I'm interested in understanding the nature of the combinatorial function." L's pessimistic view of OT is unjustified since it is based on the entirely unreasonable requirement that GEN in OT should explain the same things that Chomsky's C$_{HL}$ does. Different theories impose different organizations on the world, and so individual components of those theories, taken in isolation, obviously cannot be compared in this way.

9. This formulation comes from Smolensky (1993).

10. Nor is the relative frequency of certain sound patterns evidence for markedness constraints in OT. Factorial typology predicts nothing about relative frequency, distinguishing only those patterns with a frequency of zero from everything else. (Thus, factorial typology can account for what are traditionally called absolute universals but not for universal tendencies.) One proposed interpretation of tied rankings (§4.5), however, does predict frequencies in some situations.

11. Conflict among markedness constraints, though not anticipated by the Prague School, was also recognized in Natural Phonology (§2.1), as when Stampe (1973a: 23) speaks of the "contrary teleologies of contrary processes."

12. Grimshaw (1997b) and Speas (1997) make similar points. Jane Grimshaw supplied several valuable suggestions about how to cover the syntactic end of this discussion.

13. For the same reason, claims about specific constraints cannot be attributed to OT as a whole. This is a category error, exemplified by the following remark from Breen and Pensalfini (1999: 15 n): "However, these constraints [No-Onset and Coda – JJMc] are quite explicitly ruled out in OT. . . ." This statement confounds OT in general with a specific hypothesis about Con (i.e., that it contains the constraints Onset and No-Coda, but not their opposites). The confusion is particularly apparent once it is realized that nearly every syllable theory since Jakobson's day adopts the same hypothesis, in one form or another. That hypothesis may be wrong, as Breen and Pensalfini maintain, but it is not some ineluctable idiosyncrasy of OT.

14. Alignment constraints have a somewhat ambiguous status in markedness/faithfulness constraint typology. The Alignment constraints in McCarthy and Prince (1993a) and much subsequent work include some that evaluate only outputs and some that evaluate input/output relations. The Anchor constraints of McCarthy and Prince (1995a, 1999) redefine the input/output Alignment constraints in terms of correspondence theory. Some Alignment effects are also subsumed under positional faithfulness (§1.3.3, §3.1.3.5, §3.1.4.3).

15. Alan Prince observes that local self-conjunction allows the finite set Con to be expanded into the denumerable set $\{[C1]_D, [C1\&C1]_D, [C1\&C1\&C1]_D, \ldots\}$. Prince has conjectured, and Paul Smolensky has proven, that a denumerable set of constraints yields $2^{\aleph_0}$ possible grammars under ranking permutation. The proof goes like this. Assume two fixed constraint hierarchies of countably infinite length. Each hierarchy is by itself impermutable, but the two hierarchies can be intercalated in various ways. By substituting 0 for all the constraints in one hierarchy and 1 for all the constraints in the other, each intercalation can be mapped onto a countably infinite string of 0's and 1's: 00000111 . . . , 011000 . . . , 1101000 . . . , etc. Prepose a decimal point, and you now have a representation of all the $2^{\aleph_0}$ real numbers between 0 and 1. The implications for language learning and language typology of permitting uncountably many possible grammars have not yet been studied.

16. Discussions with Paul de Lacy shaped my understanding of this material.

17. The universality of $[\![C1 \gg C2]\!]$ means that no possible language has the ranking $[\![C2 \gg C1]\!]$. It does not mean that C1 immediately dominates C2 (other constraints can intervene), nor does it mean that every language will supply evidence for $[\![C1 \gg C2]\!]$.

18. For a different approach to natural linguistic scales, based on ternary-valued distinctive features with their accompanying markedness and faithfulness constraints, see Gnanadesikan (1997).

19. The symbol "." marks the end of one syllable and the beginning of another. There is also an implicit "." at the beginning and end of each word. So *a.pa.ta* consists of three syllables, *a* (which lacks an onset), *pa*, and *ta*.

20. What if the language does not permit inputs like /apata/? *Richness of the base* (§3.1.2) excludes the possibility of systematic, language-particular restrictions on inputs.

21. This example is based on Ito (1986, 1989).

22. This example is based on an OT analysis by Grimshaw (1997a), who attributes several of the observations to Bonet (1991).

23. The observations about Dutch, somewhat simplified here, come from Booij (1995). Also see Rosenthall (1994) and Smith (2001).

24. The Axininca Campa data come from Payne (1981). The analysis sketched here is approximately the one in McCarthy and Prince (1993a, 1993b).
25. The Hindi example is based on the OT analysis in Woolford (to appear).
26. Answers: (a, b, c, e) All no. There is no conflict between constraints B and C because they agree in their assessment of at least one candidate. (d) Yes. The absolute number of violations does not matter, but the relative number of violations does. (f) No. Because A dominates C and A concurs with B, these candidates cannot be used to prove that B dominates C. (g) Yes. A does not distinguish the two candidates, so it does not invalidate the argument for ranking B over C. (h) Yes. Because A is ranked below C, it cannot invalidate the argument for B over C.
27. Following the discussion in §1.3.3, I have replaced the dummy constraint C_F with an actual positional faithfulness constraint. The material here is based on discussions with Alan Prince and on Prince (2000).
28. Furthermore, every row of a comparative tableau must contain at least one filled cell, unless the intention is for the candidates compared in that row to both be optimal.
29. Overspecified rankings often lead to trouble further down the line: if one has, without justification, ranked A above B, the later discovery of a ranking argument proving that B dominates A will seem like a problem when in fact it is not.
30. In principle, CON could be universal but not innate if it could be reliably induced from the universally shared experiences of learners (§4.6 ¶14).
31. The examples cited here are from Kirchner (1996: 347), Broselow, Chen, and Huffman (1997: 65), Chomsky (1981), and Pesetsky (1998: 357), respectively.
32. The temptation to describe the state of affairs rather than to seek an insightful analysis is not some new vice introduced by OT. Rather, Newmeyer (1996: Chapter 5) finds it to be a recurring problem in the history of generative grammar. For example, in much syntactic research of the 1960s, "[t]he author identified a construction, then wrote a transformational rule which came close to mimicking its surface characteristics" (p. 45). Recent research is no less immune to this vice, though it expresses itself in other forms, such as "the language-specificity of some parameters that have been proposed within GB" (p. 65). (I am indebted to Jane Grimshaw for discussion of this material and for suggesting the phrase "state-of-affairs constraint.")
33. Prince and Smolensky (1993: Chapter 3, n. 13, citing a personal communication from Cheryl Zoll) discuss the idea that there is a broad family of constraints *STRUC (pronounced "star-struck") that militate against all structure whatsoever, thereby implementing a very general representational markedness theory. They note that possible applications of this idea extend beyond phonology: witness Chomsky's (1986: 4) prohibition on nonbranching N" or Grimshaw's (1993, 1994) constraint MINIMAL-PROJECTION (though see Grimshaw 1997b: 381 for an alternative view). Causley (1999a) pursues a representational approach to phonological markedness in OT.
34. Example (24) is based loosely on Speas (to appear).

2

The Context of
Optimality Theory

The goal of this chapter is to give a sense of the intellectual environment from which OT emerged. In what respects does OT continue earlier ideas and in what respects does it depart from them? The orientation of this chapter is historical rather than polemical; see Chapter 3 passim for comparison of OT with other theories.

2.1 Developments in Phonological Theory

For many years, the standard theory of generative phonology was the one developed in *The Sound Pattern of English* (Chomsky and Halle 1968).📖§2.5¶1 The *SPE* theory is *segmental*, *rule based*, and *derivational*. Though later research moved away from *SPE*'s segmental orientation, there has been a persistent assumption that phonology is, at least partly, rule based and derivational.

SPE is a segmental theory because the principal element of phonological representation is the individual speech sound, a segment. Segments are bundles of values for universal distinctive features (e.g., *t* is [+coronal, −continuant, −voice, . . .]), but the features have only a classificatory role, with no autonomous existence outside of the segment.

Phonological processes in *SPE* are expressed by rules. A rule is a transformational operation that describes an input configuration (e.g., a word-final voiced obstruent *b/d/g*) and something to do to it (e.g., a change to voiceless, as in German, Dutch, Russian, Polish, etc.). Rules are expressed using the universal feature vocabulary and a set of *abbreviatory conventions* (mostly adopted from Chomsky 1951) that allow certain kinds of rules to be stated using fewer features. A key claim is that, with the right abbreviatory conventions, rules requiring fewer features will be more natural, in the sense that they will be observed more frequently in the world's languages. This claim is embodied in the feature-counting *Evaluation Metric* of *SPE*. Apart from this universal measure of rule naturalness or likelihood, the rules are entirely language particular, to be deduced somehow by learners equipped only with the features, the abbreviatory conventions, and the Evaluation Metric.

SPE rules apply in a sequential derivation. The rules are ordered in a language-particular list: the first rule takes the input, applies if its structural description is met, and emits an output that is submitted to the next rule. The derivation ends when the last rule has had a chance to apply. The only departure from this strict ordering occurs when certain rules are designated as cyclic, which allows them to reapply to successively larger morphosyntactic constituents.

Though the need for language-particular rule ordering was doubted throughout the early 1970s, almost all research during the following two decades retained the idea of a sequential derivation. Only in the 1990s was there much serious study of nearly or fully parallel theories, like Harmonic Phonology, Two-Level Phonology, Declarative Phonology, or OT.□ §2.5¶2

The principal descriptive and typological successes of the *SPE* theory come from the abbreviatory conventions and rule ordering. For example, one abbreviatory convention, the parenthesis notation, is claimed to lead always to disjunctive interaction among its subparts. Another example: rule ordering has been used to explain differences between dialects or historical stages, on the assumption that languages can change by reordering rules without altering their form (cf. §4.5).

There is one other element of *SPE* important to this discussion: the theory of markedness introduced in that book's final chapter. It is a late imposition of substantive constraints on an overall formalist program, motivated by the following considerations:

> The entire discussion of phonology in this book suffers from a fundamental theoretical inadequacy. . . . The problem is that our approach to features, to rules, and to evaluation has been overly formal. Suppose, for example, that we were systematically to interchange features or to replace [αF] by [−αF] (where α = +, and F is a feature) throughout our description of English structure. There is nothing in our account of linguistic theory to indicate that the result would be the description of a system that violates certain principles governing human languages. To the extent that this is true, we have failed to formulate the principles of linguistic theory, of universal grammar, in a satisfactory manner. In particular, we have not made any use of the fact that the features have intrinsic content. (Chomsky and Halle 1968: 400)

In other words, inverting the observed rules of English phonology produces a system that should be just as natural, according to the formal Evaluation Metric, but is actually impossible. The source of this problem: the "intrinsic content" of features (and rules) – that is, their substantive, phonetic, or functional characteristics, traditionally called "markedness" (cf. §4.4) – is not recognized in *SPE*'s formalist program.

Chapter 9 of *SPE* sketches the beginnings of a solution to this problem, supplementing the formalism with a set of substantively motivated featural marking

conventions and a technique, called "linking," for using them to make natural
rules simpler so that they are more highly valued under the Evaluation Metric.
But the theory sketched in Chapter 9 never claimed many adherents. More than
a decade later, the standard textbook for the *SPE* theory regarded this whole
issue as an unsolved, poorly understood research problem:

> Any adequate theory of phonology must contain postulates that will define
> natural sound changes. Although many of these can be expressed by appeal
> to the notion of assimilation defined over the features of a feature system,
> it is clear that not all natural sound changes fit into this mold. For example,
> many languages have a rule converting consonants to ʔ or *h* in preconso-
> nantal and final position. Such a process is clearly not assimilatory in nature.
> Nevertheless phonological theory must have some apparatus for expressing
> the fact that neutralization to a glottal stop in these positions is a natural
> rule as opposed to, say, neutralization to *l*. (Kenstowicz and Kisseberth
> 1979: 251)

Indeed, as recently as 1995, it was still being suggested that the notion "possible phonological rule" embodies "assumptions about natural processes"
(Chomsky 1995: 380 n). These hypothetical postulates are external to the rule
system, rarely even stated, and of largely unknown character, but much of
phonological typology is said to fall on their shoulders.

In the meantime, the theory of *Natural Phonology*, which was developed
by Stampe (1973a) and others, emerged as a way of addressing this shortcom-
ing.📖 §2.5¶3 The central idea of Natural Phonology is that learners begin with a
set of innate *natural processes*, such as the final devoicing rule of German and
other languages.[1] At the outset of learning, all of the innate processes are active,
and so children's early productions tend to be highly reduced and unmarked.
Learning consists of total or partial suppression of the innate processes after
exposure to positive evidence in the ambient language (cf. §3.1.2, §4.2.1). For
example, learners of English will, upon encountering words like *bad* or *bag*,
eventually suppress the natural process of final devoicing, but learners of
German will not, since they never hear final voiced obstruents. Interestingly, the
theory predicts that learners of Japanese, who are not exposed to any final
obstruents whatsoever, will also have no reason to suppress this innate process
and should tend to devoice final obstruents when learning English as a second
language (§4.2.2).

The tension between applying natural processes and suppressing them is
understood in Natural Phonology as the difference between phonetic (= articulatory) ease and phonological intention. Natural processes "are mental substitutions . . . which respond to physical phonetic difficulties" (Donegan and
Stampe 1979: 136). Processes tend to eliminate contrasts for phonetic reasons;
antithetically, phonological intention (i.e., the lexicon) requires the preservation
of contrasts. Donegan and Stampe compare this functionalist approach (cf. §4.4)
with *SPE*'s formalist program.

The tension between clarity and ease is one of the most obvious, and oldest, explanatory principles in phonology. Modern theories, however, to the extent that they incorporate analogous principles, tend to make them monolithic, like the principle of . . . simplicity in generative phonology. . . . In that framework, positing conflicting criteria would be like pitting Ockham's razor against an anti-Ockham who multiplies entities as fast as the razor can shave them off: it would defeat their purpose of evaluating alternative analyses. (Donegan and Stampe 1979: 130)

Natural Phonology, then, has no truck with the abbreviatory conventions and feature-counting Evaluation Metric of *SPE*.

OT has closer affinities to Natural Phonology than to *SPE*. Although OT shares with *SPE*, and with generative grammar as a whole, the goal of developing an explicit theory of language competence, the principal modes of analysis and explanation in OT and *SPE* have little in common. *SPE* is focused on the formal properties of language-particular rules, developing a set of notational conventions that encode claims about which phonologies are less likely. OT is focused on the interactional properties of simple universal constraints through language-particular ranking. Likewise, Natural Phonology recognizes a set of universal processes that can be suppressed on a language-particular basis.

The affinities between OT and Natural Phonology become even clearer when learning (§4.2) and the role of functionalism (§4.4) are considered, but there are also important differences. A Natural Phonology process, like an *SPE* rule, is a "package" consisting of an input configuration (a structural description) and an operation to perform on it (a structural change). In OT, though, this package is unpacked and reorganized into separate constraints (§1.2.2): markedness constraints, which describe output configurations, and faithfulness constraints, which prohibit operations on the input. The markedness/faithfulness split is essential to OT's explanation for homogeneity of target/heterogeneity of process (§1.3.2, §3.1.4.2), an issue that did not figure in the development of Natural Phonology.

Another difference between OT and Natural Phonology is that the two theories have different ways of limiting the activity of their respective markedness constraints and natural processes. In OT, the activity of a markedness constraint is limited under crucial domination by a faithfulness constraint or another markedness constraint (§1.3), and complete inactivity cannot usually be guaranteed (§1.3.4, §3.2.2, §3.2.3). In Natural Phonology, complete inactivity is easily attained by suppressing a process. Natural Phonology also recognizes partial suppression or constrained application of processes, but because it does not work out the details, direct comparison is not possible. In any event, partial suppression is quite different from the interactional effects of constraint ranking in OT.

A final difference between OT and Natural Phonology is that only OT has a class of faithfulness constraints. "Phonological intention," which is Natural

Phonology's closest analogue to faithfulness, plays a role only in learning, where it motivates suppression of process activity. Natural Phonology provides no place for phonological intention in the grammar itself, unlike OT, which puts faithfulness and markedness constraints on a par.

Another development in the post-*SPE* period was the intensive study of phonological representations. This trend continues up to the present day under rubrics like autosegmental phonology, feature geometry, metrical phonology, dependency phonology, and so on.$_{§2.5¶4}$ Nonlinear phonology, as this overall research program is sometimes called, seeks to combine a fairly rich theory of representations and constraints on representations with an impoverished theory of rules. The program is successful to the extent that all and only the natural phonological processes ("natural" = observed in nature) can be reduced to elementary operations on the enriched representations.

The common process of assimilation is a typical example. In autosegmental phonology, where features are independent of segments, assimilation involves the elementary operation of adding an association between a feature and a segment that does not already bear that association line. Diagram (1) represents the process of place-of-articulation assimilation graphically.

(1) Assimilation as autosegmental spreading

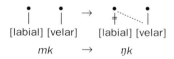

$$mk \quad \rightarrow \quad \eta k$$

The scope or span of the place feature [velar] is expanded at the expense of the place feature [labial]. Assimilation, then, is a simple change in the coordination of the segmental and featural tiers.

For present purposes, the most important property of this research program is the emphasis it places on *constraints on representations*.$_{§2.5¶5}$ The autosegmental Well-Formedness Condition, the metrical Clash Filter, and the Obligatory Contour Principle,[2] among others, all serve to limit possible phonological representations and, indirectly, to constrain rule application. To put it optimistically, "if the representations are right, then the rules will follow" (McCarthy 1988: 84).

This optimism was not justified. In actual descriptive practice, the enriched representations of nonlinear phonology were often manipulated by rules that retained all of the notational complexity and language-particular ordering of *SPE*. (Archangeli and Pulleyblank 1994 is an important exception.) The hope of simplifying the rules by complicating the representations was never fulfilled. Furthermore, nearly every proposed constraint on phonological representations encountered three fundamental problems: between-language differences in constraint applicability, within-language differences in constraint applicability, and difficulty reconciling the blocking and triggering functions of the constraints. Here, in brief, are the details of these three problems.

With few exceptions, every proposed constraint on phonological representations that was studied long enough was found to differ in its force from language to language (cf. §3.2.1.4).[3] The exception that proves the rule is the autosegmental Line-Crossing Prohibition of Goldsmith (1976a, 1976b). It is generally accepted that this constraint holds in all languages, but it has been argued to follow from considerations that lie entirely outside of phonological theory (Hammond 1988; Sagey 1988). If so, then it is not a linguistic constraint at all.

Within a language, proposed constraints have been found to be fully active in some contexts and less than fully active in others. For example, Ito (1989: 223) distinguishes "relative" and "absolute" versions of the Onset Principle: "Avoid onsetless syllables" versus "Onsetless syllables are impossible." In a language subject only to the weaker constraint, onsetless syllables will be eschewed whenever possible, but they will not be actively eliminated. Similarly, Hayes (1995: 87) distinguishes strong and weak versions of a prohibition on degenerate stress feet. (A degenerate foot is monosyllabic or monomoraic, consisting of a single rhythmic unit.) Some languages enforce the strong version of this constraint, prohibiting degenerate feet under all circumstances, while other languages impose only the weak version, permitting degenerate feet under main stress though not otherwise.

But the most serious problem with representational constraints in nonlinear phonology is that they are called on both to block rules and to trigger them. In the *SPE* theory of derivations, a rule is an obligatory transformation that applies to an input if and only if the input meets the rule's structural description. There are no true representational constraints in *SPE*, and so there is no possibility of recognizing notions like blocking and triggering. Nonlinear phonology essentially retained the *SPE* theory of rules and derivations but with representational constraints grafted onto them. The resulting chimera never really managed to fit together for reasons recognized in the literature on *conspiracies* (see §3.1.4.3 and the related discussion of the Duplication Problem in §3.1.2.2).

In an important paper, Kisseberth (1970a) observed that several phonological rules in Yawelmani Yokuts (an extinct language of California) serve a similar purpose: they actively eliminate or passively fail to create sequences of three adjacent consonants (i.e., *CCC). In the geopolitical environment of the 1960s and 1970s, the word "conspiracy" was the natural choice to describe this covert collusion among diverse rules. 📖 §2.5¶6

For the *SPE* theory, conspiracies are a serious problem: there is no mechanism for making connections among rules coexisting in a grammar, and there is no such thing as an output target, such as the avoidance of triconsonantal clusters. Kisseberth's solution was to modify the *SPE* theory: grammars can specify output targets, and rules are simplified by eliminating those aspects of their structural descriptions that can be inferred from any ambient output target. In Yawelmani, for example, a rule that *SPE* would formulate as

V → Ø/VC___CV (a medial vowel deletes when preceded and followed by a single consonant) can be reformulated as V → Ø/C___C. The simpler formulation is possible because the bracketing V's are predictable from the *CCC target. Under *SPE*'s Evaluation Metric (simple = natural) this is a successful explanation. Subsequent work in nonlinear phonology improved the explanation still further, by showing that the target has a syllabic basis, preferring unmarked syllable structures and exhaustive parsing.

The problem with this explanation is its incompleteness: it works for the fellow travelers, those rules like vowel deletion that passively acquiesce in the conspiracy, but it does not work for the active conspirators, those rules that alter forms to conform to the output target. For example, Yawelmani also has a rule of vowel epenthesis, Ø → i/C___CC. It clearly supports the output target by eliminating forbidden CCC clusters, but there is no mechanism for simplifying it. The obvious move, radical simplification to context-free Ø → *i*, will not work because there is no economy mechanism in the *SPE* theory or in Kisseberth's model (1970a), no way to say "epenthesize *only when* required by the target." In short, though there was progress on the blocking side of the conspiracy problem, there was no comparable progress on the triggering side.

Later on, constraint-and-repair theories emerged as a way of extending *SPE*'s rule-based framework to accommodate "only when" or triggering effects.📖$_{§2.5¶7}$ The idea is that a process like vowel epenthesis in Yawelmani is a special kind of rule, sometimes called a repair, that applies only when needed to fix a constraint violation. The blocking phenomenon is accommodated differently, or not at all, and other rules may be allowed that are independent of the repair system. These mixed rule-and-constraint-based theories are compared with OT at various places in Chapter 3.

The upshot was that the conspiracy problem was never fully resolved in the 1980s and 1990s. The intuitions about a successful solution were reasonably clear, but the formal properties were never worked out. Some progress was made in using syllabic structure to deal with cases like Yawelmani, but the overall conspiracy problem was much broader and more pervasive than that. It remained a serious impediment to further development of phonological theory.

The conspiracy problem constitutes the single biggest phonological influence on the emergence of OT. Here is what Prince and Smolensky have to say about it:

> As the theory of representations in syntax has ramified, the theory of operations has dwindled in content, even to triviality and, for some, nonexistence. The parallel development in phonology and morphology has been underway for a number of years, but the outcome is perhaps less clear. . . . What is clear is that any serious theory of phonology must rely heavily on well-formedness constraints. . . . What remains in dispute, or in subformal obscurity, is the character of the interaction among the posited well-

formedness constraints, as well as the relation between such constraints and whatever derivational rules they are meant to influence. Given the pervasiveness of this unclarity, and the extent to which it impedes understanding even the most basic functioning of the grammar, it is not excessively dramatic to speak of the issues surrounding the role of well-formedness constraints as involving a kind of conceptual crisis at the center of phonological thought. (Prince and Smolensky 1993: 1)

A major goal of OT is to resolve this "conceptual crisis." Chapter 3 explains how OT accomplishes this; see especially §3.1.2.2 on the Duplication Problem, §3.1.4.2 on homogeneity of target/heterogeneity of process, and §3.1.4.3 on conspiracies.

2.2 Syntactic Theory Contrasted with Phonological Theory

As the quotation at the end of the preceding section implies, syntactic theory was well ahead of phonological theory in finding a central, explanatory role for well-formedness constraints. For some time now, the thinking in syntax has been that rules are language-particular devices suitable only for description; real explanations are obtained from universal *principles*.⌨§2.5¶8

It was not always so. Generative syntax and phonology started in approximately the same spot: the *Aspects* model (Chomsky 1965) is as rich in its theory of rules, and as limited in its principles, as the *SPE* model. But the subsequent development of syntactic theory – in works like Perlmutter (1971) or Chomsky and Lasnik (1977), and in the context of entire research programs like P&P, Relational Grammar, LFG (Lexical-Functional Grammar), and GPSG (Generalized Phrase-Structure Grammar) – shifted more and more of the analytic and explanatory burden away from rules and onto constraints.[4] The GB (Government-Binding Theory) hypothesis that there is just one transformation, Move-α, supplemented by a rich theory of principles, had no counterpart in phonological theory.

Together with its emphasis on universal principles, contemporary syntactic theory has also tried to get a better handle on the language particular than the *Aspects* model had. The *parameters* of P&P are perhaps the best-known example, but other frameworks have similar strategies for simultaneously permitting and restricting variation between languages. Parameters provide a far more explanatory theory of between-language variation than the language-particular rules of *Aspects*. In phonology, parametric models were proposed for specific domains, such as the parametric theory of stress in Hayes (1980). In phonology, though, parameters were not seen as enduring commitments; the parameter settings of a language could be overridden derivationally by language-particular rules. Needless to say, this considerably complicates the task of the learner and makes the parametric theory much less predictive.

A final point of difference is that contemporary syntactic theory, across frameworks, has rejected or greatly reduced the role of the sequential derivation as a significant explanatory device. The last syntactic analysis that depended crucially on language-particular rule ordering is lost in the mists of history, and even the idea of sequential interaction of any kind has been seriously questioned and rejected in many frameworks (though cf. Chomsky 1995: 223, and §3.3.3.1). In phonology, though nonderivational theories like Constraint-Based or Declarative Phonology had been proposed⊞§2.5¶5.¶7 and though there was a long tradition of attempting to predict the course of derivations with rule-ordering principles (§2.1),⊞§2.5¶2 most work throughout the 1970s and 1980s continued to presuppose a serial derivation with at least some language-particular rules applying in a language-particular order.

This was also the situation at the beginning of the 1990s, as characterized in the quotation from Prince and Smolensky at the end of §2.1. The dominant phonological framework, though it had an improved theory of representations and representational parameters and constraints, retained the apparatus of language-particular rules and rule ordering inherited from *SPE*. In contrast, serious research in syntax across frameworks had shifted far from the kinds of analyses and explanations proposed in *Aspects*, with an increasing emphasis on universal principles and sharply curtailed possibilities for between-language variation.

2.3 Rules and Constraints in Phonology and Syntax

We have seen that phonology and syntax took two different paths of development since the late 1960s. One reason for this difference is surely methodological: phonologists have tended to be preoccupied with achieving exhaustive descriptive coverage, even at considerable cost in explanation; conversely, their syntactic colleagues have pushed toward the goal of developing interesting explanations even at the expense of descriptive incompleteness. Consequently, it sometimes seems as if the debunking of a proposed principle in phonology is an accomplishment as much prized as positing one in syntax. Readers can decide for themselves which is more to be admired.

There is also a deeper source of difference, however. The vexed question of how constraints can both block and trigger rules has an easier answer when all the rules are optional.[5] This observation is of great relevance to OT, and so we will look at it closely.

In Chomsky and Lasnik (1977) and GB, all transformations are optional. A transformation, then, is a choice-point in a syntactic derivation. The diagram in (2) is a kind of meta-derivation, showing several such choice-points representing the different paths that input *A* can take on the way to surface *A*, *B*, *C*, or *D*.

(2) Derivational choice-points

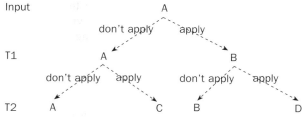

If the optional transformation T1 applies, then *A* is transformed into *B*; if it does not apply, *A* remains unchanged. Similarly with T2. The result is, in effect, a set of "candidate" surface structures, {*A, B, C, D*}, that have been obtained from input *A* by all combinations of applying or not applying these optional transformations. The surface structures in this set are submitted to the filters, which mark some of them as ill formed.

Suppose some filter marks *A* and *C* in (2) as ill formed, leaving the reduced set {*B, D*}. Because the only licit surface structures in this inventory are those that have undergone T1, the filter will seem to trigger T1. To the naive observer, T1 looks like an obligatory transformation, but it is technically optional, like all transformations. No literal triggering or constraint/repair relation is involved, since the filter is enforced long after T1 has applied. Similarly, if a filter marks *C* and *D* as ill formed, it will appear to "block" T2, but again the filter does not act directly on the transformation. Because all transformations are optional, their function approximates that of GEN, and the filters act as unranked, inviolable markedness constraints on the outputs of the transformations.[6] (The situation is different in Minimalism, which *compares* rather than *selects* among derivational paths. On the comparative, Economy-based ideas of Minimalism in relation to OT, see §3.2.3.)

The success of this research program depends, to a great extent, on the naturalness of the filters required. When a transformation is observed to be notionally triggered or blocked, the requisite filters ought to make sense as output conditions. The central claim, then, is "that the consequences of ordering, obligatoriness, and contextual dependency can be captured in terms of surface filters . . . and further, that these properties can be expressed in a natural way at this level" (Chomsky and Lasnik 1977: 433). Taking this hypothesis to its limit, as in GB, the transformational component is reduced to near triviality, the single optional context-free operation Move-α.

From a purely technical standpoint, there is no reason why a GB-style approach could not be implemented in phonology. Why not construct a phonological model where a few context-free rules apply optionally, overgenerating outputs that are filtered downstream? This could be a promising line of attack on the conspiracy problem (§2.1, §3.1.4.3), but in fact it is hard to find much work in phonology that has pursued this idea seriously. Two main factors seem to have discouraged most phonologists from following up this obvious and seemingly promising line of inquiry.

First, because the processes that receive the most attention in phonology are almost always obligatory, every rule context will have to be directly translated into a filter, with no apparent improvement in insight. For example, one of the rules in the Yawelmani conspiracy (§2.1) is V → Ø/VC___CV. Suppose, in the spirit of the GB approach, that this context-sensitive rule is replaced by a context-free optional rule V → Ø. It is blocked from overapplying by Kisseberth's original *CCC filter. But how is it blocked from underapplying? That is, since the rule is technically optional, there must be another filter to rule out forms where the rule should have applied but did not. This other filter will have to be *VCVCV – identical to the original rule's structural description. The *CCC filter will block outputs where V → Ø has applied excessively, but the *VCVCV filter is needed to ensure that it applies sufficiently. Skepticism about filters like this one tended to foreclose further developments along this line.

Second, context-free rules and surface filters have trouble dealing with all of the language-particular details of conspiracies. Recall that Yawelmani also has an epenthesis rule, Ø → i/C___CC. The context free rule Ø → i is reasonable enough, and the requisite filter, *CCC (or its syllabic equivalent), is independently motivated. But there is no way to ensure that epenthesis produces CiCC and not *CCiC, since both CiCC and CCiC do occur independently in Yawelmani. (In other words, CCiC is fine – just not as the output of epenthesis.) Yawelmani, then, exhibits an unexpected and seemingly unanalyzable *homogeneity* of process. It seems as if the epenthesis rule must still have its context to sort this out correctly, but that defeats the whole purpose of the filter.[7]

These problems suggest that obligatoriness and context-dependency, as they play out in phonology, cannot "be expressed in a natural way" with optional, context-free rules and surface filters. Arguably, though, both of these problems emanate from the assumption that the filters are inviolable. If instead they are ranked and violable, as in OT, the filters can be much simpler, answering the first objection, and they can be used to select among competing rule outputs, answering the second. Concretely, the inviolable filter *VCVCV in Yawelmani could be replaced by a much simpler violable filter, perhaps as simple as *V, but with *V crucially ranked below *CCC or its equivalent, to rule out candidates with excessive vowel deletion. And the choice between two epenthesis sites – CiCC versus *CCiC – can be understood as an instance of emergence of the unmarked (§3.2.2), where a violable filter (i.e., an OT markedness constraint) is ranked below faithfulness but is nevertheless decisive in situations where faithfulness is not relevant.[8]

Do similar problems arise in syntactic theory, and do they require the same solution? The checking theory of Minimalism is perhaps one indication that the goal of reducing all obligatoriness to natural surface filters is unattainable, as is the more general problem in P&P of surrounding putatively natural filters with protective hedges and parameters (see §1.2.2; Grimshaw 1997b; Speas 1997). The syntactic applications of OT discussed in Chapter 3 indicate that there is an important role for violable output constraints in syntax and that this role is abstractly the same as OT's solution to the problem of phonological conspiracies like Yawelmani's. From the OT perspective, phonology and syntax are not that different, and one of the principal themes throughout Chapter 3 is the strength of the parallels between phonological and syntactic consequences of the theory.

2.4 Harmony Theory

Harmony Theory, Harmonic Grammar, and Harmonic Phonology are important precursors to OT. (Harmony Theory was developed by Smolensky. Its linguistic extensions and applications are the work of Smolensky, Legendre, Goldsmith, and others.☐§2.5¶9) Harmony Theory provides insight into the workings of certain connectionist networks, allowing them to be understood symbolically as realizing "soft" constraints. This theory, then, represents a kind of nexus of numerical connectionism and symbolic cognitive science. Harmonic Grammar is a specifically linguistic application and realization of Harmony Theory.[9]

A simple connectionist network can be described as a kind of pattern associator with the structure in (3). Every member of the set of input nodes $\{in_1, in_2, \ldots, in_m\}$ is connected with every member of the set of output nodes $\{out_1, out_2, \ldots, out_n\}$.

(3) A simple connectionist model

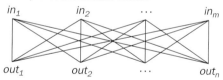

The input nodes stand for various properties that the input form might have (e.g., begins with a vowel, begins with a consonant, etc.), and the output nodes stand for properties of the output form. Each node has a numerical activation value. The activation values of the input nodes are fixed for a given input, so they effectively represent that input. Similarly, the activation values of the output nodes represent the output form. For example, if the output node standing for "begins with a vowel" has a higher activation value than the output node standing for "begins with a consonant," the output will begin with a vowel.

Each link between the two layers has associated with it a numerical weight. The weight of the link between in_i and out_j is conventionally designated w_{ij}. The activation of a specific output node out_j – which ultimately translates into some linguistic property of the predicted output form – is a function of the activation of all the input nodes in_i linked to it and the weights associated with those links w_{ij}. If w_{ij} is positive, then activation of in_i will tend to excite out_j; conversely, if

w_{ij} is negative, then activation of in_i will tend to inhibit out_j. Training a network like this one consists of taking known input-output pairs and adjusting the weights until the correct outputs are predicted. The trained network can then be tried out on novel inputs to see whether it works.

Each connection in the network is a soft constraint: if the input is this, then the output is preferably (not) that. The absolute value of the weight on the connection is an indication of how soft or hard that particular constraint is relative to the other constraints. Because the weights are numerical and can be combined, weaker constraints can join forces against a stronger constraint.

Numerical optimization is the main thing that distinguishes connectionist models from OT. OT has strict domination hierarchies rather than weighted constraints, eliminating the possibility of additive effects among constraints (except perhaps for the more limited case of local conjunction [§1.2.3]). This difference between OT and connectionism makes it much easier in OT to understand the workings of grammars, to deal with categorical, symbolic data, and to develop effective learning algorithms.

The interpretation of connectionist networks and their applicability to linguistic data are greatly enhanced by Smolensky's notion of *harmony*. Harmony is a way of abstracting over a whole network, giving it the kind of high-level interpretation that can be matched up with symbolic theories of cognition, such as linguistic theory. The harmony of the network in (3) is defined as the sum of the product $in_i*w_{ij}*out_j$ for all i and j (where in_i and out_j stand for the activation values of the respective nodes). For the entire network to yield a relatively high harmony value, then, there must be many specific connections where in_i, w_{ij}, and out_j have high absolute values.

Now comes the interpretation of the harmony notion. A connection where in_i, w_{ij}, and out_j have high values means that a robust soft constraint is being obeyed. The constraint is robust, because the absolute value of the weight is high. The constraint is being obeyed because the presence of the input property represented by the node in_i is exciting the presence of the output property out_j. The same goes, *mutatis mutandis*, for inhibition, when w_{ij} and out_j are negative and have relatively high absolute values. The interpretation: obedience to a robust negative soft constraint. So a high harmony value means that lots of relatively robust soft constraints are being obeyed throughout the network.

That is the idea. The harmony of the individual connections, thought of as soft constraints, is a combined measure of how hard or soft they are and how much they are being respected. The harmony of the entire network, which is the sum of the harmony of its individual connections, is a measure of how well all of its soft constraints are being respected, with the strongest constraints (those where $|w_{ij}|$ is largest) contributing the most. Selecting an output that maximizes the harmony of the network is a way of best satisfying the soft constraints that the network expresses. Before going on, readers might want to take a moment to think about how maximization of harmony resembles and differs from EVAL.

Harmony Theory is distinct from OT, but also connected to it, as Prince and Smolensky explain:

> Optimality Theory, by contrast, seeks to strengthen the higher-level theory of grammatical form. It can be viewed as abstracting the core idea of the principle of Harmony Maximization and making it work formally and empirically in a purely symbolic theory of grammar. . . . The property of strict domination is a new element, one quite unexpected and currently unexplainable from the connectionist perspective, and one which is crucial to the success of the enterprise. (Prince and Smolensky 1993: 202)

Harmony Theory and OT are both about finding optima in systems of soft constraints. But OT is symbolic, not numerical, and concomitantly it has strict domination constraint hierarchies, not weights.

Applications of Harmonic Grammar exploit the capacity of Harmony Theory to do numerical optimization. Legendre, Miyata, and Smolensky (1990a) describe an application of Harmonic Grammar to the problem of predicting which French verbs are unergative and which are unaccusative.[10] This example nicely illustrates Harmonic Grammar because there is no simple mapping from the lexical properties of verbs (such as telicity or animacy of the argument) to the unaccusative/unergative split. Furthermore, the split itself is not so sharp, since putatively unaccusative verbs differ in how they perform on various syntactic tests of unaccusativity, and the syntactic acceptability judgments are graded. The connectionist network they use is more complicated than (3): its inputs are the properties of the verbs (and the test to be applied) and its outputs are graded acceptability judgments, but there is an intermediate layer (so-called hidden units) of two nodes, one standing for unaccusativity and the other for unergativity. The soft constraints embedded in this system classify a verb as relatively unaccusative or relatively unergative by maximizing the harmony of the sub-network consisting of all the nodes in the input and hidden layers. The harmony values of this sub-network are then mapped onto the output acceptability judgments: the higher the harmony, the better the sentence. (For approaches to gradient data or optionality in OT proper, see §4.5.)

2.5   For Further Reading

¶1   *The Sound Pattern of English*

SPE is tough going even for experienced phonologists, so it is better to start with a textbook treatment. Of the various 1970s-era textbooks, Dell (1973) and its English translation (Dell 1980) are the best at giving a sense of the broader enterprise, Schane (1973) is the most compact and accessible, Hyman (1975) is most helpful for those who need a review of concepts once known and now forgotten, and Kenstowicz and Kisseberth (1979) is richest in data and analyses. For developments since about 1975, the best and most comprehensive resources are Goldsmith (1995) and Kenstowicz (1994a).

Concerning the content of *SPE* specifically, Goyvaerts and Pullum (1975) is a collection of critical essays, McCawley (1973) attacks *SPE*'s formalist program (with a reply by Prince 1975), and Stampe (1973b) criticizes the *SPE* markedness theory (with a reply by Kean 1977). Anderson (1979, 1985: Chapter 13) gives a good sense of the intellectual history of this period, and Dinnsen (1979) is a good overview of the state of the art a decade after *SPE*.

¶2   Rule Ordering, Derivations, and Parallelism
The literature from the early 1970s attempting to eliminate or reduce the role of language-particular rule ordering is abundant; Iverson (1995) gives a useful survey with all of the main references (e.g., Anderson 1974; Chafe 1968; Iverson 1974; Kenstowicz and Kisseberth 1971, 1977; Kiparsky 1968; Kisseberth 1973; Koutsoudas 1976; Koutsoudas, Sanders, and Noll 1974). More recent research has focused on reducing or eliminating the sequential derivations of *SPE*. Some of the frameworks where this is a matter of particular emphasis include Constraint-Based or Declarative Phonology (Bird 1990; Coleman 1991; Scobbie 1991, 1993), Harmonic Phonology (Bosch 1991; Goldsmith 1990, 1991, 1993a; Wiltshire 1992), and Two-Level or Cognitive Phonology (Karttunen 1993; Koskenniemi 1983; Lakoff 1993; Wheeler and Touretzky 1993). Also see §3.3.3 for related discussion.

¶3   Natural Phonology
The locus classicus of Natural Phonology is Stampe (1973a). Other important works include Donegan (1978), Donegan and Stampe (1979), Lovins (1973), Nathan (1984), Stampe (1969), many of the contributions to Bruck, Fox, and La Galy (1974), and Dressler's (1985) extension of the theory to morphology. For further discussion of the differences between constraint ranking in OT and process suppression or limitation in Natural Phonology, see Pater (1997: 234).

Natural Phonology should not be confused with Natural *Generative* Phonology (Hooper [Bybee] 1976, 1979; Vennemann 1974), which is based on very different premises with little relevance to OT.

¶4   Nonlinear Phonology
The literature on this topic is too large to summarize here, but fortunately the contributions to and bibliography of Goldsmith (1995) do the job very well. There are also many recent textbooks; I have found Gussenhoven and Jacobs (1998) to be unusually accessible, while Goldsmith (1990) and Kenstowicz (1994a) offer particularly comprehensive and authoritative coverage.

¶5   The Role of Well-Formedness Constraints in Phonology
Other approaches to the "conceptual crisis" include those cited in ¶2, ¶3, and ¶7 in this section, as well as Government and Dependency Phonology (Anderson 1986; Anderson and Ewen 1987; Charette 1988; Durand 1986; Ewen

1995; Harris 1990b, 1994; van der Hulst 1989; Kaye 1990; Kaye and Lowenstamm 1984, 1985; Kaye, Lowenstamm, and Vergnaud 1985; Polgardi 1998), and Montague Phonology (Bach and Wheeler 1981; Wheeler 1981, 1988). There have been many other attempts to grapple with particular aspects of the problem, such as Archangeli and Pulleyblank (1994), Broselow (1976, 1992), Burzio (1994b: 363 s.v. "constraints, violable/hierarchically ranked/ sometimes in conflict"), Goldsmith (1976a, 1976b), Hammond (1984), Ito (1986, 1989), Kiparsky (1981, 1985), McCarthy (1986), Prince (1983), Singh (1987), and, as well as many of the works cited in ¶6. See Burzio (1995) for another perspective on how studies of well-formedness constraints in phonology figured into the development of OT.

¶6   *Conspiracies*

Using Csik and Papa's (1979) excellent bibliography, I have prepared the following exhaustive list of 1970s-era works on conspiracies and related notions: Abdul-Ghani (1976), Bhat (1976), Bladon (1971), Clayton (1976), Clifton (1975), Dalgish (1975), Devine and Stephens (1974), Haiman (1972), Hale (1973), Hock (1975), Kim (1972), Kiparsky (1972, 1973a), Kisseberth (1970a, 1970b, 1972), Klausenburger (1974), Kučera (1973), Lehman (1973), Lovins (1971), Morin (1976), Nessly (1973), Pyle (1974), Robson (1971), Ross (1973), Schourup (1974), Shibatani (1973), and Sommerstein (1974). The papers by Kiparsky, Kisseberth, and Sommerstein are of particular importance. Also see the references about the Duplication Problem in §3.4 ¶2.

¶7   *Constraint and Repair Theories in Phonology*

Harmonic Phonology (references in ¶2, this section) and the Theory of Constraints and Repair Strategies (TCRS) (Paradis 1988a, Paradis and LaCharité 1993) both employ the idea of a constraint triggering a repair rule, as do Calabrese (1987, 1988, 1995), Mester (1994), Rice (1987), Yip (1988), and many others. Persistent rules (Chafe 1968: 131; Halle and Vergnaud 1987: 135; Myers 1991) are a little different, though addressed to similar situations: a persistent rule applies throughout the derivation, like a constraint, but unlike a constraint it incorporates a statement of its own repair.

¶8   *Rules, Constraints, and Parameters in Syntactic Theory*

Newmeyer (1996: Chapter 5 [originally published in 1991]) nicely reviews the history of the tension between rules and principles (i.e., constraints) in generative syntax from *Syntactic Structures* (Chomsky 1957) through GB. Marantz (1995) provides an accessible overview of the subsequent development of P&P from GB through Minimalism. There is much recent literature containing overt comparison of P&P and OT; see Grimshaw (1997b), Pesetsky (1997, 1998), Samek-Lodovici (1998), and Speas (1997). Also see the cross-references in the FAQ about parameters.

¶9   *Harmony Theory and Harmonic Grammar*

Harmony Theory is developed in Smolensky (1983, 1984a, 1984b, 1986), while Harmonic Grammar is the topic of Legendre, Miyata, and Smolensky (1990a, 1990b, 1990c, 1991a, 1991b). Harmonic Phonology (references in ¶2) is a related approach, as is Goldsmith and Larson's Dynamic Linear Model (Goldsmith 1992, Goldsmith and Larson 1990, Larson 1990, 1992, Prince 1993a). Works specifically dealing with the relationships among OT, Harmony Theory, and connectionism include Smolensky, Legendre, and Miyata (1992), Prince and Smolensky (1993: Chapter 10, 1997), and Smolensky (1988, 1995a).

Though their results are not couched within Harmony Theory, Burzio (1994b) and Gibson and Broihier (1998) also use weighted constraints; research on stochastic constraints and grammars is also relevant (e.g., Boersma 1998; Broe, Frisch, and Pierrehumbert 1995; Frisch 1996, 2000). See §4.5 for some related discussion.

Notes

1. Natural Phonology additionally recognizes a class of *learned rules*. They deal with the lexicalized residue of defunct natural processes, such as the *f/v* alternation in *leaf/leaves*.
2. For these constraints, see, respectively, Goldsmith (1976a, 1976b), Prince (1983), and Leben (1973).
3. This observation is no less true for the constraints mentioned in the preceding paragraph. On the Well-Formedness Condition, see Pulleyblank (1986); on the Clash Filter, see Nespor and Vogel (1989) and Hayes (1984, 1995); on the Obligatory Contour Principle, see Odden (1986) and cf. Myers (1997b).
4. This one-sentence sketch of the history of syntactic thought obviously simplifies a complex situation. For a much more nuanced and accurate view of the shifting roles of rules and principles, see Newmeyer (1996: Chapter 5).
5. See Bromberger and Halle (1989) for a different view.
6. Technically, "[t]he transformational rules of the core grammar are unordered and optional. . . . The operations are restricted to movement, left- and right-adjunction, and substitution of a designated element" (Chomsky and Lasnik 1977: 431). Since unordered, optional rules can be freely reapplied to their own outputs, and since Chomsky-adjunction is a type of recursion, the transformational component can deform a finite input in infinitely many ways. Though the infinity of the candidate set has figured prominently in critiques of OT (§1.1.3, §4.3), the issue was not raised in this earlier context.
7. Kiparsky (1973a) and Myers (1991) make the same point in their discussion of conspiracies and constraint-and-repair theories, respectively.
8. There are several proposals in the literature for how to distinguish C*i*CC from *CC*i*C using independently motivated constraints (see Broselow 1992; Farwaneh 1995: 125ff.; Ito 1986, 1989; Kiparsky to appear-b; Kirchner 1996; Mester and Padgett 1994; Selkirk 1981).
9. The use of the word "harmony" in Harmonic Grammar and OT completes a circle going back to Smolensky's undergraduate days at Harvard (Paul Smolensky, per-

sonal communication). He first encountered the field of linguistics while taking a general education course taught by Jorge Hankamer. Smolensky was much impressed by the process of vowel harmony in Turkish, and the word stuck with him as a description for a kind of global well-formedness.

10. Unergatives and unaccusatives are two types of intransitive verbs (Perlmutter 1974). Very roughly, the grammatical subjects of unergatives are agents (e.g., *work*) and those of unaccusatives are not (e.g., *melt* in *the ice melted*). This distinction is important in the syntax of many languages.

3

The Results of Optimality Theory

In this chapter, I describe the main consequences of OT. In keeping with the overall goals of this book, the focus throughout the chapter is on results that are broadly applicable and on examples that clearly and simply illustrate those results. For the same reason, particular attention is given to *architectural (near-)imperatives*: results that follow from the basic structure of OT, as described in Chapter 1, without too much reliance on parochial assumptions about linguistic representations or constraints.

This chapter is organized around the properties of the theory that lead to these results rather than around particular linguistic phenomena. There are three main sections: markedness/faithfulness interaction (§3.1), constraint violability (§3.2), and globality and parallelism (§3.3). Since these aspects of OT are not isolated from one another, there is inevitably some overlap among the sections and some room for disagreement about where to put particular topics. The cross-references and the FAQs will, I hope, aid readers in pulling the threads together.

3.1 Consequences of Markedness/Faithfulness Interaction

OT has two main types of constraints, markedness and faithfulness (§1.2.2). Markedness constraints evaluate the well-formedness of output candidates. Faithfulness constraints prohibit disparity between output candidates and the inputs that underlie them. The interaction of markedness and faithfulness constraints through language-particular ranking (§1.3) is essential to description and explanation in OT.

The effects of markedness/faithfulness interaction are diverse, and so the contents of this section range widely. The section begins (§3.1.1) with a review of the basics of interaction, covering some of the same ground as §1.3 but more rigorously. The discussion then turns to one of the main, overarching linguistic problems: language-particular restrictions on the inventory (§3.1.2) and distribution (§3.1.3) of linguistic objects. OT, in contrast with most recent thinking in phonology and syntax, recognizes no role for the lexicon in addressing these problems. Section 3.1.4 looks at the other main, overarching linguistic problem: the character of processes and their role in linguistic systems. OT has no primitive notion of a process, rule, or transformation; relatedly, it makes important claims about the interaction and coexistence of processes in a language. Finally, §3.1.5 examines the consequences of ranking permutation for language typology. It also addresses an important question: how does a theory based on violable constraints account for truly universal properties of human language?

3.1.1   The Basics: Ranking Prerequisites for an Unfaithful Mapping

Mappings from inputs to outputs may be faithful or unfaithful. The mapping /abc/ → [abc] is faithful, since every element of the input is exactly replicated in the output, and vice versa, with no additions, alterations, transpositions, or subtractions.[1] The mapping /abc/ → [adc] is unfaithful, so the candidate [adc] incurs a violation of some faithfulness constraint. Unfaithful mappings are particularly important because it takes an unfaithful mapping to "make things happen." The topics to be discussed below – restrictions on inventories (§3.1.2), distribution (§3.1.3), and processes (§3.1.4) – depend on understanding the role of unfaithful mappings. The goal of this section is to get the basics in place by establishing the ranking conditions that produce an unfaithful mapping. These conditions are entirely independent of the empirical domain under investigation, with equal applicability to phonology, morphology, or syntax.

Whether a particular grammar maps the input /abc/ onto the faithful output [abc] or the unfaithful output [adc] depends on the details of the constraints supplied by UG and how they are ranked in that grammar. A necessary condition for an unfaithful mapping is the basic ⟦M ≫ F⟧ ranking seen throughout chapter 1 (e.g., (10)). But because constraints interact, necessary and sufficient conditions for an unfaithful mapping to occur, include all of the requirements in (1).

(1) Conditions for an unfaithful mapping
   The unfaithful mapping /a/ → [b] will occur if and only if all of the following conditions are met:
   a. Con includes some markedness constraint M that favors [b] over [a]. (M *favors* X over Y if and only if M assigns fewer violation-marks to X than Y.)
   b. M is ranked above every faithfulness constraint that is violated by the /a/ → [b] mapping.
   c. M is ranked above every markedness constraint that favors [a] over [b].
   d. For all candidates [x] (where [x] is not [a] or [b]), no mapping /a/ → [x] is more harmonic than /a/ → [b]. This is assured in two situations.
      i. The candidate [x] is more marked than [b]. That is, the highest-ranking constraint that distinguishes them is a markedness constraint favoring [b] over [x].

ii. The mapping /a/ → [x] is less faithful than /a/ → [b]. That is, the highest-ranking constraint that distinguishes them is a faithfulness constraint favoring /a/ → [b] over /a/ → [x].

These requirements derive from the basic structure of the theory; ultimately, all can be understood as consequences of the Cancellation/Domination Lemma ((15) in §1.3), which itself follows from EVAL.

Clauses (1a–b) say that any unfaithful mapping requires the basic ⟦M ≫ F⟧ ranking. The markedness constraint must dominate *some* relevant faithfulness constraint, because unfaithfulness is never gratuitous; rather, it is always the price paid for concomitant improvement in markedness (§3.1.4.5). Clause (1b) also excludes the blocking configuration ⟦C_F ≫ M ≫ F⟧ (such as (14) in §1.3), where M dominates some but not all faithfulness constraints that the unfaithful mapping /a/ → [b] violates.

As was just noted, the only reason for an unfaithful mapping to be optimal is if it does better than the faithful candidate on the markedness constraints as they are ranked in the language under investigation. A fortiori, an unfaithful mapping cannot be optimal if it produces worse performance on the ranked markedness constraints. That is the import of clause (1c): if unfaithful [b] is more marked than faithful [a], then the unfaithful mapping cannot be more harmonic than the faithful one. This clause also excludes a blocking configuration, the ⟦C_M ≫ M ≫ F⟧ ranking exemplified by (13) in §1.3.

Clause (1d) recognizes the effects of homogeneity of target/heterogeneity of process (§1.3.2, §3.1.4.2). Many unfaithful mappings could in principle satisfy the markedness constraint M, but the mapping to [b] is the one that is actually observed. The various alternative mappings must be less harmonic because they involve candidates that are more marked or less faithful than [b] (again, relative to the language's particular constraint hierarchy). A concrete example, where the alternatives are less faithful, can be found in (13) and (14) of §1.3.

In summary, all of these requirements must be met to guarantee that /a/ maps most harmonically onto [b]. If (1a–c) do not hold, then /a/ will map faithfully to [a]. If (1d) is not met, then /a/ will receive unfaithful treatment, but it will end up as something other than [b].

3.1.2   Inventories and Richness of the Base

3.1.2.1   Basic Concepts

As used here, the term *inventory* refers to the set of linguistic objects that are permitted in the output representations of a language. It is often useful to speak of the inventory of objects of some specific type, such as the inventory of vowels in English or the inventory of clitic pronouns in Spanish. Some members of an inventory may have a restricted *distribution*, meaning that they are limited to (or prohibited from) appearing in certain contexts. The theory of inventories in OT is the topic of this section, and distributional restrictions are addressed in §3.1.3.

These terms are probably used more in phonology than in syntax, but the underlying concepts are relevant throughout linguistics. In every language and at every level of analysis – phonological, morphological, or syntactic – there are limitations on what elements are permitted in surface structure and where they are permitted. Any linguistic theory needs a way of accounting for these observations and the associated typological generalizations (§3.1.5).

An observed inventory restriction can be described schematically as follows. Suppose that the free combination of primitive linguistic objects (e.g., phonological or morphosyntactic features) allows for the four-way distinction A/B/C/D. But in the language under investigation, only the three-way distinction A/B/C is actually observed in surface structures. The inventory of this language is restricted by the absence of D. In principle, this gap could be accidental, like missing *blick* in English, but let us suppose further that familiar criteria like productivity tests or typological consistency show that it is not.

In both phonology and syntax, inventory restrictions have usually been analyzed by imposing a filter on the input side, barring D from the lexicon or other source of inputs. Lexical redundancy rules, morpheme structure constraints, or simply the lexicon itself impose structure on the freely combined linguistic primitives that we see in (2).

(2) Free combination   Input   Output
    of linguistic
    primitives

    A   ———————→   A   ———————→   A

    B   ———————→   B   ———————→   B

    C   ═══════→   C   ———————→   C
    D   ━━━━━━━↗

If the input is identified with the lexicon, we would say that the lexicon of this language systematically fails to exploit an option that UG supplies. Other languages may, of course, differ on this point by including D in the lexicon. This is a standard way to account for between-language variation in both phonology and syntax; in fact, according to one view (Chomsky 1993), this might be the *only* way of accounting for between-language variation. Some examples from English: the lexicon is subject to a phonological redundancy rule prohibiting front rounded vowels (*ü, ö*); the lexicon lacks a Q element, and so *wh*-phrases must be fronted (Chomsky 1995:69).[2]

Most work in OT, however, recognizes no distinction between the free combination of linguistic primitives and the input. D is absent from surface structure because input D is unfaithfully mapped to something else – either some other member of the inventory or the null output (§4.1.2). For the purpose of discussion, assume that D is mapped to C, as in (3).

(3) Free combination   Output
    of linguistic primitives
    = Input

    A   ⟶   A

    B   ⟶   B

    C   ⟶   C
    D   ⟶

The absence of D from surface forms is here a consequence of the unfaithful mapping of D to C, which absolutely neutralizes any possible distinction between them. Examples like this can be found throughout this book, such as (14) in §3.1.2.5 (morphosyntax), (21) in §3.1.3.5 (phonology), and (4) in §4.1.3 (syntax).

The hypothesis that the free combination of linguistic primitives and the input are identical is called *richness of the base* (ROTB).[3] 📖$_{§3.4¶1}$ Equivalently, ROTB says that there are no language-particular restrictions on the input, no linguistically significant generalizations about the lexicon, no principled lexical gaps, no lexical redundancy rules, morpheme structure constraints, or similar devices. All generalizations about the inventory of elements permitted in surface structure must be derived from markedness/faithfulness interaction, which controls the faithful and unfaithful mappings that preserve or merge the potential contrasts present in the rich base.

This material presents abundant opportunities for terminological confusion, which I here attempt to sort out. The *inventory* of a language is the set of permitted surface structures. Except for accidental gaps, the observed inventory of a language should exactly match the output of EVAL for that language's constraint hierarchy. The inventory, then, is derived or *emerges* from applying the hierarchy to a set of inputs. The *base* is the universal set of inputs. If a language's constraint hierarchy has been correctly analyzed, then applying GEN and EVAL to any input chosen from the universal base will yield some surface structure in that language's inventory. The *lexicon* should really be called the *vocabulary*: because of accidental gaps, the observed inventory is a proper subset of the inventory that emerges from EVAL. The grammar is responsible for systematic gaps (*bnick* is not a possible word of English) but not for accidental ones (*blick* is not a word of English), nor does the grammar purport to explain accidental properties of lexical meaning (*brick* is an object made of clay). These accidental properties are recorded in the lexicon, which, however, lacks the internal principles familiar from other theories of phonology and syntax. Hence the term vocabulary. There will be much more about all of this in §3.1.2.

ROTB is a natural consequence of one of the central ideas in OT – that languages differ only in constraint ranking. It is, moreover, the most parsimonious hypothesis: the input (the base or lexicon) freely combines the primitive elements of linguistic representation, and then the grammar, which is needed anyway, reduces this profusion to the observed inventory.

3.1.2.2 The Duplication Problem, with Examples

Apart from the conceptual arguments for assuming ROTB, there is also a powerful empirical reason that was first recognized in phonological research of the 1970s. The *Duplication Problem* is a particular kind of conspiracy (§2.1).📖₃.₄¶₂ Merely eliminating D from the lexicon, as in the standard theory (2), is not enough to ensure the absence of D from the inventory. It is also necessary to take precautions against any rules of the grammar creating D's in the mapping from the lexicon to surface structure. Consider, for example, a language that, like English, has no front rounded vowels (*ü, ö*) in its inventory. According to the standard model, this language has the lexical redundancy rule in (4a). Now suppose that the same language also has a fronting or umlaut rule that changes *u* and *o* into *i* and *e*, respectively, when the next syllable contains *i*. That rule is exemplified in (4b) and formulated in (4c).

(4) a. Lexical redundancy rule
    if [−back], then [−round]
   b. Fronting rule exemplified
      /put + i/   →   piti
      /kop + i/   →   kepi
   c. Fronting rule
         V   → $\begin{bmatrix} -\text{back} \\ -\text{round} \end{bmatrix}$ /_____C_0 i

There is a correlation here: *ü* and *ö* are banned from the inventory of this language, and the fronting rule produces *i*'s and *e*'s rather than *ü*'s and *ö*'s. This correlation is surely not an accident, yet it is entirely unexplained in the standard theory (2). Formally, the problem is that the [−round] specification in the output of the fronting rule duplicates the [−round] specification in the consequent of the lexical redundancy rule. Since the standard theory equates simplicity with naturalness under the Evaluation Metric (§2.1), a simpler and putatively more natural fronting rule would change *u* into *ü* and *o* into *ö*. In other words, the fronting rule must be made more complicated and consequently less natural looking, to bring it into accord with the lexical redundancy rule. This is an instance of the Duplication Problem: a lexical redundancy rule and a rule of the phonology act together in service of the same surface target.

The Duplication Problem, then, is the observation that rules of grammar often duplicate in their dynamic mappings the restrictions that are imposed statically by lexical redundancy rules. "In many respects, [lexical redundancy rules] seem to be exactly like ordinary phonological rules, in form and function" (Chomsky and Halle 1968: 382). ROTB avoids the Duplication Problem simply by denying that there is any such thing as a lexical redundancy rule or the equivalent. ROTB recognizes no distinction between the mappings that enforce static inventory restrictions and those that produce dynamic alternations; the Duplication Problem shows that this distinction is in any case illusory.

In OT, a single markedness constraint, suitably ranked, is responsible for the absence of *ü*'s and *ö*'s from the inventory of the language in (4). This constraint, call it FRT/*RND, is identical to the lexical redundancy rule (4a), but it evaluates outputs rather than inputs. If FRT/*RND is to compel unfaithful mappings, as it must if it is to affect the inventory, it must be ranked above some faithfulness constraint. Suppose that the low-ranking faithfulness constraint is IDENT(back), which requires input and output to agree in their values for the feature [back]. If FRT/*RND dominates IDENT(back), and if in addition IDENT(round) dominates IDENT(back) (cf. (1c)), then input /tük/ will map unfaithfully to *tuk*, as illustrated in (5).

(5) FRT/*RND, IDENT(round) ≫ IDENT(back)

/tük/	FRT/*RND	IDENT(round)	IDENT(back)	Remarks
a. ☞ tuk			*	Backing of /ü/
b. tük	*			Faithful
c. tik		*		Unrounding of /ü/

The rich base freely combines all of the elements of phonological representation, so it must contain the input /tük/ even if the surface inventory does not. (This is not to say that /tük/ is a literal underlying representation in the vocabulary of this language. See §3.1.2.4.) But /tük/ is mapped unfaithfully to *tuk*, so one possible source of *ü*'s in the inventory is thereby foreclosed. With the opposite ranking, putting faithfulness on top, /tük/ will survive to the surface unscathed. That is the situation in German, which does allow *ü* in its inventory and has a three-way surface contrast among *i*, *u*, and *ü*.

Input /ü/ is not the only possible source of output *ü*, since the effects of the fronting process must be contended with. Assume for the sake of discussion an ad hoc markedness constraint FRONT that penalizes back vowels before *i* (as in (6)). It is ranked above the faithfulness constraint IDENT(back).

(6) FRONT ≫ IDENT(back)

/put + i/	FRONT	IDENT(back)	Remarks
a. ☞ piti		*	Fronting of /u/ before /i/
b. puti	*		Faithful

The interesting action in OT involves constraint interaction, and this case is no exception. We already know from (5) that FRT/*RND dominates IDENT(back).

If, in addition, FRONT dominates IDENT(round), as it does in (7), then the fronting process will correctly yield *piti* rather than *püti*.

(7) FRONT ≫ IDENT(round)

/put + i/		FRONT	FRT/*RND	IDENT(round)	IDENT(back)
a.	☞ piti			*	*
b.	puti	*			
c.	püti		*		*

The optimal form in (7) violates both of the low-ranking faithfulness constraints, but its competitors do worse.

The rankings required in this language are summarized in (8).

(8)

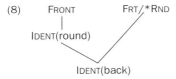

Diagrams like this are probably the best way to summarize the accumulated inferences about the constraint hierarchy of a language. It shows the constraints in a partial ordering, which is often all that can be determined (§1.1.2). Higher-ranking constraints are written at the top. If there is a strictly downward path between two constraints, then the higher one dominates the lower. For example, FRONT dominates the two faithfulness constraints in (8). If there is no strictly downward path between two constraints, then no ranking between them has been established. That is the case with FRT/*RND and all other constraints except IDENT(back). Depicting the constraint hierarchy by flattening it out, though unavoidable in a tableau like (7), loses this fine structure and can be misleading.

Taken together, tableaux (5) and (7) show that the same constraints in the same hierarchy are responsible for the static restriction – *ü* and *ö* do not occur in underived contexts – and for the dynamic one – *ü* and *ö* are not created by applying processes. There is no Duplication Problem, because the observed inventory restriction is accounted for once and only once in the grammar since there are no language-particular restrictions on inputs. The overall idea is that static and dynamic restrictions on inventories have the same source as each other and as all other aspects of between-language variation in OT: the interaction of markedness and faithfulness constraints.

ROTB does not deny the possibility of *universal* restrictions on input. Like putative restrictions on GEN (§1.1.3), though, they should be approached skeptically. It undoubtedly makes sense to impose some very general restrictions on inputs, such as providing a universal alphabet of phonological or morphosyntactic features. But there are alternative interpretations of many narrower restrictions. For example, because no known language has a contrast in syllabification between tautomorphemic *pa.ta* and *pat.a* or *pa.kla* and *pak.la*, it is often proposed that syllabification is universally absent from underlying representations.[4] But OT offers a different approach to this observation. Suppose that Con has no constraints demanding faithfulness to syllable structure. Markedness constraints will fully determine the syllabification of every input, without interference from faithfulness constraints. The non-contrastiveness of syllabification follows from this: inputs can contain all the syllabification they want, or none, or something in between, but no input syllabification will have any influence on the surface outcome if there are no syllabic faithfulness constraints to transmit that influence.

Before going on to look at a syntactic example, we need to consider an alternative solution to the Duplication Problem found in the phonological literature. Global rules or derivational constraints (Kisseberth 1970a, 1970b), linking rules (Chomsky and Halle 1968), persistent rules (Chafe 1968: 131; Halle and Vergnaud 1987: 135; Myers 1991), and underspecification (Archangeli 1984; Kiparsky 1981) share a common approach to languages like (4): details aside, they give the lexical redundancy rule (4a) a special durable status, so that it can "fix up" *ü*'s and *ö*'s, regardless of their source, by changing them into *i*'s and *e*'s. On this view, the fronting rule produces the prohibited segments *ü* and *ö* (or their underspecified counterparts), but the durable fix-up rule is immediately triggered, further changing them to *i* and *e*. Similar ideas are also common in syntactic analysis, though the fix-up theory itself (e.g., the mapping from S-Structure to PF) has until recently received less attention than its phonological counterparts.

The problem with the fix-up approach is that it accounts only for situations like (4) where the inventory restriction has a triggering effect (§1.3, §2.1, §2.3, §3.1.4). But inventory restrictions can also have blocking effects, stopping a process from applying when its output would escape from the licit inventory. Kiparsky (1982a, 1982b) calls this property structure preservation because of its resemblance to the syntactic principle with that name (Emonds 1970). In OT, whether a markedness constraint has a triggering effect, as in (7), or a blocking effect, as in (9), is a matter of interaction.

(9) Blocking from Ident(round) ≫ Front

/put + i/		Frt/*Rnd	Ident(round)	Front	Ident(back)
a.	piti		*		*
b.	☞ puti			*	
c.	püti	*			*

By swapping the ranking of Front and Ident(round), two distinct interactional possibilities are realized. With the ranking ⟦Front ≫ Ident(round)⟧ in (7), the fronting process can go ahead even when it leads to unfaithfulness in rounding as a consequence of further interaction with FRT/*RND. With the opposite ranking in (9), the fronting process cannot proceed under those conditions; it is simply blocked. Both types of interaction are well attested, and no criteria have been discovered that can consistently predict whether a given inventory restriction will apply in triggering or blocking mode. From the OT perspective, this is exactly as expected: blocking versus triggering is a matter of constraint ranking, and constraint ranking differs across languages.

The Duplication Problem does not seem to have been recognized in the pre-OT syntactic literature, but it has figured in applications of OT to syntax. Grimshaw (1997b: 409) discusses a couple of situations where independently necessary properties of the grammar render a parallel lexical restriction superfluous. For example, English has no complementizer in embedded questions: *I wonder who **that** he saw. This fact is standardly taken to mean that the English lexicon lacks [+wh] complementizers, but that kind of systematic, language-particular restriction on inputs is incompatible with ROTB. In OT, then, the grammar must supply the explanation for the impossibility of complementizers in embedded questions, and indeed it does. In English, heads are usually at the left edge of their phrases, unless some higher-ranking constraint compels minimal displacement (see (74) in §3.3.1). This observation shows that the edge Alignment constraint (§1.2.2.) HEAD-LEFT dominates its symmetric counterpart HEAD-RIGHT. The complementizer *that*, as head of CP, will maximally satisfy HEAD-LEFT if it is at the left edge of CP. But in embedded questions, there is a *wh*-word at the left edge of CP, so perfect satisfaction of HEAD-LEFT is not possible. In consequence, English has no complementizer at all, because HEAD-LEFT dominates OB-HD (which, short for obligatory heads, requires every projection to have a head – see (26) in §3.1.3.6).

(10) HEAD-LEFT ≫ OB-HD

	HEAD-LEFT	OB-HD
a. ☞ I wonder [CP who he saw		*
b. I wonder [CP who that he saw	*	

By deriving this observation from the grammar, as in (10), it is related to English's general left-headedness. Compare this to theories that simply say the lexicon lacks [+wh] complementizers. This is a covert instance of the Duplication Problem: the lexicon stipulates something that could be explained in other terms. The absence of a complementizer for embedded questions from the English inventory is a fact about the grammar, not the lexicon. The rich base provides such a complementizer, but the grammar rejects it.

In summary, observed inventory restrictions are a consequence of unfaithful mappings that neutralize potential distinctions present in the rich base. The base, then, can be universal, since inventory differences are sufficiently accounted for by the language-particular constraint rankings responsible for those unfaithful mappings.

3.1.2.3   Absolute Ill-Formedness

This discussion of unfaithful mappings and the limited role of the lexicon is important for another reason. It shows how *absolute ill-formedness* or ungrammaticality is obtained in OT.⊞§3.4¶3 A word, sentence, or other linguistic object (LO) is absolutely ill formed in some language if it never occurs in surface structures of that language – that is, it is absent from the inventory. Absolute ill-formedness might initially seem like a problem for a theory that is based on comparing candidates: how can LO be completely bad if well-formedness is always relative? This question misconceives the issue. If LO qua candidate is never optimal in any of its competitions against other candidates, then it is absolutely ill formed in the sense just defined – it will never be observed in that language. Absolute ill-formedness, then, is really absolute neutralization. If /A/ and /B/ both map onto [A], and if [B] loses not only in this competition but in all others, then [B] is absolutely ill formed. This is a comparative theory of absolute ungrammaticality, in keeping with the overall structure of OT.

For example, if the grammars in (7) and (9) are assumed to be complete, they will never select an output containing *ü* or *ö* as optimal. In real-life examples, which are typically more complicated, pronouncements like this need to be made cautiously. The seemingly attractive route of just checking that LO will never be obtained from a fully faithful mapping is not sufficient to establish its absolute ill-formedness. For example, if the ranking in (8) is replaced by ⟦FRONT, IDENT(round) ≫ FRT/*RND ≫ IDENT(back)⟧, then /tük/ will map unfaithfully to [tuk], as desired, but /put + i/ will map to [püti]. Hence, it may require methods of formal proof to show that some LO is absolutely ill formed relative to some constraint hierarchy H and the full range of inputs.

For further discussion of absolute ill-formedness in syntax, see §4.4.1.2.

3.1.2.4   The Lexicon and Richness of the Base

According to ROTB, all languages share the same set of potential inputs. This is sometimes taken to mean, absurdly, that all languages have literally the same *vocabulary* – that every language has the vocabulary entry /kæt/ with the meaning *Felis catus*. ROTB does not dispense with the need for a language-particular vocabulary with its myriad accidental sound-meaning associations. But ROTB does assert that no linguistically significant regularities have their source in the lexicon. This means, for example, that the grammar of Maori, a language without syllable-final consonants, must unfaithfully map input /kæt/ onto some output that is possible in the Maori inventory, such as [ka] or [kati]. To repeat the point, there is no suggestion here that Maori has the *word* /kæt/, with or without the meaning *Felis catus*. Rather, what ROTB says is that the grammar of Maori must be able to contend with inputs like /kæt/ if it is to accurately model what Maori speakers know about their language's pronunciation.

A related source of anxiety concerns the possibility of unfaithful mappings from the rich base.[5] Is the English word *peat* (phonetically [pit]) derived from the underlying representation /püt/ by an unfaithful mapping? Since English has no *i*/*ü* alternations, what does the learner do? What underlying representation does the learner of English actually impute to the surface form [pit], and why?

This concern was anticipated in work on Natural Phonology during the early 1970s (§2.1). Suppose that the rich base offers the inputs /A/ and /B/, both of which are mapped to [A] by the grammar. Obviously, learners will achieve nothing by positing distinct vocabulary items /A/ and /B/, since they will always be neutralized. If having a determinate underlying representation for [A] is important, then the choice can be made during language learning by a procedure that Prince and Smolensky call *lexicon optimization*: choose the underlying representation that gives the most harmonic mapping.[6] 📖§3.4¶4 The mapping /A/ → [A] is fully faithful, while the /B/ → [A] mapping incurs at least one faithfulness violation. Since these two mappings have otherwise identical violation-marks, the /A/ → [A] mapping is the more harmonic one. The underlying form /A/ is said to *occult* the underlying form /B/. The overall effect is much the same as an anti-B lexical redundancy rule in the standard theory but without positing constraints on inputs. Any apparent restriction on inputs is then an epiphenomenon of the markedness/faithfulness interactions that are responsible for these mappings.

Here is a concrete example, which can be traced back to Stampe (1973a: 32–33, 1973b: 50–51). English has no words beginning with the velar nasal ŋ. The rich base offers both /ŋaw/ and /naw/, but this distinction is always neutralized to surface [naw] *now*. Neutralization of a potential underlying distinction indicates crucial domination of a faithfulness constraint, as in (11).

(11) /ŋaw/ → [naw]

	/ŋaw/	*[ŋ	IDENT(velar)
a.	☞ naw		*
b.	ŋaw	*	

In this way, the grammar asserts that there are no initial ŋ's in surface forms of English, mapping them onto *n*'s (as in the Anglicized pronunciation of the Vietnamese surname *Nguyen*). The "actual" underlying representation of [naw] can be selected by lexicon optimization, applying the *tableau des tableaux* technique in (12) (Ito, Mester, and Padgett 1995), which compares the mappings to [naw] from the two inputs.

(12) *Tableau des tableaux* showing /nɑw/ → [nɑw] ≻ /ŋɑw/ → [nɑw]

			*[ŋ	IDENT(velar)
a.	☞ /nɑw/	☞ nɑw		
		ŋɑw	*	*
b.	/ŋɑw/	☞ nɑw		*
		ŋɑw	*	

The *tableau des tableaux* compares two inputs, /nɑw/ and /ŋɑw/, asking which one maps more harmonically to the output [nɑw]. Since the /nɑw/ → [nɑw] mapping incurs a proper subset of the /ŋɑw/ → [nɑw] mapping's marks, the /nɑw/ → [nɑw] mapping is more harmonic. Therefore, /nɑw/ is selected as the "actual" underlying form for [nɑw], occulting /ŋɑw/.

Lexicon optimization exists mainly to provide reassurance that the familiar underlying forms are still identifiable in the rich base. It is not an empirical hypothesis of the usual sort because the claims it makes are not testable with ordinary linguistic evidence.[7] As a learning strategy rather than as a principle of grammar, it is decisive only in situations where the learner has no evidence in the primary data about which potential underlying form is the "actual" one. In fact, when there is real evidence for the underlying form – such as alternations within a paradigm – learners must attend to that evidence and ignore lexicon optimization. For example, lexicon optimization says that German [unt] 'and' is derived from the underlying form /unt/ (despite the spelling *und*), since there are no alternations affecting this uninflectable word. But [runt] 'round (sg.)' comes from underlying /rund/ by a process of final devoicing, because the paradigm of this word includes [rundə] 'round (pl.)' (see the references at the end of §4.2.2).

Because lexicon optimization is only a learning strategy to be invoked when the evidence fails, it is illegitimate to use it to draw inferences or construct arguments about the synchronic grammars of adults. Here is an example of this "pseudo-lexicon-optimization," loosely based on several situations I have encountered in readings or discussions. Suppose there is a language with two kinds of root morphemes. Words containing accented roots have consistent stress on the final syllable of the root: *padót, padóta*. Words containing unaccented roots have consistent stress on the final syllable of the word: *batúk, batuká*. The difference between accented and unaccented roots is made in the lexicon: /padót/ versus /batuk/. Three constraints are required: MAX(acc), which requires faithful preservation of /padót/'s underlying accent; HEAD(PWd), which says that each phonological word must have a unique head and therefore exactly one accent; and ALIGN-R(PWd, Accent), which says that the last syllable of every phonological word must be accented. The constraints are ranked as in (13).

(13) MAX(acc), HEAD(PWd) ≫ ALIGN-R(PWd, Accent)

a.

/padót + a/		MAX(acc)	HEAD(PWd)	ALIGN-R
i.	☞ padóta			*
ii.	padótá		*	
iii.	padotá	*		

b.

/batuk + a/		MAX(acc)	HEAD(PWd)	ALIGN-R
i.	☞ batuká			
ii.	batúká		*	
iii.	batuka		*	*

As (13b) shows, where the root is unaccented, the default pattern of final stress (ALIGN-R) emerges. Otherwise, the root accent is faithfully preserved.

So far, so good, but now comes the pseudo-lexicon-optimization. Why are there no roots with underlying nonfinal accent, such as */bálit/? For the pseudo-optimizer, the answer is obvious: learners hearing words like *padót/padóta* and *batúk/batuká* will, by lexicon optimization, set up the underlying forms /padót/ and /batuk/, since these underlying forms map most harmonically onto the observed surface forms. Learners never hear words like */bálit/bálita*, so, by pseudo-lexicon-optimization, they are never moved to construct lexical entries like */bálit/. QED – not!

This sort of reasoning is superficially appealing because it resonates so well with traditional ideas about how the grammar and the lexicon are integrated via redundancy rules, underspecification, or similar devices (§2.1). In reality, pseudo-lexicon-optimization is circular, with a very short circumference. Boiled down to its essentials, the argument goes like this: "learners never hear */bálit/bálita*, so learners never produce */bálit/bálita*." That would be fine, if learning a language were just a matter of memorizing a dictionary, but obviously it is more than that. The hypothetical speakers of this language know that */bálit/bálita* is not merely nonoccurring but impossible, just as English speakers can tell the difference between nonoccurring *blick* and impossible *bnick*. This means that the grammar supplies productive knowledge of the impossibility of roots with nonfinal accent. When /bálit/ is drawn from the rich base, the grammar must map it onto something actually occurring. That is only possible if the hierarchy in (13) is augmented with a further markedness constraint, ranked above MAX(acc), that permits accent only on the last two syllables of an output form. Though lexicon optimization helps the learner to choose the "right" underlying form for a given surface form, it does not absolve the grammar (or the analyst) from dealing with the full range of inputs present in the rich base. In short, lexicon optimization works as a learning strategy from outputs to inputs, but it has no role in helping the grammar control the profusion of inputs, mapping them only onto possible outputs.

An issue related to lexicon optimization is *how exactly* to be unfaithful to the rich base (cf. Prince and Tesar 1999: Section 3). For instance, does the grammar of English map /ŋaw/ most harmonically to [naw], [maw], [aw], or something else entirely? Because unfaithful mappings can only occur to achieve markedness improvement (§3.1.1), we know that /ŋaw/ maps to something less marked than [ŋaw], and some outputs will be harmonically bounded (§1.3.1, §3.1.5) by others, particularly when faithfulness constraints stand in a stringency relation (§1.2.3, §3.1.3.5). Other processes in the language, especially those supported by overt alternations, may also narrow down the space of possibilities, because processes interact (§3.1.4). But there is certainly no guarantee that these factors, taken together, will suffice to determine uniquely what it is that /ŋaw/ maps to (cf. Chao 1934).

Lexicon optimization provides a way of resolving a somewhat trivial indeterminacy in the lexicon. But there is a more serious indeterminacy that affects the grammar itself. Without alternations, learners are not privy to any evidence in the primary data about *whether* to be unfaithful to the rich base. Starting from a grammar that permits [naw] and [ŋaw], how can a learner who receives only positive evidence manage to zero in on the subset language that permits only [naw]? This is an instance of the *subset problem* (Angluin 1980; Baker 1979), and the standard solution is to have learners start from the subset language, working toward the superset language by expanding the repertoire in response to positive evidence. This idea can be carried over to OT by assuming that the learner starts from an initial state in which all markedness constraints dominate all faithfulness constraints, schematically ⟦M ≫ F⟧. This assumption fits rather well with the familiar observation that children's early productions are unmarked relative to the adult models that they hear (Jakobson 1941). Acquisition then proceeds by demoting certain markedness constraints below antagonistic faithfulness constraints upon exposure to positive evidence. For more on this topic, see §4.2 and the references in §4.6 ¶5.

The ranking in (11) is just an instantiation of that innate initial state ⟦M ≫ F⟧. Learners of English will never encounter any reason for departing from (11), and so it persists into adulthood. Learners of Vietnamese are exposed to abundant exemplars of word-initial ŋ, and this leads them to demote the markedness constraint *[ŋ below IDENT(velar) and other antagonistic faithfulness constraints. In short, all learners start out knowing that initial ŋ is not permitted, and they must unlearn this in the course of acquiring a language like Vietnamese. (cf. learning by process suppression in Natural Phonology (§2.1).)

3.1.2.5 Syntactic Applications

These ideas are no less important in (morpho)syntax, even if the term "inventory" is not so much used as in phonology.📖§3.4 ¶5 Consider, for example, the inventory of pronominal clitics in the Romance languages (also see §1.3.2).[8] The third person nonreflexive clitics are distinguished for number, gender, and case. There is, in addition, a third person reflexive clitic that neutralizes all of these distinctions. The first and second person clitics are distinguished for number, but they neutralize distinctions of gender, case, and reflexivity.

Suppose, in accordance with ROTB, that the input consists of the free combination of the morphosyntactic features [person], [plural], [feminine], [dative], and [reflexive]. Some of the neutralizations are shown in (14), using Spanish as the language for the output forms (compare (3), which is the phonological counterpart of this diagram).

(14) Featural decomposition of some Spanish clitics

[3person, −plural, −feminine, −dative, −reflexive]	→	*lo*
[3person, −plural, +feminine, −dative, −reflexive]	→	*la*
[3person, +plural, −feminine, −dative, −reflexive]	→	*los*
[3person, +plural, +feminine, −dative, −reflexive]	→	*las*
[3person, −plural, −feminine, +dative, −reflexive]	↘	*le*
[3person, −plural, +feminine, +dative, −reflexive]	↗	
[3person, +plural, −feminine, +dative, −reflexive]	↘	*les*
[3person, +plural, +feminine, +dative, −reflexive]	↗	

This is a classic system of neutralization, quite comparable to what is observed in phonology. As in many other languages, the relatively unmarked categories (such as accusative) tend to support finer-grained distinctions than do their marked counterparts. Or, to put it differently, the "worst of the worst" feature combinations – those that are marked on several different dimensions at once – are ruled out.

Local constraint conjunction (§1.2.3) is well suited to bringing worst-of-the-worst behavior under grammatical control. Suppose that UG supplies constraints militating against only the marked members of these oppositions, such as *FEM and *DAT. The local conjunction of *FEM and *DAT, written [*FEM&*DAT]$_{Word}$, characterizes one of these worst-of-the-worst situations. It dominates the constraint demanding faithfulness to gender, leading to neutralization of gender distinctions in Spanish and French third person dative pronouns. In this way, markedness/faithfulness interactions filter the rich morphosyntactic base exactly as they do in phonology. With permuted ranking, of course, different results are obtained. In Italian, for instance, where there is a gender distinction among singular dative clitics, the ranking of [*FEM&*DAT]$_{Word}$ and faithfulness is the opposite.[9] Other generalizations are obtained similarly.

In P&P, the lexicon is seen as the locus of all or almost all that is language particular, with the grammar tending much more strongly toward the universal. (This is an expansion of the *Aspects* thesis that the lexicon is the repository of irregularity.) In OT, however, the perspective is rather different: the base is universal, and it is the grammar – a ranking of universal constraints – that filters this rich base to yield the surface inventory. The implications of this idea for syntactic theory are now just beginning to be studied (see the references in §3.4 ¶1).

3.1.2.6 *Summary and Methodological Remark*

The inventory is an *emergent* property of OT grammars (cf. §3.2.2). No language-particular restrictions are imposed on the input, and so all linguistically significant generalizations about the inventory must emerge from the grammar itself. This hypothesis is necessary if OT is to be true to its boast that all typology comes from language-particular ranking and if it is to solve the Duplication Problem. Significantly, it also means that the theory of inventories is tightly integrated into OT's account of other emergent properties: distribution (§3.1.3), processes and their interaction (§3.1.4), and typological distinctions and universals (§3.1.5). This leads to a range of claims and predictions that cannot be matched by theories that attribute some or all inventory restrictions to the lexicon and not the grammar.

ROTB is a central property of this explanation; it follows from the basic architecture and typological claims of the theory. For this reason, all OT analyses need to be tested against a range of inputs that have not been restricted artificially. This methodology can seem quite alien to anyone approaching OT with a background in P&P, *SPE*, or underspecification theory – but it is nonetheless essential. The only workable research strategy is to integrate ROTB into the analysis from the outset and not attempt to graft it on at the end.

3.1.3 Distributional Restrictions

3.1.3.1 *Basic Notions*

Restricted distribution is another classic linguistic problem, dating back to the time of the American structuralists. The distribution of an item is the set of linguistically relevant contexts in which it appears: syllable-initially, but never syllable-finally (e.g., *h* in English); alone, but never with an auxiliary (e.g., *do*-support in English). Discussions of distribution usually focus on the relative distribution of two items, A and B, one of which may be zero. The distribution of A and B can be usefully classified by comparing the contexts C_A and C_B in which they occur, as in (15).

(15) Types of distributional restrictions

	Characterization	Description
a. Identical distribution	$C_A = C_B$	A and B have identical distributions (except for accidental gaps). The A/B distinction is maintained in all contexts where they occur.
b. Complementary distribution	$C_A \cap C_B = \emptyset$	A and B never occur in the same context. The A/B distinction is neutralized everywhere.
c. Contextual neutralization	$C_A \subsetneq C_B$	There are contexts that permit both A and B, but there are also contexts that permit only B. The A/B distinction is neutralized contextually in favor of B.

There are other distributional possibilities, but these are the most important ones.

For concreteness, we will examine the effects of oral and nasal consonants (*b* vs. *m*) on the distribution of following oral and nasal vowels (*a* vs. *ã*).[10] To simplify the exposition, several artificial limitations will be imposed: input forms and output candidates will be limited to the set {*ba, bã, a, ã, ma, mã*}; the only unfaithful mapping emitted by GEN will be a change in the nasality of a vowel, /a/ → *ã* or /ã/ → *a*; and CON will consist of the constraints *V$_{NAS}$, *NV$_{ORAL}$, and IDENT(nasal). *V$_{NAS}$ and *NV$_{ORAL}$ are markedness constraints. The justification for *V$_{NAS}$ is a classic Praguian markedness effect: some languages have oral vowels only, some have both oral and nasal vowels, but no language has only nasal vowels. From this we infer that UG contains a markedness constraint militating against nasal vowels – *V$_{NAS}$ – and that there is no corresponding constraint against oral vowels.[11] But in certain contexts, even oral vowels are marked, such as the position after a nasal consonant, and that is the basis for the constraint *NV$_{ORAL}$. It is violated by any sequence like *ma* (vs. *mã*).

For present purposes, I assume that the faithfulness constraint IDENT(nasal) is symmetric, meaning that it is violated by both of the unfaithful mappings /a/ → *ã* and /ã/ → *a*. Recall that these are the only unfaithful mappings permitted by our artificially limited GEN, so mappings like /b/ → *m* or /m/ → Ø will not even be considered. (Obviously they would be addressed in a more complete analysis.)

3.1.3.2 Factorial Typology

With the modest constraint set *V$_{NAS}$, *NV$_{ORAL}$, and IDENT(nasal), it is possible and desirable to begin by computing the typology that is predicted by ranking permutation. There are just 3! = 6 possibilities, of which two pairs produce identical results, as shown in (16).

(16) Factorial typology of $*V_{NAS}$, $*NV_{ORAL}$, and IDENT(nasal)

	Ranking	Inventory
a. Identical distribution	IDENT(nasal) $\gg$ $*NV_{ORAL}$ $\gg$ $*V_{NAS}$ IDENT(nasal) $\gg$ $*V_{NAS}$ $\gg$ $*NV_{ORAL}$	$\{ba, b\tilde{a}, a, \tilde{a}, ma, m\tilde{a}\}$
b. Complementary distribution	$*NV_{ORAL} \gg * V_{NAS} \gg$ IDENT(nasal)	$\{ba, a, m\tilde{a}\}$
	$*V_{NAS} \gg *NV_{ORAL} \gg$ IDENT(nasal) $*V_{NAS} \gg$ IDENT(nasal) $\gg *NV_{ORAL}$	$\{ba, a, ma\}$
c. Contextual neutralization	$*NV_{ORAL} \gg$ IDENT(nasal) $\gg *V_{NAS}$	$\{ba, b\tilde{a}, a, \tilde{a}, m\tilde{a}\}$

We will consider each of these distributions in turn.

3.1.3.3 Identical Distribution

If A and B have identical distributions, then nothing about the A/B distinction is predictable. Unpredictability is a sure sign of activity by faithfulness constraints, which act to protect the free combination of elements that make up the rich input.

Concretely, nasal and oral vowels have identical distribution when faithfulness stands at the zenith of the hierarchy (16a). With IDENT(nasal) top ranked, the markedness constraints cannot be active over the candidate sets being considered here. In that situation, all of the potential contrasts present in the rich base arrive at the surface unscathed (see (17)).

(17) Mappings for identical distribution

/ba/	$\rightarrow$	ba
/bã/	$\rightarrow$	bã
/a/	$\rightarrow$	a
/ã/	$\rightarrow$	ã
/ma/	$\rightarrow$	ma
/mã/	$\rightarrow$	mã

Because all the mappings are faithful, the relative markedness of *ma* versus *mã* is never an issue, and so the ranking of $*NV_{ORAL}$ with respect to $*V_{NAS}$ cannot be determined. For that reason, (16a) includes two different permutations that produce identical results.

3.1.3.4 Complementary Distribution

Complementary distribution of A and B means full predictability, with lack of respect for faithfulness when it conflicts with markedness. Two different situations of complementary distribution are covered by the rankings in (16b). The first, with faithfulness at the bottom and $*NV_{ORAL}$ dominating $*V_{NAS}$, is the classic situation of complementary distribution: nasalized vowels occur only when needed, where "when needed" is defined by the context-sensitive markedness constraint $*NV_{ORAL}$. The second ranking in (16b) – actually a pair of rankings that produce identical results – is a trivial situation of complementary distribution, with oral vowels occurring in all contexts and nasal vowels in no context.[12]

Here is an example of nontrivial complementary distribution from Madurese (Austronesian, Java), slightly simplified.[13] Oral and nasal vowels are in complementary distribution: oral vowels occur only after oral consonants (*ba*, *bã) or after no consonant at all (*a*, *ã); nasal vowels occur only after nasal consonants (*nã*, *na). The rich base includes, as inputs, both the forbidden and the permitted output forms: /ba/, /bã/, /a/, /ã/, /ma/, and /mã/. Example (18) presents the required mappings.

(18) Mappings in Madurese

/ba/	↘	*ba*
/bã/	↗	

/a/	↘	*a*
/ã/	↗	

/ma/	↘	*mã*
/mã/	↗	

As in §3.1.2, (18) shows mappings to the output from a rich base and not overt alternations. This diagram establishes that nasality and orality in Madurese vowels are fully under grammatical control, which means that markedness constraints are dispositive in all contexts, so faithfulness inevitably suffers. Two unfaithful mappings are observed from the rich base: /a/ → *ã* after a nasal consonant and /ã/ → *a* elsewhere. The analysis must contend with both.

At this point, readers might find it helpful to review the conditions for an unfaithful mapping given in (1) of §3.1.1, keeping in mind that complementary distribution requires two unfaithful mappings. The first condition (1a) says that unfaithful mappings are based on ⟦M ≫ F⟧ rankings. Two such rankings, shown in (19a–b), are relevant to Madurese.

(19) a. *V_{NAS} ≫ IDENT(nasal)

/bã/		*V_{NAS}	IDENT(nasal)
i.	☞ ba		*
ii.	bã	*	

b. *NV_{ORAL} ≫ IDENT(nasal)

/ma/		*NV_{ORAL}	IDENT(nasal)
i.	☞ mã		*
ii.	ma	*	

The rich base includes inputs like /bã/ or /ma/, with the "wrong" vowel. These inputs must be unfaithfully mapped to outputs that conform to the observed distribution. The tableaux in (19) exemplify that, under ROTB, complementary distribution requires at least two unfaithful mappings.[14]

Another of the prerequisites for an unfaithful mapping, (1b), says that any unfaithful mapping must result in an improvement in markedness relative to the markedness constraints of UG as ranked in the language under discussion. Mapping /bã/ to *ba* is an obvious markedness improvement, as (19a) shows, but mapping /ma/ to *mã* must also improve markedness. The argument in (20) shows how the two markedness constraints are ranked in Madurese.

(20) $*NV_{ORAL} \gg *V_{NAS}$

/ma/		$*NV_{ORAL}$	$*V_{NAS}$
a.	☞ mã		*
b.	ma	*	

Because $*NV_{ORAL}$ dominates $*V_{NAS}$, *mã* is less marked than *ma* in this language. Of course, with the opposite ranking of these constraints, there would be no nasalized vowels in any context.

The remaining ranking prerequisite, (1c), says that a specific unfaithful mapping is guaranteed only if all other ways of satisfying the relevant markedness constraint(s) are foreclosed by other constraints. For expository purposes, I have assumed that GEN offers no other options, but in real life we would need to call on appropriate markedness or faithfulness constraints to rule out mappings like /bã/ → *b* or /ma/ → *ba*.

That completes the picture of Madurese. With the ranking ⟦$*NV_{ORAL} \gg *V_{NAS}$ $\gg$ IDENT(nasal)⟧, nasalized vowels appear only when needed, as demanded by top-ranked $*NV_{ORAL}$. Otherwise, vowels are oral, in obedience to $*V_{NAS}$. Orality, then, is the default (§3.2.2.3).

To sum up the essence of complementary distribution: the ⟦M $\gg$ F⟧ rankings must be sufficient to dispose of all A's occurring in B's context and all B's occurring in A's context. Suppose CON supplies two markedness constraints, M(A ≻ B) and M(B ≻ A), where M(X ≻ Y) means "M favors X over Y; M assigns fewer violation-marks to X than Y." Often, these two constraints will conflict. M(A ≻ B) favors A over B generally, with M(B ≻ A) favoring B over A in a specific context (like $*V_{NAS}$ and $*NV_{ORAL}$, respectively). Nontrivial complementary distribution will only be achieved if faithfulness is at the bottom and contextually restricted M(B ≻ A) dominates context-free M(A ≻ B). In traditional terms, A is the default relative to B: B occurs in limited circumstances, as defined by M(B ≻ A), and complementarily A occurs everywhere else. 📖 §3.4 ¶6

Keep in mind that, since both A and B are present in the rich base, where they can be found in all possible contexts, complementary distribution requires *both* /A/ and /B/ to be unfaithfully mapped in some contexts. This can be a source of confusion, since traditional approaches to complementarity take various precautions, such as lexical redundancy rules or underspecification, to make sure that the contrast between /A/ and /B/ is not available in the lexicon (§3.1.2).

3.1.3.5 Contextual Neutralization

A contrast may be preserved in some contexts and neutralized in others. The responsible ranking, as in (16c), is one where the specific, context-sensitive constraint M(B≻A) is ranked above faithfulness, while the general, context-free constraint M(A≻B) is ranked below faithfulness. Yoruba (Niger-Congo, Nigeria) is the contextually neutralized counterpart of Madurese, and its mappings are shown in (21).

(21) Mappings in Yoruba

/ba/	→	ba
/bã/	→	bã
/a/	→	a
/ã/	→	ã
/ma/	↘	mã
/mã/	↗	

The distinction between oral and nasal vowels is neutralized in the context after a nasal consonant, but it is faithfully preserved elsewhere.

Because /bã/ and /ã/ are mapped faithfully in Yoruba, it is immediately apparent that IDENT(nasal) dominates *V_{NAS}. The real action, then, involves the ranking of *NV_{ORAL} relative to faithfulness. Since /ma/ maps unfaithfully to *mã*, the ranking must be as in (22).

(22) *NV_{ORAL} ≫ IDENT(nasal)

/ma/		*NV_{ORAL}	IDENT(nasal)
a.	☞ mã		*
b.	ma	*	

With *V_{NAS} ranked below IDENT(nasal), the latent *a/ã* contrast is maintained, except in a postnasal context, where the demands of *NV_{ORAL} take precedence.

The analysis of Yoruba just sketched typifies one kind of approach to contextual neutralization. It is based on positing context-sensitive markedness constraints like *NV_{ORAL}. Another, less obvious line of attack is to derive context sensitivity from interaction of context-free markedness constraints with *positional faithfulness* constraints.📖 §3.4 ¶7 The central idea behind positional faithfulness is that faithfulness constraints may be relativized to certain prominent positions, such as stressed syllables or root morphemes.

Here is an example. In Nancowry (Austro-Asiatic, Nicobar Islands) stress falls predictably on the final syllable of the root. In stressed syllables, there is a contrast between nasal and oral vowels, but in unstressed syllables, all vowels are oral. The required mappings, faithful and unfaithful, are in (23).[15]

(23) Mappings in Nancowry

/bata/	→	batá
/batã/	→	batá̃
/bata/	↘	
/bãta/	↗	batá

In other words, an output oral vowel in a stressed syllable can be reliably projected back to an input oral vowel, but an oral vowel in an unstressed syllable cannot. Stressed syllables and other prominent positions are a locus of particularly robust faithfulness.

The idea is that UG distinguishes between a stressed-syllable-specific version of IDENT(nasal) and its nonspecific counterpart. (This is a stringency relation – see §1.2.3.) In Nancowry, these constraints are ranked with $*V_{Nas}$ in between: ⟦IDENT$_\sigma$(nasal) ≫ $*V_{Nas}$ ≫ IDENT(nasal)⟧. In this way, $*V_{Nas}$ can compel unfaithfulness to nasality in unstressed syllables, but not in stressed ones, as we see in (24a–b).

(24) a. /batã/ → batá̃

/batã/	IDENT$_\sigma$(nasal)	$*V_{Nas}$	IDENT(nasal)
i. ☞ batá̃		*	
ii. batá	*		*

b. /bãta/ → batá

/batã/	IDENT$_\sigma$(nasal)	$*V_{Nas}$	IDENT(nasal)
i. ☞ batá			*
ii. bãtá		*	

Tableau (24a) shows why the nasal/oral contrast is preserved in stressed syllables (because of ⟦IDENT$_\sigma$(nasal) ≫ $*V_{Nas}$⟧), and tableau (24b) shows why this contrast is neutralized in unstressed syllables (because of ⟦$*V_{Nas}$ ≫ IDENT(nasal)⟧).

3.1.3.6 A Syntactic Example: Only-When-Needed Behavior

Though the term "distribution" does not figure very much in discussions of contemporary syntactic theory, distributional concerns are still very much in evidence. An example is the distribution of unstressed *dŏ* – that is, *do*-support – in English. The central insight is that *dŏ* appears only when it is needed: in constructions where an auxiliary is required but none is available (e.g., inversion: *Dĭd Dana leave?*, *What dĭd Dana eat?*; and negation: *Dana dĭdn't leave.*).

A linguistic object that is present only when needed and otherwise absent completely is in complementary distribution with zero. The phonological analogue of English *dŏ* is the vowel ə in the Salish languages of the Pacific Northwest. It is typically described as occurring only when there is no other vowel available to support a syllable. At a sufficiently abstract level, English *dŏ* and Salish ə are analyzed identically. The minimal ranking conditions for some linguistic object LO to be in complementary distribution with zero are given in (25).

(25) Schematic ranking for only-when-needed distribution

PRO-LO and ANTI-LO denote markedness constraints that respectively demand the linguistic object LO in some particular context and militate against LO generally. F(∅⇸LO) and F(LO⇸∅) are the antagonistic faithfulness constraints against inserting or deleting LO, respectively. According to this ranking, LO will appear only when needed, where "need" is expressed by top-ranked PRO-LO. Both English *dŏ* and Salish ə conform to this schematic ranking, and abstractly both are the same as the analysis of Madurese in §3.1.3.4, which says that nasal vowels also appear only when needed.

Grimshaw (1997b) presents an OT analysis of *do*-support that uses a ranking similar to (25) to account for *dŏ*'s only-when-needed distribution.[16] The constraint with PRO-LO force is OB-HD: every projection has a head. In inversion constructions, *dŏ* and its trace serve as the heads of CP and IP, respectively, as shown in (26).

(26) Application of Oʙ-Hᴅ to English *do*-support

Candidates	Oʙ-Hᴅ	Remarks
a. ☞ [_CP_ *wh* **do**ᵢ [_IP_ DP **e**ᵢ [_VP_ V *t*]]]		E.g., *What dĭd Dana eat?* *Dŏ* is head of CP, and its trace is head of IP.
b. [_CP_ *wh* **e** [_IP_ DP **e** [_VP_ V *t*]]]	**	E.g., **What Dana ate?* Neither CP nor IP is headed, because there is no *dŏ*-support or inversion. Oʙ-Hᴅ is violated by both of the headless projections.
c. [_CP_ *wh* **e** [_VP_ DP V *t*]]	*	E.g., **What Dana ate?* Different structure, but CP is still headless.
d. [_CP_ *wh* **e** [_IP_ DP **do** [_VP_ V *t*]]]	*	E.g., **What Dana dĭd eat?* *dŏ* is head of IP, but CP is headless, because no inversion.

Though Oʙ-Hᴅ favors the right output in tableau (26), it is by no means the whole story, since Oʙ-Hᴅ alone cannot explain why *do*-support is found only when it is required. Situations not requiring, and therefore prohibiting, *dŏ* include simple declaratives (**Dana dĭd eat.*) and inversion constructions with another auxiliary (**What dŏes Dana will eat?*, **What will Dana dŏ eat?*). Examples like these establish that the default condition is to have no *dŏ* at all.

In Grimshaw's analysis, the default-defining anti-*dŏ* constraint is Fᴜʟʟ-Iɴᴛ (full interpretation), which requires that lexical conceptual structure be parsed (also see §3.1.4). The lexical conceptual structure of output items must be given a semantic interpretation, and for a verb, this includes assignment of its theta-roles. Supporting *dŏ* violates Fᴜʟʟ-Iɴᴛ under the assumption that it is the same as main verb *do* but without its theta-roles assigned. In sum, Fᴜʟʟ-Iɴᴛ militates against semantically and functionally empty items like *dŏ*. There are, of course, other ways to achieve the same result, but this constraint is sufficient for present purposes.

Interactions of the special case/default case type fall under the ⟦Pʀᴏ-LO ≫ Aɴᴛɪ-LO⟧ rubric in (25). Oʙ-Hᴅ must dominate Fᴜʟʟ-Iɴᴛ to force *do*-support when CP and IP have no other head, as shown in (27).

(27) Oʙ-Hᴅ ≫ Fᴜʟʟ-Iɴᴛ

	Oʙ-Hᴅ	Fᴜʟʟ-Iɴᴛ
a. ☞ [_CP_ *wh* **do**ᵢ [_IP_ DP **e**ᵢ [_VP_ V *t*]]]		*
b. [_CP_ *wh* **e** [_IP_ DP **e** [_VP_ V *t*]]]	**	

Do-support does not co-occur with another auxiliary, though, because the interesting candidates tie on OB-HD, and so *dŏ*'s violation of FULL-INT is unnecessary (see (28)).

(28) FULL-INT decisive

	OB-HD	FULL-INT
a. ☞ [CP *wh* **will**i [IP DP **e**i [VP V *t*]]]		
b. [CP *wh* **will**i [IP DP **e**i [XP do [VP V *t*]]]]		*
c. [CP *wh* **do**i [IP DP **e**i [XP will [VP V *t*]]]]		*

For the same reason, *dŏ* in simple declaratives, multiple *dŏ*'s, and other gratuitous uses of *dŏ* are all prohibited. *Do*-support occurs only when truly needed to satisfy OB-HD.

As for faithfulness, the general idea is pretty clear (also see §4.1). In conformity with (25), any faithfulness constraints that militate against inserting or deleting *dŏ* must be ranked below OB-HD and FULL-INT, respectively. In this way, the constraints OB-HD and FULL-INT will fully control *dŏ*'s surface distribution, establishing a strong formal parallel between *do*-support in English and analogous systems of epenthesis in phonology.

3.1.3.7 *Summary*

To sum up: all possible linguistic distinctions are already present in the rich base. The job of the grammar is to map these diverse inputs onto the more restricted inventory and distributional patterns of a particular language. Let P stand for some potentially contrastive linguistic property, such as nasality in vowels. On the one hand, if faithfulness to P dominates all markedness constraints that would limit P, then there is overlapping distribution of the elements distinguished by P (16a). On the other hand, if faithfulness to P is ranked below markedness constraints that are fully dispositive of P in all environments, then the distribution is complementary (16b), (18)–(20). Neutralization of P in some contexts but not others (16c) has two potential sources: context-free faithfulness to P is dominated by a context-sensitive markedness constraint (21)–(22) or context-free markedness of P is dominated by a context-sensitive faithfulness constraint (23)–(24). (When or whether these two different accounts of contextual neutralization are appropriate is a matter of current research.⌸§3.4 ¶7)

3.1.4 Processes and Systems of Processes

3.1.4.1 *Basic Notions*

The term "process" is pre-theoretical and therefore to be approached cautiously. It refers to a particular change that occurs when an output is derived from an input, along with all the conditions that trigger or prevent that change.

Processes are primitives of standard generative phonology or early syntactic theory (§2.1, §2.2), because an *SPE* phonological rule or an *Aspects* syntactic transformation is a package that combines some operation and conditions necessary and sufficient for that operation to apply. But processes are certainly not primitives of OT. As we saw in §3.1.1, the closest OT can come to characterizing a process, if that should prove desirable, is to provide the rather complex set of conditions for unfaithful mappings given in (1).

A central claim of OT, embodied in (1), is that unfaithful mappings are the result of markedness/faithfulness interactions. The rule package of classical phonological or syntactic theory is unrecognizably decomposed in OT, leading to three key differences between OT and rule-based theories:

(i) OT defines the triggering and blocking conditions in terms of attained output targets (using the term "target" loosely to describe a required or prohibited output configuration) rather than in terms of input contexts. A rule $A \rightarrow B/C\_\_\_\_D$ says that A changes into B if it is in the $C\_\_\_\_D$ context at the derivational instant when the rule applies. A constraint *CAD is violated by any output form containing the string *CAD*.

(ii) OT decouples the operation, which faithfulness constraints regulate, from the conditions that trigger or block it, which are determined through interaction with markedness constraints and other faithfulness constraints. The rule $A \rightarrow B/C\_\_\_\_D$ inextricably links the $A \rightarrow B$ transformation with the *CAD* input configuration that triggers it.

(iii) While the classical rule or transformation is an entirely autonomous entity, free to be plugged into any language, there is no effective way to isolate one process from another in a single OT grammar, since all processes must derive from constraints that are ranked together in a single strict domination hierarchy. The classical rule is a free agent, but an OT grammar is a coherent system. For this reason, OT makes predictions about coexistence and interaction of processes that are unattainable in rule-based theories.

These three consequences of OT are the topic of this section (also see §1.3 for a more basic introduction to these matters).

OT is output oriented, requiring all processes to have an overt teleology. This claim follows from the observation (§1.3, §3.1.1, and §3.1.4.5) that unfaithful mappings are only possible when they achieve improvement in markedness. Therefore, only markedness constraints, which evaluate the well-formedness of output structures, are able to trigger processes. This property of OT constitutes a clean break from rule-based theories. A rule, as the term is typically used, describes an operation and the input-side conditions leading to its applicability. In OT, the output-side conditions are decisive.

OT's output orientation sometimes leads to the presumption that OT is much more amenable to the study of linguistic performance than are previous competence-based theories in the generative tradition (cf. §4.4). Regardless of whether this assumption is viewed with sanguinity or jaundice, it is wrong. It is akin to the suggestion that LFG or GPSG "are more congenial to the functionalist world view than P&P, given that they share with functionalism a 'surfacey' approach to characterizing grammatical form. . . ." (Newmeyer 1998: 12 citing Croft 1998). The source of this confusion may be the ordinary-language meaning of "output" or "surface," which are terms of art in their respective theories. The output is exactly what the theory says it is – no more, no less. To the chagrin of some and the delight of others, the output could (but need not) be in a rather remote relationship to sense data, with thick layers of interpretation, execution, and perception in between. A rule-based theory is equally able to posit a more or less surfacey output. OT brings with it no special commitment to hugging the sensory ground – though OT's ability to give formal structure to otherwise fuzzy tendencies does encourage exploration of phonetic or functionalist approaches that had been all but abandoned in formal linguistics (§4.4).

3.1.4.2 Homogeneity of Target/Heterogeneity of Process

The output orientation of OT is closely linked to another property of the theory, the decoupling of the operational side of a process from the conditions that trigger or block the operation. Taken together, these properties lead to a basic typological claim of OT, which I have been calling homogeneity of target/heterogeneity of process (§1.3.2). It says that the same output configuration may be achieved in different ways across languages or even across contexts within a language. This prediction is an unavoidable consequence of two of OT's basic premises: the markedness/faithfulness dichotomy and factorial typology. 📖 §3.4¶8

I briefly mentioned some of the evidence for this claim in §1.3.2. Diola Fogny and Ponapean both enforce a markedness constraint that prohibits certain consonant clusters in the output, but they differ in how they enforce this requirement. In Diola Fogny, the offending clusters are simplified by deleting one of the consonants (/let-ku-jaw/ → *lekujaw* 'they won't go'), while in Ponapean, the cluster is broken up by vowel epenthesis (/pet-pet/ → *petepet* 'be squeezed'). Similarly, the Romance languages differ in their treatment of sequences of identical clitics. In Spanish, one of the clitics is deleted, but in Italian, it is altered so it is no longer identical to its neighbor. Phonological dissimilation, a close parallel, shows the same heterogeneity of process (Suzuki 1998: 152ff.).

We will now look in greater depth at a few other cases of homogeneity of target/heterogeneity of process, involving both between-language and within-language heterogeneity effects. The between-language example involves a constraint, dubbed *NC̦, that militates against consonant clusters of a nasal followed by a voiceless consonant (e.g., *mp, nt, ŋk*).[17]

The constraint *NC̦ can be satisfied in diverse ways. As a matter of logic, there are many different unfaithful mappings that input /mp/ could undergo to ensure the absence of output *mp* from the inventory. And as a matter of fact, many of these logical possibilities are actually attested in different languages. Some examples are given in (29).

(29) a. Toba Batak (Austronesian, Sumatra) (Hayes 1986)
     Nasal consonant changes to oral.

     /maŋinum tuak/   →   maŋinu**p** tuak   'drink palm wine'
     /holom saɔtik/   →   holo**p** saɔtik   'somewhat dark'

   b. Kelantan Malay (Austronesian, Malaysia) (Teoh 1988)[18]
     Nasal consonant deletes.

     /pintu/   →   pitu   'door'
     /hampas/   →   hapas   'husk'

   c. Japanese (Ito et al. 1995)
     Voiceless consonant becomes voiced.

     /sin-ta/   →   šin**d**a   'died'
     /yom-ta/   →   yon**d**a   'read (past)'

The same markedness constraint is active in all three languages, but the unfaithful mappings that bring satisfaction of this constraint are different. This is homogeneity of target/heterogeneity of process.

OT accounts for homogeneity of target/heterogeneity of process by permuting different faithfulness constraints around a fixed point, the markedness constraint. In addition to the markedness constraint *NÇ, UG supplies the faithfulness constraints IDENT(nasal), MAX, and IDENT(voice). If *NÇ crucially dominates at least one faithfulness constraint, it "triggers" violation of the lowest-ranking faithfulness constraint in that set (see (1c) in §3.1.1). The grammars of the three languages in (29), then, must assert at least the rankings in (30).

(30) a. Toba Batak
     *NÇ, IDENT(voice), MAX ≫ IDENT(nasal)

   b. Kelantan Malay
     *NÇ, IDENT(nasal), IDENT(voice) ≫ MAX

   c. Japanese
     *NÇ, IDENT(nasal), MAX ≫ IDENT(voice)

   d. English
     IDENT(nasal), IDENT(voice), MAX ≫ *NÇ

The ranking for English has been thrown in at the end. In English, all three faithfulness constraints dominate *NÇ, so it cannot compel unfaithful mappings, and therefore surface nasal + voiceless stop clusters are predicted to exist (*hamper, canter, tinker*).[19]

Though *NÇ is responsible for a range of unfaithful mappings, the observed options exemplified in (29) do not include all of the logical possibilities. For example, no known language enforces *NÇ by deleting both of the offending consonants (/sin-ta/ → *sia*).[20] There is, then, a mismatch between the observed and imaginable processes involving *NÇ. Because OT is inherently typological, it calls attention to the limits as well as the range of between-

language variation. This matter is held in abeyance for now, to be taken up again
in §3.1.5.

Heterogeneity of process can also be observed within a single language. The
simplest case is blocking, as in Axininca Campa (§1.3.3), Nancowry (§3.1.3.5),
or English (§3.1.3.6). Axininca Campa epenthesizes a consonant in onsetless
syllables by virtue of [[Onset ≫ Dep]]. But there is no epenthesis word-initially
because a positional faithfulness constraint dominates Onset. So the response
to Onset violation is heterogeneous: epenthesize in one context, but do nothing
in another. Likewise, Nancowry has a process of vowel denasalization, which
is defined by the ranking [[*V$_{\text{NAS}}$ ≫ Ident(nasal)]]. But denasalization is blocked
in stressed syllables by the top-ranked positional faithfulness constraint
Ident$_\sigma$(nasal). Similarly, English has a process deleting *dŏ*, because Full-Int
dominates faithfulness. This process is blocked by Ob-Hd, though. Blocking
might almost be regarded as the most extreme form of process heterogeneity:
under certain conditions, the process does not happen at all.

3.1.4.3 *Conspiracies*

The most interesting cases of process heterogeneity are the *conspiracies*
(§2.1): even within a single language, the same markedness constraint may be
satisfied in different ways depending on the context. (Also see the related discussion of nonuniformity effects in §3.2.1.) To get this type of process heterogeneity, the markedness constraint "driving" the process must dominate two
faithfulness constraints, which are themselves ranked: [[M ≫ F1 ≫ F2]]. This
implies that M could be satisfied by violating either F1 or F2. Because F1 dominates F2, violation of the latter is preferred, and so the default M-triggered
process involves unfaithfulness on the F2 dimension.

With this ranking, it is not necessary to violate F1 as long as violation of
F2 is available instead. But sometimes it may not be possible to violate F2:
violation of F2 could be blocked by a high-ranking markedness constraint;
violation of F2 could be blocked by some more specific faithfulness constraint,
such as positional faithfulness, ranked above F2; or violation of F2 could be just
irrelevant to some input. In any of these situations, the usual F2-violating map is
blocked or useless, and the F1-violating map steps into the breach as a kind of last
resort, ensuring that the winning candidate satisfies M in one way or another.

Hiatus resolution – i.e., satisfying Onset at V$_1$ + V$_2$ juncture – frequently
involves heterogeneous processes. The following example comes from Emai
(Benue-Congo, Nigeria).[21] Under various conditions (see (31)), the first vowel
deletes, or the second vowel deletes, or the first vowel changes into a glide.

(31) Hiatus resolution in Emai

    a. If V$_1$ is final in a functional morpheme and V$_2$ is initial in a lexical
       morpheme, delete V$_1$:

        ... V$_1$]$_{\text{Fnc}}$ [$_{\text{Lex}}$V$_2$ ...
        ↓
        ∅

b. If V_1 is final in a lexical morpheme and V_2 is initial in a functional
morpheme, delete V_2:

$$\ldots V_1]_{Lex} [_{Fnc} V_2 \ldots$$
$$\downarrow$$
$$\varnothing$$

c. If V_1 and V_2 are both in lexical morphemes or both in functional
morphemes, delete V_1:

$$\ldots V_1]_{Lex} [_{Lex} V_2 \ldots \qquad \ldots V_1]_{Fnc} [_{Fnc} V_2 \ldots$$
$$\downarrow \qquad\qquad\qquad \downarrow$$
$$\varnothing \qquad\qquad\qquad \varnothing$$

d. But if V_1 is high (*i* or *u*) and in a lexical (though not functional) morpheme,
it changes into the corresponding glide (*y* or *w*):

$$\ldots i]_{Lex} [_{Lex} V_2 \ldots \qquad \ldots u]_{Lex} [_{Lex} V_2 \ldots$$
$$\downarrow \qquad\qquad\qquad \downarrow$$
$$y \qquad\qquad\qquad w$$

Undominated constraints establish the context in which these alternations
are played out. Markedness constraints allow only the high glides *y* and *w*
to appear in Emai. The faithfulness constraint IDENT(high) allows only /i/
and /u/, which are already high, to turn into *y* and *w*. Candidates that violate
these undominated constraints are of little interest and will not be mentioned
again.

It is apparent that ONSET can be satisfied in many different ways in Emai.
But the pattern is quite systematic and can be readily summarized with the informal hierarchy in (32).

(32) Dispreferred responses to ONSET organized hierarchically

Don't delete ≫	Don't change a ≫	Don't delete ≫	Don't delete
segments in	vowel into a	segments in	any
lexical	glide.	morpheme-	segments.
morphemes.		initial position.	

I will first explain informally how to arrive at this hierarchy and then develop
the analysis with tableaux.

Deleting segments from lexical morphemes is least favored. It only happens
when all of the other possibilities are foreclosed. The $\ldots \cancel{V}_1]_{Lex} [_{Lex} V_2 \ldots$ configuration in (31c) is an example. V_1 cannot become a glide because it is non-
high, so deletion is the only option left. Since it is V_1 that is deleted and not V_2,
we can conclude that there is a bias against morpheme-initial deletions. The
same bias is seen when two functional morphemes meet, as in $\ldots \cancel{V}_1]_{Fnc} [_{Fnc} V_2$
$\ldots$ of (31c). But a mere bias or tie breaker does not tell us anything about
ranking (for the reason why, see (21c) in §1.4.3).

Other examples help to sort out the ranking. In the $\ldots i]_{Lex} [_{Lex} V_2 \ldots$
situation, where the first vowel is high, it changes into a glide (see (31d)).
This means that deleting a lexical vowel is less harmonic than changing it into

a glide, all else being equal. So "don't change into a glide" must be ranked below "don't delete segments from lexical morphemes."

In the parallel situation involving two functional morphemes with high V_1 (that is, . . . $i]_{Fnc}$ $[_{Fnc}$ V_2 . . .), the first vowel does not change into a glide but instead deletes. The top-ranked constraint "don't delete segments from lexical morphemes" is irrelevant when both vowels are in functional morphemes, so the ranking justified in the preceding paragraph is irrelevant. Instead, this example proves that "don't change into a glide" is ranked above the general constraint "don't delete."

So far, we have established that "don't delete segments from lexical morphemes" dominates "don't change into a glide," which itself dominates "don't delete." Though "don't delete morpheme-initial segments" was recruited to break ties in . . . $\Psi_1]_X$ $[_X V_2$ . . . situations, its ranking relative to the other constraints has not yet been ascertained. Constraint ranking requires conflict, so it is necessary to find examples where "don't delete morpheme-initial segments" is at odds with "don't delete segments from lexical morphemes" and "don't change into a glide."

One such situation pits a lexical V_1 against a functional V_2. In the . . . $V_1]_{Lex}$ $[_{Fnc}V_2$ . . . configuration of (31b), there is a choice between deleting a lexical final vowel or deleting a nonlexical initial vowel. In fact, V_2 deletes, proving that "don't delete segments from lexical morphemes" is ranked higher than "don't delete morpheme-initial segments." Similarly, if high V_1 in a lexical morpheme meets V_2 in a functional morpheme (that is, . . . $i]_{Lex}$ $[_{Fnc}V_2$ . . .), the choice is between changing a vowel into a glide or deleting a nonlexical initial vowel. Examples of this type are not reported by Casali (1996); for present purposes, I simply assume that V_2 deletes. If further investigation bears this assumption out, it proves that "don't change into a glide" is ranked above "don't delete morpheme-initial segments."

These four informal constraints correspond to four faithfulness constraints in the actual analysis. Two of them are positional faithfulness constraints, $M_{AX_{LEX}}$ and $M_{AX_{INIT}}$. They protect lexical and morpheme-initial vowels, respectively. Both are frequently encountered under similar conditions in other languages. 📖$_{\S3.4\P9}$ An I_{DENT} constraint bars the vowel $\rightarrow$ glide mapping. At the bottom of the hierarchy is the general anti-deletion constraint M_{AX}, which is more stringent (§1.2.3, §3.1.3.5) than its positionally restricted counterparts.

Tableaux (33)–(36) work through the various cases, providing a formal basis for the ranking argument. They are in comparative format (§1.4.1) because this allows a more compact presentation of an example that would otherwise drag on for many pages. Comparative tableaux permit ranking arguments to be seen even in relatively complex tableaux involving several candidates and many constraints. Keep in mind that the first column contains the winner on the left and a failed competitor on the right. A "W" marks constraints favoring the winner, while an "L" marks constraints favoring the loser.

In tableau (33) we see the encounter between two lexical morphemes, the first of which ends in a high vowel, so glide formation is permitted by the undominated constraint IDENT(high).

(33) Emai I: MAX$_{Lex}$ ≫ IDENT

/...ku]$_{Lex}$ [$_{Lex}$ a.../	ONSET	MAX$_{LEX}$	IDENT	MAX$_{INIT}$	MAX	Description of failed candidate
a. ...kwa...~...ka...		W	L		W	V$_1$ deletes.
b. ...kwa...~...ku...		W	L	W	W	V$_2$ deletes.
c. ...kwa...~...ku.a...	W		L			Faithful

The crucial comparison is outlined in (33a): MAX$_{Lex}$ must dominate IDENT ("don't change a vowel into a glide"), favoring glide formation over deletion. If IDENT can be independently shown to outrank MAX (see (34a–b)), then this tableau supplies a valid argument for the ranking ⟦MAX$_{Lex}$ ≫ IDENT⟧.

Tableau (33) shows that glide formation is preferred when both morphemes are lexical, since glide formation avoids MAX$_{Lex}$ violation. But suppose that one or both morphemes are nonlexical, keeping V$_1$ high so as to give glide formation a fair test. There are three configurations represented by the three tableaux in (34): functional + lexical, functional + functional, and lexical + functional. Glide formation is known not to occur in the first two cases and, by assumption, the third. The rankings responsible for these failures of glide formation are outlined in (34).

(34) Emai II

a. IDENT ≫ MAX

/...βi]$_{Fnc}$ [$_{Lex}$o.../	ONSET	MAX$_{LEX}$	IDENT	MAX$_{INIT}$	MAX	Description of failed candidate
i. ...βo...~...βyo...			W		L	V$_1$ → glide.
ii. ...βo...~...βi...		W		W		V$_2$ deletes.
iii. ...βo...~...βi.o...	W				L	Faithful

b. IDENT ≫ MAX

/...si]$_{Fnc}$ [$_{Fnc}$ɔ.../	ONSET	MAX$_{LEX}$	IDENT	MAX$_{INIT}$	MAX	Description of failed candidate
i. ...sɔ...~...syɔ...			W		L	V$_1$ → glide.
ii. ...sɔ...~...si...				W		V$_2$ deletes.
iii. ...sɔ...~...si.ɔ...	W				L	Faithful

c. IDENT ≫ MAX_INIT (conjectured)

/ . . . ku]_Lex [_Fnc a . . . /	ONSET	MAX_LEX	IDENT	MAX_INIT	MAX	Description of failed candidate
i. . . . ku . . . ~ . . . kwa . . .			W	L	L	V_1 → glide.
ii. . . . ku . . . ~ . . . ka . . .		W		L		V_2 deletes.
iii. . . . ku . . . ~ . . . ku.a . . .	W				L	Faithful

When the first morpheme is functional, as in (34a–b), it loses its vowel in preference to glide formation. This is sufficient to establish that IDENT dominates MAX. And if the data assumed in (34c) are borne out, then this tableau proves that IDENT must also dominate MAX_INIT, since every loser-favoring constraint must be dominated by some winner-favoring constraint (see (15) in §1.3.3).

When V_1 is non-high, only deletion is possible because undominated constraints rule out glide formation. Whether deletion targets V_1 or V_2 depends on the sub-hierarchy ⟦MAX_LEX ≫ MAX_INIT⟧. Tableau (35) supplies the ranking argument: if a vowel in a functional morpheme meets a vowel in a lexical morpheme, in either order, then the vowel in the functional morpheme loses, because MAX_LEX is the highest-ranking faithfulness constraint.

(35) Emai III: MAX_LEX ≫ MAX_INIT

/ . . . be]_Lex [_Fnc ɔ . . . /	ONSET	MAX_LEX	IDENT	MAX_INIT	MAX	Description of failed candidate
a. . . . be . . . ~ . . . bɔ . . .		W		L		V_1 deletes.
b. . . . be . . . ~ . . . be.ɔ . . .	W			L	L	Faithful

But if the two vowels come from morphemes of equal status – both lexical or both functional – then the candidates with deletion tie on MAX_LEX, and so MAX_INIT is decisive. Tableau (36) shows this for a configuration with two lexical morphemes; an example involving two functional morphemes was already analyzed in (34b).

(36) Both candidates violate MAX_LEX

/ . . . kɔ]_Lex [_Lex e . . . /	ONSET	MAX_LEX	IDENT	MAX_INIT	MAX	Description of failed candidate
a. . . . ke . . . ~ . . . kɔ . . .				W		V_2 deletes.
b. . . . ke . . . ~ . . . kɔ.e . . .	W	L			L	Faithful

The comparative format makes it particularly obvious that the candidate in (36a) is tied with the winner on all constraints except MAX_{INIT} – no other cell in that row contains a W or L entry.

This analysis of Emai shows how a complex system of processes, all in service of the same output target, can be brought under grammatical control through the ranking of faithfulness constraints. This is a typical conspiracy that could not be satisfactorily explained in terms of traditional rewrite rules.

In rule-based theories of the *SPE* variety, Emai would require at least three and as many as five rules: deletion of V_1 under three different grammatical conditions, deletion of V_2, and devocalization of V_1. The number of rules is not a problem, but their form is: all of the rules specify a V-V sequence in their structural descriptions and eliminate it in their structural changes. The hiatus-resolving force of these various rules is a conspiracy so secret that it is unknown to the conspirators; the formal and functional resemblances among these various rules are purely accidental in the context of that theory.

Of course, the analyst, pulling the strings behind the scenes, is well aware that these rules all produce the same result. And sometimes the analyst's awareness can lead to a delusion of explanation: even though neither the theory nor the grammar says anywhere that these rules all serve the same end, that truth is so self-evident that it can seem as if it has been explained when it has not. Formal grammatical theories, such as OT or *SPE*, have no way to explain anything except through their formal grammatical mechanisms. In the OT analysis of Emai, all of the processes discussed serve the same end because the unfaithful mappings are all compelled by ONSET, sitting at the top of the hierarchy. In rule-based phonology, each process is a separate rule with no connection to other rules except accidental coexistence in the grammar. Such connections among rules are not obtainable using formal grammatical mechanisms.

Constraint-and-repair theories (§2.1) can get a somewhat better handle on conspiracies, including Emai's. As in OT, a single output constraint is responsible for the alternations: this constraint triggers certain repairs, which are rewrite rules that are applied only when needed to satisfy a constraint. But constraint-and-repair theories encounter a somewhat more subtle problem with conspiracies. Typically, these theories have very general economy principles for deciding which repair to use in which situation (§3.2.3). It is quite difficult to see how principles of such generality can be used to obtain an articulated hierarchy of repair preferences like (32) or the variations seen in other languages documented by Casali (1996, 1997). Something very much like constraint ranking would seem to be necessary.

A final remark on conspiracies. There are cases where the same markedness constraint, in the same language, both triggers some unfaithful mappings and blocks others. Suppose we have a ranking $[\![M1 \gg F1]\!]$ that characterizes the conditions for some unfaithful mapping (that is, some process). Suppose we also have a ranking $[\![M2 \gg F2]\!]$ (another process). Now, if M1 happens to conflict with and dominate M2, then M1 will appear to trigger one process and block another. Kisseberth's (1970a) original Yawelmani Yokuts example (§2.1) is a conspiracy of this type. Recast in OT terms,[22] the constraint in the M1 role is Kisseberth's prohibition on triconsonantal clusters, updated as a constraint on syllable structure. It dominates the faithfulness constraint DEP, so it can force epenthesis, and it also dominates the markedness constraint responsible for the syncope alternation, so it can block syncope.

3.1.4.4 *Interim Summary*

This discussion of conspiracies provides a glimpse into the broad vista of process interaction in OT. For anyone schooled in other approaches to phonology and syntax, it is sometimes difficult to appreciate exactly how interactive an OT grammar is. The methods and analytic resources of the other theories encourage a localistic approach to linguistic problems. Some notionally distinct phenomenon is isolated on pre-theoretic grounds, and then rules or similar devices are postulated until the phenomenon has been exhausted. This localistic strategy is legitimate in P&P, for example, because it fits P&P's strongly modular organization, and it is legitimate in *SPE* because positing one rule in a language says nothing whatsoever about any other rules that might coexist with it. But it is not possible in OT.

OT by virtue of its inherently interactive character places strong limitations on what a grammar can do. A whole grammar – the whole phonology of a language, for instance – consists of a single strict ranking of the constraints of CON (§1.1.2). This means that no process exists in isolation from any other process; all processes potentially interact. The situation in OT, then, is very different from *SPE*, where each rule is fully autonomous, or P&P, where modularity confines and limits the interactional possibilities. See §3.3 for further discussion of OT's integrated, global character.

3.1.4.5 *Harmonic Ascent*

Some of the consequences of OT's interactional nature have been discussed already, such as conspiracies. Others will be examined in §3.2 and §3.3. The goal now is to discuss some of the limits that interaction places on the systems of processes that can coexist in a single language.

One of the most striking results is the property of *harmonic ascent*, from Moreton (1996/1999).▢§3.4¶10 A classic OT grammar is a ranking of markedness constraints and faithfulness constraints – nothing more. By definition, a markedness constraint evaluates output candidates without reference to the input, while a faithfulness constraint evaluates input/output disparity, favoring the candidate with the least disparity (i.e., none at all). From this fact, and from the further assumption that there is some fully faithful candidate (a corollary to ROTB and the nature of GEN), Moreton proves formally that, for any OT grammar G and any input I, the output of G from I, G(I), is either identical to I or less marked than I relative to the ranking of the markedness constraints in

G. The underlying intuition is clear: the only reason to violate a faithfulness constraint is if violation leads to improvement in markedness. For details of the proof, see Moreton's work.[23]

Harmonic ascent has several empirical consequences. For one thing, it means that no OT grammar can describe a process of unconditional augmentation, where every form grows in size (e.g., /ba/ → *baʔ*, /bat/ → *batə*, /bata/ → *bataʔ*, . . .). The reason: augmentation is an unfaithful mapping, and unfaithful mappings must improve markedness. But markedness constraints evaluate output forms without reference to the input, and "getting longer" is not evaluable on output forms, so there can be no markedness constraint in CON to demand this unfaithfulness.[24]

Harmonic ascent also means that there can be no symmetrical processes of metathesis in a single language (e.g., /ia/ → *ai* and /ai/ → *ia*), nor can there be symmetrical deletion and insertion processes (e.g., /bilə/ → *bil*, /bil/ → *bilə*). If /ia/ maps unfaithfully to *ai*, then the unfaithful candidate *ai* must be less marked than the faithful candidate **ia*. And if /ai/ maps to *ia*, then the unfaithful candidate *ia* must be less marked than the faithful candidate **ai*. That is a contradiction: since markedness constraints evaluate output forms without reference to the input, it is impossible for *ai* to be less marked than *ia* and for *ia* to be less marked than *ai*. The situation with symmetrical deletion and insertion processes is similar.

More generally, harmonic ascent entails that no single OT grammar can describe any process or set of processes characterizing a circular chain shift, such as /a/ → *i* coexisting with /i/ → *a*. Symmetric and circular processes are inconsistent with harmonic ascent because the ranking in a grammar must be consistent: there is no way for both of the unfaithful mappings /A/ → *B*, *A* and /B/ → *A*, *B* to improve markedness relative to a single constraint hierarchy.

Surprisingly, these empirical consequences follow from the basic architecture of OT, requiring no special assumptions about CON except that it contains only markedness and faithfulness constraints. Harmonic ascent is therefore relevant to all domains of inquiry, not just to phonology. Even more surprisingly, these empirical consequences appear to be correct, or at least arguably so. Processes of unconditional augmentation or symmetric insertion/deletion have never been reported. There is one putative example of symmetrical metathesis that Moreton reanalyzes.

This leaves circular chain shifts, which were the focus of considerable study in the early 1970s. 📖 §3.4¶11 The *SPE* theory included a special notation, variables over feature coefficients ("alpha variables"), for expressing circular chain shifts of the /A/ → *B* and /B/ → *A* variety as a single rule. These were called *exchange rules*. But Anderson and Browne (1973) subsequently argued that no phonological exchange rule survives close scrutiny.[25] This is what we would expect, if harmonic ascent is a property of OT grammars that contain only markedness and faithfulness constraints.

By the way, merely eliminating phonological exchange rules from the *SPE* theory, perhaps by curtailing the notation that permits them, is not sufficient to rule out the mappings that they would produce – and of course it is the mappings themselves, and not the rules, that the theory must exclude. An exchange rule allows /A/ → B and /B/ → A to be done in a single step, but it is fully consistent with the tenets of *SPE* to decompose these mappings into three derivational steps: /A/ changes into the otherwise nonoccurring segment C, waits out the change from /B/ to A, and then changes A into B (cf. Chomsky and Halle 1968: 204). This point emphasizes that the global properties of an *SPE*-style grammar cannot be effectively restricted, because each rule is autonomous from the others. In contrast, OT's interactive nature means that no process can be certain of its autonomy.

Anderson and Browne also argued that there are *morphological* exchange rules, such as ablaut. The full implications of this observation are not yet fully clear, but they suggest an appeal to modularity (cf. §3.3.3.4). Perhaps the CON that pertains to the morphological module contains a third type of constraint, *anti-faithfulness* (Alderete 1998).⌨§3.4¶12 The morphology prizes a certain degree of difference or alternation within paradigms to make different members of the paradigm distinct. Anti-faithfulness constraints express that preference formally. With anti-faithfulness in the mix, harmonic ascent is not to be expected of the morphology and evidently is not observed.

3.1.4.6 *Incomplete Process-Specificity of Blocking*

Harmonic ascent is an architectural (near-)imperative of OT because it follows from the most basic assumptions about the architecture of this theory. Another architectural imperative is *limited process-specificity*.⌨§3.4¶13

For several decades, it has been known that output constraints or filters can block processes from applying (§1.3.3, §2.1, §3.1.2, §3.1.4.2). Now suppose a language has two similar processes – similar enough for the same output constraints in principle to block both. If an output constraint blocks one of these processes but not the other, its effect can be described as *process specific*. OT places a limit on process-specificity: if two similar processes coexist in a language, they cannot both be subject to process-specific blocking effects. This result, as we shall see, follows from one of OT's core premises, constraint ranking.

First, some background. If a language has two similar processes, in OT terms the grammar of that language must crucially rank two different markedness constraints, M1 and M2, above the same faithfulness constraint, F. Each of the rankings ⟦M1 ≫ F⟧ and ⟦M2 ≫ F⟧ approximates the effect of a process (cf. §3.1.1), and these two processes are similar in the sense that both involve the same unfaithful mapping under different conditions.

Now add a blocking constraint B to the mix. (B can be a markedness constraint or a positional faithfulness constraint. See §1.3 and §3.1.2 for exemplification of blocking through constraint ranking.) If B1 is to block only one of the processes, it must be ranked between M1 and M2 to compel violation of only the lower-ranking one. For example, with the ranking [M1 ≫ B ≫ M2 ≫ F], one of the processes (the one that is motivated by M1) will proceed without interference from B, but the other will be blocked by B.

Here is an example.[26] In Southern Palestinian Arabic, there are processes of assimilation that spread the feature of tongue-root retraction [RTR] leftward and rightward from a consonant. For example, tongue-root retraction (indicated by capitalization) spreads leftward in the unfaithful mapping /balla:S/ → *BALLA:S* and rightward in /Saba:ħ/ → *SABA:Ħ*. The sounds *i, y, š,* and *ǰ* resist taking on the feature [RTR], and they are observed to stop rightward spreading: /Sayya:d/ → *SAyya:d, *SAYYA:D*. But these same sounds do not stop leftward spreading: /xayya:T/ → *XAYYA:T, *xayyA:T*. In short, interference by *i/y/š/ǰ* is process specific: they stop rightward spreading but not leftward spreading.

As we just saw, process-specificity of blocking requires a ranking with the general form [M1 ≫ B ≫ M2 ≫ F]. In (37), the constraints M1 and M2 are based on the edge Alignment schema (§1.2.3), and the bottom-ranked faithfulness constraint is IDENT(RTR).

(37) Ranking for blocking in Southern Palestinian Arabic
ALIGN-L(RTR) ≫ B ≫ ALIGN-R(RTR) ≫ IDENT(RTR)

The blocking constraint B militates against combining the feature [RTR] with the sounds *i, y, š,* and *ǰ* . (These sounds have a high, front tongue position, which is antagonistic to [RTR] (Archangeli and Pulleyblank 1994).) By dominating ALIGN-R(RTR), B stops rightward spreading in its tracks, but has no influence over leftward spreading because it is itself dominated by ALIGN-L(RTR). The effect of the blocking constraint B, then, is process specific – it is specific to the process of rightward spreading.

At the next level of complexity are rankings with two processes and two blocking constraints, B1 and B2. For example, B1 might prohibit combining [RTR] with high segments, while B2 would prohibit combining [RTR] with front segments. Under the ranking in (38), B1 will stop spreading in both directions, but B2 will stop only rightward spreading.

(38) Ranking for general and process-specific blocking
B1 ≫ ALIGN-L(RTR) ≫ B2 ≫ ALIGN-R(RTR) ≫ IDENT(RTR)

So leftward spreading is stopped only by high segments (B1 dominates ALIGN-L(RTR)), while rightward spreading is stopped by high or front segments (B1 and B2 dominate ALIGN-R(RTR)). What this means, in effect, is that rightward spreading is the weaker process, because it is enforced by the lower-ranking Alignment constraint. Interpolated into this ranking, the blocking constraints differ in process-specificity: B2 is specific to rightward spreading, but B1 is nonspecific, affecting both directions of spreading. (Northern Palestinian Arabic is a real-life example that approximates (38).)

Another logical possibility is complete process-specificity: B1 blocks only one process and B2 blocks only the other. For example, suppose that leftward spreading is stopped by high segments and that rightward spreading is stopped by front segments, but leftward spreading is indifferent to whether a segment is front or not and rightward spreading is indifferent to whether it is high or not.

This logical possibility, though simple to describe, cannot be analyzed in OT using the constraints we have been assuming. For basic architectural reasons, OT places limits on process-specificity, offering no guarantees that each process can have its own suite of blocking constraints. The blocking effects will in principle overlap. To see why, consider the rankings in (39) required to analyze the hypothetical system just sketched.

(39) Ranking prerequisites for complete process-specificity
    a. Two similar processes
        M1 ≫ F
        M2 ≫ F
    b. B1 blocks ⟦M1 ≫ F⟧ process, but not ⟦M2 ≫ F⟧ process
        B1 ≫ M1
        M2 ≫ B1
    c. B2 blocks ⟦M2 ≫ F⟧ process, but not ⟦M1 ≫ F⟧ process
        B2 ≫ M2
        M1 ≫ B2

Complete process-specificity cannot be obtained, because these ranking prerequisites are mutually inconsistent. From transitivity of domination, we get both ⟦B1 ≫ M1 ≫ B2⟧ and ⟦B2 ≫ M2 ≫ B1⟧. This is a contradiction, and so no such grammar can exist. To put it somewhat more directly, it is in the nature of constraint hierarchies that M1 and M2 be in *some* ranking with respect to one another, and whichever of them is ranked higher characterizes the "stronger" of the two processes. No constraint can block the stronger process unless it also has the potential to block the weaker process. (Whether it does in fact block the weaker process in any particular case depends obviously on details of the constraints involved and the candidates under evaluation.)

Rule-based and rule-and-constraint-based linguistic theories make no such prediction. In general, these theories treat the coexistence of processes within a grammar as purely accidental, asserting no connection between the coexistent processes in terms of applicability. There is no necessity or even possibility of ranking processes for relative strength, and so there is no claim about how output constraints can or cannot affect the application of different processes.

The process-specificity result is not unique to phonology; obviously, nothing in (39) depends on the substantive properties of the empirical domain under analysis. This result is so general because it follows from OT's essential character – the claim that a grammar of a language is a constraint hierarchy. All hierarchies will have the property of limiting process-specificity effects in this way. It is, then, an architectural imperative of OT.

3.1.4.7 No Constraint-Specificity of Repair

Constraint-and-repair theories (§2.1) sometimes allow each output constraint to trigger its own specific repair operation. Like complete process-specificity, and for much the same reason, constraint-specific repairs are not in general possible in OT.

Consider a hypothetical language that prohibits syllable-final consonants but that disposes of them in two different ways. Obstruents are deleted, but sonorants trigger epenthesis, as in (40).

(40) Hypothetical case of constraint-specific repairs
    a. Syllable-final obstruent deletes
       /pat/   →   pa
    b. Syllable-final sonorant triggers epenthesis
       /pan/   →   panə

Suppose CON supplies distinct markedness constraints for these two situations, NO-CODA(obst) and NO-CODA(son). Suppose further that the faithfulness constraints MAX and DEP are not sensitive to the obstruent/sonorant distinction. Is there any way to rank these constraints to characterize this hypothetical language?

The answer is no. Because constraint ranking is a total ordering, we can be sure that either MAX dominates DEP or DEP dominates MAX. NO-CODA(obst) and NO-CODA(son) can compel violation of MAX or DEP, but EVAL ensures that the optimal form will violate the lower ranking of these two faithfulness constraints. Tableaux (41a–b) show this for one possible permutation of the constraints.

(41) a. /pat/ → pa (as in (40a))

/pat/		NO-CODA(son)	DEP	NO-CODA(obst)	MAX
i.	☞ pa				*
ii.	patə		*		
iii.	pat			*	

    b. /pan/ → pa (but cf. (40b))

/pan/		NO-CODA(son)	DEP	NO-CODA(obst)	MAX
i.	☞ pa				*
ii.	panə		*		
iii.	pan	*			

These tableaux represent one failed attempt to supply a grammar for the language in (40). Although DEP has been carefully ranked below NO-CODA(son) and above NO-CODA(obst), that is a pointless exercise. Because MAX is ranked even lower than DEP, it is the preferred constraint to violate. The repair, then, must be the same for both markedness constraints. As this example shows, OT cannot link repairs to targets, and so there are logically possible pairings of similar targets with different repairs that OT cannot analyze.[27] (A related issue is the exclusion of logically possible but nonoccurring repairs. See 3.1.5.2.)

3.1.4.8 *No Construction-Specificity of Interactions*

The integrality of the OT grammar has important implications in syntax, as the following quotation explains. (It refers to the constraints FULL-INT, which is violated by uninterpretable elements like expletives, and SUBJECT, which requires SpecIP to be structurally realized. See §3.1.3.6, §3.1.5.3, and §4.1.2 for more about these constraints.)

> [Some u]niversals arise from the identification of language grammars with constraint hierarchies, and from the corollary that constraint hierarchies are invariant across the distinct syntactic structures of a language. It is this requirement that underlies the prediction of the language universal banning overt expletives in null subject languages. . . . [N]ull subjects are possible only if FULL-INT is ranked above SUBJECT, else the subject position would be realized by an expletive. But, once this ranking is established, it must hold throughout the syntactic structures of the language, thus disallowing overt expletives also in prototypical expletive contexts, such as those involving raising verbs. (Samek-Lodovici 1996a: 218) (Also see Grimshaw and Samek-Lodovici 1995, 1998: 207.)

Just as there are no guarantees of process-specific blocking effects or repairs, so also there are no guarantees of construction-specific constraint interactions. The interaction of FULL-INT and SUBJECT yields a typology of null subjects and expletives. The ranking [[FULL-INT ≫ SUBJECT]] is a necessary condition for null subjects to be possible, but this ranking also rules out expletives generally. This predicted correlation follows from the substantive claim that CON contains these particular constraints and from the basic architecture of the theory, which posits a single grammar to evaluate all outputs.

This universal, like several of the other architectural imperatives mentioned here, is of a somewhat subtle and abstract character, and so the search for potential counterexamples will require some deftness. For example, positional faithfulness constraints (§3.1.3.5) can, in some cases, produce construction-specific effects, but that is no contradiction. The universal says that *interaction* of constraints is not specific to constructions – a different matter than making the constraints themselves construction specific. Of course, a sufficiently rich theory of construction-specific markedness and faithfulness constraints could render this universal empirically empty, though still technically valid. Thus, any proposed enrichments of CON along these lines need to be weighed against the potential loss of explanation through eating away at this universal.

3.1.4.9   Peroration

These results emphasize that, because of OT's interactive character, an OT grammar is much more of an integrated system than collections of rules or modules are. No doubt many other, similar implications of OT's architecture remain to be found. This is a matter of ongoing research.

3.1.5   Typology and Universals

3.1.5.1   Overview

OT is inherently typological. The constraints of CON are universal, and ROTB ensures that the inputs are universal too. Therefore, all variation between languages has a single cause: language-particular ranking. If the grammar of one language is known exhaustively, then in principle the grammars of all possible human languages are known. Analysis of one language can never be carried out without consideration of the broader typological context.

OT derives language universals from the same source as typology: ranking permutation (also see §1.1 on GEN). If no permutation of the constraints in CON produces a language with property P, then languages with P are predicted not to exist. P is outside of the typology, unlearnable and unknowable. This is the key insight and perhaps the central claim of OT.

The language universals discussed in §3.1.4.5–3.1.4.7 illustrate this point, as do other examples discussed in this section. Harmonic ascent, the limits on process-specificity, and the limits on construction-specificity are all consequences of factorial typology. In fact, results like these are often amenable to methods of formal proof, as is the case with harmonic ascent.

The discussion in §3.1.4 also hints at a further nuance of the theory of universals in OT: all universals follow from factorial typology, which is central to OT, but universals differ in how much they depend on particular substantive assumptions about the constraints in CON.[28] Harmonic ascent, for example, makes only the most meager assumptions about CON: that it contains markedness constraints and faithfulness constraints, but nothing else. Harmonic ascent, then, is an architectural imperative. The process-specificity results are the same. But the inverse correlation of overt expletives and null subjects requires CON to contain the particular constraints FULL-INT and SUBJECT, and not other imaginable constraints. Implicational universals, as will be shown in §3.1.5.4 (also see §1.2.3), similarly require substantive assumptions about CON, such as nonpermutable ranking of constraints corresponding to natural linguistic scales. I will use this rough classification of universals by their source, borrowed from Alan Prince, to serve as a framework for discussing further examples and refinements.

3.1.5.2 Architectural Imperatives

First, the architectural (near-)imperatives. These are universals that follow from the core elements of OT (§1.1): GEN's freedom of analysis, EVAL's comparative function and minimal violation, the markedness/faithfulness dichotomy, the strict domination hierarchy, and the claim that permuted ranking is the sole basis of between-language variation, with its corollaries of ROTB and universal CON. Such universals are necessarily somewhat abstract and general, but they may have repercussions that are quite specific, such as the prohibition of circular chain shifts (§3.1.4.5) or the impossibility of certain blocking patterns with assimilation processes (§3.1.4.6). They are also some of the most surprising; since OT was not designed with these results in mind, they are unanticipated, making them all the more intriguing.

One of the clearest examples of this type of universal was first noted by Vieri Samek-Lodovici:

> In OT, crosslinguistic variation occurs when two conflicting constraints are reranked relative to each other. This analysis makes an interesting prediction: given two conflicting constraints C1 and C2, there are two groups of languages where C1 will be satisfied and its effect visible. The first is constituted of all those languages where C1 outranks C2 (assuming of course that higher ranked constraints do not conflict with C1). The second and less obvious group is constituted of languages with the reverse ranking ⟦C2 ≫ C1⟧: in these languages C1 has a chance to be satisfied whenever the higher ranked constraint C2 is either vacuously satisfied by all competing candidates, and therefore not conflicting with C1, or it is violated by pressure of a higher constraint compatible with the satisfaction of C1. In more intuitive terms, this means that linguistic variations across languages and within a single language mirror each other, and are determined by the satisfaction of the same constraints. (Samek-Lodovici 1996a: 216)

To be more specific, consider a constraint C that is unviolated and therefore undominated in some language. This universal says that, because ranking is free, there should also be languages where C is crucially dominated and therefore sometimes violated. But since constraints can still be visibly active even when dominated (§1.2, §1.3, §3.2, and examples in §3.1), we should sometimes find situations where C decisively affects the choice of the optimal candidate even in languages that do not respect C generally.

This universal, which derives from the most basic properties of OT, is one way in which constraint ranking differs from parametrization.📖₍§3.4¶14₎ Let [C] stand for the parametric doppelgänger of the constraint C. The effects of the [+C] parameter value in the parametric theory are the same as the effects of undominated C in OT. But the effects of the [−C] parameter value are not the same as the effects, real or potential, of dominated C. In a language with the [−C] setting, [+C] of course has no consequences. But the constraint C is still an "attractor" even when dominated. Parameters are either on or off, but ranking provides much finer control over constraint activity. Similar control can be obtained in parametric theories only by proliferating parameters, eventually to absurdity (cf. §3.2.2.2 and the FAQ on parameters).

Samek-Lodovici goes on to cite several concrete instantiations of this prediction. For example, we saw in §3.1.4.8 that a necessary condition for null subjects is the ranking [[FULL-INT ≫ SUBJECT]]. In Italian, null subjects occur only with topic antecedents, and in that case they are not just permitted but required by the constraint DROP-TOPIC, which is violated by any structurally realized argument whose antecedent is a topic. The ranking for Italian under this analysis is given in (42a). Its English counterpart appears in (42b).

(42) Ranking for null subjects in Italian vs. English

In Italian, DROP-TOPIC is ranked above its antagonistic faithfulness constraint MAX. In English, which disallows null subjects even when they have topic antecedents, the ranking is just the opposite. Permuting these constraints, then, is responsible for one aspect of between-language variation. But there is also within-language variation in Italian: null subjects occur sometimes but not always. When a subject does not have a topic antecedent, it is preserved to satisfy low-ranking MAX, because the candidates with and without a subject tie by satisfying DROP-TOPIC vacuously. This is one respect in which the variation within a language mirrors variation across languages.

Again, this is a point of difference between OT and parametric theories. As in emergence of the unmarked (§3.2.2), a constraint that is crucially dominated is nonetheless decisive in situations where higher-ranking constraints are not. In other languages, the same constraint is undominated and hence obeyed consistently. From the perspective of between-language variation, this constraint looks like a parameter – but no parameter can also account for within-language variation. Parameters are either on or off, active or irrelevant. There is no middle ground.

The null-subject universal identifies a locus of predicted between-language variation. There are also situations where between-language variation is *not* predicted and is, in fact, impossible.[29] Among the candidates that GEN derives from input /A/ is fully faithful [A] (see §3.1.4.5 concerning this point). By hypothesis, the candidate [A] violates no faithfulness constraints, and let us further suppose that it violates no markedness constraints. This is certainly a possible situation, and it has an interesting consequence: [A] will always be the optimal output from input /A/ in any language. Since the /A/ → [A] mapping violates no faithfulness or markedness constraints, it harmonically bounds /A/ → [X] for any X ≠ A, since [X] cannot possibly be more faithful or less marked than [A], and there is no other way for [X] to be optimal (§3.1.4.5).

Another architectural imperative of OT might be called economy of deriva-tion or minimality of repair, recruiting the terminology though not the concepts of theories that combine constraints with rules (§2.1). Recall how EVAL com-pares two candidates: the more harmonic candidate is the one that performs better on the highest-ranking constraint where a difference is made between them. If the highest-ranking constraint that distinguishes the two candidates is a faithfulness constraint, then of course the more faithful candidate will be chosen.

This is not just idle rumination or scholasticism – the choice between the last two candidates, after all the others have been winnowed out, is often a matter of which is more faithful. Recall, for example, the question raised in the discussion of (29) in §3.1.4: why does no known language enforce *NÇ by deleting both of the offending consonants (/sin-ta/ → *sia)? The answer is that *sia always competes against a more faithful candidate, sita. Since *sia fares no better on markedness, it is harmonically bounded by sita with respect to the given input and constraint set. (On harmonic bounding, see §1.3.1, §3.1.2.4, and the references in §1.5 ¶9.) Tableau (43) shows this.

(43) An overkill effect

/sin-ta/		*NÇ	MAX
a.	☞ sita		*
b.	sia		**
c.	sinta	*	

Under either permutation of *NÇ and MAX, the candidate *sia cannot win, because it incurs a proper superset of sita's violation-marks. Informally, *sia is overkill, more unfaithful than it needs to be merely to satisfy *NÇ.

To the extent that notions like economy of derivation or minimality of repair (§3.2.3) can be made precise, their principal effects are captured by minimality of faithfulness violation in OT. When two candidates fare equally on the higher-ranking markedness constraints, and the decision comes down to a faithfulness constraint, the more faithful one is optimal. This situation is just a special case of the action of EVAL (§1.1). Minimality of faithfulness violation is simply a consequence of the way EVAL works, indistinguishable from minimality of markedness violation. In contrast, economy of derivation or minimality of repair are special impositions on the operational side of mixed rule/constraint theories (see §3.2.3).

Through EVAL, OT unites its economy principles with its "filters." This unity comes ultimately from another architectural imperative of OT: grammars consist of faithfulness and markedness constraints interacting in a single hierarchy.

3.1.5.3 Universals from Factorial Typology

Other universals emerge from factorial typology under the assumption that CON includes (or excludes) certain specific constraints. 📖$_{\S3.4\P15}$ A syntactic example, which depends on including FULL-INT and SUBJECT in CON, was given in §3.1.4.6. To complement this case, we will look here at two other applications of this approach, one in phonology and the other in morphology.

Final devoicing is a phonological process changing voiced obstruents *b/d/g* into their voiceless counterparts *p/t/k* at the end of a syllable. It is found in Russian, Polish, German, Dutch, Catalan, and many less familiar languages. Now, suppose CON includes a constraint prohibiting syllable-final voiced obstruents – call it]$_\sigma$/*VOICE. In languages with final devoicing, this markedness constraint is ranked above the antagonistic faithfulness constraint IDENT(voice), illustrated in (44).

(44)]$_\sigma$/*VOICE ≫ IDENT(voice) (Example: German /bad/ → [bat] 'bath')

/bad/		]$_\sigma$/*VOICE	IDENT(voice)
a.	☞ bat		*
b.	bad	*	

Languages like English that distinguish *bad* from *bat* have the opposite ranking of these two constraints.

When placed in a wider context, though, this system makes a problematic prediction that was first noted by Lombardi (to appear). CON also contains the faithfulness constraint MAX, which prohibits deletion. By free ranking permutation, there should exist languages where]$_\sigma$/*VOICE and IDENT(voice) both dominate MAX. We know from (1c) in §3.1.1 that a markedness constraint will compel violation of the lowest-ranking relevant faithfulness constraint that it dominates. So languages with this ranking delete rather than devoice syllable-final voiced obstruents (see (45)).

(45)]$_\sigma$/*VOICE, IDENT(voice) ≫ MAX

/bad/		]$_\sigma$/*VOICE	IDENT(voice)	MAX
a.	☞ ba			*
b.	bad	*		
c.	bat		*	

Under this regime, the most harmonic mapping is /bad/ → [ba]. The problem is that no known language enforces]$_\sigma$/*VOICE in this way.[30]

This example shows that the processes leading to satisfaction of the]$_\sigma$/*VOICE target are not as heterogeneous as one would expect: there is devoicing in many languages, but deletion in none. This observation demands an explanation, and Lombardi provides one by calling on harmonic bounding in a way that is abstractly identical to the *sita*/**sia* example (43).[31] The problem in (45) is that the optimal candidate vacuously satisfies IDENT(voice), since deleting /d/ obviates the possibility of changing its voicing, just as death puts an end to all worries about aging. Suppose, though, that the distinctive features in a segment S are regarded as objects or particles assembled together in S, rather than as attributes of S. This is approximately the difference between the *SPE* and autosegmental views of features.

Under the autosegmental view of features as autonomous entities, to delete /d/ is also to delete its [voice] feature,[32] while to devoice /d/ is merely to delete its [voice] feature, as in (46), preserving the rest of it.

(46) Unattested devoicing by deletion: /bad/ → **ba*

/bad/	]$_\sigma$/*VOICE	MAX(voice)	MAX(segment)
a. ☞ ba		*	*
b. bad	*		
c. bat		*	

MAX(voice) and MAX(segment) are in a stringency relationship (§1.2.3): MAX(voice) is violated whenever MAX(segment) is violated, but not vice versa. Logically, the relationship between these two constraints is equivalent to the inference "if I have lost an arm, then I have lost some fingers" (unless I am already adactylous).

Because MAX(voice) and MAX(segment) are in a stringency relationship, the candidate *bat* harmonically bounds the candidate *ba* with respect to the input and constraints in (46). This means that]$_\sigma$/*VOICE cannot force the mapping /bad/ → *ba* under any permutation of these constraints, because there is always a more harmonic mapping, /bad/ → *bat*. The nonexistence of languages that satisfy]$_\sigma$/*VOICE by deletion receives a principled explanation from factorial typology and a quasi-autosegmental view of featural faithfulness. Deletion in these circumstances is another instance of overkill.

It has sometimes been suggested that examples like this constitute a problem for OT. The idea seems to be that OT, by separating targets from processes, is predicting a broader range of possibilities than rule-based grammars do, since rules unite context and process into a single package. But of course a rule-based grammar can equally well contain a rule deleting syllable-final voiced obstruents, so rules are not the better way to go. Rather, the real difference is that OT, because of its inherently typological nature, calls attention to this problem and suggests where to look for a solution, based on harmonic bounding. In contrast, rule-based theories, at least in phonology, rarely address typological matters and offer no general solution to this problem, beyond the pious hope that future research will supply substantive constraints on rule form (see §2.1).

Stringency relationships are not the only source of universals, and in fact the wrong stringency relationship can actually subvert the desired typology. This is illustrated by the promised morphological example of a universal derived from factorial typology and specific assumptions about Con. Reduplication is a morphological process that copies part or all of a word. Infixation is the appearance of an affix inside a root rather than in the usual peripheral position of prefixes and suffixes. 📖 §3.4¶16 In a particularly complex though well-attested pattern, a reduplicative prefix alternates systematically with a reduplicative infix (see (47)).[33]

(47) Reduplicative pre- and infixation in Timugon Murut (Austronesian, Malaysia)
    a. Word begins with consonant ⇒ reduplicative prefix

| bulud | **bu**-bulud | 'hill/ridge' |
| limo | **li**-limo | 'five/about five' |

    b. Word begins with a vowel ⇒ reduplicative infix

| abalan | a-**ba**-balan | 'bathes/often bathes' |
| ulampoy | u-**la**-lampoy | no gloss |

The same morphological process is occurring in (47a) and (47b). The difference in placement of the reduplicated material is determined by the phonology of the base word, whether it starts with a consonant (C) or a vowel (V).

The reduplicative affix in Timugon Murut can be said to have post-initial onsetless syllable (PIOS) distribution, defined as follows: a PIOS affix is infixed after the initial syllable if the initial syllable is onsetless, and otherwise it is prefixed. PIOS affixes occur in various languages, and without exception they are reduplicative. No known language has a PIOS affix that is non-reduplicative. This typological skew is particularly surprising because, except for PIOS affixes, ordinary non-reduplicative affixes are far more common than reduplicative affixes.

The explanation for this typological generalization lies with the constraints on syllable structure and the theory of infixation in OT. The theory of infixation in OT, due to Prince and Smolensky (1993), holds that infixes are failed prefixes or suffixes – failed because the constraint aligning them peripherally is crucially dominated and hence violated. The key constraints on syllable structure, Onset and No-Coda (§1.2), are responsible for compelling that violation. In Timugon Murut, Onset dominates Align-Pfx, which requires the left edge of a prefix to coincide with the left edge of the word, as shown in (48a–b) (see §1.2.3 on edge Alignment constraints and §3.2.2.1 for more about Timugon Murut).[34]

(48) Onset ≫ Align-Pfx
    a.

		Onset	Align-Pfx
i.	☞ **bu**-bulud		
ii.	bu-**lu**-lud		∗∗

b.

	ONSET	ALIGN-PFX
i. ☞ a-**ba**-balan	*	*
ii. **a**-abalan	**	

In (48a), there is no reason to displace the reduplicative prefix, because both candidates tie by satisfying ONSET. But in (48b), ONSET and ALIGN-PFX are in conflict. Candidate (ii) fares worse on ONSET because it reduplicates an onset-less syllable, while candidate (i) skips over that syllable, dealigning the prefix. Candidate (i) still violates ONSET, but its better performance on ONSET is sufficient to establish the ranking 〖ONSET ≫ ALIGN-PFX〗. (Incidentally, this example shows that even violated constraints can be decisive in some circumstances. This is a fundamental prediction of OT – see §3.2.1.2 for further discussion.)

With this analysis of Timugon Murut in hand, we can return to the broader typological question: why is PIOS distribution only possible with reduplicative affixes? The answer is apparent from (48b): only reduplicative affixes are in danger of duplicating a preexisting ONSET violation. Ordinary non-reduplicative affixes will, at worst, preserve the ONSET violations of the base word, and so it will never pay to give a non-reduplicative prefix the PIOS distribution. Consider, for example, a non-reduplicative prefix of the form CV, like *ta-* in (49a–b).

(49) Attempting PIOS distribution with a non-reduplicative CV prefix

a.

	ONSET	ALIGN-PFX
i. ☞ **ta**-bulud		
ii. bu-**ta**-lud		**

b.

	ONSET	ALIGN-PFX
i. a-**ta**-balan	*	*
ii. ☞ **ta**-abalan	*	

This is not PIOS distribution. Instead, *ta-* ends up being prefixed to both C-initial and V-initial words. The same goes for a prefix like *a-* in (50a–b).

(50) Attempting PIOS distribution with a non-reduplicative V prefix

a.

		ONSET	ALIGN-PFX
i.	☞ **a**-bulud	*	
ii.	bu-**a**-lud	*	**

b.

		ONSET	ALIGN-PFX
i.	a-**a**-balan	**	*
ii.	☞ **a**-abalan	**	

In both tableaux, the optimal candidate is one where *a-* is simply prefixed, because both candidates tie on ONSET, leaving the choice up to ALIGN-PFX. It is easy to show the same result with the other simple affix shapes, VC and CVC, and then to generalize the result by induction to all possible shapes of affixes and roots. Furthermore, throwing NO-CODA into the pot does not change things.

Here, then, we have another typological result that depends on exactly what is in CON. Under the assumption that UG supplies the basic syllable structure constraints ONSET and NO-CODA and the affixal alignment constraint ALIGN-PFX, PIOS distribution is possible only with reduplicative prefixes. Interestingly, this result also requires that CON *not* contain another imaginable and even plausible constraint, NO-HIATUS, a more specific version of ONSET that prohibits heterosyllabic V-V sequences. Though the two candidates in (49b) perform equally on ONSET, they are distinguished by the putative constraint NO-HIATUS in (51a–b).

(51) NO-HIATUS substituted for ONSET in (49)

a.

		NO-HIATUS	ALIGN-PFX
i.	☞ **ta**-bulud		
ii.	bu-**ta**-lud		**

b.

		NO-HIATUS	ALIGN-PFX
i.	☞ a-**ta**-balan		*
ii.	**ta**-abalan	*	

The ground has shifted in (51). With No-Hiatus in Con, regardless of whether it replaces or supplements the more general constraint Onset, PIOS distribution is attainable with a non-reduplicative affix like *ta-*. To preserve the typological generalization, then, it is necessary to insist that the putative constraint No-Hiatus is not in Con. When it comes to explaining universals through factorial typology, what is *not* in Con can be as important as what *is* in Con.

3.1.5.4 Universals from Fixed Hierarchies

The last source of typological universals to be discussed is the presence of universally fixed rankings in Con (§1.2.3). These impermutable rankings are derived from natural linguistic scales, such as the sonority or animacy hierarchies. 📖 §3.4¶17

The story begins with explanation for typological observations of the form "any language that has *A* also has *B*, but not vice versa" (§1.2.2). To get this observation to follow from factorial typology, Con must meet certain requirements. First, it must not include any *A*-specific faithfulness constraint that would protect input /A/ despite its marked status. Second, Con must meet one of the following criteria:

* *B* incurs a proper subset of *A*'s markedness violations, or
* any markedness constraint favoring *A* over *B* is consistently and impermutably ranked below some markedness constraint favoring *B* over *A*. (A markedness constraint favors *A* over *B* if it assigns fewer violation-marks to *A* than *B*.)

If Con meets these conditions, it is said to be *harmonically complete* with respect to the observed implicational relation between *A* and *B*. That is, it allows languages with inventories {*B*} and {*A, B*}, but not *{*A*}.[35]

The second bullet in the preceding paragraph refers to fixed rankings in Con. These rankings are, arguably in every case, derived by combining natural linguistic scales using harmonic alignment or related techniques. Scales are orderings of linguistic objects; harmonic alignment combines two scales to form a universally impermutable constraint hierarchy. (At this time, readers might find it helpful to review the material in §1.2.3.)

The interaction between natural scales of persons and grammatical relations in (52) supplies a nice example.[36]

(52) Person Scale (PS): 1st, 2nd > 3rd
      Grammatical Relation Scale (GRS): Subject > Non-Subject

The relation ">" stands for the intentionally vague "is more prominent than." To combine two scales, it is necessary to orient them similarly, and this relation supplies that orientation. The orientation itself also has a substantive basis: in this case, items that are more central to the discourse – actual participants and subjects – appear at the prominent ends of the scales.

Scales are combined by harmonic alignment. The harmonic alignment of GRS with PS, in that order, consists of the two scales in (53a) (where ">" stands for "is more harmonic than"), and their constraint alignment consists of the two fixed universal hierarchies in (53b).

(53) a. Harmonic alignment of GRS with PS

H_{subj} = Subject/1st,2nd ≻ Subject/3rd
H_{Obj} = Non-Subject/3rd ≻ Non-Subject/1st,2nd

    b. Constraint alignment of GRS with PS

C_{Subj} = *SUBJECT/3RD ≫ *SUBJECT/1ST,2ND
C_{Obj} = *NON-SUBJ/1ST,2ND ≫ *NON-SUBJ/3RD

If this is correct, and if no other markedness constraints interfere, it is universally more marked for a subject to refer to the third person than the first or second, and conversely it is universally more marked for a non-subject (object or oblique) to refer to the first or second person than to the third.

For example, in Lummi (Salish, Pacific Northwest) active and passive are in near-complementary distribution. A sentence with a first or second person agent must be active, while a sentence that combines a third person agent with a first or second person patient must be passive. In other words, a first or second person agent or patient must be in subject position. The responsible ranking is in (54a), with some representative tableaux in (54b–c).

(54) Lummi person/voice relations

    a. *NON-SUBJ/1ST,2ND ≫ Faith, *NON-SUBJ/3RD, *SUBJECT/1ST,2ND

    b.

	1st Agent Subj	3rd Patient Obj	*NON-SUBJ/ 1ST,2ND	Faith	*NON-SUBJ/ 3RD	*SUBJECT/ 1ST,2ND
i. ☞ Active	1st Agent Subj	3rd Patient Obj			*	*
ii. Passive	1st Agent Obl	3rd Patient Subj	*	*		

    c.

	3rd Agent Subj	2nd Patient Obj	*NON-SUBJ/ 1ST,2ND	Faith	*NON-SUBJ/ 3RD	*SUBJECT/ 1ST,2ND
i. ☞ Passive	3rd Agent Obl	1st Patient Subj		*	*	*
ii. Active	3rd Agent Subj	2nd Patient Obj	*			

Tableau (54c) proves the ranking. An input with a third person subject and a second person object must receive an unfaithful analysis as a passive clause with an oblique (Obl) agent because the prohibition on second person non-subjects dominates faithfulness and the antagonistic markedness constraints.[37]

By interacting with faithfulness constraints and each other, the constraint hierarchies in (53b) predict a typology of inventories (cf. §3.1.2). Suppose, in accordance with ROTB, that inputs freely combine persons with grammatical roles. By ranking the two hierarchies with respect to one another and a faithfulness constraint, as in (54), a limited range of inventories can be produced. The four constraints in (53b) can in principle be permuted in just six ways (see (55)) (the formula is $m!/2^n$, where m is the number of constraints and n is the number of non-overlapping impermutable constraint pairs).

(55) Ranking permutations from (53b)

    a. *Subject/3rd ≫ *Subject/1st,2nd ≫ *Non-Subj/1st,2nd ≫ *Non-Subj/3rd

    b. *Subject/3rd ≫ *Non-Subj/1st,2nd ≫ *Subject/1st,2nd ≫ *Non-Subj/3rd

    c. *Subject/3rd ≫ *Non-Subj/1st,2nd ≫ *Non-Subj/3rd ≫ *Subject/1st,2nd

    d. *Non-Subj/1st,2nd ≫ *Subject/3rd ≫ *Subject/1st,2nd ≫ *Non-Subj/3rd

    e. *Non-Subj/1st,2nd ≫ *Subject/3rd ≫ *Non-Subj/3rd ≫ *Subject/1st,2nd

    f. *Non-Subj/1st,2nd ≫ *Non-Subj/3rd ≫ *Subject/3rd ≫ *Subject/1st,2nd

By inserting a single faithfulness constraint into any one of the five available "slots" in each of these hierarchies, we obtain a harmonically complete typology. For example, some languages allow passive *John was seen by me*, but no language requires it. Languages of the latter type are impossible because none of the licit permutations in (55) would judge *John was seen by me* to be less marked than its competitor *I saw John*.

Harmonic alignment and other techniques for scale combination (see the references in §1.5 ¶7) are useful tools for dealing with natural linguistic scales in phonology and syntax. Harmonic alignment is particularly appropriate for dealing with implicational universals about slots and their preferred fillers. Any language that allows third person subjects also allows first and second person subjects, so first and second person are the preferred filler for the subject slot. Or all languages allow vocoids (*a, i, u*) to be syllable nuclei, but only some languages allow liquids (*r, l*) to be nuclei, so vocoids are preferred fillers for the nucleus slot.

3.1.5.5 *Summary*

To sum up, OT derives universals from factorial typology. Universally required or prohibited configurations are those that emerge from, respectively, all licit permutations of the constraints in Con or no licit permutations of the constraints in Con. Implicational universals also emerge from ranking permutation and the structure of Con: if A implies the presence of B, and not vice versa, then B is never more marked than A in any licit permutation of the constraints in Con. In general, the explanations for universals should be sought in factorial typology under a particular theory of CON and not in GEN or other "universal" aspects of OT.

These results emphasize a theme that has been important throughout: OT is inherently typological, and so the very act of analysis within it makes significant typological and universalist claims. Universals in OT are intrinsic to the theories of EVAL and CON; they are not external impositions, to be modified or dropped with relative ease. Descriptive universals are not stated directly, and they may not be easy to discover, because they emerge indirectly from the very stuff that grammars are made of, violable constraints interacting in language-particular rankings.

3.2   Consequences of Constraint Violability

I mete and dole
unequal laws unto a savage race.
– Tennyson, Ulysses

In OT, unlike many other linguistic theories, constraints are universal but violable. Universality depends on violability: since languages differ in systematic ways, CON can be universal only if its constraints are obeyed in some languages but violated in others. The conditions under which some constraint C will be violated in some language L can be determined by considering C's place in the constraint hierarchy H_L under the definition of EVAL (§1.1.2, §1.3). The optimal candidate will violate C only if none of its surviving competitors obeys C. As a matter of logic, this can happen under two different circumstances: either all C-obeying candidates are ruled out by constraints ranked higher than C in H_L, or there is no C-obeying candidate among those emitted by GEN for a specific input. In practice, only the first circumstance is usually relevant, since the second will probably never occur if GEN is granted full freedom of analysis (§1.1.3).

Even if C is crucially dominated and therefore sometimes violated in L, violation of C is never gratuitous. So whenever C is presented with a mix of candidates, it will favor those that obey it, or if none do, it will favor those that violate it least. This is an architectural imperative of OT that follows from EVAL. Constraint ranking in OT and parametrization in other theories differ sharply on just this point (see the cross-references in the parameters FAQ). Parameters that have been turned off have no latent effects – they are simply inert. But even when crucially dominated, C can be active under the circumstances just described. Indeed, depending on what other constraints are in CON, it may be impossible to produce any ranking that guarantees C's inactivity over all inputs and all candidates, especially with the added challenge of ROTB and freedom of analysis.

My goal in this section is to explore three main consequences of constraint violability in OT: nonuniformity of structure, emergence of the unmarked, and extremism and economy. These terms come, respectively, from Prince (1993b), McCarthy and Prince (1994a), and Prince (1998). The three sections below explain and illustrate each of them in turn.

3.2.1 Nonuniformity of Structure

3.2.1.1 The Basics

Because constraints are violable, OT predicts that some languages may allow a considerable degree of conditioned variation in the form of output structures, while other languages may impose rigid formal requirements on the same structures. This difference follows from ranking permutation, since the same markedness constraint M may be undominated and unviolated in one language but crucially dominated in another. Languages with the latter ranking will permit *nonuniformity of structure* with respect to M.📖_{§3.4¶18}

In the clearest cases, the M-obeying and M-violating structures are in complementary distribution. Consider in this light some of the examples discussed in §3.1.3. In Madurese (§3.1.3.4), nasal vowels are forbidden except when they are required, after a nasal consonant. The markedness constraint $*V_{Nas}$ is M, and it is crucially dominated by $*NV_{Oral}$. In English (§3.1.3.6), *do*-support is forbidden except when it is required, in inversion constructions with no other auxiliary. The markedness constraint Full-Int is M, and it is crucially dominated by Ob-Hd. English and Madurese are structurally nonuniform, prohibiting nasalized vowels or expletive verbs except when their presence is triggered by higher-ranking constraints.

3.2.1.2 Exemplification

Four examples are discussed in this subsection. Two involve nonuniformity arising when constraints compete over the same piece of linguistic turf, such as requiring that the same syllable belong to a foot and not belong to a foot. The conflict is resolved by ranking, yielding a consistent outcome when there actually is a conflict. But when circumstances allow the conflict to be sidestepped completely, nonuniformity can result from satisfying both of the constraints at once. The other two examples involve the interface between grammatical components, each of which imposes inconsistent requirements on the output, again leading to nonuniformity when conditions are right.

First, an example of competition over the same chunk of a linguistic structure. In some languages, final syllables are said to be *extrametrical*, meaning that they are disregarded when words are parsed into metrical feet. But extrametricality is blocked or revoked in shorter words, when making the final syllable extrametrical would leave too little intrametrical material to construct even a single foot. Hayes (1995: 110–13) calls this the "unstressable word syndrome."

Latin supplies a nice example of the syndrome in action.[38] In Latin, the final syllable is extrametrical, and the syllable(s) preceding it are parsed into a foot called the moraic trochee. This foot can consist of two light CV syllables, as in *au(rícu)la* 'outer ear', or it can consist of a single heavy CV: or CVC syllable, as in *re(fé:)kit* 'he did again' or *re(fék)tus* 'done again'. But extrametricality is blocked in two kinds of words that would otherwise be unstressable. Monosyllabic words like *(lúx)* 'light' could not support a foot at all if they were entirely extrametrical, so footless *lux* is impossible. And disyllabic words whose penultimate syllable is light, such as *pede* 'foot', are exhaustively parsed into a foot *(péde)*. The alternative parsing, *(pé)de*, is ruled out because it involves a degenerate foot *(pé)*. The responsible constraint is Foot Binarity (FT-BIN), which requires stress feet to contain at least two light syllables or one heavy syllable.[39]

Latin words, then, are nonuniform with respect to extrametricality of the final syllable. This means that the markedness constraint responsible for extrametricality effects, called NON-FINALITY, is crucially dominated. NON-FINALITY says that the stress foot cannot be final, forcing the metrical parse to avoid the final syllable. In Latin, NON-FINALITY is dominated by HEAD(PWd), which says that every phonological word must contain at least one foot to serve as its head. For this reason, monosyllables like *(lúx)* have no alternative but to violate NON-FINALITY, as shown in (56).

(56) HEAD(PWd) ≫ NON-FINALITY

		HEAD(PWd)	NON-FINALITY
a.	☞ [(lúx)_{Ft}]_{PWd}		*
b.	[lux]_{PWd}	*	

By positing no feet at all, candidate (56b) manages to satisfy NON-FINALITY – but to no purpose, since HEAD(PWd) is higher ranked. With words like *péde*, there is a third interesting candidate, (57c), which fatally violates FT-BIN.

(57) HEAD(PWd), FT-BIN ≫ NON-FINALITY

		HEAD(PWd)	FT-BIN	NON-FINALITY
a.	☞ [(péde)_{Ft}]_{PWd}			*
b.	[pede]_{PWd}	*		
c.	[(pé)de]_{PWd}		*	

In longer words like *au(rícu)la* in (58), though, there is no difficulty in satisfying all three constraints, and so they are obeyed.

(58) HEAD(PWd), FT-BIN ≫ NON-FINALITY

		HEAD(PWd)	FT-BIN	NON-FINALITY
a.	☞ [au(rícu)_{Ft}la]_{PWd}			
b.	[auricula]_{PWd}	*		
c.	[auri(cú)_{Ft}la]_{PWd}		*	
d.	[auri(cúla)_{Ft}]_{PWd}			*

The structural property of extrametricality, then, is nonuniform across the vocabulary of Latin. In short words, extrametricality is "revoked" – actually, never present – because NON-FINALITY is crucially dominated. But when a word is long enough, all three constraints can be satisfied, and so they are.

The Latin example shows how a nonuniformity effect can emerge from the competition between two constraints imposing structural requirements that are sometimes, but not always, inconsistent. It is also possible to get similar results from a single constraint competing with itself. This happens in cliticization.[40] 📖 §3.4¶19 Clitics typically bunch up or cluster in certain favored locations, such as second position. Clustering is a nonuniformity effect: all clitics are attracted to second position, but only one can actually be there. The others come as close to second position as possible.

Most clitics in Bulgarian appear in second position, with multiple clitics clustering in that slot: *Penka ja e dala na Petko* 'Penka gave it to Petko'. The attraction of clitics to second position is obtained by ranking NON-INITIALITY above ALIGN-L. But since every clitic is subject to ALIGN-L, nonuniformity – that is, clustering – is observed when, as in (59), there is more than one clitic in the clause.

(59) NON-INITIALITY ≫ ALIGN-L

		NON-INITIALITY	ALIGN-L
a.	☞ Penka **ja e** dala . . .		***
b.	Penka **ja** dala **e** . . .		****
c.	**Ja e** Penka dala . . .	*	*
d.	Penka **e ja** dala . . .		***

As a matter of simple logic, both clitics cannot be in second position, so some violation of ALIGN-L must be tolerated (unless a clitic is deleted). Though candidate (59c) has the best attainable performance on ALIGN-L, it is not optimal because it violates higher-ranking NON-INITIALITY. Though dominated, ALIGN-L is still active, ruling out candidates like (59b) with unclustered clitics. The analysis is not quite complete, though, because (59a) and (59d) are equally harmonic and some tie breaker is required (see (21c) in §1.4.3 for general discussion of breaking ties and Legendre 1999 for this specific case).

The interfaces between grammatical components, such as phonology/morphology or phonology/syntax, are also rife with nonuniformity effects. For example, though the phonemic inventory of a language is often thought of as a relatively uncomplicated notion, it is not unusual to find sounds in complementary distribution except under some fairly specific morphological conditions (cf. §3.1.2, §3.1.3). Two examples are given in (60a–b).[41]

(60) a. Madurese
Oral and nasal vowels are in complementary distribution (see §3.1.3.4), except in reduplicative affixes: *ȳāt-nēȳāt* 'intentions', *w̃ã-mōw̃ã* 'faces'. This breach of complementarity improves resemblance between the affix and the base word that it is copying.

b. Terena (Arawakan, Brazil)
Except for *m, n, ŋ*, all segments are predictably oral. But the characteristic morphology of the 1st singular is nasalization of the initial portion of the word up through the first oral obstruent (which becomes prenasalized).

owoku	ōw̃ōŋgu	'house'/'my house'
arine	ār̃īnē	'sickness'/'my sickness'
nokone	nōŋgone	'need'/'I need'

In these cases and others like them, an otherwise simple distribution is disrupted under specific morphological circumstances. The result looks like phonemic polysystemy: two different systems of phonemes for different morphological conditions. The phonemic system is nonuniform across different morphological categories.

In OT, phonemic nonuniformity is derived from constraint interaction. A distribution is fully predictable if $[\![M \gg F]\!]$ rankings are dispositive of all inputs drawn from the rich base (§3.1.2, §3.1.3). A distribution is nonuniform, in the sense just exemplified, if the top-ranked M constraint is itself dominated by interface constraints requiring surface identity or morphological realization.[42] The surface identity constraints, which extend the notion of faithfulness to relations among output strings, come from correspondence theory (§1.2.2, §3.3.3.5). One class of these constraints requires resemblance between a base word and the reduplicative affix attached to it, as in Madurese (60a). A constraint demanding that every morpheme be realized overtly (MORPH-REAL) is responsible for the nonuniformity effect in Terena (60b), under the assumption that the first singular morpheme consists only of the distinctive feature [+nasal]. In each case, one of these correspondence constraints dominates the highest-ranking markedness constraint controlling the distribution. The result is nonuniformity of distribution or polysystemy without multiple systems: a distribution that is mostly predictable from purely phonological criteria is overridden under specific morphological conditions.

Nonuniformity effects can also be observed at the phonology/syntax interface (§3.3.2.4).[43] In English, functional elements like *to* or *do* are usually not
freestanding phonological words (PWd's). Instead, they are procliticized to a
following lexical word to make a single PWd unit: *I gave the book [tŏ Bill]$_{PWd}$,
[Dŏes Bill]$_{PWd}$ eat meat?* We know this because the function word is unstressed
and has a reduced vowel: [tə bíl], [dəz bíl]. But when the supporting lexical
word is removed by syntactic movement or deletion processes, the function
word is promoted to full-fledged PWd status: *Who did you give the book
[tó]$_{PWd}$?, Bill [dóes]$_{PWd}$.* So the phonological projection of syntactic function
words is nonuniform across contexts.

The usual, proclitic status of function words in English is determined by
constraint interaction. PWDCON asserts that every PWd must contain some
lexical word.[44] This constraint is obeyed by *[Bill]$_{PWd}$* or *[tŏ Bill]$_{PWd}$*, but it is violated by *[to]$_{PWd}$*. Two other constraints are part of the typology of pro- versus
enclitics. ALIGN-R(Lex, PWd) says that the right edge of every lexical word
must coincide with the right edge of some PWd, and ALIGN-L(Lex, PWd) is its
symmetric counterpart. Ranked as ⟦ALIGN-R ≫ ALIGN-L⟧, they favor procliticization – *John gave the book [tŏ Bill]$_{PWd}$* – over encliticization – **John gave
the [book tŏ]$_{PWd}$ [Bill]$_{PWd}$.*

Examples like *Bill [dóes]$_{PWd}$*, with a PWd that contains no lexical word,
show that PWDCON is not always obeyed. The source of this nonuniformity
effect is crucial domination of PWDCON by ALIGN-R(Lex, PWd) and another
constraint, EXH(PPh), which says that the immediate constituents of phonological phrases are PWd's and nothing else. Tableau (61) supplies the basis for this
ranking argument.

(61) ALIGN-R(Lex, PWd), EXH(PPh) ≫ PWDCON

		ALIGN-R	EXH(PPh)	PWDCON
a. ☞	[[Bill]$_{PWd}$ [dóes]$_{PWd}$]$_{PPh}$			*
b.	[[Bill dŏes]$_{PWd}$]$_{PPh}$	*		
c.	[[Bill]$_{PWd}$ dŏes]$_{PPh}$		*	

When a function word occurs phrase-finally in English, some kind of nonuniformity is unavoidable, since the normal function-word behavior, procliticization, is
not an option. The role of (61), then, is to bow to the inevitable but make the best
of it, selecting a candidate that best satisfies these constraints as they are ranked
in English. Through permuted ranking, other languages should show other
responses in equivalent situations. And indeed they do (Selkirk 1995, 1996).

3.2.1.3 Opposite Constraints

The most radical kind of nonuniformity is complete reversal: a structure is
found generally, but its exact opposite or mirror image occurs under restricted

conditions. In Kanakuru (Chadic, Nigeria), the position of focused constituents has this reversal property (62a–c).[45]

(62) a. Focused phrase *before* clausal complement

neigon	**nuŋ**	[ka	Aish	watʊg	Billiri]
said	**who**	that	Aisha	went-to	Billiri

'**Who** said that Aisha went to Billiri?'

b. Focused phrase *before* modifier of complex DP complement

aɗe	shiruwoi	**ŋgadlai**	[mɔ	shee	wura]	ane
ate	fish-the	**cat-the**	that	she	fried	up

'**The cat** ate up the fish that she fried.'

c. Focused phrase *after* simplex DP complement

tui	[worom	mono]	**shire**
ate	bean	my	**she**

'**She** ate my beans.'

The simplest situation is exemplified by (62a): focus precedes any complements of the verb. This position can be construed as adjunction at the left edge of VP (out of which the verb has been moved, so the left edge of VP is equivalent to postverbal position). Example (62b) is the same thing, but with a complication. The naive expectation is **aɗe ŋgadlai shiruwoi mɔ shee wura ane*, but this is ruled out by a requirement that the nominal object *shiruwoi* be adjacent to the verb to receive case. But *shiruwoi* can be incorporated into the verb, leaving the focused constituent free to lodge in its preferred locus without interfering with case assignment.

Now, the interesting case is obviously (62c), since that is where the reversal happens. Placing focus at the left edge of VP is not possible, because the adjacency requirement on case assignment would be violated. Incorporation is blocked by the Empty Category Principle (ECP) (see Samek-Lodovici 1996a: 128–29 for why). With these otherwise attractive options foreclosed, one might expect the language simply to leave *shire* in clause-initial position, which is usual for subjects, but that is not what happens in Kanakuru. Rather, focus shifts to the opposite edge of VP.

Formally, two edge Alignment constraints (§1.2.3, §3.1.5.3, §3.2.3) are in action here, and they are tugging *shire* in opposite directions. The higher-ranking constraint is ALIGN-L(Focus, VP). It characterizes the more general situation in (62a–b), where focus is left-adjoined to VP. But ALIGN-L is crucially dominated by the ECP and by a constraint requiring adjacency for case assignment. When these constraints conflict with ALIGN-L, all surviving candidates will end up violating ALIGN-L. Then the next lower constraint in the hierarchy, ALIGN-R, steps into the breach, as evidenced in (63).

(63) CASE-ADJ, ECP ≫ ALIGN-L(Focus, VP) ≫ ALIGN-R(Focus, VP)

	CASE-ADJ	ECP	ALIGN-L (Focus, VP)	ALIGN-R (Focus, VP)
a. ☞ tui [worom mono] **shire** ate bean my **she**			*	
b. tui **shire** [worom mono] ate **she** bean my	*			*
c. tui + worom **shire** [mono] ate + bean **she** my		*		*
d. **shire** tui [worom mono] **she** ate bean my			*	*

What is left of the VP after verb raising is bracketed in these examples. In this situation, ALIGN-L is violated equally by both surviving candidates,[46] so the disposition of this tie goes to ALIGN-R. The last candidate shows *shire* left in place, a disposition that ALIGN-R decisively rejects. In addition to the constraints shown, any markedness or faithfulness constraint that would encourage *shire* to remain in preverbal subject position must be ranked below ALIGN-R to rule out this fourth candidate.

The basic OT architecture is entirely consistent with the possibility of two constraints with sometimes opposite effects coexisting and being active in a single grammar. If all constraints are universal and universally available, then any pairs of opposed constraints that are in CON will be present in every grammar. Though obviously many constraints in CON will not have opposites, some will. This is especially true of Alignment constraints, which generally come in symmetric pairs. Indeed, Samek-Lodovici's Kanakuru example of focus alignment is complemented by de Lacy's (2000c) Maori example of phrasal alignment. In Maori, the phonology/syntax interface constraints ALIGN-R(XP, PPh) and ALIGN-L(XP, PPh) are both present and active in determining the phonological phrasing, which has direct, readily observable effects on the intonation contour.

Samek-Lodovici and de Lacy make an important point about how opposite constraints distinguish OT from parametric theories. Though most parameters are said to have on and off values, some have left and right symmetry. For example, research on the phonology/syntax interface by Chen (1987) and Selkirk (1986) led to an edge-based theory that anticipates Alignment in important respects. But there is a difference: prior to OT, the choice of edge was done with a left/right parameter, while in OT ALIGN-L and ALIGN-R are present in every grammar but differently ranked. The parametric theory has no way to obtain the effects derived by ranking opposite constraints. Those effects are only possible in a theory that allows constraints to be violated, since the lower-ranking Alignment constraint is going to be active only when the optimal candidate and its close competitors violate the higher-ranking Alignment constraint (as in (63)).

Another difference between opposite constraints and parameters is that the former are not really opposites at all. There is a situation where ALIGN-R(X, Y) and ALIGN-L(X, Y) are in agreement rather than conflict: if the constituents X and Y are of exactly the same size, in a configuration like $[X]_Y$. Concretely, if ALIGN-R(X, Y) and ALIGN-L(X, Y) are both ranked above faithfulness to X, then X will be expanded or truncated as needed to fit the Procrustean bed of Y. This sort of behavior is observed with morphological templates (§3.4 ¶20, §4.2.2).

3.2.1.4 *Summary and Comparative Remarks*

To sum up, structural nonuniformity is an architectural imperative of OT in the sense that some nonuniformity is an inevitable consequence of constraint interaction. The source of nonuniformity is crucial domination of a markedness constraint. In the most extreme case, two constraints expressing nearly opposite imperatives can both be active.

The existence of structural nonuniformity sometimes suggests that the putative structural property does not exist at all. This inference has been particularly important in the study of phonology. The recent history of phonology prior to OT saw a burgeoning of structural or representational models (§2.1), such as autosegmental phonology, underspecification theory, and feature geometry. Research in OT has questioned these representational theories precisely because of nonuniformity effects. For example, some versions of underspecification theory treat unmarked feature values as absent, and therefore phonologically inert, during the early stages of a derivation. Later on, these feature values are filled in by default rules, and so they become active. The problem with this view is that (in)activity of unmarked feature values correlates rather poorly with derivational stages and in general seems to be nonuniform both early and late in the derivation (McCarthy and Taub 1992; Mohanan 1991). This has led to the conclusion that a representational theory of markedness – i.e., underspecification theory – should be set aside in favor of a substantive theory of markedness – violable constraints in OT (Prince and Smolensky 1993: 188; Smolensky 1993) (cf. Causley 1999a). Along the same lines, Padgett (1995a, 1995b) has argued that the representational "class nodes" of feature geometry should be replaced by a substantive, constraint-based theory of feature classes. Again, the evidence comes from nonuniformity effects.

At this point, it makes sense to pause and reflect on how nonuniformity is obtained in rule-based and rule-and-constraint-based theories (§2.1, §2.2). In general, nonuniformity presents no challenge to rule-based theories that incorporate a serial derivation and structure-changing operations. *SPE* and *Aspects* are examples of such theories. Nonuniformity is unremarkable because one rule can fully or partially undo the effects of a previous rule. A typical analysis would assign the prevalent structure early in the derivation, with later rules changing or replacing it under specific conditions.

But theories of the *SPE* and *Aspects* genre are the least successful in accounting for language typology, and so they have been largely replaced by theories that mix rules or repairs with inviolable, possibly parametric constraints. Nonuniformity is much more problematic for these later theories, precisely because the constraints are inviolable. For example, though something like PWDCON is surely a constraint of English phonology in any of these theories, its application is somehow nonuniform across contexts. The constraint cannot be violated, because ranking and violability are not elements of these theories. In the face of problems like this, two alternative strategies can be observed in the literature. One strategy is to complicate or parametrize the statement of PWDCON so that it does not need to be violated. For example, redefining PWDCON to say "every *nonfinal* PWd must contain some lexical word" would do the trick for English, but it gives up on the goal of providing a restrictive, explanatory typology. The other strategy is to call on modularity and serialism, recognizing successive components in the grammar where constraints are or are not in force. For example, one might say that PWDCON is "on" in the module controlling word phonology but "off" in the phrase-phonology module. This technique was pioneered in the theory of Lexical Phonology (§3.3.3.3). It too has problems with typology, since the differences between levels are unprincipled, as well as with learning (§4.2). It has also been known to lead to the positing of modules for which there is no evidence other than differences in activity of a single constraint or rule.

3.2.2 Emergence of the Unmarked

3.2.2.1 *The Basics*

Just because a constraint is crucially dominated does not mean it is inactive. Even low-ranking constraints can be decisive if higher-ranking ones are not able to select a unique optimal candidate. When the low-ranking constraint is from the markedness family, this phenomenon is called *the emergence of the unmarked* (TETU). The scenario goes like this. A markedness constraint M is crucially dominated in some language L, so M-violating structures are abundant in L. In particular, M may be ranked below its antagonistic faithfulness constraints, so M never induces an unfaithful mapping from any input (§3.1.1). But there may be situations where several candidates tie on all the constraints dominating M. In just those situations, M can be visibly active, favoring the optimal candidate over some or all of its competitors. The structure that is unmarked with respect to M is then said to *emerge*, even though M's presence in the grammar is generally hidden.📖§3.4 ¶20

TETU is an architectural imperative of OT; that is, given OT's basic premises, it is inevitable that markedness constraints will sometimes emerge in the sense just described. TETU follows from the premise that all constraints are present in all grammars and from the activity of EVAL, which will dig as far down in the hierarchy as it needs to in order to select the optimal candidate.

TETU is closely linked with OT's typological claims. Any markedness constraint that is undominated in one language can, if conditions permit, be emergent in another language (cf. §3.1.5.2). Likewise, any markedness constraint that is emergent in one language should, through permuted ranking, be undominated in another. These predicted correlations provide a further test of putative markedness constraints in CON and of the theory as a whole.

TETU effects are so pervasive in OT that they can be observed in nearly all of the examples discussed previously. Many of them involve special/general interactions (§1.2, §1.3, §3.1.3, §3.1.4, §3.1.5), where the lower-ranking general constraint emerges only in situations where the higher-ranking special constraint is not decisive. Here are some cases.

ONSET does not state a categorical truth about Axininca Campa (§1.3.3) because initial syllables can be onsetless. Nevertheless, ONSET is active in this language, emerging in medial position, where it is obeyed consistently. The constraint interactions responsible for this TETU behavior are shown in (14) of §1.3.3: a positional faithfulness constraint dominates ONSET, so it cannot be satisfied by unfaithful mappings initially. But in noninitial syllables, the positional faithfulness constraint is irrelevant, and so the ranking ⟦ONSET ≫ DEP⟧ is decisive in selecting candidates with medial consonant epenthesis. In this way, the limited activity of ONSET in languages like Axininca Campa is connected directly and formally with its broader activity in languages like Arabic that prohibit onsetless syllables categorically. This is one instance of the typological basis for TETU.

TETU is essential to the OT account of distributional restrictions (§3.1.3), since an emergent markedness constraint typically characterizes the default distribution. In English, for example, *dǒ* occurs only when needed, and so it must be prevented from co-occurring with another auxiliary. OB-HD demands that every projection have a head, forcing the appearance of *dǒ* when there is no other auxiliary in inversion constructions. But when there is another auxiliary, lower-ranking FULL-INT emerges to prohibit *dǒ* (28). Similarly, in Madurese (19a), *V_{Nas} emerges in vowels that are not preceded by nasal consonants, where higher-ranking *NV_{ORAL} is irrelevant. And in Nancowry (24b), *V_{Nas} emerges in unstressed syllables, where the positional faithfulness constraint is irrelevant.

TETU is also the source of many nonuniformity effects (§3.2.1). In Kanakuru, ALIGN-R emerges when its opposite, ALIGN-L, is not decisive (63).

Extremism (§3.2.3) is another source of TETU effects. In Timugon Murut (48b) (also see §3.1.5.3), ONSET dominates ALIGN-PFX, but ALIGN-PFX is still decisive in favoring a candidate where the prefix is as far to the left as possible while still obeying ONSET. This TETU effect can be seen in the comparative tableau (64).

(64) Emergence of ALIGN-PFX

		ONSET	ALIGN-PFX
a.	a-**ba**-balan ~ **a**-abalan	W	L
b.	a-**ba**-balan ~ aba-**la**-lan		W

Though ALIGN-PFX is crucially dominated, it is not irrelevant or inactive. It favors the candidate where the reduplicative morpheme is closer to the preferred prefixal position.

There is another respect in which Timugon Murut exhibits TETU. ONSET itself is also an emergent constraint. ONSET is unable to compel unfaithful mappings in this language, as is shown by examples like *ambilú.o*, *nansú.i*, and *lógo.i*, with initial and medial onsetless syllables.[47] So ONSET must, at a minimum, be dominated by the faithfulness constraints MAX and DEP, as illustrated in (65).

(65) Emergence of ONSET and ALIGN-PFX

		MAX	DEP	ONSET	ALIGN-PFX
a.	a-**ba**-balan ~ **a**-abalan			W	L
b.	a-**ba**-balan ~ aba-**la**-lan				W
c.	a-**ba**-balan ~ **ba**-balan	W		L	L
d.	a-**ba**-balan ~ ?**a**-?abalan		W	L	L

This is a striking TETU effect, modeled after Prince and Smolensky's (1991, 1993) original Tagalog example. Timugon Murut flagrantly violates ONSET, but still ONSET is decisive in determining the position of the reduplicative prefix. This difference in activity of ONSET is simply a matter of ranking.

The role of ONSET in Timugon Murut nicely illustrates the connection between TETU and typology. (See Bresnan to appear-a for a parallel syntactic example.) Though Timugon Murut presents abundant evidence *against* this constraint, we know from the study of language typology that it must exist. By one of the core hypotheses of OT (§1.1), every constraint in CON is present in the grammar of every language. So ONSET must be present in the grammar of Timugon Murut. In (65), we see confirmation of this hypothesis: in a little corner of the language where faithfulness is not relevant, ONSET emerges to decide in favor of the candidate with infixation. This is what we expect to find: constraints that are motivated by typological evidence should also be active, even when dominated, when the right ranking conditions obtain.

3.2.2.2 Comparison with Parameters

What if there were an [Onset] parameter instead of a violable constraint?[48] Languages that are [+Onset] would require all syllables to have onsets, and lan-

guages that are [−Onset] would not impose that requirement, permitting syllables with and without onsets. Learners would start with the subset [+Onset]
value, switching to the superset value [−Onset] in the face of disconfirm-
ing evidence (cf. §3.1.2.4). The gross typology given by this parameter is
sound, but it lacks the fine structure given by constraint ranking. The simple
[Onset] parameter says nothing about languages like Axininca Campa or
Timugon Murut, where (in OT terms) the constraint ONSET is dominated but
emergent. 📖 §3.4 ¶14

The dedicated parametrizer has only one real option at this point: expand
the set of parameters. For example, the difference between Axininca Campa,
which allows initial onsetless syllables, and languages that allow no onsetless
syllables, might be accommodated with a more specific parameter like
[Onset-Medial]. And Timugon Murut, where ONSET emerges only in deciding
the placement of the reduplicative affix, would require an [Onset] parameter
whose force is limited to this specific affix (cf. Steriade 1988). By relativizing
parameters to positions, morphological categories, or other domains, it is
possible to get some of the fine control over parametric activity that ranking
provides for constraints.

Relativizing parameters in these ways may work descriptively, but it has
a distinct disadvantage in comparison to ranking in OT (also see §1.2.3).
Superficially, relativized parameters might seem equivalent to relativized
versions of constraints, such as positional faithfulness (§1.3.3, §3.1.3.5).
But there is an important difference: the relativized parameter [Onset-
Medial] is the end of discussion, but the positional constraint FAITH$_{INIT-σ}$ is just
the beginning. The relativized parameter merely restates the observation,
explaining the explanandum and nothing more. Positional faithfulness
makes perilous predictions, such as the preservation of contrasts in initial
syllables when they are neutralized elsewhere, or incomplete positional
faithfulness effects through crucial domination of the positional faithfulness
constraint itself. In other words, the relativized parameter adds little to our
understanding of the typology, while the relativized constraint affects the
typology in diverse and often unexpected ways. Relativized parameters,
though they may offer short-term descriptive success, do not seem to yield a
very interesting or productive approach to the finer shades of between-language
differences.[49]

3.2.2.3 *Comparison with Default Rules*

A somewhat more promising line of attack on TETU effects in rule-and-
constraint-based theories involves *default* or *last resort* rules. The idea is that
there is some inviolable condition on output forms C(O), and certain rules are
favored as the way to bring representations into conformity with C(O). But
when those favored rules are inapplicable, irrelevant, or blocked, the default/last
resort rule steps in to ensure that C(O) gets satisfied anyway. Rule-and-

constraint-based theories of phonology and syntax share this basic idea, though they implement it in exactly opposite ways.

In rule-and-constraint-based phonology, default rules are part of underspecification theory (§1.4.4, §3.1.2.2, §3.1.2.4). The idea is that a feature that is fully predictable in some language is absent, or underspecified, in the lexicon of that language. Specific, context-sensitive phonological rules fill in some values of that feature, and a context-free default rule takes care of the rest. Rules of both types are constrained to be feature filling, which means that they cannot alter feature values already present in the lexicon or derived by previous rules. The output condition C(O) that forces the default rule to apply when the more specific rules have not is a requirement that output representations be fully specified for all features.[50]

For example, nasal vowels in Madurese appear only after a nasal consonant; vowels are otherwise oral. In underspecification theory, one would say that the nasal/oral distinction is underspecified for vowels in the lexicon, so the vowels of /ba/, /a/, and /ma/ are all [Ønasal]. A rule of the phonology spells out the vowel of [mã] as [+nasal] because of the preceding nasal consonant, and then the universal default rule V → [−nasal] applies to all vowels that are still underspecified. The unmarked feature value emerges at the *end* of the derivation, when the universal default rule applies.[51]

The approach to defaults taken in contemporary syntactic theory is rather different (Chomsky 1995: 138ff.). Feature checking is the overriding output condition that compels movement or other operations. If some operation must be performed to ensure that features are checked, universal rules take precedence, but if no universal rule is successful, then a language-particular rule steps in as the last resort. This means that unmarked values emerge at the *beginning* of the derivation, when the universal rules apply.

From these remarks, it becomes clear that the approaches to TETU taken in rule-and-constraint-based phonology and Minimalist syntax are almost exact opposites. The rule-based phonological model gives precedence to language-particular rules, letting universal ones apply only when the language-particular rules have failed. Minimalist syntax gives precedence to universal operations, recruiting language-particular operations only when the universal ones are blocked.

This difference can be related to the traditional assumption that phonological derivations always succeed, but syntactic derivations may fail (cf. §2.3, §4.1.2). The featural default rules of underspecification theory are context-free operations, so they always manage to correct any lingering underspecification. In fact, they are so effective that there is no reason to impose an output constraint requiring full specification – it has no work to do, except to reassure the analyst that the default rules have a purpose. In syntax, though, progressing from the universal to the language particular may not be enough to ensure that the derivation converges, in Chomsky's (1995: 171) sense. If neither universal nor language-particular operations can bring the output into conformity with the feature-checking requirement, then the derivation crashes.

In OT, there is no such difference. All derivations "succeed" in the sense of yielding some output (§4.1.2), though some fail to yield a distinctive output (§3.1.2). Both phonological and syntactic defaults come from the same source: when higher-ranking faithfulness and/or markedness constraints are not fully decisive in selecting a unique output, the determination of the optimal candidate may be left up to a low-ranking markedness constraint. Precedence, then, is a matter of ranking rather than of serial ordering, and it is unrelated to universal versus language-particular status. As usual, the constraints are universal and their ranking is language particular.

3.2.2.4 Summary

TETU is one of the most distinctive properties of OT. No other linguistic theory has anything quite like it, since it follows from constraint violability under domination. TETU yields some surprising analyses, where even constraints that are frequently violated and unable to compel unfaithful mappings are nonetheless decisive under limited conditions. Higher-ranking constraints define the precise conditions where the low-ranking markedness constraint can emerge. TETU gives OT a consistent account of defaults in phonology and syntax, and it establishes a direct connection, via ranking permutation, between defaults and language typology.

3.2.3 Extremism and Economy

I would remind you that extremism . . . is no vice.
– Barry Goldwater, 1964 Republican presidential
nomination acceptance speech

Constraints are violable in OT, but violation is minimal. Minimality of violation is fundamental to OT, because it follows from the way EVAL works (§1.1.2). Minimal violation of a constraint C means that, when several candidates tie on all constraints ranked higher than C, the candidate(s) that incur the fewest violations of C will be favored. In most cases discussed so far in this chapter, the candidate that is most harmonic under C simply obeys C, while competing candidates violate C. But "fewest" may be greater than zero. Even a candidate that violates C can be favored over its competitors, as long as it violates C less than they do.

The two tableau formats (§1.4.1) focus on different aspects of the candidates' performance under a constraint. Imagine that C is crucially dominated and that all surviving candidates violate C, but they differ in extent of violation. This situation is schematized in tableaux (66a–b).

(66) a. Violation tableau   b. Comparative tableau

	...	C
i. ☞ Cand$_1$		*
ii. Cand$_2$		**
iii. Cand$_3$		***

	...	C
i. Cand$_1$ ~ Cand$_2$		W
ii. Cand$_1$ ~ Cand$_3$		W

The violation tableau (66a) ranks all of the candidates according to their degree of C performance, with Cand$_1$ at the top, while the comparative tableau (66b) extracts the central datum: that Cand$_1$ bests all comers with respect to C. The situation where the optimal candidate does not violate C is merely a special case of this more general application of EVAL.

This section focuses on cases where C, as in (66), is violated to differing extents by various candidates and least of all by the optimal candidate. Differences in extent of constraint violation are part and parcel of OT, and they have two sources (§1.1):

(i) Any constraint can be violated to different extents when candidates are big enough to contain several potential loci of violation. For example, the markedness constraint ONSET is violated worse by a candidate with two onsetless syllables than a candidate with one onsetless syllable. So, when presented with the forms ʔa.ʔu, ʔa.u, and a.u, this constraint orders them as ʔa.ʔu ≻ ʔa.u ≻ a.u, assigning them zero, one, and two violation-marks, respectively. The same goes for the faithfulness constraints. For instance, if the input is /au/, the constraint DEP imposes exactly the opposite ordering on these candidates – a.u ≻ ʔa.u ≻ ʔa.ʔu – because it is more faithful to have fewer epenthetic consonants.

(ii) Certain constraints are evaluated *gradiently*.[52] These constraints rank candidates for relative satisfaction even when there is just a single locus of violation. They describe some desired configuration that candidates can match to a greater or lesser degree, and they define a metric for translating the goodness of match into varying numbers of violation-marks. Edge Alignment constraints (§1.2.3, §3.1.5.3, §3.2.1.3) are the most conspicuous examples of gradience. They assign no violation-marks to candidates with perfect alignment, and they measure imperfect violation in terms of the number of linguistic units (e.g., segments, syllables, XP's) intervening between the designated constituent-edges. Though some constraints, such as ONSET, cannot be given a sensible gradient interpretation, this notion has also been applied to some faithfulness constraints and to some markedness constraints other than alignment.

When C produces multiple violations for either of these reasons, minimal violation in accordance with EVAL will favor the surviving candidate that bears the fewest violation-marks. Minimal violation under these conditions yields two kinds of empirical consequences that can be called *extremism* and *economy*. 📖 §3.4¶21 Extremism and economy are formally the same thing but notionally opposite. Extremism is "as-much-as-possible" behavior, where there is a push toward some limit. Economy is "as-little-as-possible" behavior, where the limit exerts some kind of pull. The division between these two kinds of behavior is often rather blurry and is of no consequence when it comes to analysis, but it is useful expositorily.

The Timugon Murut infixation example ((64)–(65) in §3.2.2.1) presents a typical extremism effect. The infix is placed as close to the beginning of the word as possible, as long as it does not create an additional onsetless syllable. The constraint ALIGN-PFX asserts that the infix must appear exactly at the beginning of the word, and nonconforming candidates are assessed gradiently for their deviance from this requirement. The extremism as-close-as-possible effect is given by the interaction of ALIGN-PFX with ONSET, which dominates it. The optimal candidate is the one with the infix farthest to the left among those that tie on ONSET. No special mechanism is needed to get this extremism effect or others like it, since it requires nothing more than a banal application of EVAL. The as-close bit is just minimal violation of ALIGN-PFX, and the as-possible bit is just minimal violation of ONSET. The connection between the two is made by ranking, and the very meaning of constraint ranking comes from EVAL.

Economy of derivation and its relationship to minimal violation were discussed in §3.1.5.2. When C in (66) is a faithfulness constraint, minimal violation of C ensures that no more is done than needed, where "no more" is given by applying C under EVAL and "than needed" comes from the constraints dominating C. For example, a language with onset-filling epenthesis has the ranking ⟦ONSET ≫ DEP⟧, and minimal violation of DEP eliminates gratuitous epenthesis, favoring the mappings /bai/ → [baʔi] and /bati/ → [bati] over competitors like *[baʔiʔiʔiʔi] or *[batiʔi].

Minimal violation of a markedness constraint can also produce economy effects. As we saw in §3.1.3.6, English *dŏ* occurs only as needed, because violation of FULL-INT is minimized as long as higher-ranking OB-HD is satisfied. Tableau (67), which adds another candidate to (27), illustrates one aspect of this.

(67) OB-HD ≫ FULL-INT

		OB-HD	FULL-INT
a.	☞ [CP *wh* **do**ᵢ [IP DP **e**ᵢ [VP V *t*]]]		*
b.	[CP *wh* **e** [IP DP **e** [VP V *t*]]]	**	
c.	[CP *wh* **do** [IP DP **do** [VP V *t*]]]		**

Since the trace of inversion supplies a satisfactory head for IP in (67a), there is no need for the multiple *dŏ*s in (67c). But OB-HD guarantees that at least one dŏ appears. The upshot: dŏ occurs no more than needed, with "no more" and "than needed" deriving from the way EVAL operates over this constraint hierarchy.

Extremism and economy are not unique to OT, but they have been worked out in very different ways in other linguistic theories. On the one hand, some approaches take a localistic view of extremism and economy, building them into specific rules or niches of the grammar. For example, research in metrical phonology has turned up domain-specific conditions like Halle and Vergnaud's (1987: 15) Exhaustivity and Maximality Conditions, which require exhaustive and maximal metrical parsing, subject to other constraints, or Selkirk's (1981: 215) principle requiring that the number of degenerate (i.e., epenthetic) syllables be minimized, all else being equal.

On the other hand, some approaches to extremism and economy effects are of very great generality and applicability. For example, Economy in the sense of Chomsky (1995) is understood to require minimal structures, fewer derivational steps, and shorter movements, all of course subject to other constraints. And in phonology, the constraint-and-repair theory TCRS (§2.5 ¶7) imposes general Minimality and Preservation Principles on repairs. Repairs must "involve as few strategies (steps) as possible," and their application is limited by the requirement that "[u]nderlying phonological information is maximally preserved" (Paradis 1997: 546). The problem with principles of such generality is that it is often not clear how to apply them in specific situations. Without an explicit theory of how to compare the economy of any representation or derivation with that of its competitors, there is the danger of unconscious appeal to an analyst behind the curtain filling in the details needed to achieve the desired outcomes.

Here is an example that illustrates the pitfalls of an overly general approach to economy. Recall hiatus resolution in Emai from §3.1.4.3. One observation that needs to be accounted for is the preference for glide formation over deletion in cases like /. . . ku]$_{Lex}$ [$_{Lex}$ a . . . /. It is fairly easy to see how general considerations of economy might favor the output [. . . kwa . . .], which fairly well preserves the underlying /u/, over *[. . . ka . . .], which obliterates the /u/ entirely. But how will general economy principles account for the mapping /. . . βi]$_{Fnc}$ [$_{Lex}$ o . . ./ → [. . . βo . . .], *[. . . βyo . . .], where the membership of /i/ in a functional morpheme forces deletion instead of glide formation? And what of languages that resemble Emai in many respects but differ on details like this one (Casali 1996, 1997)? In OT, it is clear how these differences will be obtained – language-particular ranking of universal constraints – but they present an obvious challenge to universal, invariable economy principles.

The would-be theorist of extremism and economy must navigate between the Scylla of an overly specific approach and the Charybdis of an overly general one. The various extremism and economy effects clearly have something in common. Approaches that are specific to a domain, a rule, or a phenomenon inevitably miss this commonality. Very general approaches, though, are in danger of saying little more of substance than Strunk and White's (1972) infamous Rule 17: "Omit needless words. Omit needless words. Omit needless words." The problem is not with Rule 17 itself, but with applying it to specific cases. Generality of formulation may be accompanied by vagueness and imprecision about how to compare actual structures or derivations for complexity, length, or other properties being pushed or pulled to their limits. Nonformulation is, of course, even worse.

EVAL sets OT's course through the Strait of Messina. Minimal violation details precisely what it means to minimize or maximize along some dimension, and ranking takes care of the "as possible" or "as needed" clauses. There are no special or general economy principles, because economy and extremism derive from the very nature of the theory.

3.3 Consequences of Globality and Parallelism

Globality and parallelism may be the most controversial aspects of OT. Most – but not all – research in OT assumes a basically flat derivation, mapping inputs directly onto outputs with no intermediate stages. This is a significant departure from the serial derivation and the concomitant chronological metaphor that have guided much research in generative linguistics since the 1950s (though see §2.2).

The nature of the derivation is less central to OT than matters discussed previously, and so it has not proven difficult to set this topic aside until now. The time has come, though, to address this aspect of the theory. The discussion is organized as follows. The first order of business (§3.3.1) is to explain what globality and parallelism are, how they connect with OT, and how OT differs in this respect from some other linguistic theories. Next (§3.3.2), we will look at the consequences of globality and parallelism, recalling results discussed previously and introducing new ones. Finally (§3.3.3), we examine the serialist critique of globality and parallelism and various responses to it, including alternative OT architectures.

3.3.1 Globality and Parallelism Explained

Recall the basic OT architecture in (3) of §1.1, repeated in (68).

(68) Basic OT architecture

$$input \longrightarrow \boxed{\text{GEN}} \longrightarrow candidates \longrightarrow \boxed{\text{EVAL}} \longrightarrow output$$

This model is *parallel* and *global*. It is parallel primarily because of the way GEN works: respecting inclusivity or freedom of analysis, and emitting candidates that differ from the input in diverse ways. Candidates are fully formed, in the sense that they can stand as finished outputs of the grammar, and they can differ from the input by showing the effects of several notionally distinct processes simultaneously.

This model is global because of the way EVAL works: taking a *single* language-particular hierarchy H and applying it to every candidate set from every input. This means that every constraint of UG, depending on how it is ranked in H, has the potential to determine which candidate is most harmonic. Every candidate is evaluated by the whole hierarchy for every aspect of its well-formedness.

The best way to understand these properties of OT is to compare them to the rule-based serial derivation of the *SPE* and *Aspects* models. In *SPE/Aspects*, a grammar is a list of extrinsically ordered rules. The first rule takes an underlying representation I_0 as input and emits an intermediate representation I_1 that has been transformed in accordance with that rule. The second rule takes I_1 as input and emits I_2, and so on. The derivation terminates when the last rule applies; its output, I_L, is the surface representation.

The *SPE/Aspects* model is *serial* and *local*. It is serial because each notionally distinct operation is accorded its own step in the derivation. Distinct operations are sequential rather than simultaneous. It is local because the statement that a rule makes about well-formedness is not durable; apart from the input it receives and the output it emits, a rule has no connection whatsoever to the rest of the derivation in which it resides. The application or formulation of one rule is strictly local to a particular derivational step, with no influence over or from other rules. (Modifications of *SPE/Aspects* often retreat from strict locality by way of principles like the Elsewhere Condition or Strict Cyclicity (§3.3.2.4).)

An example drawn from the phonology of Nootka (Wakashan, Vancouver Island) nicely illustrates this difference in perspective.[53] In Nootka, dorsal consonants (velars like *k* and uvulars like *q*) become rounded after round vowels (69a). There are also underlying rounded dorsals in Nootka, and they lose their rounding at the end of a syllable (69b). Now consider the situation where a dorsal consonant is both preceded by a round vowel and followed by a syllable boundary (indicated by "."), so it meets the structural conditions of both rules. What happens is that unrounding takes precedence (69c).

(69) Nootka rounding and unrounding
    a. Dorsals become rounded after round vowels
        K → Kʷ / o__   ʔo.**kʷ**iːɬ   'making it'
                        cf. **ki**ːɬ   'making'
    b. Syllable-final dorsals become unrounded
        Kʷ → K / __.   ɬaːk.šiƛ   'to take pity on'
                        cf. ɬaː.**kʷ**iqnak 'pitiful'
    c. Interaction: Unrounding "wins"
        m̓oː**q**.   'throwing off sparks'
        cf.m̓o.**qʷ**ak   'phosphorescent'

In a serial derivation like (70), unrounding wins because it is ordered after rounding.

(70) Serial derivation for Nootka

Underlying	/m̓oːq/	cf.	/ʔokiːɬ/	/ɬaːkʷšiƛ/
Rounding	m̓oːqʷ.		ʔo.kʷiːɬ	—
Unrounding	m̓oːq.		—	ɬaːk.šiƛ

These two rules are local and serial in their effects. The rounding rule causes /q/ to become [qʷ] after a round vowel, but it has no other, lingering influence on the subsequent course of the derivation. In other words, the rounding rule states a generalization that is guaranteed to be true only at the derivational instant when it applies. Later, the unrounding rule is free to undo the effects of the earlier rule, treating all rounded dorsals equally, whatever their source.

In OT, the interaction between these processes is a matter of conflicting markedness constraints, and this conflict is resolved, like all constraint conflicts, by ranking. Two markedness constraints are visibly active in Nootka. One asserts that plain dorsals cannot occur after round vowels (71a). The other prohibits rounded dorsals syllable-finally (71b).

(71) Markedness constraints for Nootka

    a. "ROUNDING"

       *oK

    b. "UNROUNDING"

       *Kʷ.

These markedness constraints dominate the faithfulness constraint IDENT(round), producing the alternations in (69a–b), as shown in (72a–b).

(72) a. "ROUNDING" ≫ IDENT(round)

/ʔokiːɬ/	"ROUNDING"	IDENT(round)
i. ☞ ʔo.kʷiːɬ		*
ii. ʔo.kiːɬ	*	

    b. "UNROUNDING" ≫ IDENT(round)

/ɬaːkʷši(ƛ)/	"UNROUNDING"	IDENT(round)
i. ☞ ɬaːk.ši(ƛ)		*
ii. ɬaːkʷ.ši(ƛ)	*	

Now, if "UNROUNDING" dominates "ROUNDING," as in (73), the output is unrounded in situations of conflict like /m̓oːq/ (69c).

(73) "UNROUNDING" ≫ "ROUNDING" ≫ IDENT(round)

/mo:q/	"UNROUNDING"	"ROUNDING"	IDENT(round)
a. ☞ mo:q.		*	
b. mo:qʷ.	*		*

This OT analysis is global and parallel. The effects of the rounding and unrounding processes are evaluated simultaneously by a single constraint hierarchy. The precedence relation between these two processes is a matter of ranking the relevant markedness constraints.

There are analogous situations in syntax.[54] Suppose that the three components of a phrase – specifier (Spec), head (Hd), and complement (YP) – are freely permuted in different candidates emitted by GEN, with the choice among those candidates left up to the grammar. The typological difference between the order Spec-Hd-YP and Hd-Spec-YP is due to permuted ranking of the Alignment constraints SPEC-LEFT and HEAD-LEFT; see (74a–b).

(74) a. SPEC-LEFT ≫ HEAD-LEFT

	SPEC-LEFT	HEAD-LEFT
i. ☞ Spec-Hd-YP		*
ii. Hd-Spec-YP	*	
iii. Spec-YP-Hd		**

b. HEAD-LEFT ≫ SPEC-LEFT

	HEAD-LEFT	SPEC-LEFT
i. Spec-Hd-YP	*	
ii. ☞ Hd-Spec-YP		*
iii. Hd-YP-Spec		**

Whichever constraint is higher ranking determines which of the specifier or head is initial. The other then settles for second-best.

Derivationally oriented approaches to syntax derive this typological difference using a kind of implicit rule ordering. The input is assumed to be identical in both types, but one type also has a movement rule. This is a kind of rule ordering, because the fixing of the input must happen before movement. The only difference from the phonological situation is that the ordering is obtained from modularity rather than from mere stipulation.

These phonological and syntactic examples share a common theme. In serial theories, precedence relations among processes are analyzed in terms of rule ordering: the last rule to get its hands on the representation has precedence, in the sense that it reliably states a surface-true generalization. In OT, however, precedence relations among constraints are accounted for by ranking: the highest-ranking constraint has precedence, in the same sense that it reliably states a surface-true generalization.[55] There is, then, some overlap, though certainly not equivalence, in the functions of constraint ranking and rule ordering.

Since OT has constraint ranking anyway, it makes sense to start from the assumption that this is the only way to encode precedence relations in the grammar. In other words, the parallel, global architecture in (68) is the null hypothesis for implementing OT. Alternative implementations and the evidence for them will be discussed in §3.3.2.6 and §3.3.3, but for now we will stick to exploring the results obtained from the basic model (68).

3.3.2 Exemplification

3.3.2.1 Consequences of Globality

The basic OT architecture in (68) is global in the sense that EVAL applies a single language-particular constraint hierarchy H to all constructions from all inputs. A strictly global theory would be fully integral, with no modularity whatsoever. By common consent, all research in OT assumes a more limited globality, distinguishing at least between phonological and syntactic modules. I will ignore this largely irrelevant complication in subsequent discussion, but modularity questions will arise again in §3.3.3.

The main consequences of globality can be presented fairly quickly, since they are also discussed in §3.1.4.5–3.1.4.9. In those sections, several architectural imperatives of OT are noted, all of which presuppose globality (or integrality, as the same property is referred to in that context). Harmonic ascent says that the output must be either identical to a fully faithful analysis of the input or less marked than it. Restricted process-specificity says that it is not generally possible to isolate blocking effects on different processes. And construction-independence of evaluation says that constraint interactions must in principle generalize to all applicable linguistic structures.

All three of these universals depend upon generalizing over the results of evaluation with a single constraint hierarchy. For example, harmonic ascent could easily be subverted if distinct hierarchies, with different rankings of markedness constraints, were operative under different conditions or at different stages of a derivation. The same goes for the other two universals, showing that nontrivial empirical claims follow from the globality property of the basic OT architecture. (There will be more to say about globality in §3.3.2.8.)

3.3.2.2 Consequences of Parallelism: Overview

Parallelism is a more complicated business than globality and requires a correspondingly greater amount of attention. In the basic OT architecture (68), there is only one pass through GEN and EVAL. GEN has the property called freedom of analysis or inclusivity (§1.1.3), meaning that it can construct candidates that differ in many ways from the input. The candidates emitted by GEN will therefore include some that are changed in several different ways at once. These candidates would have required several derivational steps to reach in a rule-based theory. The whole of this diverse candidate set is then submitted to EVAL, which selects its most harmonic member as the final output. This is a parallel theory because, given these assumptions about GEN and EVAL, the effects of notionally distinct linguistic operations are evaluated together, in parallel. In comparison, rule-based serial theories perform one operation at a time, stepping through a succession of intermediate stages. Parallelism, then, is the submission of complete output candidates to the grammar, without intermediate stages.

The known consequences of parallelism in OT can be loosely grouped into the four overlapping categories in (75), which will serve as the basis for subsequent discussion.

(75) Consequences of parallelism
  a. *Chicken-egg effects.* The application of process A depends on knowing the output of process B, and the application of process B depends on knowing the output of process A. Under parallelism, the effects of both processes can and must be considered simultaneously.
  b. *Top-down effects* (noncompositionality). Constituent X dominates constituent Y, and the well-formedness of X depends on Y (bottom up), but the well-formedness of Y is also influenced by X (top down). Under parallelism, there is no distinction between top-down and bottom-up effects, because various candidate parsings into X and Y constituents are evaluated.
  c. *Remote interaction.* Because fully formed output candidates are evaluated by the whole grammar, remote interactions are expected. Remoteness refers here not only to structural or stringwise distance but also to derivational remoteness, when two competing candidates differ in substantial ways from one another.
  d. *Globality effects.* Some further consequences of globality also depend on parallelism. This is shown by examining the predictions of a global but serial implementation of OT.

Chicken-egg and top-down effects (75a–b) are pretty much the same thing, but in different empirical or analytic domains. They include many of the ordering paradoxes in the literature on rule-based serialism, where there is inconsistent ordering of two rules. Remote interaction (75c) is a consequence of the kinds of candidates that GEN supplies and how they are evaluated. As we will see, although there are some compelling examples of remote interaction, there are also some problematic predictions. Finally, the effects of globality that depend on parallelism (75d) can be identified by decoupling the two, positing an architecture identical to (68) except that the output of EVAL is looped back into GEN. Each of these topics is addressed in the following sections.

3.3.2.3 Consequences of Parallelism I: Chicken-Egg Effects

Chicken-egg effects involve two or more notionally distinct processes that mutually depend on each other's output. If these processes are expressed by separate rules in a serial derivation, there is a problem: no ordering of the rules will work.⧠ §3.4¶22

There is a chicken-egg effect in the morphophonology of Southern Paiute (Uto-Aztecan, Utah). This language imposes strong restrictions on coda consonants. The only permitted codas are the first half of a doubled consonant or a nasal that shares place of articulation with a following stop or affricate: *tuŋ.qōn.nuq.qʷI* 'Paiute name'. (The syllable boundaries are shown by ".".) Typologically, this restricted syllable structure is quite common (e.g., Japanese). The restriction of nasals to positions before stops and affricates is also typical, since assimilation of nasals to continuants is somewhat unusual (cf. English *impose* vs. *infer*).[56]

This limited syllable structure carries over to the reduplicative morphology of Southern Paiute. The reduplicative prefix usually copies the first consonant and vowel of the root: ***ma**-maqa* 'to give', ***qa**-qaiva* 'mountain', ***wi**-winni* 'to stand'. But the second consonant of the root is copied only if two conditions are both met: the first consonant of the root is a stop or affricate and the second consonant is a nasal. Examples of this CVN-reduplication include ***pim**-pinti* 'to hang onto', ***ton**-tonna* 'to hit', and ***tun**-tuŋqutto* 'to become numb'. The generalization is that CVN-reduplication is possible only when it produces an independently permitted consonant cluster consisting of a nasal and stop that share place of articulation.

This generalization cannot be captured in a serial derivation. Two basic processes are at work: reduplicative copying and nasal assimilation. The problem, in chicken-egg terms, is that it is impossible to know how much to copy until nasal assimilation has applied, but it is impossible to apply nasal assimilation unless the nasal has been copied, so neither ordering works, as we see in (76a–b).

(76) Southern Paiute serially

a. Underlying representation	/Redup + pinti/	/Redup + winni/
Reduplication	**pi**-pinti	**wi**-winni
Nasal assimilation	*does not apply*	*does not apply*
Output	***pi**-pinti	**wi**-winni
b. Underlying representation	/Redup + pinti/	/Redup + winni/
Nasal assimilation	*does not apply*	*does not apply*
Reduplication	**pi**-pinti	**wi**-winni
Output	***pi**-pinti	**wi**-winni

The *n* of *pinti* is not copyable because it is not homorganic with the initial *p*. Nasal assimilation would make it homorganic, but nasal assimilation never sees

the requisite *n-p* sequence that it needs in order to apply, no matter how it is
ordered relative to reduplication.[57]

No such problem arises in parallel OT. The effects of the copying and assimilation operations are evaluated simultaneously. The winning candidate is one
that copies maximally (satisfying the base-reduplicant identity constraint
$\textsc{Max}_{\textsc{br}}$) while still obeying the undominated syllable-structure constraints
($\textsc{Coda-Cond}$) (see (77a–b)).[58]

(77) a. /Redup + pinti/ → *pim-pinti*

		Coda-Cond	Max$_{\text{BR}}$
i.	☞ pim-pinti		**
ii.	pin-pinti	*	**
iii.	pi-pinti		***

b. /Redup + winni/ → *wi-winni*

		Coda-Cond	Max$_{\text{BR}}$
i.	☞ wi-winni		***
ii.	win-winni	*	**
iii.	wim-winni	*	**

The constraint $\textsc{Max}_{\textsc{br}}$ assigns one violation-mark for each uncopied segment.
It therefore favors maximality of copying but only within the limits set by
undominated $\textsc{Coda-Cond}$. The latter constraint only permits nasal codas when
they are followed by a homorganic stop. So it chooses the assimilated candidate *pim-pinti* over unassimilated **pin-pinti*, while rejecting both unassimilated
**win-winni* and unassimilated **wim-winni* because the following consonant is
not a stop. Crucially, the winning candidate *pim-pinti* shows the simultaneous
effects of two processes, reduplication and assimilation, and those effects are
evaluated in parallel by the constraint hierarchy under Eval.

In the phonological literature, there have been various attempts to deal with
cases like this by grafting some form of parallelism onto a basically serial theory
(cf. Calabrese 1995; Myers 1991; Paradis 1988a). In very general terms, the
idea is to segregate all operations into two basic types, which are sometimes
called rules and repairs (cf. §2.1). Rules apply sequentially, but repairs are
applied in parallel with rules, automatically bringing rule outputs into conformity with general structural constraints. In Southern Paiute, for instance, reduplicative copying would be a rule, but nasal assimilation would be a repair,
able to fly in under the radar, so to speak, to help effectuate reduplicative
copying. In principle, this line of analysis might be promising, but in practice

it encounters significant difficulties. The architecture of such a theory has never been described in detail and may turn out to be unattainable (cf. the discussion of the triggering problem in phonology in §2.3). And a principled basis for the rule/repair split has proven elusive. In OT, all unfaithful mappings are in some sense repairs, an essential thesis if homogeneity of target/heterogeneity of process is to be accounted for (§3.1.4.2).

To sum up, the argument for parallelism from chicken-egg effects is based on the observation that sometimes there is no possible serial ordering of two notionally distinct operations. Parallel derivation looks like the only viable alternative in these cases. The balance has now shifted to Occam's other foot: since parallel derivation is *sometimes* required, is it *all* that is required? More on this question in §3.3.3.

3.3.2.4 *Consequences of Parallelism II: Top-Down Effects*

The argument from top-down effects is a variant of the chicken-egg argument but with special relevance to the well-formedness of hierarchical constituent structure.⌑$_{§3.4¶23}$ In a serial theory, the naive expectation is that hierarchical structures should be constructed from the bottom up, with each layer of structure derived by a distinct step of a serial derivation. Conditions on well-formedness are enforced by rules that apply as each level is constructed, with no backtracking.

Consider, for example, how bottom-up serialism would apply in sentence phonology. On this view, the structures of sentence phonology would be built in successive stages corresponding to the levels of the prosodic hierarchy: phonological words (PWd), then phonological phrases (PPh), then intonation phrases (IPh), and so on. Rules creating structures at level n would depend on the presence, position, number, or size of structures at level $n - 1$, but by the nature of the derivation the properties of structures at level $n - 1$ could not depend in any way on the properties of level n structures. Bottom-up effects should be observed, but never top-down ones – or at the very least, top-down effects should be highly unusual.

Syntactic theory has mostly developed along strict bottom-up lines. The generalized transformations of Chomsky (1975) and the Strict Cycle Condition of Chomsky (1973) are ways of excluding or strictly limiting top-down effects. But contemporary phonological theory countenances many top-down effects, contrary to naive expectation about the consequences of serial derivation. In fact, some top-down effects in phonology are the modal situation, with strict bottom-up derivation being rare or even unknown.

Top-down effects in phonology typically involve nonuniformity of metrical or prosodic structure (§3.2.1.2), such as the unstressable word syndrome or the prosody of function words. To follow up on the latter example, the prosodic structure of a function word depends on the larger context in which it finds itself.[59] Take, for instance, the difference between reduced *tŏ* [tə] in (78a) and unreduced, stressed *tó* [tú] in (78b).

(78) a. Reduced *tŏ*
>> I gave the book **tŏ** Bill.
>> I went **tŏ** Boston.
>> **Tŏ** add **tŏ** his troubles . . .

>   b. Stressed *tó*
>> Who did you give the book **tó**?
>> I talked **tó**, and eventually persuaded, my most skeptical colleagues.
>> I went **tó** – and here I must dispense with modesty – tŏ very great lengths indeed assisting him in his search for employment. Alas, tŏ no avail.

The general rule is that monosyllabic function words (other than object pronouns) are stressed and consequently unreduced before an intonation break, and they are otherwise reduced in normal speech.

Here is how these facts are usually and no doubt correctly interpreted (also see §3.2.1.2). A stressed function word is a freestanding phonological word: $[tó]_{PWd}$. It is stressed for reasons having to do with the prosodic hierarchy: every PWd must contain a foot, to serve as its head; and every foot must contain a stressed syllable, to serve as *its* head. So $[tó]_{PWd}$ is stressed because it is a head all the way down. An unstressed function word is a clitic rather than an independent PWd. In English, function words are normally proclitic to a following lexical word: $[tŏ\ Bill]_{PWd}$. There is no imperative to supply proclitic *tŏ* with a foot, and so it is unstressed and its vowel becomes [ə] in accordance with general properties of English phonology.

The analysis of (78), then, reduces to the following question: under what conditions are function words in English analyzed as independent PWd's versus clitics? The answer: they are analyzed as PWd's only when they have to be. In language typology generally and in English specifically, monosyllabic function words are preferentially cliticized. In English, cliticization has a directional bias, favoring pro- over enclisis. Stressed $[tó]_{PWd}$ appears only when there is nothing to procliticize onto, because no PWd follows in the same intonation phrase. An IPh-final function word presents a conundrum: it cannot be procliticized, so should it be encliticized or promoted to PWd status? Standard English takes the latter option, though my own most casual register favors the former.

The analysis just sketched has an obvious translation into OT, since it is already couched in the language of constraint interaction. In fact, a version of this analysis can be seen in (61) of §3.2.1.2. The constraint PWDCON is violated by any PWd that, like $[tó]_{PWd}$, contains no lexical words. As part of UG, this constraint accounts for the typologically justified unmarkedness of cliticized function words. The ranking [ALIGN-R(Lex, PWd) ≫ ALIGN-L(Lex, PWd)] favors proclisis – $[book]_{PWd}\ [tŏ\ Bill]_{PWd}$ – over enclisis – *$[book\ tŏ]_{PWd}\ [Bill]_{PWd}$. Violation of PWDCON is compelled by ALIGN-R (shown in (79)).

(79) ALIGN-R(Lex, PWd) ≫ PWDCON ≫ ALIGN-L(Lex, PWd)

		ALIGN-R	PWDCON	ALIGN-L
a.	☞ I gave the book [tŏ Bill]_PWd.			*
b.	I gave the [book tŏ]_PWd Bill.	*		
c.	I gave the book [tó]_PWd Bill.		*	
x.	☞ I talked [tó]_PWd]_IPh and eventually . . .		*	
y.	I [talked tŏ]_PWd]_IPh and eventually . . .	*		

In addition to the rankings in (79), PWDCON is dominated by the constraints responsible for higher-level phrasing, requiring IPh boundaries at the edges of clauses, around parentheticals, and so on.

By virtue of PWDCON, the normal or default condition for a function word is to be a clitic. Alignment constraints can impel a function word into PWd status but only under duress. This analysis not only works for English but also yields the right typology: in all languages, function words are typically cliticized unless special conditions like these obtain.

This theory of function-word phonology depends crucially on parallel evaluation. Candidate analyses differ in the prosodic structure assigned to function words, and so constraints can evaluate those differences in the wider prosodic context. Top-down effects are both expected and observed.

Bottom-up serialism has a difficult time with this phenomenon. Because the process of reduction is irreversible (e.g., *a* and *her* both neutralize to [ə] in my speech), the standard serial analysis starts out by analyzing all words, both functional and lexical, as freestanding PWd's (cf. Selkirk 1972, 1984). Later in the derivation, as higher-level prosodic structure is erected, processes of cliticization or "destressing" apply, reducing function words in certain contexts. Derivations for the fragments *tŏ Boston* and *Where tó?* are given in (80).

(80) Serial derivation of reduced and unreduced function words

PWd-level analysis	[tó]_PWd [Boston]_PWd	[where]_PWd [tó]_PWd
Phrase-level analysis	[[tó]_PWd [Boston]_PWd]_IPh	[[where]_PWd [tó]_PWd]_IPh
Destressing	[[tŏ Boston]_PWd]_IPh	*Blocked*

Destressing is blocked in the *where to?* case by the following IPh boundary.

Though the serial theory is basically bottom-up, the destressing rule is top-down in its effects. This example shows, then, that the serial, derivational theory must permit top-down, structure-changing rules. More seriously, the derivational theory has exactly the wrong take on the typological situation. According to this approach, the normal or default case is to analyze every syntactic "word," functional or lexical, as an independent PWd. This structure is the default because it is imposed generally by the first relevant rule of the derivation, and its effects endure unless they are wiped out later by the special destressing process, which, moreover, makes the grammar more complex and therefore less highly valued under the Evaluation Metric (§2.1). This is surely the wrong prediction typologically. Across languages, the unmarked condition for function words is *not* to be freestanding PWd's, a generalization that PWDCON expresses. But out of descriptive necessity, the serial analysis must treat a highly marked system – where both lexical and function words are PWd's – as an unmarked default. That is simply backward.

There is a more general point here. Serial derivations bring with them various architectural imperatives, most of which are left tacit and unremarked on except in the "how to order rules" lecture of introductory phonology (and formerly syntax) courses. Bottom-up derivation is one imperative: for example, PWd's must be assigned before IPh's, since IPh dominates PWd in the prosodic hierarchy. Relatedly, bottom-up rules are structure building, but top-down rules can only be structure changing. Another architectural imperative of serialism involves the interaction of reversible and irreversible operations: as in the English example (80), the reversible operation must be ordered first. These imperatives sometimes force a particular analysis and, as we saw, that analysis may be implausible on typological grounds. Evaluating the empirical adequacy of serial derivation, like evaluating parallel derivation, must proceed on this basis.

A final remark. The Elsewhere Condition is often invoked in situations like this. (See §1.5 ¶6 for references.) The idea is to apply destressing and PWd assignment together, disjunctively, with the more specific rule (i.e., destressing) taking precedence. This approach is quite workable – in fact, it is basically a parallel analysis. Destressing and PWd assignment compete to apply in the same contexts, and the more specific of them wins. But even with this refinement, the typological problem remains, since the typologically unjustifiable rule assigning PWd's to all function words remains as part of the grammar.

3.3.2.5 *Consequences of Parallelism III: Structurally Remote Interaction*
Because fully formed candidates are evaluated by the whole constraint hierarchy, obtaining some local harmonic advantage may have effects that are structurally or derivationally remote from the locus of that advantage.

This is pretty vague, so an analogy might help. I play chess in a fashion that locally and serially optimizes: when it is my turn, I look for a move that will let me attack another piece, with little or no thought for future consequences. Bobby Fischer at age 13 was a massively parallel chess-playing machine who, in a celebrated game against Donald Byrne, sacrificed a queen at move 18 to obtain a checkmate at move 41. Fischer's skill allowed him to optimize globally over many futures considered in parallel, rather than to proceed locally and serially from his current position on the board.

Back to linguistics. The example of remote interactions between local and global structure comes from metrical phonology. 📖§3.4¶24 In Yidiny (Pama-Nyungan, Australia) all words fall into two categories (see (81a–b)), those with trochaic (falling) rhythm throughout and those with iambic (rising) rhythm throughout[60]

(81) a. Trochaic rhythm

    (gáliŋ)   'go (present)'

    (gúda)(gágu)   'dog (purposive)'

    (wúŋa)(bá:jiŋ)   'hunt (antipassive present)'

    (májin)(dáŋal)(ñúnda)   'walk up (comitative subordinate dative)'

   b. Iambic rhythm

    (galbí:)   'catfish'

    (bargán)(dají:ñ)   'pass by (antipassive past)'

    (magí)(riŋál)(dañú:n)da   'climb up (going comitative coming

                                subordinate dative)'

The presumed rhythmic organization of these words – the metrical foot structure – is shown by the parentheses in (80), and the stresses are marked by acute accents.

The generalization that distinguishes these two word classes depends on vowel length. If an even-numbered syllable contains a long vowel (such as *i:* or *u:*), then that syllable and all other even-numbered syllables are stressed. Otherwise, odd-numbered syllables are stressed. More formally, the whole word has iambic feet if and only if an iambic parse will allow stress and length to coincide in some syllable of the word.[61]

In this light, the generalization about Yidiny can be restated as follows: feet are iambic throughout the word if any foot has the optimal short-long iambic form; otherwise feet are trochaic. This generalization already suggests how Yidiny should be analyzed with interacting constraints. The constraint ALIGN-L(Ft, Hd(Ft)) requires every foot to have its head at the left edge. It therefore asserts the preference for or default status of trochaic feet in Yidiny. But ALIGN-L(Ft, Hd(Ft)) is crucially dominated by a constraint like LONG/STR "if long, then stressed," as in (82).

(82) LONG/STR ≫ ALIGN-L(Ft, Hd(Ft))

		LONG/STR	ALIGN-L(Ft, Hd(Ft))
a.	☞ (galbí:)		*
b.	(gálbi:)	*	

When a word contains no long vowels, or when LONG/STR and ALIGN-L concur in rejecting the iambic candidate, then the trochaic default emerges, see (83a–b).

(83) Trochaic default

a. No long vowels

		LONG/STR	ALIGN-L(Ft, Hd(Ft))
i.	☞ (gúda)(gágu)		
ii.	(gudá)(gagú)		**

b. Long vowel in even syllable

		LONG/STR	ALIGN-L(Ft, Hd(Ft))
i.	☞ (wúŋa)(bá:jiŋ)		
ii.	(wuŋá)(ba:jíŋ)	*	**

In (83a), the trochaic analysis is favored by ALIGN-L because LONG/STR is simply irrelevant with words that contain no long vowels. In (83b), the trochaic analysis and LONG/STR agree in their assessment of iambic *wuŋ ába:jíŋ, which is therefore rejected. (Compare the Kanakuru example in §3.2.1.3.)

The interaction of LONG/STR and ALIGN-L in (82)–(83) accounts for the local, bottom-up effect of vowel length on stress. But Yidiny also displays a remote effect: if LONG/STR forces one foot to be iambic, then all feet are iambic. This effect is apparent in iambic words of sufficient length, as in (84), where every foot except the one containing the long vowel is wrongly predicted to be trochaic, in conformity with ALIGN-L.

(84) A global effect

		LONG/STR	ALIGN-L(Ft, Hd(Ft))
a.	(magí)(riŋál)(dañú:n)da		***
b.	(mági)(ríŋal)(dáñu:n)da	*	
c.	(mági)(ríŋal)(dañú:n)da		*
d.	(magí)(ríŋal)(dañú:n)da		**
e.	(mági)(riŋál)(dañú:n)da		**

Candidate (84a) is the intended output form. But, according to this tableau, it is harmonically bounded by the competing candidates (84c–e). (That is, the competitors incur a proper subset of (84a)'s violation-marks – see §1.3.1, §3.1.5.3.) With the system developed so far, only a local effect of vowel length on stress is possible.

The defect in candidates (84c–e) is that they have a rhythmic lapse, a sequence of two unstressed syllables in a row. There is ample typological justification for the rhythmic constraint *Lapse and its counterpart, *Clash, which prohibits the other way of disrupting rhythm, stress on adjacent syllables. By dominating Align-L(Ft, Hd(Ft)), *Lapse rules out all of the problematic candidates in (84), thereby globalizing the local effect of Long/Str, as shown in (85).

(85) Global effect obtained with *Lapse

	Long/Str	*Lapse	Align-L(Ft, Hd(Ft))
a. ☞ (magî)(riŋál)(dañú:n)da			***
b. (mági)(ríŋal)(dáñu:n)da	*		
c. (mági)(ríŋal)(dañú:n)da		*	*
d. (magî)(ríŋal)(dañú:n)da		*	**
e. (mági)(riŋál)(dañú:n)da		*	**

This analysis relies on the assumption that Gen emits complete output candidates, with all metrical feet in place. The grammar – ⟦Long/Str, *Lapse ≫ Align-L⟧ – selects the most harmonic of these candidates according to their overall structure. Because the competing candidates are complete, local well-formedness (Long/Str) can have global effects.

When we look at how derivational theories have dealt with Yidiny, it becomes clear how problematic this interaction can prove to be. One approach is radically derivational (Hayes 1982): first iambic feet are assigned across the board, and later on feet are shifted to trochaic except in words with a stressed long vowel. But of course derivations like this do considerable violence to the claim of Hayes (1987) and others that the iambic/trochaic distinction is a parameter to be set on a language-by-language basis. Another approach is essentially parallel (Halle and Vergnaud 1987: 24): words are simultaneously parsed into trochaic and iambic feet, and subsequent rules select the preferred analysis and delete the other one. This idea of simultaneous, competing parses is strongly reminiscent of OT, but with a difference: the two parses are imposed on the same form, and consequently this difference in "candidates" is limited to competing prosodic analyses of a fixed segmental string (a little like the Parse/Fill model of Prince and Smolensky 1993 (§1.2.2)).

3.3.2.6   *Consequences of Parallelism IV: Derivationally Remote Interaction*

Yidiny provides evidence of one kind of remote interaction that is possible in parallel OT. Another kind, derivational remoteness, has been extensively studied in research on the morphosyntax and morphophonology of lexical selection or allomorphy.⊡§3.4¶25 Phenomena like these have been notoriously difficult to analyze in rule-based, derivational theories, as the following quotations emphasize:

What is most striking about [this analysis] is that the specific properties of
the output form depend upon the other surface forms (both morphological
and syntactic) that actively compete with it, and not on the details of the
derivation of its formal structure, as in the classical generative approach to
syntax. (Bresnan to appear-b)

   This paper is concerned with a long-standing theoretical . . . problem. It
is a theoretical problem because it regards the organization of the grammar;
in particular it addresses the question of where in the grammar are lexical,
unpredictable morpheme alternations to be included, and where are phonological regularities to be expressed. (Mascaró 1996: 473)

The problem is that rules make no real contribution to analyzing these phenomena, which depend on notions like competition or selection. But competition and selection find ready expression in OT. We will look at two examples,
one morphophonological and the other morphosyntactic.

   The Catalan "personal article" has two forms, *en* and *l'*.[62] Like English *a/an*
or French *beau/bel*, the choice is decided by the sound that begins the next word.
The allomorph *en* precedes consonants and the allomorph *l'* precedes vowels,
as illustrated in (86a–b).

(86) a. *en* before consonants
         en Wittgenstein
     b. *l'* before vowels
         l'Einstein

There is no regular phonological process relating the two allomorphs in
Catalan (or English or French for that matter). There is no rule mapping
some unique underlying form onto *en* in one context and *l'* in the other. So
the existence of these two allomorphs and the relation between them is a matter
for the lexicon (actually, the vocabulary – see §3.1.2.4) rather than for the
grammar. But the choice between the allomorphs makes sense phonologically,
and in fact it can be obtained through emergence of universal constraints
(cf. §3.2.2).

   Since the alternation itself is unpredictable, both alternants must be stored
in the lexicon as a set rather than as a unique underlying representation: {/en/,
/l/}. Among the properties of GEN is the obligation to supply candidates with
both alternants: *en Wittgenstein, l'Wittgenstein, en Einstein, l'Einstein*. Crucially, because both /en/ and /l/ are present in underlying representation, candidate pairs like *en Wittgenstein* and *l'Wittgenstein* are both fully faithful to the
input. Allomorph selection, then, brings no cost in faithfulness.

   These faithfulness-free alternations provide an excellent opportunity for
TETU, and that is precisely what is observed. In Catalan, onsetless syllables are
abundant, showing that ONSET is ranked below its antagonistic faithfulness constraints DEP and MAX. But ONSET, as we see in (87), emerges to decide which
allomorph of the personal article to use with a vowel-initial name.

(87) Emergence of ONSET

/{en, l} + Einstein/	ONSET
a. ☞ l'Einstein	
b. en Einstein	*

By hypothesis, these candidates do not differ in faithfulness, and so markedness decides the matter in favor of *l'Einstein*. Another candidate, *ʔen Einstein*, avoids the ONSET violation at the expense of violating the faithfulness constraint DEP. This is not an option because, as I just noted, ONSET is only emergent in Catalan allomorph selection – it cannot compel unfaithful mappings.

Similar considerations apply to consonant-initial names. Though *en Wittgenstein* incurs an ONSET violation, it harmonically bounds epenthesizing *əl Wittgenstein*, which has both ONSET and DEP violations. (The candidate *l'Wittgenstein* violates an undominated markedness constraint because of its initial cluster.) And much the same goes for the English and French examples cited earlier: *an apple* or *bel ami* (syllabified as [æ.næ.pəl] and [bɛ.la.mi]) avoid the ONSET violations of *a apple* and *beau ami*. Likewise, *an lemon* or *bel mari* incur NO-CODA violations that their competitors *a lemon* and *beau mari* successfully dodge. As in Catalan, ONSET and No-Coda are emergent constraints, unable to compel unfaithful mappings but relevant to allomorph selection.

This mode of analysis incorporates several key insights that are widely applicable to phonologically conditioned allomorphy. First, the source of the allomorphs – the lexicon/vocabulary – is entirely separate from the conditions that determine allomorph choice – CON. This is a special case of a general property of OT, homogeneity of target/heterogeneity of process (§3.1.4.2). Second, and relatedly, allomorphs are selected comparatively, rather than derived operationally, as they are in some rule-based analyses. This is a familiar effect of EVAL, which through its comparative function accounts for all phonological alternations – allomorphic, morphophonemic, or allophonic. Third, as has already been noted, the constraints responsible for allomorph selection may be only emergent and not otherwise active in the language under study. Any constraint of CON can in principle be responsible for allomorph choice, even if it is ranked too low to compel unfaithfulness.

Finally, parallelism is a necessary component of the analysis. Through parallelism, candidates derived by lexical selection have equal status with candidates derived by the operational component of GEN, and EVAL compares both, using exactly the same constraints and the same hierarchy. Derivational approaches based on selecting an allomorph at the point of lexical insertion miss the connection between the constraint(s) responsible for allomorph choice and the constraints of phonology as a whole. Parallelism, then, eliminates the derivational remoteness between the source of the allomorphs and choice between them.

Parallelism is also important for two other reasons that arise in the analysis of specific cases. The Catalan *en/l'* alternation, like English *a/an* and French *beau/bel*, is external allomorphy. Though the word – really, the morpheme – is the thing that alternates, the choice of alternant is conditioned outside the word. In modular theories like Lexical Phonology (see the references in §3.4¶31), word-internal allomorphic alternations must be completed by the end of the lexical component, and so they cannot be dependent on word-external context. In a fully parallel model, on the other hand, there is no distinction between internal and external allomorphy, nor between allomorphy and phonology (except for the input/output relation). All are treated alike, and the nature of external allomorphy suggests that they should be.

Derivational theories also encounter difficulties with ordering paradoxes (§3.3.2.3) in allomorphy/phonology interactions. In a derivational model, allomorph choice should only be sensitive to underlying phonological context, since allomorph choice is part of lexical selection. But examples of allomorphy that are conditioned by surface phonological context are not unknown. For example, in my own most natural speech, there is a contrast between *a history of the US* and *an historical fact*. The regular loss of *h* before unstressed syllables (*inhíbit/inh̆íbition*) conditions the choice of the *an* allomorph. Under parallelism, the loss of *h* and the choice of allomorph are evaluated together, simultaneously, and so allomorph choice can only be determined by surface conditions (though see §3.3.3 on opacity).

The central insights about phonologically conditioned allomorphy – the process/target dichotomy, comparison of competing allomorphs, emergence of the decisive constraints, and derivational remoteness of allomorph source and selection, eliminated through parallelism – can all be observed in morphosyntactic lexical selection phenomena as well. Here is an example taken from the pronominal system of Chicheŵa (Bantu, Malawi).[63]

Chicheŵa has both free and bound pronouns: *ndí íwó* 'with it' versus *nawó* 'with-it'. The bound pronouns are limited to anaphora with discourse topics, with the free pronouns used everywhere else. But even in contexts that demand a bound pronoun, a free pronoun is used if the vocabulary happens not to include the corresponding bound form.

This latter contingency is observed with certain prepositions. Chicheŵa has just three prepositions: *ndí* 'with, by', *mpâka* 'until, up to', *kwá* 'to'. Of these, only the first has a combining form that can be used with a bound pronoun, as in the example *nawó*. The lexicon/vocabulary happens not to supply combining forms for *mpâka* and *kwá*, and so they are followed by free pronouns even when the discourse context would demand a bound one. Examples (88a–b) illustrate this contrast.

(88) a. Lexicon supplies free *ndí* and combining *na*

mkángó	uwu	ndinapítá	**nawó**	ku	msika.
lion	this	I-went	with-it	to	market

'This lion, I went with it to market.'

vs.

?*mkángó	uwu	ndinapítá	**ndí**	**íwó**	ku	msika.
lion	this	I-went	with	it	to	market

b. Lexicon supplies only free *kwá*

mfúmú	iyi	ndikákúneněza	**kwá**	**íyo**.
chief	this	I'm-going-to-tell-on-you	to	him

'This chief, I'm going to tell on you to him.'

vs.

*mfúmú	iyi	ndikákúneněza	**kwǎyo**.
chief	this	I'm-going-to-tell-on-you	to-him

Lion and *chief* are topics, so we expect to see bound rather than free pronouns referring to them. That is certainly the situation in (88a), but not in (88b), where the desired bound form does not exist. In short, that which is not forbidden (**kwǎyo*) is required (*nawó*).

This system has characteristics that are familiar from many other examples discussed in this chapter. Bound pronouns have only-when-needed distribution (§3.1.3.6): they are required as anaphors to topics, and otherwise they are prohibited. Free pronouns are the default (§3.1.3.4) in two different ways: they occur in all contexts where bound pronouns are not required, and they occur in examples like (88b), where the bound form is lexically absent. The default status of free pronouns in Chicheŵa accords well with the associated typological universals (§1.2.3, §3.1.5.4). All languages have free pronouns; some, such as English, have only free pronouns, and others, such as Chicheŵa, have both free and bound pronouns. No language has only bound pronouns. Free pronouns, then, are in some sense the default in all languages and not just in Chicheŵa.

As in phonologically conditioned allomorphy, the competition among candidates is key. The quotation from Bresnan at the beginning of this section emphasizes that candidate competition, rather than derivational operations, is the right way to address problems like this. Candidates from both lexical and syntactic sources are evaluated in parallel, without regard for how they came into being. This is essential if Chicheŵa's complex chain of contingencies is to be analyzed, and especially if the analysis is to be connected with the unmarked status of free pronouns cross-linguistically.

3.3.2.7 *Some Challenges to Remote Interaction*

Before going on to look at further consequences of parallelism, we need to look at some potential problems that arise from OT's capacity to analyze structurally or derivationally remote interactions. The two previous sections have

shown that such interactions do indeed occur and can be analyzed in a typologically responsible way within OT. But there are also certain imaginable interactions that do not seem to occur.[64]

Here is a relatively straightforward example. When OT is applied to metrical stress theory, three basic markedness constraints are usually assumed. FT-
BIN (§3.2.1.2) requires feet to be binary, consisting of exactly two metrical units
(syllables or moras). HEAD(PWd) (§3.2.1.2) demands that every phonological
word contain at least one foot, to serve as its head. And PARSE-SYLL (§4.2.2.)
says that every syllable must belong to some foot or, equivalently for present
purposes, no syllable is immediately dominated by a PWd.

Together, FT-BIN and HEAD(PWd) are frequently observed to force epenthesis when faithfulness would produce a monosyllabic or monomoraic word. For
example, monosyllabic words in Shona receive prothetic *i* to make them big
enough to support a disyllabic foot, as in (89).

(89) Prothesis in Shona (Myers 1986)

| /pá/ | → | [(**i** pá)] | 'give!' (cf. *ku-pá* 'to give') |
| /bʸá/ | → | [(**i** bʸá)] | 'leave!' (cf. *ku-bʸá* 'to leave') |

(Recall that parentheses mark stress feet and brackets mark phonological
words.) This process, called augmentation, occurs when FT-BIN and
HEAD(PWd) both dominate DEP as in (90), forcing epenthesis to avoid a
monosyllabic foot or a footless phonological word.

(90) FT-BIN, HEAD(PWd) ≫ DEP

/pá/		FT-BIN	HEAD(PWd)	DEP
a.	☞ [(**i** pá)]			*
b.	[(pá)]	*		
c.	[pa]		*	

Ranking permutation predicts a typology, and one member of the predicted
typology has the ranking ⟦FT-BIN, PARSE-SYLL ≫ DEP⟧. This hierarchy ensures
that all words are exhaustively parsed into binary feet. That is, all words are
even syllabled on the surface, with epenthesis called on as necessary, as illustrated in (91).

(91) FT-BIN, PARSE-SYLL ≫ DEP (hypothetical example)

/tasidu/		FT-BIN	PARSE-SYLL	DEP
a.	☞ [(**í** ta)(sídu)]			*
b.	[(tá)(sídu)]	*		
c.	[ta(sídu)]		*	

Both (90) and (91) involve top-down, remote interactions, in the sense used in §3.3.2.5. They are remote because there is considerable distance structurally between the prosodic constraints triggering epenthesis and the epenthesis process itself. Despite this and other similarities between them, though, the interaction in (90) is robustly attested in many languages while the interaction in (91) is literally unknown. Clearly, this particular theory of CON overgenerates.

It is worth noting at this juncture that this kind of overgeneration is equally an issue in rule-based or rule-and-constraint-based theories (cf. §3.1.5.3). It is a trivial matter in such theories to write a rule adding a syllable to every monosyllabic foot or to designate epenthesis as a repair for violations of a foot binarity constraint. Because of its inherently typological character, OT focuses attention on these issues, but a commitment to a restrictive and explanatory typology is obviously not some new analytic burden that OT imposes.

One approach to the overgeneration problem in OT is to pursue a different theory of CON. The most likely culprit is the constraint PARSE-SYLL, since it is the locus of the difference between (90) and (91). Using general techniques introduced in §1.4.4, we can figure out in advance what any proposed replacement for PARSE-SYLL must do. It must evaluate (91c) as no less harmonic than (91a) to avoid making the wrong typological prediction: *ta(sídu)* ≥ *(íta)(sídu)*. And to retain the desirable effects of the old PARSE-SYLL, the new constraint must favor exhaustive footing over incomplete footing, such as (91b) over (91c): *(tá)(sídu)* ≻ *ta(sídu)*. Obvious replacements do not come immediately to mind, since these two demands on the new constraint are hard to reconcile.

There is a larger issue here. The difference between (90) and (91) makes sense in a way that these constraints and their interaction are not yet expressing. The constraints HEAD(PWd) and PARSE-SYLL are in a stringency relationship (§1.2.3) that their informal definitions may have obscured. When PARSE-SYLL is obeyed, the PWd contains at least one foot, so HEAD is also obeyed. But when HEAD is obeyed, PARSE-SYLL may still be violated. So HEAD imposes a narrower, more refined test than PARSE-SYLL, making PARSE-SYLL the more stringent (i.e., more easily violated) constraint. In this light, one suspects that it is no accident that HEAD can compel violation of DEP but PARSE-SYLL will not. HEAD is more exact in its requirements, making it in some vague sense more prominent or assertive (cf. §3.1.4.6).

These ruminations obviously do not constitute a theory of permissible and impermissible remote interactions, nor do they even suggest the beginnings of such a theory. The interactional capacities of OT grammars remain a subject for research and further development of the theory. See the references in §3.4 ¶26 for one recent line of attack.

3.3.2.8 Consequences of Parallelism V: Globality Effects

Throughout this section, I have found it useful to distinguish between two related properties of the basic OT architecture in (68), globality and parallelism. Globality describes the way EVAL works: it takes a single language-particular hierarchy and applies it to every candidate set. Parallelism describes the way GEN works: it emits candidates that are ready to stand as finished outputs of the grammar.

Though the basic OT architecture unites globality and parallelism, it is in principle possible to decouple them. Suppose that the output of EVAL is looped back into GEN as a new input, from which a candidate set is constructed, to which EVAL then applies, and so on. The derivation will continue like this until *convergence*, when the output of EVAL after one GEN → EVAL loop is identical to the output of the immediately preceding pass. Once that has happened, further iteration would be pointless, since no additional changes are possible.[65] The theory so described is global but not parallel; there is a serial derivation, but the same grammar is applied at each pass through the loop. This theory is one of a family of OT variants called *harmonic serialism* (§1.1.4).📖 §3.4¶28 Other variants in this family are discussed in §3.3.3.

The question to be addressed here is: under what circumstances will the GEN → EVAL → GEN loop of harmonic serialism produce different results from the one pass through GEN and EVAL that happens in classic parallel OT, keeping all else equal? Yet another way to ask this question is: when will it take more than two passes through the loop to reach convergence? Any differences between harmonic serialism and parallel OT that emerge from pondering these questions must be consequences of parallelism, since these two models are identical in all other respects. And under the right conditions, these differences do arise.

Under the assumption that GEN has full freedom of analysis (§1.1.3), the candidate set at each pass through the GEN → EVAL loop will contain the same forms as the previous pass – though with a different relationship to the input, of course, because the input is different on each iteration of the loop. This means that the markedness violations of the respective candidate forms will not change at each pass through the loop, but their faithfulness violations will change, since faithfulness is recomputed relative to the new input at each pass. Based on these observations, the schematic examples in (92a–c) give the minimal conditions for a harmonic serialist derivation to converge later than the second pass through the GEN → EVAL loop.

(92) Three-pass convergence in harmonic serialism
     a. Pass 1

/A/	F1	M	F2	F3	Remarks
[A]		**			[A] does worst on M.
☞ [E]		*	*		[E] performs better on M, violating only low-ranking F2.
[I]	*				[I] incurs no marks from M, but violates top-ranked F1.

b. Pass 2

/E/	F1	M	F2	F3	Remarks
[A]		**			Markedness violations are the same at each iteration.
[E]		*			Faithfulness violations change, because input is different.
☞ [I]				*	Now [I], which is least marked, obeys top-ranked F1.

c. Pass 3

/I/	F1	M	F2	F3	Remarks
[A]		**			Can't go back because can't become more marked.
[E]		*			
☞ [I]					Convergence. [I] is fully faithful and least marked.

F1, F2, and F3 denote faithfulness constraints and M is a markedness constraint.[66] The inputs and candidates are arbitrary expressions, though it may help to think of them as the vowels *a*, *e*, and *i*.

On pass 1 through the Gen → Eval loop, candidate [E] is the winner. It avoids a violation of the markedness constraint M, but it also obeys the top-ranked faithfulness constraint F1. The fully faithful candidate [A] does worse on markedness, while candidate [I] goes too far, satisfying the markedness constraint perfectly at the expense of fatally violating F1.

On pass 2, the output of pass 1 is now the input, /E/. The markedness violations of the various candidates have not changed, but their faithfulness violations have. Now the candidate [I] is evaluated relative to the input /E/, and its F1 violation has disappeared. Think about vowel raising: changing *a* to *i* directly is less faithful than the individual steps *a* to *e* and *e* to *i* considered separately. So [I] is the output of pass 2. Submitting /I/ as input on pass 3 leads to convergence, since further markedness improvement is not possible.

This is a situation where parallel OT and harmonic serialism produce different results. It therefore reveals one of the specific contributions that parallelism makes to classic OT. In parallel OT, this particular constraint hierarchy, given the input /A/, would produce the output [E]. But with harmonic serialism, this hierarchy eventually produces the final output [I], starting from the same input. The direct mapping from /A/ to [I] violates the high-ranking constraint F1, but the indirect mapping that goes by way of [E] violates only low-ranking faithfulness constraints along the way, as we see in (93).

(93) Parallel and serial derivational paths compared

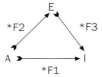

These observations can be made a bit more general. With this constraint set, it is possible to analyze a language that maps /A/ to [E] and /E/ to [I] under parallel OT but not under harmonic serialism. The grammar given in (92), if applied in parallel fashion, describes such a language (think of (92a) and (92b) as separate parallel derivations). But there is no permutation of these constraints that will allow harmonic serialism to account for that language. The problem is that high-ranking F1, which stops /A/ from changing all the way to [I] in one fell swoop, is effectively inactive in harmonic serialism because it is subverted on the next pass through the loop, as in (92b).

This difference between harmonic serialism and parallel OT turns on the question of whether CON includes constraints like F1 in (92). The essential property of this constraint is that it assign fewer violation-marks to the /A/ → [E] mapping than the /A/ → [I] mapping and no violation-marks at all to the /E/ → [I] mapping.[67] If constraints like this are an empirically necessary component of CON, then we have an argument in favor of parallel OT against harmonic serialism.

Constraints similar to F1 have been proposed in the literature on phonological chain shifts. A chain shift is a process that maps /A/ to [E] and /E/ to [I] in the same environment. For example, some languages have chain shifts that replace (literal) /a/ with [e] and /e/ with [i], as in examples (94a–b) from a dialect of Spanish spoken in northwestern Spain.[68]

(94) a. /a/ → [e]

| | /gat + u/ | → | gétu | 'cat (m. sg.)' (cf. *gáta* 'cat (f. sg.)') |
| | /blank + u/ | → | blénku | 'white (m. sg.)' (cf. *blánka* 'white (f. sg.)') |

 b. /e/ → [i]

| | /nen + u/ | → | nínu | 'child (m. sg.)' (cf. *néna* 'child (f. sg.)') |
| | /sek + u/ | → | síku | 'dry (m. sg.)' (cf. *séka* 'dry (f. sg.)') |

The generalization is that the stressed vowel moves up one step in height when followed by a high suffix vowel. This generalization is inexpressible in harmonic serialism, for the reasons just given.

To account for chain shifts in parallel OT, something must be said about the constraint standing in the role of F1. That is, CON must include some constraint with the properties attributed to F1: it must assign fewer violation-marks to the /a/ → [e] mapping than to the /a/ → [i] mapping, and it must assign no violation-marks to the /e/ → [i] mapping. Three approaches to this constraint have been taken in the literature.

(i) (From Kirchner 1996.) The vowels [a], [e], and [i] are represented by the standard binary feature combinations: [a] = [−high, +low], [e] = [−high, −low], and [i] = [+high, −low]. CON includes faithfulness constraints IDENT(high) and IDENT(low) that militate against changing the values of [high] and [low], respectively. Thus, the mapping /a/ → [i] violates both IDENT(high) and IDENT(low). The constraint functioning as F1 is the local conjunction (§1.2.3) of these two constraints in the domain of a single segment: [IDENT(low)&IDENT(high)]$_{Seg}$. Only the /a/ → [i] mapping will violate it. Tableau (95) shows the results.

(95) Analyzing chain shifts with local conjunction

/CaCi/	[IDENT(low) & IDENT(high)]$_{Seg}$	M	IDENT(low)	IDENT(high)
CaCi		**		
☞ CeCi		*	*	
CiCi	*		*	*
/CeCi/				
CaCi		**	*	
CeCi		*		
☞ CiCi				*

(ii) (From Gnanadesikan 1997.) The vowels [a], [e], and [i] are represented by positions on a phonological scale: low > mid > high. CON supplies two kinds of faithfulness constraints for this or other scales: IDENT(height) is violated by any shift on the vowel height scale, but less stringent IDENT-ADJ(height) is violated only by shifts to nonadjacent positions on the scale (i.e., low → high and high → low mappings). By substituting IDENT-ADJ(height) for the conjoined constraint in (95) and IDENT(height) for the two low-ranking faithfulness constraints, the same results are obtained.

(iii) (From Orgun 1996a.) The vowels are represented by binary features, as in (95). But instead of constraint conjunction or scalar faithfulness, CON supplies faithfulness constraints that are sensitive to input context.[69] For example, the constraint IDENT(high)$_{low}$ would be defined as "an input low vowel cannot change its value of [high]." Substituting this constraint for the conjoined constraint in (95) again yields the same results.

Any one of these proposals would accommodate chain shifts and thereby show that OT grammars cannot be permitted to iterate serially if chain shifts are to be analyzed successfully. Parallel OT emerges as superior to its global but serial counterpart, harmonic serialism.

3.3.2.9 Summary

Globality and parallelism are perhaps the most controversial properties of OT. Though alternatives will be considered in the next section, globality and parallelism follow from the simplest model, the basic OT architecture in (68). This architecture is global because a single grammar – that is, a single ranking of the constraints in Con – is in force throughout the derivation. It is parallel because the derivation is flat, mapping input directly to output without further applications of the grammar.

Globality is important to the integrity of many of the architectural imperatives in §3.1.4 and §3.1.5. These universals, such as harmonic ascent, describe the properties of OT when the mapping from input to final output involves just a single grammar applied to all candidates. Departures from globality would dilute or even eliminate these results.

The consequences of parallelism are more diverse, but most come down to parallelism's greater capacity for remote interaction. Top-down and cross-module interactions like those exemplified thus far are the expected result of parallel evaluation of fully formed and diverse output candidates. The nature of and limits on these interactions, a vexed question throughout the history of generative grammar, is just beginning to be studied in OT.

3.3.3 Other Architectures for OT

Though we have focused throughout on the original and simplest OT architecture, with its properties of globality and parallelism, the literature includes variant architectures that have been introduced to correct perceived inadequacies of the theory. These variants dispense with globality or parallelism or both. Not all variants have been studied in sufficient depth to bear reexamination here, but it is certainly worth looking at the most prominent ones and the issues they are intended to address.

This section begins (§3.3.3.1) by looking briefly at the historical context from which serial and parallel models have emerged and the principal issue that challenges parallel OT, opacity.▭$_{§3.4¶27}$ Subsequent sections describe the variants: another implementation of harmonic serialism with closer resemblance to derivations in GB and Minimalism (§3.3.3.2); cyclic evaluation (§3.3.3.3); a modularized version of OT along the lines of the theory of Lexical Phonology (§3.3.3.4); and a range of alternative, nonserial approaches to opacity (§3.3.3.5).

3.3.3.1 The Context and the Issues

The serial derivation has shown a remarkable durability in linguistic thought. It remains a prominent feature in much of contemporary phonological and syntactic theory. Here, for example, is how Chomsky frames the issue in recent work:

A related question is whether C_{HL} is derivational or representational: does it involve successive operations leading to (π, λ) (if it converges), or does it operate in one of any number of other ways – say, selecting two such representations and then computing to determine whether they are properly paired, selecting one and deriving the other, and so on? . . . My own judgment is that a derivational approach is . . . correct, and the particular version of a minimalist program I am considering assigns it even greater prominence. . . . There are certain properties of language, which appear to be fundamental, that suggest this conclusion. Viewed derivationally, computation typically involves simple steps expressible in terms of natural relations and properties, with the context that makes them natural "wiped out" by later operations, hence not visible in the representations to which the derivation converges. (Chomsky 1995: 223)

This view is even more widespread in the field of phonology.

Nevertheless, the standard conception of the serial derivation has not gone unquestioned. For some time, there has been a consensus that extrinsic rule ordering is not required in syntax (§2.2), even if the serial derivation is retained. But serial derivation plays no role in many other contemporary syntactic theories, such as Relational or Arc-Pair Grammar, LFG, or GPSG. In phonology, extrinsic rule ordering was scrutinized closely, though with less effect on the subsequent development of the field, during the 1970s (see the references in §2.5 ¶2). The need for the serial derivation has also been questioned in phonology, as one may observe from Goldsmith (1993b), Koskenniemi (1983), or the literature on Declarative Phonology (Coleman 1998 and references there).

One of the main functions of the serial derivation is to allow rules to state temporary truths. Rules express true generalizations, but only at the derivational instant when they apply. Subsequent rules can obscure the truth that the rule expresses, making it only temporary. In OT, however, violability under domination provides a way for a constraint to be active yet not always true. In this way, constraint ranking can take over many of the functions of the serial derivation. The Occamite argument then says: if ranking can take over some of the functions of the serial derivation, perhaps it can take over all of them.

Constraint ranking and rule ordering are not equivalent, though. Serial ordering does more than negotiate precedence relations among rules. As Chomsky notes in the quotation at the beginning of this subsection, later operations can "wipe out" the context of earlier ones. This also allows hidden, underlying or derived conditions to influence the outcome in ways that go well beyond what faithfulness constraints can do in OT. For example, imagine that there is a language with epenthesis of *t* in response to onsetless syllables. Suppose, too, that onsetless syllables do appear on the surface under the following conditions:

(i) Word-initial onsetless syllables are permitted freely: /aka-i/ → *akati, *takati* (cf. Axininca Campa in §1.3.3).

(ii) Medial onsetless syllables can be created by deletion of intervocalic *h*: /mapuh-i/ → *mapu.i*.

Both of these conditions are accounted for with extrinsic rule ordering in a serial theory. The first would be a result of marking initial vowels as extrametrical before applying the *t*-epenthesis rule,[70] and the second would be a result of ordering *h* deletion after *t*-epenthesis. But only the first can be accounted for straightforwardly with constraint interaction, by ranking a positional faithfulness constraint that prohibits epenthesis into initial syllables above ONSET ((18) in §1.4.1). In contrast, it seems most improbable that CON supplies a faithfulness constraint prohibiting epenthesis into a position that once held an *h* – in fact, if faithfulness constraints are understood to require identity between input and output and if markedness constraints can refer only to outputs (§1.2.2), then such a constraint is not merely improbable but impossible. Yet without such a constraint, there is no obvious way to compel *mapu.i*'s ONSET violation.

Chomsky (1995: 224) sketches a different argument along the same general lines. Suppose a noun incorporates into a verb, creating the complex verb [V-N]$_V$. This complex verb subsequently raises to I. By the end of the derivation, then, there is a nonlocal relation between N and its trace, though locality was properly but temporarily respected when N first moved. So locality of movement cannot be evaluated by inspection of outputs without reference to an intermediate stage of a serial derivation.[71]

The hypothetical *mapu.i* case and Chomsky's incorporation example are called *opaque interactions* in the phonological literature. A definition of opacity in terms of rule application is given in (96).

> (96) Opacity (after Kiparsky 1973C: 79)
>   A phonological rule $\mathscr{P}$ of the form $A → B / C\_\_\_\_D$ is *opaque* if there are surface structures with either of the following characteristics:
>   a. instances of A in the environment $C\_\_\_\_D$.
>   b. instances of B derived by $\mathscr{P}$ that occur in environments other than $C\_\_\_\_D$.

Intuitively, a rule is opaque if there are surface forms that look like they should have undergone it but did not (96a) or surface forms that underwent the rule but look like they should not have (96b). The *mapu.i* case is opacity of the first type and the incorporation example is more like the second type.

Opacity poses a challenge to the basic OT architecture. The reasons why have already been hinted at, but here they are with full explicitness. In opacity of the (96a) type, an otherwise general process fails in certain cases, even though its surface conditions are met. In the hypothetical case (i, ii), we can use transparent mappings like /paka + i/ → *pakati* to establish the hierarchy in (97), where MAX and ONSET dominate DEP.

(97) Background to opaque interaction

/paka + i/		MAX	ONSET	DEP
a.	☞ pakati			*
b.	paka paki	*		
c.	paka.i		*	

But given this independently motivated ranking, there is no way to prevent the loss of *h* from engendering the insertion of *t* that we see in (98).

(98) Opaque interaction

/mapuh + i/		*V*h*V	MAX	ONSET	DEP
a.	maputi		*		*
b.	mapuhi	*			
c.	mapu.i		*	*	

The constraint *V*h*V is an ad hoc expedient for the purposes of this discussion. The important point is that the intended winner, *mapu.i*, ends up losing to *maputi. The intended output *mapu.i* has a seemingly gratuitous violation of ONSET that is avoidable merely by violating low-ranking DEP.

Opacity of the (96b) type is a bit different: a general process goes through even in certain cases where surface conditions do not seem favorable. In the head-movement example, the output configuration is . . . [V-N]$_V$ . . . t_V . . . t_N. The locality requirement – a head cannot be separated from its trace by an intervening head – is violated by the (N, t_N) chain. This violation of locality seems without motivation when just the surface structure is inspected.

Opacity in various guises is the main and perhaps only challenge to parallelism. §3.3.3.2—3.3.3.5 explore alternatives and refinements of the basic model and offer a different perspective on opacity and related issues.

3.3.3.2 Harmonic Serialism

In §3.3.2.8, we considered the consequences of allowing the output of EVAL to loop back into GEN until convergence.[72] A more sophisticated version of this OT variant, called *harmonic serialism*, is described in the following quotation.

> Universal grammar must also provide a function Gen that admits the candidates to be evaluated. . . . [W]e have entertained two different conceptions of Gen. The first, closer to standard generative theory, is based on serial or derivational processing: some general procedure (Do-α) is allowed to make a certain single modification to the input, producing the candidate set of all possible outcomes of such modification. This is then evaluated; and

the process continues with the output so determined. . . . In the second, parallel-processing conception of Gen, all possible ultimate outputs are contemplated at once. . . . Much of the analysis given in this book will be in the parallel mode, and some of the results will absolutely require it. But it is important to keep in mind that the serial/parallel distinction pertains to Gen and not to the issue of harmonic evaluation per se. It is an empirical question of no little interest how Gen is to be construed, and one to which the answer will become clear only as the characteristics of harmonic evaluation emerge in the context of detailed, full-scale, depth-plumbing, scholarly, and responsible analyses. (Prince and Smolensky 1993: 79)

Prince and Smolensky are contrasting serial and parallel executions of the basic ideas of optimality. In the parallel version, GEN emits candidates that may combine the effects of several notionally distinct processes, and EVAL considers those effects together when it assesses a candidate. In the serial version, though, the effects of notionally distinct processes are evaluated separately, because GEN is limited to performing one operation at a time. For example, one candidate may be faithful, another may have epenthesis, and another may have deletion, but no candidate at this stage has both epenthesis and deletion. EVAL, defined exactly as in the parallel theory, selects the most harmonic member of this candidate set. But this winner is not the ultimate output; it is an intermediate step of a serial derivation. It is fed back into GEN for another pass through the grammar. This GEN/EVAL loop continues until convergence.[73] The limitation on GEN distinguishes this version of harmonic serialism from the one described in §3.3.2.8. For that reason, I will refer to it as *limited harmonic serialism* (LHS).

LHS bears some resemblance to rule-based or rule-and-constraint-based theories in syntax and phonology. The similarities to P&P are obvious, as Prince and Smolensky's allusion to "Do-α" suggests. Certain recent ideas in phonology also look a lot like *Move-α* or *Move/Merge*.

> The elementary rule types required for the processes above are linking, delinking, and default insertion. . . . To summarize, the feature theory presented here assumes a small set of elementary rule types which carry out single operations on feature representations. (Clements and Hume 1995: 265)
>
> The rule parameters are {INSERT, DELETE} × {PATH, F-ELEMENT}. (Archangeli and Pulleyblank 1994: 286)
>
> Structure-changing rules are to be decomposed into deletion (delinking) plus structure-building. . . . (Kiparsky 1993a: 285, citing Cho 1990a; Mascaró 1987; Poser 1982)

Some measure of agreement is evident here: a phonological rule can insert or delete a single distinctive feature or autosegmental association line, but no more than that. Rules are limited to just these elementary operations.

The idea behind LHS, then, is to impose restrictions like these on GEN: output candidates can differ from the input by virtue of a single application of Move-α or Move/Merge, or by virtue of a single added or deleted feature or association line. With GEN limited in this way, EVAL will have a much smaller candidate set to choose from, and it may require a lengthy serial derivation to converge on the final output. The resulting hybrid theory should be closer to rule-based phonology or P&P than classic OT is.

It turns out, somewhat surprisingly, that LHS is not particularly helpful in addressing opacity and that it also presents some problems of its own. We will take a brief look at each of these results in turn.

Recall the hypothetical example in (97–98): underlying /mapuh + i/ becomes *mapu.i* and not **maputi*, even though the language has *t*-epenthesis otherwise (e.g., /paka + i/ → *pakati*). Rule-based phonology obtains this result with the ordering in (99).

(99) Opaque interaction via rule ordering

Underlying	/mapuh + i/	/paka + i/
Ø → t / V___V	—	pakati
h → Ø /V___V	mapu.i	—

The *t*-epenthesis rule has already had its chance by the time *h* is deleted. Rules like these are temporary, not durable, generalizations (§3.1.2.2, §3.3.1), which is why conspiracies are so problematic for rule-based phonology (§2.1).

Despite its superficial resemblance to derivational theories, LHS is not capable of replicating the derivation in (99). The constraint hierarchy has already been given in (98); the only difference is that LHS limits the comparison to candidates with no more than one unfaithful mapping at a time, as shown in (100).

(100) Attempt at opaque interaction with harmonic serialism

	Underlying	/mapuh + i/	/paka + i/
Pass 1			
GEN receives		mapuhi	pakai
GEN emits		{mapuhi, mapui}	{pakai, pakati, paka}
EVAL selects		mapui	pakati
Pass 2			
GEN receives		mapui	pakati
GEN emits		{maputi, mapui, mapi}	{pakati, pakat, pakai}
EVAL selects		maputi	pakati *Convergence*
Pass 3			
GEN receives		maputi	
GEN emits		{maputi, maput, mapui}	
EVAL selects		*maputi *Convergence*	

At each pass, GEN is limited to performing at most a single deletion or insertion on each candidate. The candidate sets, then, include a faithful member and others with a single unfaithful mapping. (The candidate sets given in (100) are not exhaustive.) EVAL at each pass selects the most harmonic member of this set.

The results initially look promising. On the first pass through EVAL, the hoped-for outcomes do indeed emerge. In the problematically opaque case of /mapuh + i/, the candidate set on the first pass does not include the vexatious *maputi*, and so *mapui* is obtained, as desired. (Compare the standard parallel OT analysis in (98), where *maputi* wrongly wins in one fell swoop.) Unfortunately, the derivation does not converge after the first pass, because on pass 2 the candidate set now includes *maputi*, which easily wins over the intended output *mapui*. Since /mapuh + i/ maps ultimately to *maputi*, it is clear that LHS has failed to simulate the opaque derivation of rule-based phonology. It has failed because LHS is a *global* theory, in the sense defined in §3.3.2.1. The same constraint hierarchy is applied on each pass through EVAL, and the hierarchy that maps the original input /pakai/ to *pakati* cannot avoid also mapping the intermediate-stage input /mapui/ onto *maputi*. There is no way to stop the derivation at *mapui*, because the ranking ⟦ONSET ≫ DEP⟧, which is justified by the /pakai/ → *pakati* mapping, keeps on tugging away at *mapui*, replacing it with *maputi* on pass 2.

In traditional serial, rule-based phonology, there are no global or durable generalizations. A rule mapping /VV/ onto V*t*V is a temporary truth, with no implications for V-V sequences arising later in the derivation. But because LHS is a global theory, the consequences of the ranking ⟦ONSET ≫ DEP⟧ persist, affecting the output of the *h*-deletion process. In fact, this sort of opacity presents much the same problem for LHS as it did for the phonological rule-ordering theories of the 1970s, which maximized rule application by allowing rules to apply and reapply freely until convergence (e.g., Koutsoudas, Sanders, and Noll 1974).

LHS has another important property that follows as a joint consequence of globality and harmonic ascent (§3.1.4.5). Harmonic ascent says that the output of a classic OT grammar must be fully faithful to the input or else less marked relative to the language's constraint hierarchy. In LHS, a classic OT grammar is looped back, taking its own output as a further input. So each pass in an LHS derivation must respect harmonic ascent. Furthermore, since the theory is global, applying the same grammar on each pass through the loop, the markedness of outputs at any pass can be sensibly compared to any other pass. Each intermediate stage of the LHS derivation must be less marked, relative to the language-particular hierarchy in which it is embedded, than all of its derivational predecessors, until convergence. For instance, if the successive passes of a LHS derivation produce /A/ → B → C → D → E → E, then B is less marked than A, C is less marked than A and B, and so on.

Rule-based derivations in phonology typically do not show this characteristic of steady harmonic ascent. On the contrary, rules often create highly marked structures that subsequent rules fix up. For example, it is not unusual

to find processes of vowel deletion creating complex clusters that are broken up
by vowel epenthesis in a different place, such as /yiktibu/ → *yiktbu* → *yikitbu*
in some dialects of Arabic. A derivation like this presents no problem for rule-
based theories, since rules do not have global force, but it presents serious difficulties for LHS.[74]

Although the focus here has been on potential applications of LHS in
phonology, the results follow from the basic architecture of the theory and so
they are independent of the domain of inquiry. There has been relatively little
study of LHS in phonology, 📖 §3.4¶28 and none to my knowledge in syntax. This
would seem to be a promising line of inquiry, if the issues raised in this section
are kept in mind.

3.3.3.3 *Cyclic Evaluation*

The *SPE* and *Aspects* models include a mode of *cyclic* rule application. A
cyclic phonological rule or syntactic transformation first applies to the most
deeply embedded grammatical constituent, with successive applications having
scope over successively larger constituents, in bottom-up fashion. Cyclic
application limits the domain of a rule or transformation and, in the case of
phonology, provides a way for grammatical structure to indirectly influence
phonological form.

Cyclic constraint evaluation has been proposed as a way of implementing a
similar notion in OT. 📖 §3.4¶29 The idea is that each successive layer of constituent
structure, from the bottom up, is submitted to a GEN → EVAL loop. The output
of EVAL after each iteration becomes, in the context of the next higher layer of
constituent structure, the input to another pass through GEN. The derivation terminates when the highest level of (cyclic) constituent structure is reached. The
output of EVAL at that point is the actual output form.

Like harmonic serialism, cyclic evaluation is a global, serial theory. It is
global because the same constraint hierarchy is applied on each pass through
EVAL, and it is serial because there can be more than one pass through GEN and
EVAL on the way to the final output. Because it is a serial theory, cyclic constraint evaluation can accommodate certain kinds of opacity in much the same
way as rule-based derivational theories do. For instance, in the head-movement
example of §3.3.3.1, a constraint demanding locality of movement would be
properly satisfied when the result of incorporation is evaluated on the lower
cycle and again when the complex verb raises to IP on the higher cycle, even
though the resulting chain looks nonlocal. In this way, cyclic evaluation essentially replicates the serial derivation that Chomsky describes.

There is a significant disadvantage to cyclic evaluation, though: it introduces
a major redundancy into the theory. In phonology, as I just noted, cyclicity
allows grammatical structure to exert an indirect influence on the output. But
edge Alignment constraints (§1.2.3) accomplish much the same thing by direct
influence. Since the edge Alignment constraints appear to be necessary for other
reasons, introducing cyclic evaluation places learners in the same uncomfort-

able state as the analyst, hunting for subtle clues as to which account is appropriate in any given situation.

For example, in Axininca Campa (§1.3.3),[75] vowel sequences derived from
different morphemes are parsed into different syllables, with epenthesis, even
when parsing them into the same syllable would obey all high-ranking markedness constraints; see (101).

(101) Morphology affects syllabification

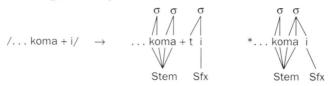

Though syllables like *mai* are in general possible in Axininca Campa, showing
that DEP dominates any markedness constraint that they violate, these syllables
cannot be created from heteromorphemic vowel sequences. Hence, *komati*'s
DEP violation looks unmotivated unless the morphological structure is taken
into account.

This case of morphology influencing syllabification can be understood in
two ways. If constraint evaluation proceeds cyclically, then the stem /. . . koma/
will pass through GEN and EVAL prior to suffixation. The winning candidate
after the first cycle will be . . . [$_\sigma$ko][$_\sigma$ma]. When the suffix /-i/ is added on the
next cycle, the candidate . . . [$_\sigma$ko][$_\sigma$ma][$_\sigma$ti] will win if some constraint demanding faithfulness to the inherited syllabification is ranked above DEP. The
otherwise attractive candidate *. . . [$_\sigma$ko][$_\sigma$mai] is unfaithful to the inherited
syllabification, and so it fails.

In a cyclic analysis of Axininca Campa, morphological structure influences
prosodic structure indirectly. Edge Alignment constraints allow the same influence to be felt directly. The constraint ALIGN-R(Stem, Syllable) is violated
by any stem whose right edge is not syllable-final. The two candidates
. . . [$_\sigma$ko][$_\sigma$ma][$_\sigma$ti] and *. . . [$_\sigma$ko][$_\sigma$mai] differ on exactly this point. (The difference is particularly apparent from the diagrams in (101).) By ranking ALIGN-
R above DEP, these two candidates can be correctly compared without the cycle
or other derivational history.

There are some subtle conditions where cyclic and Alignment approaches
to facts like these yield different empirical predictions. But a more central difference is that Alignment constraints are also applicable to situations where
cyclic analyses are probably not viable. For example, for the reasons given in
§3.3.2.4, it is not possible to give a typologically responsible bottom-up analysis of the prosodic structure of English function words. But a cyclic analysis is
by its very nature bottom up. Rather, the key to the analysis presented there is
ALIGN-R(Lex, PWd), which is an exact match formally with ALIGN-R(Stem,
Syllable) in the analysis of Axininca Campa. Both of these Alignment con-

straints assert that every token of some grammatical category (lexical word, morphological stem) should end (or begin) with the edge of some prosodic category. In general, Alignment constraints like these have turned out to be useful in the study of sentence phonology; in contrast, there is a broad consensus, antedating OT, that sentence phonology is not cyclic. 📖§3.4¶30

3.3.3.4 Modular Architectures

A modular OT architecture is one that is neither global nor parallel. The general idea is that, say, the whole phonology of a language may consist of several OT constraint hierarchies connected serially, with the output of one serving as the input to the next. Each of these serially linked modules is a grammar in the technical sense: it is a distinct ranking of the constraints in CON. The modular architecture, then, extends factorial typology from between-language to within-language differences, and combines this with the derivational structure of harmonic serialism (§1.1.4, §3.3.2.8, §3.3.3.2).

Implementations of this basic idea have all been worked out under the auspices of the theory of Lexical Phonology, 📖§3.4¶31 and so it is not inappropriate to refer to this research program as *OT-LP*. Details differ in various executions of the idea: how many modules, which are called levels or strata in OT-LP; the relationship of the levels to the morphology and syntax, as in the lexical/postlexical distinction of classic LP; whether any levels are also cyclic, in the sense of §3.3.3.3; and so on. The remarks here are necessarily focused on the general properties of the OT-LP program rather than on the specifics of some implementation.

Because it is neither global nor parallel, OT-LP can often directly replicate the rule-ordering analysis of opacity. Take another look at the hypothetical example in (99). Now imagine that the whole grammar consists of two levels, Level 1 and Level 2, which apply in that order. Because Level 1 and Level 2 are distinct modules, they rank the constraints in CON differently. Because Level 1 includes the ranking [ONSET ≫ DEP], it will map /paka + i/ to *pakati*. But Level 1 must also map /mapuh + i/ faithfully to *mapuhi*, so MAX dominates the markedness constraint against intervocalic *h*. Both rankings are reversed in Level 2: to obtain the mapping from the Level-1 output *mapuhi* to the Level-2 output *mapu.i*, MAX must dominate ONSET and be dominated by the markedness constraint against intervocalic *h*.

As this example makes clear, OT-LP places certain conditions on the analyzability of opacity. Rule-based phonology allows any two rules to be ordered in any way, permitting a wide range of opaque interactions. But OT-LP can obtain opaque interactions only if, as in the hypothetical example just described, the two processes occur at different levels. Within-level opacity, if it exists, will present exactly the same problems (reviewed in §3.3.3.1) for OT-LP as it does for classic OT. Conversely, if two processes are forced to be in different levels by other criteria, then opaque interaction will be unavoidable if the processes interact in the right way. It remains to be seen whether these predictions are generally correct.

There is a broader theme here. Imagine that a rule-based grammar consists of just the single rule $A \rightarrow B/C\_\_D$, with no other constraints, conditions, or anything else. Because by assumption there is just this one rule in the grammar, rule interaction is not possible, and by applying the ranking criteria for an unfaithful mapping in (1) of §3.1.1, this rule can be literally translated into a set of constraint rankings.[76] Now imagine a series of such grammars linked like the levels of OT-LP. The result is an exact match to the derivation of rule-based phonology. Each OT grammar is used to obtain the effect of a single rule, and rule ordering is simulated by linking those OT grammars serially. This is a reductio ad absurdum of modular implementations of OT. In reality, OT-LP stops well short of the absurdum by placing limits on the levels that may be posited and, more speculatively, by requiring some uniformity of ranking across levels within a single language.

Beyond opacity, OT-LP is directed toward the analysis of *paradigm uniformity effects*. It is frequently observed that regular phonological patterns are disrupted to obtain greater resemblance between morphologically related forms (cf. §3.2.1.2) – that is, greater uniformity of realization of a morpheme within its paradigm. For example, long and short vowels are in complementary distribution in the Scottish dialect of English:[77] vowels are long word-finally (*agree* has long [iː]) and in certain other contexts not discussed here, and they are short otherwise (*grid* and *greed* are homophonous, both being pronounced with short [i]). The interesting thing for present purposes is that word-final long vowels are preserved before inflectional suffixes, so *agreed* has long [iː] just like *agree*. Consequently, vowel length is uniform within an inflectional paradigm.

In OT-LP, this observation indicates that two different grammars are involved. In the Level-1 grammar, vowel length is fully predictable, so any constraint demanding faithfulness to vowel length must be ranked below markedness constraints that are fully dispositive of vowel length in all contexts (cf. §3.1.3.4). The Level-2 grammar reverses this ranking, elevating faithfulness to vowel length above those markedness constraints. Level 2 receives as inputs the outputs of Level 1, and it simply preserves the vowel-length distribution that was assigned at Level 1.

Correlatively, OT-LP asserts that inflectional morphology like the suffix /-d/ of *agreed* is not added until Level 2. For this reason, the Level-1 phonology operates on simple *agree* even when the ultimate goal of the derivation is *agreed*. This correlation of phonological grammars with morphology – the inputs to Level 1 lack certain morphology not added until Level 2, and the two levels have different grammars because they rank CON differently – is the basis of OT-LP's explanation for paradigm uniformity effects. Though implementational details differ, this explanation is much the same as in classic rule-based LP.

There are, however, some important differences between classic LP and OT-LP. One of the main achievements of classic LP is the discovery of principled limits on how levels can differ from each other within a single language. The

Strong Domain Hypothesis asserts that rules of the lexical phonology can only be switched off, never on, and then only at the end of a level (Borowsky 1986; Kiparsky 1984). Rules of the lexical phonology are said to be limited in various ways: they apply only in derived environments, they are subject to the Elsewhere Condition, they apply only to members of lexical categories, they tolerate exceptions, and they are structure preserving (Kiparsky 1982b, 1985; Mohanan 1982). None of these principles is reconstructible in OT-LP because of basic architectural differences between rule-based phonology (which includes classic LP) and OT. For instance, the notion of turning a process or constraint off has no counterpart in OT, where all constraints are available in all grammars and are at least potentially active in spite of low rank (§1.3.4, §3.1.5.2, §3.2.1.3). The assumption that a grammar is a collection of language-particular rules and some parameter settings is an important aspect of classic LP with relevance to many of its principles, but this assumption is neither present nor reconstructible in OT. The consequences of this and other differences between LP and OT-LP remain to be explored.[78]

3.3.3.5 *Other Approaches to Opacity in OT*

Four other general approaches to opacity in OT can be identified in the literature. This section will describe each briefly and take note of some of the research questions it engenders.[79]

The problem of opacity for a parallel theory was recognized from the very beginning in OT, and so a partial solution was incorporated into the original PARSE/FILL implementation of faithfulness (§1.2.2).⌂§3.4¶27 Under the PARSE/FILL regime, the properties of the input are encoded structurally in the output. Deleted segments are present in the output but syllabically unparsed; epenthetic segments are not present in the output, but their syllabic positions are. The constraints PARSE and FILL militate against these two types of unfaithfulness. Compare trace theory (Chomsky 1973) and some versions of autosegmental phonology (e.g., Selkirk 1981; Steriade 1982), which implement similar ideas. For a skeptical view, see note 71.

The input that is immanent within the output offers a handle on a range of opacity phenomena. For instance, Sea Dayak (Austronesian, Indonesia) has a process that spreads nasality from a nasal consonant onto following vowels, just like Madurese in §3.1.3.4.[80] Nasal spreading is blocked by oral consonants – even when they are deleted. In a rule-based theory, this opaque interaction is obtained by ordering nasal spreading before the rule that deletes oral consonants, as depicted in (102).

(102) Sea Dayak derivationally

Underlying	/naŋga?/	
V → [+nasal] / N___	nãŋga?	Nasal spreading (cf. (19b))
b, d, g → Ø / N___	nãŋa?	Deletion

Under the assumptions of the PARSE/FILL faithfulness theory, deletion is not literal, and so a "deleted" oral consonant is present in output candidates, though phonetically uninterpreted. So the seemingly opaque mapping /naŋgaʔ/ → nāŋaʔ is actually a mapping to nāŋ⟨g⟩aʔ, with a latent, syllabically unparsed g. The unparsed g blocks nasal spreading, since its continued presence means that ŋ and a are not literally adjacent, and so they vacuously satisfy the markedness constraint that is responsible for the nasal-spreading process. By enriching the representation of candidates, opaque interactions are rendered transparent and thus present no difficulties for parallel evaluation. And since there is ample precedent in both phonology and syntax for this sort of enrichment, nothing new is required to accommodate opacity.

This approach can in principle account for a broad range of opaque interactions, though it raises two important questions. One concerns truly transparent interactions. It seems reasonable to suppose that there could be another language identical to Sea Dayak except that /naŋgaʔ/ surfaces as nāŋā́ʔ. If deletion is always nonparsing, the winning candidate must be nāŋ⟨g⟩ā́ʔ. It is hard to see how this candidate could ever be optimal, since nasal spreading is universally blocked by intervening oral consonants (Walker 1998). Additional theoretical development is required, either to allow candidates with literal deletion or to differentiate languages by the visibility of unparsed material.

The other question raised by this approach to opacity involves extensions to other opaque interactions. For example, analyzing the hypothetical example in (99) in these terms would require that /mapuh-i/ map most harmonically to mapu⟨h⟩.i. To get this result, it is necessary to use the presence of unparsed h to block epenthesis – that is, mapu⟨h⟩.i must be more harmonic than *mapu⟨h⟩ti, with epenthetic t, while still allowing the /paka-i/ → pakati mapping. This and similar questions arise when the PARSE/FILL approach is generalized to other opaque interactions.[81]

Another approach to opacity via faithfulness extends the theory of correspondence (§1.2.2). Though faithfulness was originally an input/output relation only, the paradigm uniformity effects mentioned in §3.3.3.4 can be understood as faithfulness effects across related output forms. The idea is that paradigmatically related output forms stand in an *output-output correspondence relation*, which is regulated by the family of *OO-Faith* constraints.📖§1.5¶3, §3.4¶31 If one member of a paradigm undergoes a process transparently, then the other members can be forced to resemble it by appropriate ranking of some OO-Faith constraints. In the Scottish English example of §3.3.3.4, the word *agree* has a final long vowel transparently, since [i] is always long at the end of a word. By positing an OO correspondence relation between *agree* and *agreed*, and enforcing resemblance with the constraint OO-IDENT(long), the transparent long [iː] of *agree* is carried over opaquely to the related word *agreed*. The key is to rank OO-IDENT(long) above any markedness that would militate against long vowels before *d* – in particular, the markedness constraint that is responsible for the short vowel in *greed*.

Like OT-LP, this approach associates opacity with certain kinds of morphological complexity. In OT-LP, opaque interactions are only possible when processes apply at different levels, and each level is usually identified with some layer of morphological derivation. OO-Faith says approximately the same thing: an opaque interaction is possible whenever a transparent process in a morphologically simplex form is carried over to a morphologically derived form. As in OT-LP, the principal question needing investigation is whether all observed opaque interactions involve the right morphological conditions to allow this kind of analysis to go through.

Sympathy theory takes a very different line on the opacity issue.⬚§3.4¶32 The idea in sympathy theory is that, in addition to the actual output form, EVAL may select a sympathetic candidate, which is the most harmonic candidate that obeys some specified faithfulness constraint, called the selector. Rankable constraints require the output form to resemble the sympathetic candidate in some respect, and in this way the sympathetic candidate, even if not the winner itself, may exercise an indirect influence over the outcome.

For instance, among the candidates obtained from input /naŋga?/ is *nãŋga?. Because it retains all of the input segments and correctly nasalizes the vowel after *n*, this candidate is the most harmonic one that obeys the faithfulness constraint MAX. If MAX is designated as the selector, then *nãŋga? will be chosen as the sympathetic candidate. It is not the actual output form, since it violates some markedness constraint that militates against ŋg and that is ranked above MAX, but it is available to exercise sympathetic influence over the actual output form. Output candidates are evaluated for their resemblance to *nãŋga?, and on this criterion nãŋa? is more harmonic than *nãŋã?. By appropriate ranking, forced resemblance to the sympathetic candidate overrides the constraint demanding that nasal consonants be followed by nasalized vowels.

Because it represents a more radical departure from the standard conception of EVAL than the other approaches to opacity, sympathy theory raises more difficult questions. The workings of EVAL need to be rethought in this context, as does the mechanism of selection and the nature of the constraints demanding intercandidate resemblance. And as with all the other approaches, there are questions about the match between observed and predicted opaque interactions. (See the references in §3.4 ¶32 for exploration of these issues and some proposals for addressing them.)

Local constraint conjunction (§1.2.3, §3.1.2.5, §3.3.2.8) offers yet another take on opacity.⬚§1.5¶5 The tableau in (95) applies local conjunction to one kind of opaque interaction, a chain shift. As in that example, the conjunction of two faithfulness constraints prohibits the piling up of faithfulness violations in close proximity. Many opaque interactions have this character. For example, the transparent mapping /mapuh-i/ → *maputi has two nearby faithfulness violations –

MAX for the loss of /h/, and DEP for the insertion of *t* – but the opaque candidate *mapu.i* has just one. By ranking the conjoined constraint [MAX&DEP]$_\delta$ above ONSET, the otherwise more attractive candidate **maputi* can be ruled out, as in (103).

(103) An account of opacity using local conjunction

/mapuh + i/		*VhV	[MAX&DEP]$_\delta$	MAX	ONSET	DEP
a.	maputi		*	*		*
b.	mapuhi	*				
c.	☞ mapu.i				*	*

A similar point can be made about the mapping /naŋgaʔ/ → *nãŋaʔ* versus **nãŋãʔ*: the failed candidate violates [MAX&IDENT(nasal)]$_\delta$.

Two typological issues are in the background of all applications of local conjunction, including this one (§1.2.3): conjoinability of constraints and domains of conjunction. The domain issue is particularly important, since the wrong choice of domain can easily produce absurd results. For example, it is crucial that the domain δ in which [MAX&IDENT(nasal)]$_\delta$ is evaluated include the highlighted sequence in /naŋgaʔ/ and not /naŋgaʔ/. If the situation were reversed, violation of MAX in the second syllable would block nasalization in the first syllable – an interaction that is not only unattested but almost surely impossible. Questions about conjoinability and the associated domains of conjunction are again a matter of current research.

3.3.3.6   Final Remarks

Though the opacity issue in OT is not yet fully resolved, it is clear that there are several promising lines of inquiry now under study. But perhaps more important than these parochial concerns is the light that this research sheds on questions that had long ago been abandoned. Though syntactic theory showed a steady progression away from the rich derivational model of *Aspects*, much of phonological theory remained in a kind of stasis (§2.3). In the 1970s, there was serious study of limitations on *SPE*'s derivational richness under the rubrics of predicting rule order, limiting abstractness, and similar ideas.📖$_{§2.5¶2}$. But this work had almost no influence on the subsequent development of the field, which tended to marry an increasingly articulated theory of representations with a loose derivational model harking back to *SPE*. Efforts to restrict the theory of derivations, such as the strict division between lexical and post-lexical rules in the theory of Lexical Phonology, were often undermined by subsequent developments, such as the word level (Booij and Rubach 1987; Borowsky 1993) or stipulated noncyclic levels (Halle and Mohanan 1985; Halle and Vergnaud 1987). To the extent that the "problem" of opacity in OT has forced a reexamination of the limits of interaction, it has brought new attention to a matter that has wrongly been considered settled and has too long been neglected.

3.4   For Further Reading

¶1   *Richness of the Base*

Precursors to ROTB and lexicon optimization can be found in the work of Dell (1973, 1980), Hudson (1974b), Myers (1991), and Stampe (1973a: 32–33, 1973b: 50–51). (Though see Kaye 1974, 1975 for a defense of morpheme structure constraints.) The original OT discussion appears in Prince and Smolensky (1993: Chapter 4, Section 3.1 and Chapter 9, Section 3). Relevant phonological analyses are too numerous to mention. In the syntactic literature, ROTB receives special attention from Aissen (1999), Bakovic and Keer (to appear), Bresnan (to appear-a, to appear-b), Grimshaw (1997b, to appear: 385ff.), Grimshaw and Samek-Lodovici (1995, 1998), Legendre, Smolensky, and Wilson (1998), and Samek-Lodovici (1996a: 219).

For some critical reflections on ROTB and lexicon optimization, see Archangeli and Suzuki (1997), Hammond (1997b), and Roca (1997b). Radically different approaches to underlying representations in OT are entertained by Archangeli and Langendoen (1997a), Burzio (1996, 1997), Golston (1996), Hammond (1995, 1997b), and Russell (1995).

The claim that syllabification is universally absent from underlying representations comes from Blevins (1995: 221), Clements (1986: 318), and Hayes (1989: 260), among others. An interpretation of this observation in terms of faithfulness in OT is in Keer (1999a) and McCarthy (to appear). The observation that reduplication never copies syllables is due to Moravcsik (1978) and Marantz (1982).

¶2   *The Duplication Problem*

The original treatments of the Duplication Problem are Clayton (1976) and Kenstowicz and Kisseberth (1977). The alternative proposals mentioned in the text include global rules or derivational constraints (Kisseberth 1970a, 1970b), linking rules (Chomsky and Halle 1968), persistent rules (Chafe 1968: 131; Halle and Vergnaud 1987: 135; Myers 1991), and underspecification (Archangeli 1984; Kiparsky 1981). Also see the references in §2.5 ¶6.

¶3   *Absolute Ill-Formedness*

The notion of absolute ill-formedness is utterly pervasive, though sometimes only implicit, in work on OT. Explicit discussions can be found in Prince and Smolensky (1993: Chapter 4, Section 3.1), Ackema and Neeleman (2000), Bakovic and Keer (to appear), Legendre, Smolensky, and Wilson (1998), and Legendre et al. (1995). Orgun and Sprouse (1999) and Pesetsky (1997: 147–52, 1998: 377–81) argue that the standard OT approach to absolute ill-formedness is insufficient. See §4.1.2 for further discussion and §4.6 ¶1.

¶4 *Lexicon Optimization*

Several works explore ramifications of lexicon optimization: Inkelas (1994) and Inkelas, Orgun, and Zoll (1997) relate it to underspecification and the treatment of lexical exceptions; Ito, Mester, and Padgett (1995) further develop its formal basis; McCarthy (1998) and Tesar and Smolensky (2000: 77ff.) extend it to whole paradigms; Yip (1996) uses external evidence to test the underlying representations it gives. For more on the problem of learning underlying representations and a grammar together, see §4.2.2 and the references in §4.6 ¶6,7.

¶5 *Markedness in Morphosyntax*

Jakobson (1971), which was originally published in 1932, is the first work to extend Trubetzkoy's (1939) ideas about markedness to morphology and syntax. Newmeyer (1998: 196ff.) supplies a useful review of contemporary thought on the subject, and Williams (1981) pursues similar ideas, though couched in different terms. Some OT works using morphosyntactic markedness hierarchies to account for typological generalizations include Aissen (1999), Artstein (1998), Bresnan (to appear-b), Grimshaw (to appear), Lee (2000), and Woolford (to appear).

¶6 *Analyzing Distributional Generalizations in OT*

Some of the key references presenting the general approach to distributional generalizations sketched in the text include Ito and Mester (1995, 1997a), Kirchner (1997, 1998a), McCarthy and Prince (1995a), Prince and Smolensky (1993: Chapter 9), and Prince and Tesar (1999). Samek-Lodovici (1996a) analyzes the distribution of expletives and null, focused, and canonical subjects, placing particular emphasis on parallels between within-language and between-language variation.

¶7 *Positional Faithfulness and Positional Markedness*

The loci classici for positional faithfulness are Beckman (1995, 1997, 1998) and Casali (1996, 1997); other works treating positional faithfulness, positional markedness, and similar notions include Alderete (1998, 1999, to appear-b), de Lacy (2000b), Lombardi (1999, to appear), Padgett (1995b), Revithiadou (1999), Smith (2000a, 2000b, 2001), Steriade (1999a, 1999c), Zoll (1997, 1998), and (in syntax) Woolford (to appear). Dresher and van der Hulst (1998) study similar phenomena from a different perspective. Also see the references in §1.5 ¶3.

¶8 *Homogeneity of Target/Heterogeneity of Process*

Works placing special emphasis on homogeneity of target/heterogeneity of process include Alber and Plag (1999), Bresnan (to appear-b), Grimshaw (1997a), Lombardi (to appear), McCarthy (2000c), Mester (1994), Myers (1997b), Pater (1999a), and Wilson (1999).

¶9   Faithfulness to Lexical versus Functional Morphemes

A distinction between root and affix faithfulness was proposed in McCarthy and Prince (1995a). Significant discussion can be found in Alderete (1998, to appear-b), Bakovic (2000), Beckman (1998), Casali (1996, 1997), Dresher and van der Hulst (1998), Futagi (1998), Revithiadou (1999), Smith (1998, 2000a, 2001), Struijke (1998, 2000a), and Walker (1997a).

¶10   Harmonic Ascent

The original paper on harmonic ascent, combining formal proofs and extensive empirical analysis, is Moreton (1996/1999). There is further discussion in McCarthy (2000b) and Prince (1997a). On the relation of harmonic ascent to sympathy theory (§3.3.3.5), see McCarthy (to appear: Appendix).

¶11   Exchange Rules

Exchange or alpha-switching rules were introduced in *SPE*. The argument that they are limited to morphological processes is developed in Anderson (1974, 1975) and Anderson and Browne (1973). Other 1970s-vintage works on the exchange rules controversy include Dressler (1971), Gregersen (1974), Malone (1972), Stockwell (1975), Wolfe (1970, 1975), and Zonneveld (1976).

¶12   Anti-Faithfulness Constraints

The original anti-faithfulness constraint is Prince and Smolensky's (1993) FREE-V, which requires an underlying final vowel to be absent at the surface in the Lardil nominative case. This constraint is obviously morphological in character, and more recently, Alderete (1998, to appear-a) has advanced the hypothesis that anti-faithfulness is always morphological, refining it and applying it extensively to alternations in accentual systems. Horwood (1999) extends this idea to morphological truncation processes. On the phonological side, Bakovic (1996) proposes that anti-faithfulness is involved in stressed-syllable augmentation in Yup'ik Eskimo.

¶13   Process-Specific Constraints

The discussion in the text on process-specific constraints is based on a proposal by Alan Prince (see Prince 1997b), which was prompted by a question raised by Stuart Davis (see Davis 1995). There is fuller discussion and exemplification in McCarthy (1997) and Bakovic (2000: Chapter 4).

¶14   Parameters Compared with Ranking

Quite a number of works develop more or less explicit comparisons of OT with parametric models in phonology (Alber 1999; Crowhurst and Hewitt 1994; de Lacy 2000c; Harrikari 1999; McCarthy and Prince 1994a; Paradis 1996; Revithiadou 1999; Rosenthall and van der Hulst 1999; Spaelti 1997; Suzuki 1998; Zoll 1996), in syntax (Costa 1998; Grimshaw 1997b: 405; Samek-

Lodovici 1996a: 131ff., 1996b, 1998), and in learning (Prince and Tesar 1999;
Smolensky 1996a; Tesar and Smolensky 1998, 2000; Turkel 1994).

¶15 *Language Universals from Factorial Typology*
   The idea of deriving universal restrictions on language from factorial typology is first explored in the context of Prince and Smolensky's (1993: Chapter
6) analysis of basic syllable typology. Some of the works placing particular
emphasis on this topic include Alderete (1998, 1999), Alderete et al. (1999:
Section 2.1), Bakovic (1998b, 2000: Chapter 1), Beckman (1998: Chapter 1),
Grimshaw (1997b), Grimshaw and Samek-Lodovici (1998: 214–17), Keer
(1999a), Keer and Bakovic (1997), Legendre, Raymond, and Smolensky (1993),
Lombardi (1999, to appear), McCarthy (1999), McCarthy and Prince (1993b:
125–35, 1999: 258–67), Morelli (1998), Nelson (1998), Samek-Lodovici (to
appear), Smith (1998), Struijke (2000a), Walker (1997b), Woolford (to appear:
Section 3.5), and Zoll (1997: Section 5).

¶16 *Infixation*
   The idea that infixation is a consequence of forced violation of prefix/suffix
alignment constraints is due to Prince and Smolensky (1991, 1993). Applications and extensions of this idea appear in Akinlabi (1996), Buckley (1997),
Carlson (1998), de Lacy (2000a), Fulmer (1997), McCarthy (2000a), McCarthy
and Prince (1993a, 1993b), Noyer (1993), Spaelti (1997), Stemberger and
Bernhardt (1999a), and Urbanczyk (1996).

¶17 *Implicational Universals, Scales, and Fixed Hierarchies*
   The most extensive discussion of implicational universals and related
matters in OT appears in Chapters 8 and 9 of Prince and Smolensky (1993).
There is a gentler introduction in their Chapter 2, but it can be confusing
because, as a temporary expedient, it introduces a type of constraint that is not
in general use in OT. For this reason, the first few sections of their Chapter 5
may be the best place to begin. Phonological works prominently featuring this
topic include Anttila (1997a), de Lacy (1999), Green (1993), Kenstowicz
(1994b), Kirchner (1998a), Morén (1999), and Walker (1998, 1999). (For a different view, see Gnanadesikan 1997.) These notions are, if anything, even more
important in works applying OT to syntactic or morphosyntactic problems:
Aissen (1999), Artstein (1998), Bakovic (1998a), Bresnan (to appear-a), Burzio
(1998), Grimshaw (to appear), Lee (2000), Legendre et al. (1995), Legendre,
Smolensky, and Wilson (1998), and Woolford (to appear). Also see the references in §1.5 ¶7.

¶18 *Nonuniformity of Structure*
   The modest-sized body of literature discussing nonuniformity of structure
includes Alderete (1998: Chapters 4 and 5), Bermúdez-Otero (1996), McCarthy
(1995, 2000c), Mester (1994), Pater (to appear-b), and Rosenthall and van der

Hulst (1999). The recognition of nonuniformity as a basic consequence of OT is due to Prince (1993b). Harris's (1990a) notion of a "derived contrast" is also relevant.

¶19 *Cliticization*

Edge Alignment plays a role in many analyses of clitic placement, including Anderson (1996a, 1996b, 2000), Grimshaw (to appear), van der Leeuw (1997), Legendre (1998, 1999, 2000, to appear-b), and Peperkamp (1997).

¶20 *Emergence of the Unmarked*

TETU is introduced in McCarthy and Prince (1994a). Bresnan (to appear-a), Costa (to appear), Lee (2000), and Müller (1998) find emergent unmarkedness effects in the syntax. As for morphology, it has been argued that TETU is the source of all morphological templates, in what McCarthy and Prince (1994a, 1994b, 1995a, 1999) call "Generalized Template Theory." Other works discussing this theory or kindred notions include Alderete et al. (1999), Carlson (1998), Chung (1999), Downing (1999), Gafos (1998), Hendricks (1999), Ito, Kitagawa, and Mester (1996), Spaelti (1997), Struijke (1998, 2000a, 2000b), Urbanczyk (1996, 1999), Ussishkin (1999), and Walker (2000). (Cf. Hyman and Inkelas 1997; Inkelas 1999 for another view.) TETU is also important in allomorph selection (see §3.3.2.6 and the references in ¶25) and in child phonology (see §4.2.2 and the references in §4.6 ¶8).

¶21 *Extremism and Economy*

Because minimal violation – the source of extremism or economy effects in OT – is intrinsic to the theory, it is not possible to single out just a few works for special notice here. Readers interested in pursuing these topics can look at the large literature on Alignment constraints (such as the works mentioned in §1.5 ¶4 or in ¶16 and ¶19 in this section) for extremism or at the equally large literature on OT syntax for references to economy.

¶22 *Chicken-Egg Effects*

The chicken-egg effects argument for parallelism is developed by Prince and Smolensky (1993: Chapter 7, Section 4) in the context of their analysis of Lardil augmentation. Another example is the interaction of stressing and sonorant destressing in English, for which see Pater (to appear-b). McCarthy and Prince (1995a, 1999) discuss ordering paradoxes in reduplication/phonology interactions.

The original source for Southern Paiute is Sapir (1930). The ordering paradox was first noted by McDonough (1987) and Zec (1993) (who gives an OT analysis). An OT analysis of the same phenomenon in a related language, Tübatulabal, appears in Alderete et al. (1999: 346), and similar issues arise in Kitto and de Lacy's (2000) analysis of epenthesis in Cook Islands Maori.

¶23 Top-Down Effects

The top-down effects argument originates with Prince and Smolensky (1993: Chapter 3, Section 2 and Chapter 4, Section 3). The topic is discussed lucidly and at length, with extensive exemplification from prosodic structure, by Kager (1999a: Chapter 4). The literature on global effects on prosodic structure (¶24), on allomorphy (¶25), and on sentence phonology (¶30) is also relevant.

¶24 Global Effects on Prosodic Structure

Prince and Smolensky (1993: Chapter 5, Section 2.3.1) were the first to observe global effects on prosody in connection with their analysis of Berber syllable structure. Other examples, involving morphology/prosody interactions, include Axininca Campa (McCarthy and Prince 1993a: 136ff., 1993b: Chapter 4, Section 3.3), Indonesian (Cohn and McCarthy 1994/1998), Maori (de Lacy 2000c), and Rotuman (McCarthy 2000c: Section 3). Hewitt's (1992) notion of "vertical maximization" is also relevant in this respect.

The Yidiny example in the text has been discussed extensively in the literature (Crowhurst and Hewitt 1995; Halle and Vergnaud 1987; Hayes 1982, 1985, 1995; Hewitt 1992; Hung 1994; Kager 1993; McCarthy and Prince 1986/1996; Nash 1979; Poser 1986). The ranking of iambic feet for relative harmony comes from Prince (1990), based partly on Hayes (1985) and McCarthy and Prince (1986/1996). Constraints against clashes and lapses are discussed by Alber (1999), Elenbaas and Kager (1999), Green and Kenstowicz (1995), Hammond (1984), Hayes (1984, 1995), Hung (1994), Nespor and Vogel (1989), Prince (1983), Selkirk (1984), and many others.

¶25 Phonologically Conditioned Allomorphy

Spencer (1991: Chapter 4) reviews the various theories of allomorphy in generative phonology. To my knowledge, output constraints were first applied to allomorphy by Siegel (1974). Aronoff (1976: Chapters 4–5) is a rejoinder to Siegel, attempting to defend a rule-based approach to allomorphy along the lines of *SPE*'s theory of readjustment rules. The idea of lexical entries as sets of allomorphic alternants originated with Hudson (1974a) and is adopted by Hooper [Bybee] (1976) (though see Harris 1978, 1985 for rule-based and representational alternatives, respectively). Anderson's (1975) proposal that modularity is not based on ordering is also relevant here.

There is a considerable literature applying OT to problems in allomorphy or lexical selection, beginning with Mester (1994) and including Alcantará (1998), Anttila (1997b), Bresnan (to appear-a, to appear-b), Burzio (1994a, 1997), Drachman, Kager, and Drachman (1997), Grimshaw (1997a), Hargus (1995), Hargus and Tuttle (1997), Kager (1996), Lapointe and Sells (1997), Mascaró (1996), McCarthy and Prince (1993b: Chapter 7), Perlmutter (1998), Russell (1995), Tranel (1996a, 1996b, 1998), and Urbanczyk (1999).

The problems of analyzing external allomorphy within the theory of Lexical Phonology are discussed by Dresher (1983) and Hayes (1990). Skousen (1975) was the first to note the ordering paradox involving *a*/*an* and *h* deletion. English *h*/Ø alternations are analyzed in OT terms by Davis (1999).

¶26   Challenges to Remote Interaction

An interesting proposal for dealing with similar problems, involving extensive revision of EVAL, is discussed by Bakovic (2000), Bakovic and Wilson (2000), and Wilson (1999).

¶27   Opacity

Opaque rule interactions were first identified as a class by Kiparsky (1971, 1973c). They received much attention during the 1970s (see the references in §2.5 ¶2). The challenges that opacity presents for OT have been noted many times (see Archangeli and Suzuki 1996, 1997; Black 1993; Booij 1997; Cho 1995; Chomsky 1995; Clements 1997; Goldsmith 1996; Halle and Idsardi 1997; Hermans and van Oostendorp 1999; Idsardi 1997, 1998; Jensen 1995; Kager 1997, 1999b; McCarthy 1996, 1999; McCarthy and Prince 1993b; Noyer 1997; Paradis 1997; Prince and Smolensky 1993; Roca 1997b; Rubach 1997).

¶28   Harmonic Serialism

The original description of harmonic serialism appears in Prince and Smolensky (1993: Chapter 2 and pp. 79–80 n). The discussion in the text generally follows McCarthy (2000b). Black (1993) and Blevins (1997) use harmonic serialism as a vehicle to incorporate rules into OT. Moreton (2000) develops and proves some general results about the conditions under which harmonic serialism converges after two versus more passes through the GEN → EVAL loop.

¶29   The Cycle

Cyclic constraint evaluation is proposed by Booij (1996, 1997) and Kenstowicz (1995), while Orgun (1994) develops a different approach. The history and applications of the cycle are reviewed by Cole (1995), and Denton, Chan, and Canakis (1993) is a collection of recent studies. Alignment-based approaches to cyclic phenomena are foreshadowed by the large body of works making simultaneous reference to morphological and prosodic structure (Aronoff and Sridhar 1983; Booij 1988; Booij and Lieber 1993; Booij and Rubach 1984; Cohn 1989; Goldsmith 1990, 1991, 1992; Halle and Kenstowicz 1991: 479–81; Hyman 1985; Idsardi 1992; Mutaka and Hyman 1990; Odden and Odden 1985; Rubach and Booij 1990; Szpyra 1989: 178–229).

¶30   Alignment in Sentence Phonology

Chen (1987), Clements (1978: 35), and Selkirk (1986) develop ideas similar to Alignment in the analysis of sentence phonology, and this approach is also pursued in Cho (1990b), Hale and Selkirk (1987), Jun (1993), Selkirk and Shen (1990), and Selkirk and Tateishi (1988, 1991). (The literature cited in ¶29 of this section is also relevant.) Within OT, relevant works include Kenstowicz and Sohn (1997), Kim (1997), van der Leeuw (1997), Peperkamp (1997), Selkirk (1995, 1996), Truckenbrodt (1995, 1999), and Wiltshire (1998). Also see the references on Alignment in §1.5 ¶4 and on clitics in ¶19 of this section.

¶31   OT and Lexical Phonology

There is an abundance of work within the theory of Lexical Phonology (including Borowsky 1986; Hargus 1985; Hargus and Kaisse 1993; Kiparsky 1982a, 1982b, 1985; Mohanan 1986; Pulleyblank 1986; Rubach 1993; Strauss 1982). There are several good, accessible overviews of the topic, including chapters in Kenstowicz (1994a) and Spencer (1991) and articles by Kaisse and Hargus (1993), Kaisse and Shaw (1985), and Mohanan (1995).

Modular, serial implementations of OT along the lines of the theory of Lexical Phonology have been proposed or discussed in the following works: Bermúdez-Otero (1999), Cohn and McCarthy (1994/1998), Hale and Kissock (1998), Hale, Kissock, and Reiss (1998), Ito and Mester (to appear), Kenstowicz (1995), Kiparsky (to appear-a, to appear-b), McCarthy (2000c), McCarthy and Prince (1993b), Potter (1994), Rubach (2000), and many of the contributions to Hermans and van Oostendorp (1999) and Roca (1997a). For alternative approaches to some of the phenomena taken to motivate OT-LP, see Archangeli and Suzuki (1997), Benua (1997), Burzio (1994b), Crosswhite (1998), Ito, Kitagawa, and Mester (1996), Ito and Mester (1997a), Kager (1997), Kenstowicz (1996, 1997), Kraska-Szlenk (1995), McCarthy (1999, to appear), Orgun (1996b), and Steriade (1999b, 2000). Golston (1995) is relevant to the issue of modularity in the postlexical phonology.

¶32   Sympathy Theory

Sympathy theory is introduced in McCarthy (1999, to appear). Other discussions of sympathy, pro and con, include Bakovic (2000), Davis (1997), de Lacy (1998), Fukazawa (1999), Ito and Mester (1997b, 1997c), Goldrick (2000), Grijzenhout and Kraemer (1999), Harris and Kaisse (1999), Jun (1999), Karvonen and Sherman [Ussishkin] (1997, 1998), Katayama (1998), Kikuchi (1999), Lee (1999), McGarrity (1999), Merchant (1997), Sanders (1997), Shinohara (1997), and Walker (1998, 1999).

Notes

1. I am using the slashes /. . ./ and brackets [. . .] of classical phonemics to indicate inputs and outputs, respectively. But it should be understood that these stand for any kind of input and output linguistic object, not just a phonological one.
2. Compare Ackema and Neeleman (1998a, 1998b) for an account of the typology of *wh*-questions in terms of ranking permutation rather than lexical specification.

3. This usage recalls the original sense of the term "base" in Chomsky (1957).
4. This position is adopted by, among others, Blevins (1995: 221), Clements (1986: 318), and Hayes (1989: 260).
5. The following statement exemplifies this sort of objection to ROTB:

> Richness of the base is a claim about the nature of OT grammars that states that there can be great latitude in the form of UR's [underlying representations]. For example, someone with a grammar of English could have all voiceless surface velar stops stored as clicks. Given the appropriate constraint ranking (i.e., with constraints against clicks ranked high), the surface forms could still be pronounced with normal velar stops. But given Smolensky's [(1996b)] own assumption about how parsing and acquisition of UR's proceed, /kæt/, for example, could never be stored with a click. As a result, the notion of richness of the base becomes a computational curiosity of OT grammars that may be quite irrelevant to human language. (Hale and Reiss 1998: 660)

Smolensky's proposal is discussed in §4.2.2. It is based on lexicon optimization, which is explained later in this section.

6. Though lexicon optimization is a plausible learning strategy, it is certainly not the only possibility. For example, Prince and Smolensky (1993: Chapter 9, Section 3) briefly entertain an alternative that involves selecting the simplest underlying representation in the style of the feature-counting Evaluation Metric of *SPE* (§2.1). For further exploration of this line of analysis, see Keer (1998).
7. It is, however, possible to evaluate the results of lexicon optimization or alternatives against evidence of the kind that learners do not have access to, such as historical change or psycholinguistic experiments. See Archangeli and Langendoen (1997a), Bermúdez-Otero (1999), Green (1997), Holt (1997), and Yip (1996).
8. This example is based on Grimshaw (to appear). For expository purposes, I have altered and simplified her discussion considerably.
9. The grammar of Italian might instead differ from French by virtue of simply lacking the conjoined constraint [*FEM&*DAT]_Word. It is an open question whether local conjunction constitutes a kind of schema for constructing language-particular constraints from universal ones, or whether the conjunctions themselves are also universal. See §1.3, §3.1.5, and the references in §1.4 ¶5.
10. This example is based on McCarthy and Prince (1995a, 1999).
11. Another approach is to posit two markedness constraints along with a universally fixed ranking (§1.2, §3.1.5): [*V_Nas ≫ *V_Oral]. See Clements (1997) for related discussion.
12. The scenario where oral vowels occur in all contexts and nasal vowels in none is not usually thought of as complementary distribution, though technically there is complementarity. The reason: standard approaches assume that a language without surface nasal vowels has no nasal vowels in the lexicon, and so there is no reason to think of nasal vowels in that language as having any distribution, even a null one. But in OT with ROTB, even nonoccurring segments can be thought of as having a distribution that happens to be null.
13. This example is based on McCarthy and Prince (1995a, 1999) and, further back, Cohn (1990) and Stevens (1968).
14. From the perspective of earlier theories, an urgent question has not been answered: what are the *actual* lexical representations that underlie Madurese *ba* and *mã?* Lexicon optimization (§3.1.2) favors faithful mappings, so it says that the under-

lying forms are /ba/ and /mā/, respectively, if there are no overt alternations. Again from the perspective of earlier theories, it might seem odd to impute fully predictable allophones to the lexicon, but this misses the point: they are fully predictable because of the grammar, not because of the lexicon. Indeed, as the discussion in §3.1.2 emphasizes, the seemingly urgent question is in reality inconsequential.

15. For simplicity, I consider only stressless inputs. Under ROTB, though, inputs may have stress distributed at random. In Nancowry, where stress is fully predictable, all constraints demanding faithfulness to stress are ranked below some markedness constraint requiring stress on the root-final syllable. The output stress position is what matters for positional faithfulness.

16. I am grateful to Jane Grimshaw for extensive discussion of this material, which greatly aided my understanding.

17. This example comes from Pater (1999a). See Archangeli, Moll, and Ohno (1998) for a different view.

18. Teoh (1988) bases these underlying forms on Standard Malay.

19. But even in English, which shows no effect of *NÇ in the adult phonology, there is evidence that conforming clusters like *mb* or *nd* are acquired earlier than non-conforming *mp* or *nt*. This is to be expected if markedness constraints like *NÇ are at the top of the innate initial ranking (see §3.1.2.4, §4.2), but demoted in the face of contrary evidence in the adult model.

20. Three other logical possibilities are nasalization of the obstruent (/sin-ta/ → *sinna*), deletion of the obstruent (/sin-ta/ → *šina*), and epenthesis (/sin-ta/ → **šinə ta*). Nasalization is reported in Konjo (Austronesian, Sulawesi), though this example is complicated by heavy morphological conditioning (Friberg and Friberg 1991). Deletion of the obstruent occurs in Tagalog and other Austronesian languages, possibly as a kind of coalescence: /mən + pilih/ → *mə milih* 'to choose, vote'. Epenthesis to satisfy *NÇ is unattested – see Pater (1999a: 318–19) and cf. Wilson (1999).

21. This example is based on Casali (1996: 62–68). (The original source is Schaefer 1987. Also see Rosenthall 1994, 1997 for related discussion.) I have disregarded two complications; initial onsetless syllables and tautomorphemic vowel-vowel sequences are both tolerated. On the first, see Axininca Campa in §1.3.3. As for the second, Casali (1996: 64 n) suggests that ONSET violation is tolerated in underived environments (see Łubowicz 1999 for related discussion).

22. For analyses of Yawelmani within OT, see Archangeli and Suzuki (1996, 1997), Cole and Kisseberth (1995), McCarthy (1999), and Zoll (1993).

23. The phrase "harmonic ascent" is from Prince (1998).

24. Because markedness constraints evaluate outputs, CON would have to contain infinitely many of them to guarantee that augmentation improves the markedness of an input of any length. The finiteness of CON, then, ensures that there can never be unconditional augmentation.

25. See Moreton (1996/1999) for extensive discussion of two examples that were discovered subsequent to Anderson and Browne (1973): vowel-height alternations in Brussels Flemish and the Min tone circle.

26. This example is based on Davis (1995) as reanalyzed in McCarthy (1997).

27. This result can be subverted on a case-by-case basis – e.g., by tweaking CON to

distinguish MAX(obst) from MAX(son) – but that does not change the main point that, in general, constraint-specificity of repair cannot be guaranteed.

28. I owe my understanding of this distinction to Prince (1997a).

29. This argument comes from Grimshaw and Samek-Lodovici (1998).

30. Of course, many languages have segmental deletion for other causes. The point is that no language singles out all and only syllable-final voiced obstruents for deletion.

31. Lombardi also rejects the context-sensitive markedness constraint $]_\sigma$/*VOICE in favor of a combination of a context-free markedness constraint and positional faithfulness (§3.1.3.5). Her reason is again typological: no language deals with voiced coda obstruents by epenthesizing a vowel after them.

32. Except in floating feature situations, where a feature of the deleted segment is transferred to a nearby segment. See Goldsmith (1976a, 1976b) and much subsequent literature, especially Zoll (1996).

33. This example is based on McCarthy and Prince (1993a, 1993b, 1994a), which should be consulted for further details, discussion of additional candidates (such as *ab-abalan* or *a:*balan), and a formal proof of the results discussed here. The original data source is Prentice (1971).

34. On the nature of the input in reduplication and infixation, see McCarthy and Prince (1993b) and (1993a), respectively.

35. On harmonic completeness, see Prince and Smolensky (1993: Chapter 8, Section 2, and Chapter 9, Section 2) and Prince (1998).

36. This example is based on Aissen (1999), with simplifications and inevitable distortions. Also see Legendre, Raymond, and Smolensky (1993) for a similar approach. The locus classicus for these phenomena is Silverstein (1976).

37. There are further complications in Lummi, for the details of which see Aissen (1999).

38. This discussion is based on Mester (1994) and Prince and Smolensky (1993: Chapter 4, Section 3). Mester's analysis of *brevis brevians* (iambic shortening) shows why the output in (57) must be (a) and not (b).

39. FT-BIN has many blocking and triggering effects cross-linguistically, most of them falling under the general heading of word minimality. See, among others, Broselow (1982), Hayes (1995), Ito (1990), Ito, Kitagawa, and Mester (1996), McCarthy and Prince (1986/1996, 1990a, 1990b, 1993b), Mester (1994), Prince (1980), and Prince and Smolensky (1993).

40. This discussion is based on Legendre (1999). As usual, I have greatly simplified a complex empirical situation.

41. The sources for these examples are, respectively, Stevens (1968) and Bendor-Samuel (1970). They are analyzed in McCarthy and Prince (1995a, 1999) and Beckman (1998).

42. The correspondence constraints requiring resemblance between related words (OO-Faith) are discussed in Benua (1995, 1997) and other sources cited in §3.4 ¶31. Base-reduplicant correspondence constraints (BR-Faith) come from McCarthy and Prince (1993b, 1995a, 1999). The constraint MORPH-REAL is from Samek-Lodovici (1993) (also see Beckman 1998; Benua 1997; Gnanadesikan 1997).

43. This discussion follows Selkirk (1995, 1996), though with important simplifications. Previous analyses of these observations go back to Bresnan (1971). On the theory that underlies the analysis sketched here, see Chen (1987), Inkelas and Zec (1990,

1995), Nespor and Vogel (1986), Selkirk (1978, 1980a, 1986), and Truckenbrodt (1995, 1999).

44. Technically, it makes no sense to say that "every PWd must contain some lexical word"; because PWd's and lexical words come from different constituent-structure hierarchies, neither can "contain" the other. For this reason, PWDCON is actually defined as "every PWd must contain the terminal elements (i.e, the segments) of some lexical word."

45. This discussion is based on Samek-Lodovici (1996a, 1998), building on Tuller (1992). I have ruthlessly simplified the description and the analysis for expository purposes.

46. In tableau (63), it is crucial that violations of ALIGN-L be reckoned categorically rather than gradiently (cf. §1.1, §1.2.3, and especially (64)–(65) in §3.2.2.1). Although only gradient edge Alignment constraints were recognized at first (McCarthy and Prince 1993a; Prince and Smolensky 1993), subsequent research has shown the need for categorical Alignment constraints as well (Zoll 1996, 1997). We are dealing, then, with two distinct constraint families, and the name ALIGN should not be applied to both. For the categorical constraints, Zoll proposes the name COINCIDE.

47. These examples come from Prentice (1971: 24–25), and the analysis appears in McCarthy and Prince (1994a). The glosses are 'soul', 'slanting from vertical', and 'the price', respectively.

48. Parametric approaches are utterly pervasive in syntax but also pretty common in phonology. Some phonological examples include Archangeli and Pulleyblank (1994), Broselow (1992), Cho (1990a), Davis (1995), Hammond (1986), Hayes (1980, 1987), Kenstowicz (1983), Odden (1994), Piggott (1988), Rice (1992), and Walker (1996).

49. A further problem with relativized parameters is that they invite a kind of delusion of explanation. Absent an explicit theory of relativization, the connection between [Onset] and, say, [Onset-Medial] is merely typographic and accidental. Why could there not be a parameter [No-Onset-Medial]? Something is needed to ensure that what is marked in a restricted position is also marked generally. Similar problems do not arise in positional faithfulness theory (see the references in §3.4 ¶7).

50. Full output specification has been controversial ever since Pierrehumbert (1980). For a recent review and further references, see Myers (1998).

51. The precedence relation between the context-sensitive language-particular rules and the universal context-free default rule is usually attributed to the Elsewhere Condition, for which see the references in §1.5 ¶6.

52. Gradience is a term of art in OT. Despite this word's numerical overtones, gradient OT constraints assign only integral numbers of violation-marks, just like any other constraint.

53. This example is based on Campbell (1973), Pullum (1976), and Sapir and Swadesh (1978). The OT analysis is developed more fully in McCarthy (to appear). Dresher (1993: 238) discusses a similar example in Old English from the perspective of a mixed rule-and-constraint theory.

54. This example was provided to me by Jane Grimshaw.

55. Technically, an undominated constraint "reliably states a surface-true generalization" only if GEN supplies a compliant candidate. The effect of inclusivity/freedom of

analysis on GEN is such that, in all known cases, it does indeed supply a compliant candidate, so this qualification has no practical effect.

56. The restricted licensing of place in codas has been analyzed by Goldsmith (1990), Ito (1986, 1989), and Prince (1984), among others. The greater propensity of nasals to assimilate to stops versus nonstops is studied by Herbert (1986) and Padgett (1991, 1995c).

57. Marantz (1982: 454 n) hints at an analysis intended to solve the ordering problem in Southern Paiute. The idea is to separate reduplication into two parts, applying nasal assimilation between them: copy the nasal to yield *pin-pinti* and *win-winni*, then assimilate to produce *pim-pinti* (with no effect on *win-winni* because of the initial *w*), followed by deletion of unassimilated nasals to give *wi-winni*. The problem: how does the copying rule know that it should stop at the *n* of *pin-pinti*? Why not copy the whole root, giving *pinti-pinti? The typologically justifiable generalization is that the Southern Paiute reduplicative prefix is just exactly a possible syllable of the language (McCarthy and Prince 1986/1996, 1995b). But in the serial analysis just sketched, that generalization is a convenient accident. That is, it is an accident that copying stops when it yields a string that might make a single syllable, if the later rule of nasal assimilation can help it out. This makes the copying process covertly global, contrary to the basic tenets of rule-based serialism.

58. There is, in addition, a templatic requirement limiting the reduplicative morpheme to one syllable. Again, see McCarthy and Prince (1995b) and the literature reviewed there or the more recent work on Generalized Template Theory cited in §3.4 ¶20.

59. The references on which this example is based appear in note 43 of this chapter.

60. This example originates with Dixon (1977a, 1977b). See §3.4 ¶24 for further references.

61. The coincidence of stress and length in iambic feet is a well-documented desideratum (Buckley 1998; Hayes 1985, 1995). For instance, many languages lengthen the stressed vowel of iambic feet. Observations like this support the inference that the most harmonic iambic foot is one that contains a short-long sequence.

62. This example is based on Mascaró (1996).

63. This example is based on Bresnan (to appear-a), simplified as usual.

64. I have benefited at various times from discussions of this material with Eric Bakovic, Jill Beckman, Paul de Lacy, Ed Keer, Alan Prince, and Colin Wilson.

65. Convergence is guaranteed because of harmonic ascent (§3.1.4.5).

66. Other faithfulness constraints, not shown, are violated by candidate [A] in pass 2 and candidates [A] and [E] in pass 3.

67. Thanks to Elliott Moreton for pointing this out.

68. This example is from Hualde (1989).

69. Positional faithfulness constraints (§3.1.3.5) are also sensitive to context, but they do not seem to require crucial reference to *input* context. Some of the proposed faithful positions are obviously properties of the output (e.g., stressed syllable); others involve properties that are the same across all candidates (e.g., root, which is fixed among all candidates by "consistency of exponence" (McCarthy and Prince 1993b)).

70. This is approximately Spring's (1990) analysis of Axininca Campa.

71. Chomsky goes on to criticize an alternative analysis that dispenses with the intermediate stage. In this alternative, the V trace includes some record of incorporation, so that locality of movement can be correctly assessed on output structures. He dismisses this approach and similar proposals in phonology (cf. §3.3.3.5) as "artifice"

and "coding tricks," which deny what "seem to be fundamental properties of language, which should be captured, not obscured. . . ." These objections seem irrefutable, based as they are on a private and evidently quite selective aesthetic.

72. The material in this section is based on McCarthy (2000b), which may be consulted for fuller discussion.

73. Convergence in harmonic serialism is quite distinct from Chomsky's (1995) notion of the same name.

74. To put the matter somewhat more technically, a derivation /A/ → B → C implies in LHS that C is less marked than B is less marked than A, but in parallel OT the same /A/ → C mapping implies that C is less marked than both A and B (assuming, as in the LHS derivation, that B is more faithful than C). The LHS derivation, then, requires a ranking of CON where B is less marked than A, but this ranking is unnecessary in parallel OT. Interesting cases arise where the further ranking required in LHS is impossible because CON does not supply the required constraint(s) or because other rankings in the language contradict it. See McCarthy (2000b) for exemplification.

75. The Axininca Campa data come from Payne (1981). The analyses compared here are based very roughly on Spring (1990) (cycle) and McCarthy and Prince (1993a, 1993b) (Alignment).

76. Literal translation is not in general possible without these elaborate hedges and background assumptions, and so in real life it is never a good idea.

77. The original source for this example is Harris (1990a). It is also discussed by Benua (1997), Borowsky (1993), and Myers (1994).

78. It is sometimes suggested that only faithfulness constraints are re-rankable between levels in OT-LP (Kiparsky 1997, following Ito and Mester 1995), but the empirical consequences of this observation and the explanation for it are not yet known.

79. This discussion is based on §6.2 and §8 of McCarthy (1999), which may be consulted for further details and exemplification.

80. The Sea Dayak example originates with Scott (1957). There are analyses in Kenstowicz and Kisseberth (1979: 238) and McCarthy (1999).

81. These questions are addressed in ongoing research by Paul Smolensky and Matt Goldrick. See Goldrick (2000) for some initial results.

4

The Connections of
Optimality Theory

Optimality Theory has implications for a wide range of issues in linguistics and adjoining fields. The previous chapter dealt with phonological, morphological, and syntactic matters,[1] though with the focus always on the theory and results deducible from it, rather than on the phenomena. This chapter offers a synoptic view of some of the discoveries and issues that have emerged as the scope of OT research has expanded into other areas. Its relatively modest goals will be fulfilled if it helps readers to situate the most important questions and results in relation to the rest of OT and if the bibliography leads some readers to delve more deeply into these matters.

Perhaps because OT was originally and most extensively illustrated with phonological phenomena, there is relatively little theory-internal disagreement about the answers to some basic questions as they apply to phonology: What is the input? What does GEN do, and what candidates does it offer up? How do faithfulness constraints work? How does a theory with violable constraints obtain absolute ill-formedness? But when these same questions are asked about syntax, a thousand flowers bloom and many schools of thought contend. Furthermore, syntactic applications of OT must address an issue that is somewhat less important in phonology (see §2.3): how is it possible to have optionality or variation when EVAL usually supplies a unique optimal candidate (§1.1.2)? These questions are the topic of §4.1.

From the outset, OT has been coupled to an explicit theory of learning. It has also figured prominently in empirical studies of language acquisition, again almost from the outset. In §4.2.1, I review some OT work on formal learnability, on acquisition, and on their intersection. Also from the outset, OT has been associated with significant research on formal and computational matters. A smattering of this work is discussed in §4.3.

Formal grammar is sometimes seen as antithetical to the search for functional explanations for linguistic phenomena and to the study of language variation. In OT, though, the central premises of ranking and violability can be seen as a way to unite these different perspectives. §4.4 and §4.5 review some of this work.

This chapter concludes, as usual, with suggestions for further reading (§4.6). These suggestions are narrowly focused on OT; obviously, it is impossible and inappropriate here to abstract the literature from fields as huge and diverse as language acquisition or sociolinguistics. For some areas, though, it has proven possible to supply nearly exhaustive bibliographies of work discussing OT.

4.1 Further Issues in OT Syntax

OT is a linguistic theory whose properties are independent of phonology, syntax, or other empirical domains. Throughout Chapter 3, cross-disciplinary parallels were emphasized, and examples of rather diverse phenomena were used to illustrate points about the theory.

For historical and other reasons, though, there is a much larger body of work in OT on phonology than on syntax. As a consequence of this asymmetry, no consensus has yet emerged about certain basic issues in OT syntax. The goal of this section is to lay out these questions and some possible responses to them. I do not purport to review work in OT syntax generally, nor do I offer definitive answers to questions requiring further emprical investigation. Readers looking for a general picture of what OT has to say about syntax should not look here; instead, Chapter 3 is the place to find the main results of OT in syntax and other fields, and Legendre (to appear-a) is an introduction to the topic.

4.1.1 Some Controversial Questions

The questions to be discussed here are all rather closely related, so it makes sense to digest them all at once, here in (1).

(1) Some controversial questions in OT syntax
  a. What is the input?
  b. What are the candidates?
  c. What are the faithfulness constraints like?
  d. How is absolute ill-formedness obtained? (E.g., *John arrived surprised me.)
  e. How is optionality obtained? (E.g., I believe (that) she likes me.)

In keeping with the theory-driven, top-down perspective of the rest of this book, I am going to discuss the answers that OT as a whole gives for these questions. What can we deduce from OT's basic premises about the syntactic input, the syntactic candidates, and the other questions? Here are those partial answers:

(1a) *What is the input?* Richness of the base (ROTB) (§3.1.2.4) says that there are no language-particular restrictions on the input. The related overall philosophy is to avoid, as much as possible, using even *universal* restrictions on inputs as a way to capture generalizations (cf. §3.1.5). So the short answer to "what is the input?" is or ought to be "just about anything," as long as it can interface sensibly with GEN and the faithfulness constraints. This means, then, that the inputs should be the same in every language, except for the vocabulary. It also means that inputs should not be limited to particular kinds of structures; licit inputs might range in structural elaboration from something as literally minimal as the Minimalist numeration of lexical items[2] at one end to full-blown surface structures at the other (cf. note 14 in §3.1.3.4). It is up to the grammar to sort all this out, in syntax just as in phonology.

(1b) *What are the candidates?* This question could be restated as "what are the properties of GEN?" The key idea about GEN is inclusivity or freedom of analysis: GEN operates according to extremely general principles of well-formedness. GEN is usually not the appropriate repository for language universals (§1.1.3, §3.1.5). So the short answer to "what are the candidates?" is also "just about anything," as long as they can interface sensibly with the faithfulness and markedness constraints that must evaluate them. (See §1.1.3, especially note 8, for some cautions against misconceiving the role of GEN by extrapolating from other theories of grammar.)

(1c) *What are the faithfulness constraints like?* The general theory of faithfulness (§1.2) describes a set of constraints that penalize input/output disparity. Research in phonology suggests the need for some fairly specific faithfulness constraints, each of which militates against a particular kind of disparity (§1.2.2, §1.3.3, §3.1.3.5). Correspondence theory is a general framework for stating such constraints, and there is no obvious barrier to implementing correspondence in syntax as well (as in Bresnan to appear-a; Gerlach 1998). But this is an area where OT as a whole does not offer any special guidance, and so other imaginable theories of syntactic faithfulness constraints are fully compatible with OT's letter and spirit.

(1d) *How is absolute ill-formedness obtained?* Competition is the source of absolute ill-formedness (§3.1.2.3). If output *[B] never occurs in the inventory of some language, then *[B] is never optimal in any of its competitions with other candidates; that is, for any input I, there is always some candidate that is more harmonic than *[B], even if the input is /B/ itself. More extreme measures that go outside the bounds of classic OT, such as inviolable constraints or modularity (e.g., crashing at LF) may need to be considered, but only after the absolute ill-formedness effects obtainable from competition have been exhausted.

(1e) *How is optionality obtained?* Formal optionality, produced by the grammar, occurs if and only if some input /A/ maps onto two or more outputs [B], [C], . . . In classic OT, this can happen only if [B] and [C] incur identical violations on all constraints in CON, so EVAL must judge them to be equally harmonic (§1.1.2). Constraint ties, to be discussed in

§4.5, are a proposed extension of OT to accommodate a wider range of grammatical optionality. A broader issue arising in this context is whether observed and formal optionality are always the same thing.

These questions are all strongly interconnected. The trinity of input, candidates, and faithfulness constraints are all mutually dependent – assumptions about any one of them will affect the other two. Observations about absolute ill-formedness and optionality are the data on which theories of the input, candidates, and faithfulness will be built. We will now look into these questions in greater detail.

4.1.2 Absolute Ill-Formedness

Data from absolute ill-formedness can be brought to bear on these questions. Because competition is the source of absolute ill-formedness in OT, we can use observations about absolute ill-formedness to reason our way through the question of what the candidates are. According to the sketch in §4.1.1 or the more extensive development in §3.1.2.3, the absence of some sound, word, sentence, or other linguistic object from the surface inventory of a language is a result of how the grammar disposes of all candidates containing that object, no matter what the input. If output *[B] is absolutely ill formed – that is, *[B] is missing from the inventory of observed linguistic objects in a language – then the grammar does not select [B] as the optimal candidate relative to any input. One particularly important input is /B/ itself. Since fully faithful [B] must be a member of the candidate set derived from /B/ (§1.4.2, §3.1.4.5), the faithful mapping /B/ → [B] needs to be ruled out if *[B] is absolutely ill formed. (This is necessary but not sufficient to ensure *[B]'s ill-formedness.) The only way to rule out the /B/ → [B] mapping is to present some competitor [C] that is more harmonic than [B] relative to the input /B/. In fact, [C] must be less marked than [B], since it is certainly not more faithful. So now we have made some potentially useful inferences: the candidate set derived from /B/ by GEN contains at least [B] and [C]; there is some markedness constraint that [C] obeys and that [B] violates; and, by the Cancellation/Domination Lemma ((15) in §1.3.3), the [C]-favoring markedness constraint is ranked above any markedness or faithfulness constraint that favors [B] over [C].⊔§3.4¶3

A concrete example might make this anfractuous description more intelligible. The example is based on Grimshaw's analysis of English *do*-support, which was sketched in §3.1.3.6. Combinations of *dŏ* with another auxiliary verb are absolutely ill formed: *What will Bill dŏ eat?*, *What dŏes Bill will eat?* It is up to the grammar, not the input, to explain this observation. The explanation has two elements: (i) nonoccurring sentences like *What will Bill dŏ eat?* always compete against something that actually occurs; and (ii) the highest-ranking constraint deciding between them favors the occurring sentence over the nonoccurring one. In the crucial tableau, repeated as (2), *What will Bill dŏ eat?* and **What dŏes Bill will eat?* lose out to the competing candidate *What dŏes Bill eat?* They lose because the highest-ranking constraint deciding among them, FULL-INT, is violated by the sentences containing *dŏ*.

(2) FULL-INT decisive

		OB-HD	FULL-INT
a.	☞ [CP *wh* **will**i [IP DP **e**i [VP V *t*]]]		
b.	[CP *wh* **will**i [IP DP **e**i [XP do [VP V *t*]]]]		*
c.	[CP *wh* **do**i [IP DP **e**i [XP will [VP V *t*]]]]		*

By the same token, *dŏ* in simple declaratives, multiple *dŏ*'s, and other gratuitous uses of *dŏ* are all prohibited. *Do*-support occurs only when needed and only as much as needed to satisfy OB-HD, that is, to supply a head for projections that are otherwise headless.

This analysis supplies considerable information about the nature of the candidate set and GEN. The basis of absolute ill-formedness is failure in *every* competition, so (2b) and (2c) cannot be optimal in any candidate set, regardless of the input. Now suppose (2b) or (2c) is itself the input – a reasonable supposition, given OT's overall program of deriving regularities from the grammar rather than from the input. Among the candidates derived from that input, besides the fully faithful one, must be *dŏ*-less (2a), because it has to win to account for the absolute ill-formedness of its competitors. Similarly, the absolute ill-formedness of **What Bill eats?* shows that it loses the competition against *What dŏes Bill eat?* (see (27) in §3.1.3.6). In particular, the input /What Bill eats?/ must be analyzed unfaithfully, by adding *dŏ*. In short, candidates derived from the same input can differ in the presence or absence of *dŏ*, and so GEN must be able to add or remove *dŏ*. Or, generalizing, GEN can freely introduce or remove functional heads (cf. Grimshaw 1997b: 376).

This example illustrates an important form of argument about the nature of the candidate set and GEN that produces it. An absolutely ill-formed structure is a loser, and for every loser there must be some winner in the same candidate set. Therefore, *any* input that includes the loser structure among its output candidates must also include another candidate as winner.

This point might seem obvious, but the argument is not without its subtleties. One to watch out for is the possibility of different winners across different inputs. Suppose **[B]* is absolutely ill formed and is present in two different candidate sets, one derived from input /B/ and the other from input /C/. Because harmony is always determined relative to some input,[3] it is quite possible that the most harmonic member of the candidate set derived from /B/ is different from the most harmonic member of the candidate set derived from /C/. What is important for the absolute ill-formedness of **[B]* is that neither of these winners is [B].

But perhaps the most important subtlety of the argument is this. The winner in situations of absolute ill-formedness is not necessarily self-evident and must be determined in conjunction with a substantive theory of Con. In a case like (2), it seems obvious: (2b) and (2c) are absolutely ill formed because they lose out to the *dŏ*-less winner (2a). But what seems obvious is not. Nothing in the fundamentals of OT tells us in advance what the winner will be that eliminates (2b) or (2c). Rather, (2) represents a hypothesis about the relevant competitors, a hypothesis that depends on claims about Gen and Con. (What makes (2) seem obvious is probably the irrelevant fact that discussions of *do*-support typically present (2a–c) as a contrasting set of examples.)

One not-so-obvious possibility is for the winner to be the *null output*. §4.6¶1 Prince and Smolensky (1993: 48ff.) hypothesize that the null output is a member of every candidate set. In the context of their representational assumptions (§1.2.2) and the phenomena they were analyzing, the null output was called the *null parse*, and it consisted of a segmental string without prosodic structure. For instance, the word *[bnɪk] is absolutely ill formed in English, and one way to understand this observation is to hypothesize that input /bnɪk/ is mapped most harmonically to the null parse [b-n-ɪ-k], which consists of a string of segments with no overlaying prosodic structure. Under their assumptions, [b-n-ɪ-k] cannot be interpreted phonetically (it is "uniquely unsuited to life in the outside world"), and so the input /bnɪk/ is mapped to an output that is, to the learner's ear, null. Prince and Smolensky go on to generalize this idea to morphology – English *obtuser* is occulted (§3.1.2.4) by the unparsed root/affix set {*obtuse, er*} – and from there the idea readily generalizes to syntax. To avoid connecting this notion with any specific representational assumptions, though, I will refer to the null parse as the *null output* and will symbolize it in a representationally neutral way as "⊙". Of course, it should not be confused with the various phonetically null objects that are common in contemporary syntactic theory.

No matter what the input, the candidate ⊙ is among the candidates emitted by Gen. If Gen truly has freedom of analysis, then it is hard to see how ⊙ would *not* be a candidate, and if it is a candidate for some input, surely it must be for all. In other words, any reasonable way of defining Gen is likely to emit the candidate ⊙ for free and to include it in every candidate set.[4]

On the one hand, ⊙ is a surprisingly attractive candidate because it is as unmarked as can be. It vacuously satisfies every markedness constraint in Con. Markedness constraints either militate against the presence of structure – like Full-Int or No-Coda – or they require structure, when present, to have certain properties – like Ob-Hd, Onset, or many edge Alignment constraints. Since ⊙ has no structure whatsoever, it is never in danger of violating either kind of markedness constraint. On the other hand, ⊙ is quite unfaithful, since it retains (or "parses," in the earlier terminology) none of the material in the input. There are some technical problems with identifying exactly which faithfulness constraint(s) ⊙ violates, so I will dodge the issue here in favor of

Prince and Smolensky's original constraint M-PARSE, which $\odot$ always and only violates.

Though the null output has been employed insightfully in various phonological and syntactic analyses of absolute ill-formedness (see §4.6 ¶1), it cannot be the whole story. For example, suppose contrary to (2) that the null output were the candidate that trumps *What will Bill dŏ eat?* For this to happen, the faithfulness constraint that $\odot$ violates (here assumed to be M-PARSE) must be ranked below FULL-INT, as shown in (3).

(3) Null output as occulting body for supererogatory *do*-support

		OB-HD	FULL-INT	M-PARSE
a.	☞ $\odot$			*
b.	$[_{CP}$ *wh* **will**$_i$ $[_{IP}$ DP **e**$_i$ $[_{XP}$ do $[_{VP}$ V t $]]]]$		*	

This alternative analysis does not work, though, when further data are considered. The problem is that it also rules out all legitimate uses of *do*-support. Because $\odot$ is in every candidate set and by assumption incurs exactly the same violation-marks in every candidate set, it establishes a *harmony threshold* (Legendre, Smolensky, and Wilson 1998: 257 n. 9) for the entire language. To determine the harmony threshold, find the highest-ranking constraint that $\odot$ violates – i.e., M-PARSE. Then, since every candidate competes against $\odot$ and $\odot$ incurs exactly the same violation-marks in every candidate set, no candidate that violates any constraint ranked higher than M-PARSE can ever be optimal. In particular, *What dŏes Bill eat?*, which violates FULL-INT (see (27) in §3.1.3.6), would lose to $\odot$. The problem is that the null output can be *too* good a candidate, and it can be kept in check only by maintaining a sharp eye on M-PARSE or the equivalent.

Absolute ill-formedness can also be brought to bear on a more difficult question about the candidate set. Much work in OT syntax assumes a kind of Katz-Postal Hypothesis (Katz and Postal 1964) for GEN: loosely, the input establishes a fixed interpretation, and the candidates compete as the optimal syntactic expression for that fixed interpretation.📖§4.6¶2 But this otherwise reasonable limitation on the candidate set may not be reconcilable with all cases of absolute ill-formedness.[5]

Géraldine Legendre, Paul Smolensky, and their collaborators (Legendre, Smolensky, and Wilson 1998; Legendre et al. 1995) have used absolute ill-formedness to argue for expanding the candidate set to include competition among outputs with distinct interpretations. For example, some speakers of Italian find multiple *wh*-questions (e.g., *Who said what?*) to be ungrammatical. Starting from an input with multiple question operators (Q), such as $[Q_i\, Q_j\, [who_i$ *said what$_j$*]], what is the most harmonic candidate in Italian? The null output is apparently not a viable option in this case, since it runs into problems with the harmony threshold. Instead, they argue that the winning candidate superseding *Who said what?* in Italian is an output in which one of the *wh*-expressions is lost entirely, such as *Who said?* The interpretation of the output is not the same as that of the input. There is a cost in faithfulness, and that is important in the typology of multiple *wh*-questions, since not all languages (or even all speakers of Italian) reject them. So any constraint that militates against multiple *wh*-questions is in conflict with faithfulness when the input contains several Q operators. Faithfulness, then, keeps a brake on how far the winning candidate's interpretation can stray from the input's.

This added richness in the candidate set naturally raises certain concerns. Most theories of syntactic GEN, along with the assumption of fixed interpretation, take precautions to allow only functional elements to be deleted or inserted,⌑§4.6¶2 the worry being that otherwise candidates could be unfaithful to even the lexical items of the input (see, e.g., Ackema and Neeleman 1998a: 451). The problem is not self-evident, though. In phonology under correspondence theory (§1.2.2), the candidates [kæt] and [dɔg] compete as realizations of input /kæt/. This competition is unavoidable under any reasonable definition of what phonological GEN does. But the competition is also completely unproblematic: the /kæt/ → [dɔg] mapping is nonoptimal because it is unfaithful and brings no compensating improvement in markedness over the faithful candidate [kæt].[6] Likewise, the mapping from the syntactic input /The man fed the cat/ to the output [The man fed the dog] cannot be optimal unless the substitution of [dog] for /cat/ brings some improvement in syntactic or morphosyntactic markedness to compensate for its unfaithfulness. Study of this problem, then, needs to begin by identifying markedness constraints that might in principle be able to compel lexical substitutions. Constraints associating animacy or humanness with subjects (cf. §3.1.5.4) could be a good place to start.

In all of this discussion of the output candidates, the input has scarcely been mentioned. What is its status, especially in relation to conflicting hypotheses about GEN? One fairly typical assumption about the input in OT syntax is that it contains all and only those elements that contribute to the fixed interpretation of the associated candidate set:⌑§4.6¶2 lexical heads, their argument structure, and features like tense. On this view, only the predictable properties – functional heads or nonlexical Case, for example – are assigned by GEN. This approach recalls the PARSE/FILL model of early OT: it banished predictable prosodic structure from inputs and limited GEN to structure-building operations. While a syntactic analogue of the PARSE/FILL model is certainly a viable possibility, it does not seem necessary to limit inputs in this way. Predictability is a property of grammars, not of inputs (§3.1.3.4). Some aspect of linguistic structure is predictable in a language if faithfulness to that structure is ranked below markedness constraints that are fully dispositive of it. And if it is always predictable in every language, then CON supplies no faithfulness constraints that would protect it (§3.1.2.2). For this reason, it makes sense to include, but not insist on, inputs that contain functional projections and other predictable structure and to design the grammar to handle them correctly.[7]

4.1.3 Syntactic Optionality

"Optionality" is an imprecise term, so it is first necessary to be clear about what is intended. I will say there is *grammatical optionality* if and only if some input /A/ maps onto two or more outputs [B], [C], . . . And I will say there is *observational optionality* if and only if two or more outputs [B], [C], . . . have over-lapping distribution and similar form and meaning, so that an informed analyst might suspect that they exemplify grammatical optionality. Observational and grammatical optionality are not necessarily the same thing; to cite some obvious examples, the history of syntactic thought has seen some lively controversies over whether grammatical optionality is the basis for contrasts like *John killed Bill ~ John caused Bill to die* or *John gave the book to Mary ~ John gave Mary the book*.

Classic OT has only one resource for dealing with true grammatical optionality: the optional alternants must incur identical violation-marks from all the constraints in CON, so EVAL cannot distinguish among them. Real-life applications of this are rare, though, for reasons that will soon become apparent. One of the few is Grimshaw's (1997b: 410–11) analysis of *I think that it will rain ~ I think it will rain*. In her analysis, these sentences appear in the same candidate set and have identical violation-profiles. Since no third competitor is more harmonic, both of them are optimal. Noting some problems that arise when the full range of the constraints in CON are applied, Grimshaw writes, "The structure of OT makes the survival of more than one candidate a difficult result to achieve." The problem is that literally any constraint, no matter where it appears in the hierarchy, has the potential to break a tie (§1.4.3). Low rank is no guarantee of constraint inactivity, and even constraints relegated to the Ninth Circle of the hierarchy have this tie breaking potential. Guaranteeing optionality in this way is a prodigious exercise.

Moving beyond the original theory, constraint ties are another possible source of optionality. 📖 §4.6¶3 Two constraints are formally tied if their ranking can be freely permuted. The interesting cases involve conflicting constraints, so two different outputs emerge as optimal. (Formal ties should not be confused with underdetermined rankings, which always involve nonconflicting constraints (§1.1.2, §1.4.1).) The general theory of ties, though relevant to syntactic optionality, is taken up in the broader context of discussing language variation in §4.5.

There is one more way to deal with observational optionality: different inputs. If [B] and [C] have identical distributions and similar form and meaning, it does not necessarily follow that they come from the same candidate set. It is in principle possible that [B] and [C] are the unique most harmonic candidates derived from two distinct inputs present in the rich base. The grammatical fact is that these outputs are each derived from their respective inputs; the optionality itself is not grammatical.

Bakovic and Keer (to appear) take this approach to the observationally optional complementizer in *I think (that) it will rain.*[8] If the input contains *that*, then so does the output, as a matter of simple faithfulness. Likewise, if the input lacks *that*, then so does the output, also for reasons of faithfulness. Higher-ranking markedness constraints will override faithfulness in certain situations, either prohibiting *that* or requiring it.

In (4), for instance, are some of the input → output mappings that this grammar yields.

(4) Input → output mappings in Bakovic and Keer (to appear)

    a. /I think that the coat   ⟶   *I think that the coat won't fit him.*
       won't fit him/

    b. /I think the coat won't   ⟶   *I think the coat won't fit him.*
       fit him/

    c. /You know *wh*-coat   ⟶   *Which coat do you know won't fit him?*
       won't fit him/

    d. /You know that *wh*-coat
       won't fit him/

Abstractly, this situation is identical to the treatment of nasalized vowels in Yoruba illustrated in (21) of §3.1.3.5. An underlying distinction is preserved in one context ((4a) vs. (4b)) and neutralized in another ((4c) and (4d)). The rich base supplies these various inputs. Faithful treatment is expected, and actually observed in (4a–c), so long as no antagonistic markedness constraint dominates the relevant faithfulness constraint. But loss of *that* is compelled in (4d), because a markedness constraint crucially dominates faithfulness.[9]

On this view, the richness of the input is a positive virtue, since faithfulness to the presence or absence of functional elements in the input can account for their optional presence in the output. The grammar does the job of neutralization when there is no optionality, with neutralization going both ways: deleting functional elements where they are not permitted, as in (4d), and inserting them when they are required, as in *do*-support. As in the analogous phonological cases like Yoruba, the ranking of markedness relative to faithfulness in the grammar, rather than some property of the input, is key.

From the standpoint of traditional syntactic thinking, this analysis may seem to throw out baby, bathwater, tub, sink, and toilet, just as the treatment of allophony in §3.1.3.4 would seem ludicrous to a structuralist. Regardless of whatever discomfiture this analysis might evoke, though, it may simply be impossible to avoid. It relies on OT's basic premises and the null hypothesis about the input and the candidate set, so a skeptic's desire to exclude this analysis in principle may prove impossible to fulfill.

The questions posed at the outset are by no means settled in these brief remarks or in the literature generally. But we have seen that the overall structure of OT suggests how these questions should be approached within the theory, starting from its most basic premises.

4.2   Learnability and Acquisition

Research on language learning usually falls into one of two categories, *learnability* and *acquisition*. This distinction is somewhat artificial, since the main differences are methodological rather than substantive. Nevertheless, I follow this traditional distinction in this section, though I try to emphasize connections and convergence when appropriate.

4.2.1   Language Learnability

Imagine, in an idealized universe, that the process of language learning is compressed into just two points: the tabula not quite rasa of pure UG before any learning has happened, and the end point of full adult competence. Formal studies of language learnability typically start from this idealization and a particular theory of UG, and then they proceed to ask questions. Is every language learnable – that is, can learners be sure to get from point A to point B in finite time? How much data, what kind, and in what order do learners need to be assured of success? The goal of this research is usually formal proofs of learnability results for particular hypotheses about UG. And that is why the idealization is necessary: formal proofs are going to be impossible unless the huge space of external influences and independent variables is carefully delimited.

Another necessary step in studying language learnability is to adopt a divide-and-conquer strategy. The problem of language learning taken in its entirety is intractably huge – too hard to study, much less to prove results about. OT imposes some natural divisions on the overall problem. Since constraint ranking is the basis of language variation, it makes sense to start with the problem of learning a constraint hierarchy, assuming that the input and output are already known to the learner. This is a nontrivial assumption: the learner obviously does not already know which input is mapped onto which output, nor can the learner be expected to know all the inaudible structural details of the output. In fact, the learner is trying to figure out all of these things at the same time. The hope is that, by starting from the problem of learning a constraint ranking, the learning theory can be expanded to deal with the input → output mapping and the inaudible structure of the output. The most recent research suggests that this hope is not ill founded.📖 §4.6¶6

The problem of learning constraint hierarchies was addressed very early in the development of OT. Beginning in 1993, a learning theory for constraint ranking was developed by Bruce Tesar, working in collaboration with Paul Smolensky.📖 §4.6¶4 The key idea is that learning involves *constraint demotion*. In brief, the rationale for constraint demotion goes like this. Recall the Cancellation/Domination Lemma ((15) in §1.3.3): A is more harmonic than B if and only if every mark incurred by *A* is dominated by a mark incurred by *B* (disregarding shared marks, which are canceled). In other words, for *A* to beat *B*, *every* constraint favoring *B* over *A* must be dominated by *some* constraint favoring *A* over *B*. Learning a constraint hierarchy consists of bringing this state of affairs into existence: every *B*-favoring constraint is demoted below some *A*-favoring constraint. By proceeding in this way, the learner is guaranteed to find some hierarchy consistent with the data, if there is any hierarchy to find. ("Some hierarchy" and "any hierarchy" are deliberate choices – more on this shortly.)

One execution of this basic idea is the Recursive Constraint Demotion (RCD) algorithm. (There are other demotion algorithms, but here we will look only at RCD.) In accordance with the divide-and-conquer strategy, RCD starts from a set of known input-output pairs: $\{(in_1, out_1), (in_2, out_2), \ldots\}$. By applying GEN to each in_i, a set of failed candidates $\{loser_i^1, loser_i^2, \ldots\}$ can be produced as competitors to each out_i. Now construct a comparative tableau (§1.4.1) with rows for every pairing of in_i with the candidates out_i and $loser_i^{k}$.[10] The columns of the tableau will be all the constraints in CON, though as yet unranked. For clarity, I have used a real-life example from Axininca Campa (see (19) in §1.4.1). Tableau (5) is phonological, but it need not be, since RCD is appropriate for learning OT grammars in any empirical domain. And for simplicity, I have limited the tableau to candidates derived from one input, though in general RCD is applied to multiple inputs and their respective outputs.

(5) RCD learning: Before first pass

		ONSET	MAX	DEP	DEP$_{\text{INIT-}\sigma}$
a.	iŋ.ko.ma.ti ~ tiŋ.ko.ma.ti	L		W	W
b.	iŋ.ko.ma.ti ~ ko.ma.ti	L	W		
c.	iŋ.ko.ma.ti ~ iŋ.ko.ma.i	W		L	
d.	iŋ.ko.ma.ti ~ iŋ.ko.ma		W	L	
e.	iŋ.ko.ma.ti ~ tiŋ.ko.ma	L	W		W

Now comes the first demotion step. We know from the C/D Lemma that any loser-favoring constraint must be dominated by some winner-favoring constraint. So find all the constraints that favor only winners (MAX and DEP$_{\text{INIT-F}}$ in (5)) and demote all the constraints that favor some losers (ONSET and DEP) below them. This is the first ranking result: [MAX, DEP$_{\text{INIT-}\sigma}$ ≫ ONSET, DEP].

Tableau (5) is rewritten in (6) to reflect the results of the first demotion step. The partial ranking result is recorded in the order of the columns, while shading obscures constraints and candidates already disposed of. (A constraint has been disposed of if it favored only winners in the previous step through the algorithm. A candidate has been disposed of if some W dominates every L in its row.)

(6) RCD learning: Before second pass

		MAX	DEP$_{\text{INIT-}\sigma}$	ONSET	DEP
a.	iŋkomati ~ tiŋkomati		W	L	W
b.	iŋkomati ~ komati	W		L	
c.	iŋkomati ~ iŋkoma.i			W	L
d.	iŋkomati ~ iŋkoma	W			L
e.	iŋkomati ~ tiŋkoma	W	W	L	

This tableau is now ready for the recursive step of the RCD algorithm. Looking only at the unshaded portions of the tableau, again demote all loser-favoring constraints below the constraints that favor only winners. Recursion then terminates, because there are no constraints left to rank, and the resulting hierarchy is ⟦ MAX, DEP$_{\text{INIT-}\sigma}$ ≫ ONSET ≫ DEP⟧. That is correct.

Constraint demotion has several interesting properties.

- There is a built-in asymmetry: loser-favoring constraints are demoted. Instead, why not promote the winner-favoring constraints? This asymmetry harks back to the C/D Lemma: every loser-favoring constraint must be dominated by some winner-favoring constraint. Demotion is consistent with the quantificational structure of the C/D Lemma, because all loser-favoring constraints are demoted. A constraint promotion algorithm would have to pick some winner-favoring constraint to promote, and the choice is not always obvious. For instance, in (5) both DEP and DEP$_{\text{INIT-}\sigma}$ are eligible to be promoted above ONSET. Picking the wrong one would move the learner away from the correct ranking, possibly irrecoverably. This has been called the credit problem (Dresher 1999): when two constraints or principles concur in picking the right output, which one gets the credit? Constraint demotion avoids keeping track of which constraint does what simply by making sure that every loser-favoring constraint is crucially dominated by some winner-favoring one, in accord with the C/D Lemma.[11]
- RCD has been proven always to find some constraint hierarchy if there is any hierarchy to find and to require no more than $\frac{1}{2}*(N-1)*N$ winner-loser pairs to do it. (N is the number of constraints in CON.) For instance, the four constraints in (5) should be rankable with at most six winner-loser pairs. In fact, in this case only three pairs are actually necessary (such as (5a, b, c)).
- By design, RCD only works for consistent data: it always finds some hierarchy if there is any hierarchy to find. But inconsistent data, such as

variation in the ambient language, causes RCD to choke. For instance, if *iŋ.ko.ma.ti* and *iŋ.ko.ma.i* in (6c) were variant pronunciations of the same input, RCD would fail, since it could never reconcile the inconsistent W's and L's associated with these two outputs. Learning variation, then, will require some modification of the basic idea (§4.6 ¶14).

Constraint demotion, as in RCD and related algorithms, is a very simple idea that is nonetheless able to accomplish a lot of learning. Furthermore, it does so with little in the way of learning-specific apparatus. The demotion algorithms use universal components of OT – GEN, EVAL, and CON – to construct losers and to compare them with winners. The only thing specific to learning is constraint demotion itself, but this is related to the C/D Lemma, which derives from the nature of EVAL.

This simple learning theory produces rankings that are consistent with, but not quite the same as, those that an experienced analyst can produce. The rankings produced by constraint demotion are guaranteed to work and to find the important ranking relationships, but they are not guaranteed to find only the crucial ranking relationships. The ranking returned by the constraint demotion learning algorithm is a *stratified partial order*: constraints are grouped into blocks, called strata; strata are ranked relative to other strata; but constraints within a stratum are nonconflicting and therefore unrankable and unranked. Because constraints are demoted only when necessary, each constraint is ranked as high as possible in the stratified partial order.

The analyst, who has a global picture of the language, can find the crucial rankings. They are consistent with the stratified partial order found by the learning algorithm (i.e., the analyst and the algorithm will not impose opposite rankings on any constraints), but they are more narrowly specified. For example, the demotion algorithm might return the stratified partial order $[\![\{A, B\} \gg C]\!]$, when in fact the only crucial ranking is $[\![A \gg C]\!]$ because B and C do not interact. In other words, while the algorithm always produces a stratified partial order, analysts can come up with any kind of partial order (like (8) in §3.1.2.2). In general, partial orders can be incompletely connected, nonstratified, and without a top or bottom, reflecting the crucial interactions actually observed in some language.

The difference between the ranking found by constraint demotion and the ranking that an analyst finds is particularly important when it comes to learning phonotactic patterns (see §3.1.2.4 for parallel discussion of this point). Phonotactic patterns are passive restrictions on the phonological inventory: they are clearly part of adult speakers' knowledge, but they are not supported by direct evidence in the form of alternations. For instance, speakers of English know that words with initial stop + nasal clusters, such as **bnick*, are unpronounceable. Yet the rich base (§3.1.2.4) must supply these clusters, since some languages do permit them: German *Knecht* 'servant', *Gnade* 'grace', Polish *dnia* 'day (gen. sg.)', *pnie* 'trunk (nom. pl.)'. We therefore know that inputs like

/bnik/, which are present in the rich base, are mapped unfaithfully to something else in English, such as [nik]. To compel this unfaithful mapping, the grammar of English must contain an $[\![M \gg F]\!]$ ranking where the markedness constraint against initial stop + nasal clusters dominates some appropriate faithfulness constraint, such as MAX. The puzzle: how can a learner discover this ranking from positive evidence alone?

The problem is that phonotactic patterns that are unsupported by alternations are statements about what is not present in the primary data, and so exposure to positive evidence is of no assistance. This is the well-known subset problem: learners who at some stage know a superset language (e.g., {[bnik], [nik], [bik], . . .}) can never get to a subset language (e.g., {[nik], [bik], . . .}, but *[bnik]) with only positive evidence.

Here is a concrete instance of the subset problem. Suppose learning starts with the unranked initial state $[\![*\text{STOP} + \text{NASAL, MAX}]\!]$.[12] Children learning German are bound to hear [knī] *Knie* 'knee'. The constraint demotion algorithm will then force demotion of *STOP + NASAL. But children learning English never hear anything in the primary data that would tell them to demote MAX, and so their grammars will remain in the unranked initial state. This renders unattainable the adult grammar of English, which should have the ranking $[\![*\text{STOP} + \text{NASAL} \gg \text{MAX}]\!]$.

This may look like a failure of constraint demotion and a counterexample to the (formally proven) thesis that demotion will always find some hierarchy consistent with the data, if there is any hierarchy to be found. In fact, there is no counterexample. The ranking $[\![*\text{STOP} + \text{NASAL, MAX}]\!]$ is consistent with the primary data – that is, the positive evidence. It is wrong in a sense that the analyst but not the learner can detect, since only the analyst has access to negative evidence, such as the fact that adults reject words starting with [bn]. There is no literal disagreement between RCD's ranking $[\![*\text{STOP} + \text{NASAL, MAX}]\!]$ and the analyst's more completely specified ranking $[\![*\text{STOP} + \text{NASAL} \gg \text{MAX}]\!]$, but to account for the ability of speakers to judge [bn] as ill formed, it is somehow necessary to force the analyst's ranking to be the right one.

The solution to this problem, like all subset problems, is to start from a bias toward the subset language and then to expand toward the superset language only in response to positive evidence. In OT, one influential proposal for implementing this strategy is the idea that learners start from an $[\![M \gg F]\!]$ *initial state*.🕮 §4.6¶5 It describes a ranking bias present at the beginning of learning, with all markedness constraints above all faithfulness constraints. This initial ranking maximizes the unfaithful mappings, contracting the rich input set down to the minimal output set. The ontogenetically first grammar, then, produces a language that is a subset of all ontogenetically future languages. In learning, individual markedness constraints are demoted below individual faithfulness constraints on the basis of positive evidence. If all goes well, the learning process will expand and never contract the language produced on the way to the adult model.

Learners of both English and German start out with the same initial state ⟦*STOP + NASAL ≫ MAX⟧, with markedness over faithfulness. This ranking forces certain unfaithful mappings, as shown in (7).

(7) An ⟦M ≫ F⟧ ranking in the initial state

/kni/		*STOP + NASAL	MAX
a.	☞ ni		*
b.	kni	*	

Learners of English are content to remain in this state, since they never hear words like [kni] in the ambient language. The learner of German, though, is exposed to words like [kni]. This exposure forces demotion of *STOP + NASAL below MAX. The initial bias, then, allows the grammar of the subset language to be attainable without interfering with learning the superset language.

This approach recalls the idea of *process suppression* in the theory of Natural Phonology (§2.1). Natural Phonology assumes a set of innate rewrite rules, called processes. Deletion of initial stops before nasals is one of them. Learning consists of process suppression in the face of positive evidence. Exposure to the word *Knie* will cause learners of German to suppress the stop-deletion process. Learners of English, lacking that exposure, will have no reason to suppress the innate process, and so it will persist into adult competence.

Like the innate processes of Natural Phonology, the ⟦M ≫ F⟧ initial ranking establishes important connections between formal studies of learnability and empirical studies of acquisition. For more on this topic, see §4.2.2.

RCD and the related algorithms are not the whole story about learning in OT. These algorithms can only learn the ranking if presented with full structural descriptions of the outputs and a set of input → output mappings. The former is a concern in both phonology and syntax: inaudible, nonuniversal structural characteristics of outputs need to be determined by the learner in the context of also determining the grammar that yields those structures. The latter is a particular concern in phonology: how are underlying forms to be established when the properties of the underlying forms and of the grammar itself are mutually dependent? These are difficult problems, and to my knowledge no theory of language has completely solved them. But extensions of the basic constraint demotion algorithm have made considerable headway. See the suggested readings for pointers to the literature on these extensions of constraint demotion📖§4.6¶6 and for research on alternative approaches to learnability in OT.📖§4.6¶7

4.2.2 Language Acquisition

This section reviews some of the issues and results emerging from work that relates empirical research on acquisition to the predictions of OT. Nearly all of this work is about learning the phonology of a first language by normally developing children.[13] The emphasis, as in Chapter 3, is on a top-down approach: first ask what the theory says, and then relate this to empirical research. 📖§4.6¶8 Classic OT makes certain basic predictions about language acquisition. Because these predictions follow from the nature of the theory rather than from special, auxiliary assumptions about learning, they are much the same as the general results of OT discussed in Chapter 3.

> **(i)** **Continuity.** Developing grammars and mature grammars are made out of the same stuff – universal CON, GEN, and EVAL – so there should be no qualitative differences between child grammars and adult grammars. Concretely, every process or restriction at work in acquisition should also be possible in the synchronic grammars of adults.
>
> **(ii)** **Typology.** Grammars, whether in children or adults, are permuted rankings of the constraints in CON (§1.2.1, §3.1.3.2, §3.1.5.3). As a kind of corollary to continuity, the developmental stages in children's grammars ought to mimic the diversity seen in language typology. And if the ⟦M ≫ F⟧ initial state is assumed (§4.2.1), then the developmental steps ought to show demotion of markedness constraints along the way.
>
> **(iii)** **Ranking.** In language learning, one grammar replaces another. Since OT grammars are constraint hierarchies (§1.1), learning involves re-ranking, perhaps via constraint demotion (§4.2.1).
>
> **(iv)** **Violability.** Constraints are violable, but violation is minimal. A constraint that is demoted in the course of acquisition may still be visibly active in some circumstances, since demotion is no guarantee of inactivity (§1.3.4, §3.2.2, §3.2.3).
>
> **(v)** **Emergence of the unmarked** (§3.2.2). Developing grammars may show the effects of processes for which there is no evidence in the adult model. This is an expected consequence of the universality of CON.
>
> **(vi)** **Homogeneity of target/heterogeneity of process** (§1.3.2, §3.1.4.2). Different developing grammars (different children or different stages in the development of one child) may satisfy the same output target in different ways.
>
> **(vii)** **Richness of the base** (§3.1.2.4). OT shifts the emphasis from learning a lexicon to learning a grammar. This may have implications for the *comprehension/production dilemma*, in which children's ability to perceive is often far in advance of their ability to produce.

These are rich and sometimes controversial topics, so comprehensive discussion is simply not possible here. We can have brief encounters with each though, perhaps to be pursued further using the suggested readings (§4.6).

Before going on to consider each of these points, we first need to be explicit about how OT grammars function in learning phonology at around age 2. The child is seeking to master the basic inventory of segments and structures and their distribution (§3.1.2, §3.1.3). At this stage, the input to the child's developing grammar is the adult surface form, as perceived by the child. The output is the result of applying the child's developing grammar to this input. The properties of the child's grammar, then, are inferred by discrepancies between the adult model and the child's pronunciation. These assumptions are standard in much work on the acquisition of phonology before and since OT.

Now to the points (i)–(vii) themselves:

(i)–(iii). Continuity, typology, and ranking are related aspects of the same basic claim of OT: that a grammar of a language is a particular permutation of a set of universal constraints. Developing grammars should differ from each other (over time in one child, among different children acquiring the same language, and among children acquiring different languages) in the same way that the adult grammars of different languages differ. If the $[\![M \gg F]\!]$ initial ranking is also assumed, with demotion of markedness constraints in response to positive evidence, then the observed course of language development ought to begin with only unmarked outputs, followed by inclusion of progressively more marked outputs until the adult model has been matched. This is, of course, hardly a new claim (see, e.g., Jakobson 1941), but it is significant that OT provides a formal basis for it.

Explaining the course of phonological development has always been a serious and possibly insurmountable challenge to rule-based phonology. The problem is quite basic: early child phonology seems to involve many more rules than the target adult phonology, including many rules that are not supported by the adult models. If rules are acquired by learners who are outfitted only with a general theory of rule formulation and some sort of rule-acquisition device, where do all these early rules come from and where do they go later on? Except for the general theory of rule formulation and phonological representations, the learner is supposed to be a tabula rasa whose grammar should only contain rules that can be induced from the adult models. Even the most basic observations about child phonology show that this prediction is very far off the mark. For that reason, empirical research on child phonology and research on phonological theory prior to OT rarely intersected.

When we turn from this broad picture to the details, empirical research on acquisition largely bears out the predictions made by OT with the $[\![M \gg F]\!]$ initial ranking. For example, Levelt and van de Vijver (to appear) show that the observed stages in the learning of Dutch syllable structure accord well with observations about syllable-structure typology and the predictions of a plausible theory of syllabic markedness constraints in CON. Children learning Dutch start out by producing only CV syllables. These syllables are typologically unmarked, since they occur in every language, and they are unmarked in the formal sense, since they violate no markedness constraints in CON. The course of acquisition gradually introduces other syllable types as the markedness constraints NO-CODA, ONSET, and so on are each demoted below some antagonistic faithfulness constraint. The grammars at intermediate stages of development parallel the adult grammars of other languages. Other examples are easy to find.

For instance, children acquiring English are often observed to produce stops in place of fricatives: [tei] for *say*, [du] for *zoo*. Correlatively, there are languages with no fricatives, such as most of the Aboriginal languages of Australia, but all languages have stops. Fricatives are marked relative to stops – they violate more markedness constraints – both ontogenetically and typologically.

The details also reveal interesting research problems, where the match between theory and observation is imperfect. In the Dutch case, constraint demotion from an ⟦M ≫ F⟧ initial state somewhat underdetermines the course of acquisition. Dutch children consistently learn CVC syllables before they learn V syllables. Nothing in the formal grammar says that NO-CODA should be demoted before ONSET is. But since coda-bearing syllables are much more common in Dutch than onsetless ones, there is presumably an effect of frequency here on acquisition order. Dutch children also produce VC syllables after V syllables, and in general they show a pattern of first producing forms that violate only the newly demoted markedness constraint before forms that violate that constraint and some other. This is reminiscent of the worst-of-the-worst behavior that has been attributed to local constraint conjunction (§1.2.3) or, more remotely, weighted connections (§2.4, §4.5). (See Boersma and Levelt 2000 for a model that incorporates numerically weighted rankings and frequency effects.)

Perhaps the biggest challenge to continuity, in phonology at least, is the phenomenon of *consonant harmony*. In the speech of many children, the consonants in a word are obliged to have identical place and/or manner of articulation: [gɔk] for *sock*, [mayp] for *knife*, [bebu] for *table* (Amahl Smith at 2 years, 2 months). No comparable process is observed in adult speech, though there have been some interesting proposals for connecting consonant harmony in children with reduplicative and root-and-pattern morphology in adults.[14] Of course, the problem is no different for a rule-based theory: why should children be able to "acquire" a rule that is completely unprecedented in the phonology of adults?

(iv). Constraints are violable, but violation is always minimal and must be compelled (§1.1.1, §1.2.1, §3.2). Demoting a constraint is not the same as changing the setting of a parameter (see the various cross-references in the FAQ about parameters), and this has important consequences in development (Pater 1997). A demoted constraint may persist in its effects, not as some sort of developmental anachronism, but as a real part of the grammar. Indeed, the effects of a demoted constraint may persist into adulthood. Even constraints that are crucially dominated will be visibly active in circumstances where the higher-ranking constraints are irrelevant or otherwise nondecisive. To guarantee complete inactivity of a dominated constraint is at best difficult and may be impossible in some cases. Parameters, in contrast, typically have just two states, one of which is a state of complete inactivity.

Pater documents several cases where the course of development involves demoting a constraint, which leads to partial activity, rather than switching a parameter value, which leads to complete inactivity. For example, many children learning English will, at around age 2, aggressively truncate words to fit a particular preferred shape. Monosyllabic words remain unchanged, as do disyllabic words with penultimate stress (*gárbage, rábbit*). But disyllabic or trisyllabic words with an initial unstressed syllable lose it: *giráffe* → [wæːf], *spaghetti* → [géːdi]. The Procrustean bed into which these words are being forced is the trochaic stress foot, consisting of a single stressed syllable or a stressed syllable followed by an unstressed one. Monosyllables and words like *garbage* already fit the trochaic requirement, but words with an initial unstressed syllable are brought into conformity with it at the expense of faithfulness.

Truncation is also observed in adult grammars, sometimes on its own but more often as a concomitant of reduplication (e.g., *t ʲ-ílpa-t ʲílparku* in Diyari [Pama-Nyungan, Australia]). The shape of a truncated form, called its *template*, is determined by markedness constraints on prosodic structure.[15] For present purposes, the important one is PARSE-σ, which demands that the syllables of a word be exhaustively parsed into feet.

In the earlier stages of development, the markedness constraint PARSE-σ is ranked above the faithfulness constraint MAX (the ⟦M ≫ F⟧ initial state). Unfootable syllables are consequently lost, as shown in (8).

(8) Truncation in child phonology

/spa(ghétti)/		PARSE-σ	MAX
a.	☞ '(ghétti)		***
b.	spa(ghétti)	*	

Recall that the adult model is the input in early phonology. A word consisting of just a trochaic foot (indicated by the parentheses) is more harmonic than a word containing a trochaic foot plus an unfooted syllable.[16]

In the course of learning, PARSE-σ is demoted below MAX, and the adult model becomes the output of the grammar. But demotion is not annihilation. Though crucially dominated, PARSE-σ is still active in the adult phonology. It is not able to compel unfaithfulness to the input, but it is still able to force exhaustive foot parsing in words with even numbers of syllables, such as *(Àla)(báma)* or *(ìpe)(càcu)(ána)*. Minimal violation of PARSE-σ demands exhaustive footing when no higher-ranking constraint is at stake.

This example and others like it show that language learning cannot be reduced to process suppression, in the Natural Phonology sense, or parameter setting, in the manner of P&P and similar theories. Since it emerges in early acquisition, PARSE-σ would correspond to a natural process in Natural Phonology or to an unmarked parameter value in P&P. Exposure to words like *spaghetti* in the ambient language would eventually cause learners to suppress that process or to switch that parameter value, but then a suppressed process or a switched-off parameter should have no force at all. Process suppression or parameter setting are unable to make a connection between the vigorous prosecution of PARSE-σ in the language of children and its less vigorous effect in the language of adults.[17] OT, on the other hand, makes this basic connection: child phonology may show the consistent effect of a markedness constraint that is violated but still active in the language of adults.

(v). **Emergence of the unmarked** (§3.2.2) in first-language acquisition has been recognized at least since Jakobson (1941). Child phonology often shows the effects of processes for which there is no evidence in the surrounding language of adults. As we saw in (i–iii), such processes are the result of an early ⟦M ≫ F⟧ ranking.

A less-noticed phenomenon is TETU in second-language acquisition. It was first recognized in the theory of Natural Phonology (Donegan and Stampe 1979: 133; Stampe 1969: 445). Syllable-final obstruent devoicing is a natural process (§2.1, §3.1.5.3). Children learning English, French, or Arabic encounter final voiced obstruents in the primary data, and so they suppress that process. Children learning German, Polish, or Catalan are not exposed to final voiced obstruents, and so they never have reason to suppress the process.

Now, what about children learning a language with no final obstruents at all, such as Japanese, Vietnamese, Hawai'ian, or Mandarin Chinese? Lacking exposure to final voiced obstruents, these children should persist into adulthood with a potentially active but effectively inert process of final obstruent devoicing. This latent process can emerge when, as adults, they begin to learn English as a second language (or merely borrow English words [Lovins 1974: 242]).

The same prediction is made by OT with the ⟦M ≫ F⟧ initial state. Having no reason to demote the markedness constraint that prohibits final voiced obstruents, learners of Japanese or similar languages will retain the initial ranking into adulthood. Attempts to learn a second language like English should produce the same neotenous effect as in Natural Phonology.

This prediction is correct. For example, Broselow, Chen, and Wang (1998) and Wang (1995) show that Mandarin speakers learning English encounter greater difficulties with final *b/d/g* than final *p/t/k*. At one stage of learning, the markedness constraint against all final obstruents has been demoted below faithfulness, but this has merely exposed a specific constraint against final *voiced* obstruents, which was latent in the grammar of Mandarin speakers but had no opportunity to be visibly active. As in Natural Phonology, the universal constraint is there, even if it has no overt effects.[18]

Observations like this have always been problematic for theories of learning based on the acquisition of language-particular rules. Learners of Japanese or similar languages have no reason to learn a final devoicing rule, and when they study English, they find no reason to learn the rule there either. Nevertheless, they apply this unlearned and unlearnable rule to English words. The explanation given by OT (or Natural Phonology, for that matter) is that nothing is learned: because of the $[\![M \gg F]\!]$ initial state and the universality of CON, Japanese and Mandarin speakers have a latent process of final devoicing in their grammars, ready to be exposed when they attempt to pronounce English.

Expanding on this point, an OT perspective on second-language acquisition may offer a partial resolution to the vexed question of transfer versus universals. A perennial issue in the study of second-language acquisition is the relative contribution of transfer of aspects of the L1 grammar to L2 versus direct influences of UG on L2. The final devoicing case just discussed shows that both approaches are right, in a sense: the grammar of L1 is being transferred to L2, since the grammars of Japanese or Mandarin contain the $[\![M \gg F]\!]$ ranking responsible for final devoicing; but the grammars have this ranking for universal reasons, since the $[\![M \gg F]\!]$ initial state and CON are universal. Still to be addressed is the question of whether learned rankings in L1 are also transferred to L2.

(vi). **Homogeneity of target/heterogeneity of process** (§1.3.2, §3.1.4.2) is the observation that, between languages or within a language, the same output target can be satisfied in diverse ways. It is an expected consequence of the markedness/faithfulness dichotomy and the interaction of constraints through ranking. The path of acquisition shows similar diversity, as a markedness constraint is satisfied in different ways across different children, different stages of development, or different contexts.

For example, the effects of a markedness constraint prohibiting initial consonant clusters (*COMPLEX-ONSET) are conspicuous in developing phonologies at around age 2. Three different kinds of unfaithful mappings are observed in support of this constraint:[19] cluster reduction, where one of the consonants is simply dropped (Gita's [so] for *snow*, Amahl's [ŋeːk] for *snake*); epenthesis, where a vowel breaks up the cluster (d[ə]*warf*); and coalescence, where the distinctive features of the two consonants are merged into one (Gita's [pɪkəw] for *twinkle*, [fok] for *smoke*). Children may differ in this respect; Amahl consistently has reduction, but Gita has both reduction and coalescence, depending on the composition of the cluster and its local context.

Gnanadesikan (1995/to appear) and Barlow and Gierut (1999) show how these differences can be obtained from constraint interaction. According to Gnanadesikan, Gita has a rather complex hierarchy of conditions favoring coalescence or reduction. The facts, somewhat simplified, are shown in (9).

(9) Gita's disposition of initial clusters

    a. If one of the consonants is a labial, coalesce to form a labial consonant with the manner features of the least sonorous member of the cluster:

tree	[pi]	[t] is less sonorous + [r] is labial[20] → [p]
smell	[fɛw]	[s] is less sonorous + [m] is labial → [f]
squeeze	[biz]	[k] is least sonorous + [w] is labial → [b][21]

  b. But not if a round vowel follows:
      draw   [dɔ]   *[bɔ]
      straw   [dɔ]   *[bɔ]
  c. Otherwise, delete all consonants in the cluster except its least
     sonorous member:
      please   [piz]   [p] is less sonorous than [l]
      friend   [fɛn]   [f] is less sonorous than [r]
      spoon   [bun]   [p] is less sonorous than [s] (see note 21)
      snow   [so]   [s] is less sonorous than [n]
      sleep   [sip]   [s] is less sonorous than [l]

All of these outputs satisfy the markedness constraint *COMPLEX-ONSET, but
they do so in diverse ways. Gita preserves the cluster's least sonorous member,
whatever its position, deleting the rest. (Compare Amahl, who deletes *s* in *spoon*
and *snow*.) The same generalization holds in (9a), but with a twist: if the deleted
consonant is labial, it joins its labiality to the consonant that is preserved, in a
form of coalescence. But coalescence is blocked, and simple deletion occurs
instead for dissimilatory reasons, when coalescence would create a labial consonant followed by a vowel that is also labial.

In traditional terms (§2.1), this would be called a conspiracy, since several
seemingly distinct processes – deletion of the first consonant, deletion of the
second, and coalescence – are operating to achieve the same output target. In
OT, the conspiracy is unpacked into interacting markedness and faithfulness
constraints (§3.1.4.3). The markedness constraint *COMPLEX-ONSET is undominated, with other constraints determining which of the compliant candidates is
chosen. Two faithfulness constraints are involved, general MAX and its less
stringent counterpart MAX(labial), which supports preservation of labiality, possibly at the expense of other places of articulation. Markedness constraints are
also involved in controlling the outcome. The markedness hierarchy favoring
low-sonority onsets (§1.2.3) ensures, for example, [kin] over *[lin] for *clean*.
Another markedness constraint, part of the overall theory of dissimilation, crucially dominates MAX(labial), favoring [dɔ] over *[bɔ] for *draw*. Significantly,
both of these latter markedness effects are only emergent: they decide how to
simplify a cluster, where unfaithfulness is forced by *COMPLEX-ONSET, but they
do not compel unfaithful analysis of words that already begin with single consonants. The ranking and interaction of these constraints is not different in kind
from the conspiracy example discussed in §3.1.4.3; Gnanadesikan's paper can
be consulted for the details.

(vii). Richness of the base is the thesis that there are no language-
particular constraints on inputs (§3.1.2.4). The set of inputs can therefore be
thought of as universal and innate. Smolensky (1996b) has proposed that ROTB
offers a line of attack on the comprehension/production dilemma in language
acquisition.[22] Children can hear distinctions in the speech of others that they
themselves cannot produce. A child who produces [kæ] for both *cat* and *cap* is

still able to hear the difference between these words. The "dilemma" for the analyst, then, is how comprehension can be so much better than production in early acquisition.

This fact is often seen as evidence for separate comprehension and production grammars developing at different rates, but Smolensky argues that a single grammar is involved, running in both directions. What appears to be a difference in development is actually a result of differences in how constraint evaluation works when the grammar is used in one direction or the other. Throughout this section, we have been looking at productive competence: from a presumed input /kæt/, which matches the adult model, the learner's grammar selects the output [kæ]. The grammar, then, is [No-Coda ≫ Max]. No learning was required to come up with this grammar, since it is provided by the [M ≫ F] initial state.

Smolensky asks a different question: how does the learner use the [No-Coda ≫ Max] initial ranking receptively? The learner hears [kæt] and attempts to assign an input to it. The rich base supplies a set of candidate inputs. Lexicon optimization (§3.1.2.4) says that learners select the input that gives the most harmonic input → output mapping. The modified *tableau des tableaux* in (10) (cf. (12) in §3.1.2.4) compares several candidate inputs for [kæt].

(10) *Tableau des tableaux* for perceived [kæt]

Candidate Inputs	Perceived Output	No-Coda	Max
a. ☞ /kæt/		*	
b. /kæ/	[kæt]	*	*
c. /æ/		*	**
d. /dɔg/		*	***

The learner, grasping the received output form [kæt], is trying to find the optimal input for it among the space of possibilities afforded by ROTB. Markedness constraints like No-Coda are of no help, since markedness constraints evaluate only output forms, and the output form is a given. Only faithfulness constraints are relevant, so lexicon optimization will choose the input that gives the most faithful input → output mapping. Upon hearing [kæt], then, the learner will assign the input /kæt/, because the /kæt/ → [kæt] mapping has no faithfulness violations. But when the grammar is run in the productive direction, candidate outputs will differ in performance on No-Coda and other markedness constraints, and so /kæt/ will be mapped unfaithfully to [kæ]. In short, the source of the comprehension/production dilemma is a basic asymmetry in markedness constraints – they evaluate only outputs – coupled with a basic symmetry in faithfulness constraints – they evaluate input → output mappings.

This is not the whole story about the role of the lexicon in phonological development. For one thing, though receptive competence develops in advance of productive competence, it does indeed develop, and this requires some modifications of the model just sketched (Pater to appear-a). For another, this model by itself will not account for the learning of underlying representations in paradigms with alternations. (An example is the devoicing process in German, Polish, etc. See (44) in §3.1.5.3.) That lacuna is not surprising: there are virtually no empirically based, theoretically informed investigations of the later stages of phonological development, even in terms of rule-based phonology (cf. Kiparsky and Menn 1977). Dinnsen and McGarrity (1999) is the only empirically based OT work on the subject known to me, though there are various proposals addressing morphophonemic alternations as an abstract learnability problem (Hale and Reiss 1997, 1998; Hayes to appear; McCarthy 1998; Tesar and Smolensky 2000: 77ff.).

The Jakobsonian insight that markedness theory links language acquisition with language typology has generally eluded formal analysis. Although Natural Phonology made considerable headway on this matter, rule-based phonology in general shed little or no light on acquisition or its relationship to typology. OT, though, establishes a direct connection between acquisition and typology, since the same markedness constraints are involved in both. This fact, and the learnability results of §4.2.1, emphasize the extent to which OT tightly integrates a theory of grammar and a theory of learning.

4.3   Formal and Computational Analysis

Because the premises of OT are relatively simple, the theory lends itself fairly readily to formal and computational analysis of its properties and consequences. Moreton's harmonic ascent results, which were discussed in §3.1.4.5, are an excellent example of this kind of research: a claim about the relationship between the actual output and the fully faithful candidate is proven formally and related to typological observations about circular chain shifts and other phenomena. The work by Tesar and others on learnability, some of which was summarized in §4.2.1, is another fine example, showing how an aspect of OT can be analyzed formally and abstractly and also modeled computationally in a way that ultimately brings greater understanding to the theory as a whole. This section looks briefly at some other work in the same vein, focusing on one issue of broadest interest and supplying references to other research.⌑§4.6¶11

A question that often arises on first exposure to OT concerns the vastness of the candidate set: how is it possible, in a theory based on comparing candidates, to find the optimal member of the huge set of candidates derived by GEN from each input (§1.1.3)? In syntax, which uncontroversially includes recursive operations, there is no nonarbitrary bound on the length of candidates, and so there must be infinitely many of them. In phonology, the theoretical possibility of iterated epenthesis (/ba/ $\rightarrow$ *ba?i ?i ?i . . .*) likewise cannot be excluded in advance, so the phonological candidates are also of unbounded length and so of infinite number. First computing and then sorting an infinite set is not a successful strategy for producing utterances in finite time.

It is important to realize, as the discussion in §1.1.3 emphasizes, that this issue pertains to language performance and not to language competence. OT is a theory of competence in the sense and tradition of Chomsky (1965, 1968, 1995): a grammar is a function from inputs to outputs, and like any function it must be well defined. Whether the function is also efficiently computable is a matter for a performance model to address. The question of efficient computation is certainly important in its own right, but it is not a question that is properly asked of a competence model.

Research on efficiently computable performance models for OT began rather early on with the work of Tesar (1994, 1995a, 1995b) and others. 📖 §4.6¶11 Tesar's approach to finding the optimal candidate is abstractly analogous to his solution to the learnability problem (§4.2.1). The wrong way to learn an OT grammar is to start by computing all the ranking permutations and then try to find the right needle in this vast haystack; the right way is to start with *some* ranking and use a strategy like RCD that is guaranteed to find the correct one by successive approximation. The wrong way to approach optimization is to start by computing all the candidates and try to find the right needle in an infinite haystack; the right way is to start with some candidate(s) and use a strategy of successive approximation that is guaranteed to provide a small set of candidates that includes the optimal one.

Tesar's approach uses dynamic programming; here, I will describe it in very general terms, glossing over much technical detail. Candidates are constructed by analyzing the input one element at a time. For example, in phonology, the input might be analyzed segment by segment from left to right. The algorithm is initialized with a set of candidates consisting of all the ways of disposing of the initial input segment: adjoin to a syllable, delete, and so on. Then each newly exposed piece of the input is accommodated into the preexisting structure by applying one or more elementary operations, whose nature is determined by the characteristics of GEN. For example, in phonology, these operations might include adjunction to a syllable, deletion, and epenthesis. Crucially, the operations are applied only if they increase the harmony of the partially formed candidate relative to the language's constraint hierarchy. It will sometimes be the case that more than one operation is in principle applicable. When there is a conflict like this, the operation that applies is the one that yields the most harmonic result, again according to the constraint hierarchy of the language under analysis. The result is a set of candidates that have, in a sense, already been vetted by the constraint hierarchy. The optimal form is among these candidates, and it is easily chosen from among the small array of possibilities.

What about the infinity of candidates? Though the competence model recognizes infinitely many candidates with no upper bound on their length, the performance model just sketched does not need to tangle with the vastness of the candidate set because the candidate-building operations are applicable only if they increase harmony, and infinite stretches of epenthetic segments will never increase harmony. This result has been seen previously in relation to harmonic ascent (§3.1.4.5) and is formally proven by Moreton (1996/1999). The general result, then, is that infinite size of candidates is not an issue, so the infinite number of candidates is not an issue either.

Tesar's work establishes that the infinity of candidates presents no great challenge to a performance model for OT, and, indeed, computationally efficient approaches to OT are demonstrably possible. Starting from a very different point, Samek-Lodovici and Prince (1999) make considerable headway in bringing the infinity of candidates under formal control in the competence model itself.

The candidates derived from some input are infinitely many because the candidate set contains infinitely many *losers*. A loser, in the special sense I will be employing just in this section, is a candidate that cannot be optimal under any permutation of the constraints in CON; it is really a perpetual loser. (In phonology, iterated epenthesis supplies losers in abundance.) Scattered here and there throughout the candidate set are finitely many *winners*. This term is also being used in a special way to refer to those candidates that are optimal under at least one permutation of the constraints in CON.

The winner/loser distinction is important for the following reason (Samek-Lodovici and Prince 1999: 34): "all it takes [for a candidate] to be optimal for some ranking is to best all other winners, in principle freeing the learner and the analyst from comparing the winners with the infinite set of losers." In other words, the only serious competitors to the optimal form are other winners, other candidates that are optimal under at least one permutation of CON. The losers are optimal under no permutation, so they are out of the competition. The comparative effects of EVAL, then, are really only important over the quite finite set of winners, since all the losers are beyond the pale. If the winners and losers can be segregated in advance, then EVAL need never contend with infinite sets of candidates, and so the competence model itself will have a finitary cast.

Samek-Lodovici and Prince develop conditions that are necessary and sufficient for determining whether any candidate is a winner or a loser simply by applying the constraints in CON without regard to ranking. The key idea is a generalization of the notion of harmonic bounding. Recall (from (9) in §1.3.1) that B harmonically bounds C relative to some input /A/ if and only if B incurs a proper subset of C's violation-marks. This makes C categorically worse than B, in a ranking-independent way, as an output from /A/. Hence, the /A/ $\rightarrow C$ mapping is impossible or, in the terms just introduced, C is a certain loser. (Whether B is a winner depends on its relations to other candidates and other constraints.)

Any harmonically bounded candidate is a loser, but not all losers are harmonically bounded. Harmonic bounding deals only with the situation where one candidate bounds another; the more general situation involves several candidates collectively bounding the loser. Tableau (11) represents the simplest situation.

(11) Collective harmonic bounding

/A/	C1	C2
B	**	
C	*	*
D		**

Suppose there are no other constraints or candidates in this universe. *B* and *D* are winners, depending on whether C1 or C2 is ranked higher. But *C* is a loser: it cannot outperform its competitors under either ranking of the two constraints. Yet *C* is not harmonically bounded by *B* or *D* individually, since *C* does not have a proper superset of either *B*'s or *D*'s violation-marks. Rather, *C* is harmonically bounded by *B* and *D* collectively, so *B* and *D* together constitute *C*'s *bounding set*. The original sense of harmonic bounding is simply a special case of collective harmonic bounding where the bounding set contains only one candidate.

A perpetual loser is a candidate that has a non-null bounding set, such as *C* in (11). A sometime winner is a candidate that has only a null bounding set, like *B* or *D* in (11). In general, the bounding set for the loser *C* must have the following characteristics (after Samek-Lodovici and Prince 1999: (10)):

(i) Every member of the bounding set performs better than *C* on at least one of the constraints in CON.
(ii) If *C* performs better than some member of the bounding set on some constraint in CON, then some other member of the bounding set must perform better than *C* on that constraint.

In (11), *B* and *D* perform better than *C* on C1 and C2, respectively (point (i)). And although *C* beats *B* on C1, it is itself beaten by candidate *D* on the same constraint (point (ii)). Samek-Lodovici and Prince go on to show that bounding sets are guaranteed to be of limited size: they never need to be larger than the number of constraints in CON and are often smaller.

Now comes the main result. Notice that points (i) and (ii) make no mention of constraint ranking. This means that a loser's bounding set can be found by inspecting the candidates and the constraints in CON without working through all of the ranking permutations. Losers can be identified in advance of actual grammar construction or application of EVAL, simply by providing a non-null bounding set that meets these criteria. Using a procedure rooted in RCD (§4.2.1), Samek-Lodovici and Prince show how to go from CON and a set of candidates to identification of losers and determination of their bounding sets.

Their work shows that EVAL is not necessary to winnow the winners from the losers, because this winnowing can be done in a ranking-independent way. With losers out of the way, EVAL need only consider the finite set of winners, among which is the optimal candidate for any specific ranking. The infinity of the candidate set is not eliminated from the competence model – there are still infinitely many losers to identify – but it is shifted out of EVAL to be dealt with separately. Further advances in this area seem very likely.

4.4   Functionalism

4.4.1   Introduction

Functionalist approaches to linguistic phenomena look for explanations that go beyond the properties of formal grammar. In the limit, a radically functionalist view would see formal grammar as completely superfluous, but a much more widely held position is that analyses and explanations should combine formal and functional properties. OT has emerged as a significant force shaping the recent development of *functionalist phonology* (an unsatisfactory but unavoidable way of referring to a broad range of work). For reasons explored here, OT seems particularly well suited to accommodating a functional basis for formal grammar.

Functionalism is not a new idea in phonology. Its modern history begins with Ferdinand de Saussure and his students Maurice Grammont and Paul Passy. It continues into the middle of the twentieth century in work by European structuralists like André Martinet. It was even an influence on very early generative phonology, in the form of efforts to understand distinctive features in terms of the then new information theory (Cherry, Jakobson, and Halle 1952). Natural Phonology (§2.1) is a contemporary functionalist theory of phonology, and Björn Lindblom and John Ohala are perhaps the best known of those who have examined phonological issues from a phonetically based, functionalist perspective. The main thesis of functionalist phonology is contained in the first sentence of the quote from Donegan and Stampe in §2.1: "The tension between clarity and ease is one of the most obvious, and oldest, explanatory principles in phonology." In other words, phonological explanations should ultimately depend on clarity – enhancing the perceptual experience of the hearer – and ease of articulation – simplifying the task of the speaker. These two forces are often opposed, hence the "tension" between them.

Over the last several years, there has been much study of the connections between functionalist phonology and OT. My goal in this section, in keeping with the overall aims of this book, is to focus narrowly on how the core properties of OT have been applied and sometimes modified in this work.

The possibility of making these connections was realized from the beginning of OT. Prince and Smolensky (1993: 198) urge reconsideration of strict formalism in the *SPE* tradition, where the causes of phonological processes "are placed entirely outside grammar, beyond the purview of formal or theoretical analysis, inert but admired." A strict dichotomy between the rules and their causes is the standard position in the *SPE* tradition, as in the quote from Kenstowicz and Kisseberth (1979), also in §2.1: in addition to the rules themselves, which follow *SPE*'s purely formal norms, there must be an external apparatus of "postulates that ... define natural sound changes." These postulates are usually couched as tendencies, often with some kind of rationale in terms of ease of articulation or clarity of perception: syllables tend to have onsets, stressed vowels tend to be long, codas tend to be voiceless, languages tend to have triangular vowel systems (*i-a-u* or *i-e-a-o-u*), and so on. They are only tendencies because they are not matters of physiological necessity and languages can fail to observe them. But a phonological system is natural to the extent that its structure and processes conform to these tendencies.

The problem with this approach is that linguistic theory – the formal side of things – ends up doing very little of the explaining, and the external postulates end up doing almost all of it.📖$_{§4.6¶12}$ Yet the tendencies themselves cannot replace the formal grammar. Tendencies are too slippery, too hard to evaluate and balance against one another, to accomplish all that formal grammars do. Pure functionalism is to phonology what natural selection is to genetics: it can supply compelling post hoc explanations for why things ended up the way they did, but it cannot tell us how many peas from this particular plant are going to be yellow or green, round or shriveled.

OT's relevance to these issues should now be apparent. In OT, there is no need to have an apparatus of formal rules and a separate apparatus of observed tendencies, each inadequate in themselves, to evaluate the naturalness of the rules. Instead, violable constraints model the tendencies, and those constraints themselves make up the formal grammar, with constraint ranking standing in for "the tension between clarity and ease." This approach gives a formal sense to the familiar intuition that different tendencies compete with one another. The formal grammar and the substantive teleology can in principle be united in an OT constraint hierarchy.

Ranking and violability, then, are the core of OT's contribution to functionalist phonology, and a significant body of literature has grown up around this basic insight.📖$_{§4.6¶13}$ A couple of proposals made in this context bear further examination in the context of this book, since they have the potential to alter our understanding of OT as a whole. One proposal moves in the direction of greater concreteness: establishing a much more direct relationship between constraints and physical events, with consequent expansion of constraints and constraint ranking to include numerical weights. The other proposal moves in the direction of greater abstractness: using the tools of OT to evaluate whole phonological systems rather than individual utterances. We will look at each of these proposals in turn.

4.4.2   Formal Constraints and Physical Events

The closeness of the relation between the constraints and the physical events they model is an area where functionalist phonology includes a wide range of opinions. There is necessarily some connection between the formal and the physical in these models – otherwise we would not be talking about functionalism – but there can be considerable differences in the tightness of the connection.

At one end of the continuum is the requirement that constraints be functionally motivated, as a desirable or perhaps even necessary adjunct to typological motivation: "phonological markedness constraints should be *phonetically grounded* in some property of articulation and perception. That is, phonetic evidence from production should support a cross-linguistic preference for a segment (or feature value) to others in certain contexts" (Kager 1999a: 11). This statement is representative of a widely held position, echoing ideas antedating OT about the phonetic groundedness of universal (inviolable or parametric) phonological constraints (as in Archangeli and Pulleyblank 1994).

The danger with asking only that constraints be functionally motivated is that mere motivation can be something much like the external naturalness postulates of the *SPE* tradition: "inert but admired." What is wanted is causality: this constraint exists in response to that property of some physical event. But if constraints are objects in the mind and part of UG, there are very limited ways for the properties of physical events to bring constraints into existence. Indeed, the only sensible way for a physical event to motivate an innate constraint is the one proposed by Chomsky and Lasnik (1977: 437). They address the observation that the universal filter "*$[_{NP}$ NP tense VP]" might be grounded in processing considerations; when presented with the sequence "NP tense VP," the parser naturally begins to construct a sentence rather than a noun phrase. They argue that this kind of functional grounding of a UG constraint only makes sense at the level of the evolution of the species. Whatever one thinks of their explanation, the issue that Chomsky and Lasnik raise is a real one.[23]

The connection between the grammar and the physical events must be made more direct. Suppose that the constraints evaluate specific utterance tokens (i.e., specific acts of performance) for their articulatory ease or perceptual clarity. One execution of this idea is Kirchner's (1998a) theory of lenition. Kirchner identifies the traditional notion of ease of articulation with minimization of *force*. Each articulatory gesture making up an utterance token requires a certain amount of force – that is, some literal number of dynes will be required to execute that gesture in that token, depending on the mass of the articulators, the precision of movement, the velocity of movement, and so on. A family of constraints called LAZY regulates the expenditure of force in utterances. The constraints in this family, LAZY$_n$, are ranked in a fixed hierarchy from highest to lowest n, where n refers to some threshold number of force-units. LAZY$_n$ is violated by any utterance token requiring at least n force-units. So greater effort violates a higher-ranking LAZY constraint, appropriately enough.

Suppose, for example, that LAZY_{aba} is violated by a specific utterance token requiring a certain amount of force in the [aba] lip-closing gesture, and that $\text{LAZY}_{a\beta a}$ is violated by an otherwise identical utterance token requiring a certain amount of force in the [aβa] lip-approximation gesture. (Despite the shorthand, keep in mind that LAZY_{aba} and $\text{LAZY}_{a\beta a}$ actually stand for numerical thresholds measured in units of force.) Universally, LAZY_{aba} dominates $\text{LAZY}_{a\beta a}$, because, in the open-jawed [a_a] context, the jaw-raising and lip-closing gestures of [b] require greater acceleration than the jaw-raising and lip-raising gestures of [β], if speech-rate is held constant. Since the mass of the articulators is obviously the same in both conditions, force is simply a function of acceleration. This means that [aba] is universally more effortful than [aβa], all else being equal. By ranking an appropriate faithfulness constraint above or below LAZY_{aba}, we can control whether or not lenition occurs, as in (12).

(12) Partial typology of lenition with LAZY

a. Faith ≫ LAZY_{aba} ≫ $\text{LAZY}_{a\beta a}$ – No lenition

/taba/		Faith	LAZY_{aba}	$\text{LAZY}_{a\beta a}$
i.	☞ taba		*	*
ii.	taβa	*		*

b. LAZY_{aba} ≫ Faith ≫ $\text{LAZY}_{a\beta a}$ – Lenition

/taba/		LAZY_{aba}	Faith	$\text{LAZY}_{a\beta a}$
i.	☞ taβa		*	*
ii.	taba	*		*

In this way, the causes of phonological processes can be related directly to the properties of physical events. Lenition is not "motivated" by minimization of effort; it literally *is* minimization of effort, because effort is what LAZY measures.

Though the hierarchy of LAZY constraints appears to be closely analogous to other fixed universal hierarchies related to natural scales (§1.2.3, §3.1.5.4), there is an important difference. Other proposed universal hierarchies (with the exception of power hierarchies obtained by constraint self-conjunction (§1.5 ¶5)) are based on finite scales and are consequently finite in extent. But the LAZY_n constraints have real-valued coefficients n, since measurement of continua necessarily involves numbers of arbitrary precision. This means that the LAZY hierarchy is uncountably infinite in extent.

Allowing constraints with real-valued weights is one of the features of numerically optimizing connectionism (§2.4), so it is natural to ask whether a connectionist model would be superior to OT for doing this kind of analysis. Though the LAZY hierarchy has real-valued coefficients, Kirchner's theory differs from connectionism by retaining classic OT's commitment to strict domination. The model proposed by Boersma (1998) goes a step further, however. This model allows *additive ranking* of weighted articulatory effort constraints. The additive ranking idea is something like local conjunction (§1.2.3). For instance, a constraint against performing a gesture for *x* duration and a constraint against performing it with *y* precision may be combined so that the whole is worse than its parts, yielding a higher-ranking constraint that is violated only if the gesture is performed for at least *x* duration with at least *y* precision. A model with these characteristics seems indistinguishable from classic connectionism, despite its nominal association with OT. (This point is further reinforced by the model's continuous ranking scale. See §4.5.)[24]

A related issue is the difficulty of obtaining certain kinds of categorical behavior from models where the candidates being evaluated are literal utterance tokens. Kirchner (1998b) discusses this problem in the context of his theory of effort, but the broader issue is independent of details of implementation. Suppose a language has intervocalic lenition of *b*, period. In this language, by assumption, lenition is not conditioned by any other factors, even though there are several factors that can strongly affect the overall expenditure of effort. A specific example is that height of the surrounding vowels affects effort, since *aba* requires greater acceleration than *ibi*, if time is constant. Speech-rate also affects effort, since talking faster, while performing the same gestures, will require greater accelerations. In other words, lenition in this language is a phonological process of the familiar kind: it is categorical in its effects and in its sensitivity to context. Real examples like this are not hard to come by, and they frequently give evidence of productivity that puts the lie to any attempts to dismiss them as lexicalized relics.

The problem with this sort of categorical behavior, as Kirchner argues, is that there is no way to identify some specific constraint LAZY$_{VbV}$, ranked above faithfulness, that characterizes the effort required to produce an intervocalic *b* regardless of the height of the surrounding vowels and the rate of speech, because each context and each act of performance involve different amounts of effort. In other words, there is no place to rank faithfulness in the LAZY hierarchy that will ensure [aβa] is more harmonic than *[aba] and [iβi] is more harmonic than *[ibi] at every speech-rate and under all other performance conditions. It would seem that true phonological lenition cannot be modeled.[25]

The source of this problem is the assumption that the output candidates being evaluated by the LAZY hierarchy are utterance tokens, which bring with them all of the complicating performance factors. Kirchner and others have proposed to modify this assumption: constraints will not evaluate an item's realization in a specific utterance, but rather "that item's realization under canonical conditions, which we may understand to include moderate speech rate, normal loudness, upright orientation of the head, absence of nasal congestion, absence of chewing gum, and more generally, the conditions normally observed in speech, for all performance conditions. . . ." (Kirchner 1998a: 299–300). In other words, instead of positing candidates that represent real acts of performance, posit candidates representing idealized acts of performance, abstracting away from the problematic performance factors.

This idealization leads to several concerns. Although the constraints evaluate properties of physical events, the candidates themselves abstract away from those events significantly. This suggests a kind of disconnection between two parts of the theory. Another issue is the arbitrariness inherent in assuming that the output candidates exclude certain factors and include others, though factors of both types are present in every act of performance. Of course, this is the same arbitrariness seen in phonetic transcriptions generally: any symbolic representation of continuous physical events makes distinctions that are arbitrary. Perhaps the most important issue, however, is that the idealization makes one of the theory's ostensive goals unattainable. An advantage of functionalist phonology is that it promises to eliminate the blurry distinction between a phonological component, with categorical behavior, and a phonetic component, with gradient behavior. The functionalist insight is that all processes are "phonetic" in the sense that all are driven by articulatory or perceptual factors. But the idealized output forms simply reintroduce that distinction: the phonological component evaluates output candidates that describe "realization under canonical conditions," while the phonetic component deals with expressions that include performance factors like speech-rate. These problems do not seem unsolvable, but they show the need to rationalize the effects of performance to obtain both categorical and gradient behavior from a functionalist model.

4.4.3 Evaluating Phonological Systems

The other major line of development in functionalist phonology goes in a very different direction: instead of evaluating candidate surface forms or utterance tokens, the idea is to evaluate whole phonological systems, looking for those that are organized optimally. For example, it is often observed that the modal phonemic systems with three or five vowels are triangular: *i-a-u* and *i-e-a-o-u*, but not *i-ü-o* or *ɪ-e-ɛ-æ-a*. Lindblom and others showed that triangular vowel systems maximize the perceptual distance between different vowel phonemes (Liljencrants and Lindblom 1972; Lindblom 1986). For instance, in the three-vowel system *i-a-u*, *i* and *u* are each as far from each other, and both are as far from *a*, as they can get. Dispersion Theory (Flemming 1995) captures this insight in an OT-based system where competing phonemic systems are evaluated for their perceptual dispersion and other factors.[26]

Here is a much simplified example. The vowels *i* and *u* differ acoustically in the frequency of the second formant, F2. Now, suppose the F2 continuum is divided into four steps, corresponding to the F2 values (from highest to lowest) of the four high vowels *i*, *ü*, *ɯ*, and *u*. A family of markedness constraints called MinDist(F2)_n evaluates high-vowel systems for their dispersion on the F2 dimension in the following way: MinDist(F2)_n is violated by any pair of vowels that are less than *n* steps apart on the subdivided F2 continuum. These constraints select *i-u* as the optimal system with two high vowels (see (13)).

(13) Dispersion Theory evaluating competing systems with two high vowels

		MinDist(F2)_2	MinDist(F2)_3
a.	☞ *i-u*		
b.	*i-ü*	*	*
c.	*i-ɯ*		*
d.	*ü-ɯ*	*	*
e.	*ü-u*		*
f.	*ɯ-u*	*	*

A language with just two high-vowel phonemes will disperse them to the end points of the F2 continuum, thereby maximizing their perceptual distinctiveness. In the full theory, the MinDist constraints interact with constraints evaluating articulatory difficulty and with constraints setting lower bounds on system size.

Elsewhere in this book and in OT generally, the candidates under evaluation are linguistic expressions rather than linguistic generalizations. Dispersion Theory, though, must evaluate generalizations, because that is what phonemic systems are. Indeed, constraints like MinDist cannot be permitted to evaluate linguistic expressions, because if individual words were being optimized for perceptual distinctness, then we would expect to see a range of effects that could be called *local homophony avoidance*. This is avoidance of merger or similarity on a word-by-word rather than system-by-system basis. For instance, local homophony avoidance might be realized by prohibiting minimal pairs that differ in one feature (*bat/pat*) while permitting those that differ in two (*bat/cat*). Or it might block processes when they cause distinct words to become too similar or identical, as if German *Bund* 'federation' were to resist final devoicing because there is a word *bunt* 'multi-colored'. Since phenomena like these are nonexistent, it seems safe to conclude that local homophony avoidance is not a real property of human language.[27] This means that MinDist can only be permitted to affect the structure of whole systems, such as systems of phonemes or systems of possible, rather than actual, words. This is very different from the role of familiar OT constraints, which, as noted, evaluate candidate forms rather than systemwide generalizations about these forms.

If Dispersion Theory is to be brought into contact with the rest of OT, the currently obscure relationship between evaluation of systems and evaluation of candidate forms will need to be clarified. In its present form, Dispersion Theory provides something like a meta-grammar or a learning theory, responsible for evaluating candidate grammars rather than linguistic expressions. It will be interesting to see how more direct connections to OT can be made.

In summary, functionalist approaches to phonology have found in OT a way of bringing traditional functional insights about ease of articulation, clarity of perception, and the tension between them into a formal grammar. This move yields rich and interesting results, but it also brings with it important questions that bear on the fundamentals of OT.

4.5 Variation and Change

In Optimality Theory, a grammar is a specific ranking of the constraints in CON. Synchronic or diachronic variation in a language, then, must reflect differences in ranking. This idea has proven to be productive in studies of both kinds of variation, and this section briefly reviews some of that work.

As we saw in §4.1.3 (also see §1.1.2), classic OT has only very limited resources for describing optional processes. For this reason, the literature on synchronic variation in OT has focused on modifying the definition of a constraint hierarchy.📖$_{§4.6 \, ¶15}$ In the original theory, a grammar of a language is a total ordering of the constraints in CON. This means that every constraint either dominates or is dominated by every other constraint, and that there are unique top and bottom constraints.[28] In the proposed revision, a grammar is some kind of partial ordering of CON. In a partial ordering, constraints that conflict may be unranked with respect to one another, leading to variation in the output.

Let H_p stand for the grammar of some language, a partially ordered hierarchy of the constraints in CON. In the most elaborated version of the partial-ordering theory, due originally to Paul Kiparsky, each /input/ → [output] mapping is obtained by applying a totally ordered hierarchy, H_t, that is randomly sampled from the total orderings that are consistent with H_p. For example, if H_p is ⟦C1 ≫ {C2, C3}⟧, then H_t will be either ⟦C1 ≫ C2 ≫ C3⟧ or ⟦C1 ≫ C3 ≫ C2⟧, chosen randomly each time an input is mapped to an output. If the sampling is uniform (i.e., each total ordering has equal likelihood of being chosen each time), then each total ordering in this example will be in force 50 percent of the time, on average. This theory, then, not only produces variation, but it also predicts the frequency of the variants, allowing it to make contact with some aspects of quantitative sociolinguistics. For real examples, none of which is simple enough to summarize here, see the references in §4.6 ¶15.

The original approach to frequency effects in quantitative sociolinguistics was the *variable rule*, a modification of the rule formalism in *SPE* to include numerical coefficients. (See Labov 1997: 148–51 for a concise review of the history of variable rules.) This approach inherits both the strengths and the weaknesses of *SPE*: it can describe anything while explaining nothing (§2.1). The idea of uniformly sampling total orderings from a partially ordered constraint hierarchy offers formulations and predictions that are no less precise but that also have the potential of explaining which factors contribute to variation and by how much.

A very different approach to variation in OT, with more profound consequences for the theory's basic structure, is Boersma's (1998: 271, 330ff.) proposal that constraint ranking itself is numerically weighted. (Compare the discussion of connectionist models in §2.4.) His *continuous ranking scale* replaces strict domination with a scale in which every constraint is assigned to a real number that indicates its position in the hierarchy. In speech production, a normally distributed noise factor is added to each constraint's ranking value. If the noise factor is large enough, and the constraints are close enough together on the scale, then sometimes their ranking will be reversed, producing variation across otherwise identical tokens from the same speaker (also see §4.4).

Suppose, for example, that the hierarchy in (12a) is replaced by a continuous ranking scale with the coefficients in (14).

(14) A continuous ranking scale

.7 ⌐ Faith

.6 ⌐ LAZY$_{aba}$

.1 ⌐ LAZY$_{a\beta a}$

For simplicity, we will assume that the noise factor only affects LAZY$_{aba}$. Much of the time Faith will dominate LAZY$_{aba}$, so there will be no lenition, but occasionally, when the noise factor is big enough, the ranking of these two constraints will be reversed, producing lenition instead. Observed frequency effects can be obtained by adjusting the rankings and the size of the noise factor. In this way, the continuous ranking scale can model variation, though in a way that seems less principled than the partial-ordering theory.

We turn now to language change. One of the key insights of generative grammar is the idea that many changes in languages are actually changes in their grammars (Halle 1962; Kiparsky 1965, 1968). This idea is by no means uncontroversial, but this is not the place to rehearse the controversy. Instead, I will assume for the sake of argument that it is true and then proceed to discuss how this idea plays out if grammars are actually OT constraint hierarchies.

One obvious deduction is that language change (qua grammar change) must involve constraint reranking. Grammars differ by imposing different rankings on CON. If successive historical stages of a language have different grammars, then they must have different rankings. Hence, change in grammar is reranking of constraints in OT. 📖 §4.6 ¶16

Change-by-constraint-reranking is not the same thing as change-by-rule-reordering, which enjoyed some currency in the late 1960s. (On the differences between ranking and ordering, see the cross-references in the rule-ordering FAQ.) Nor is reranking the same thing as rule loss and rule addition, which were two other mechanisms of language change prominent during the same period. The main difference is that a change in ranking may affect the visible activity of some constraint, but it will not in general turn the constraint off (cf. rule loss) or on (cf. rule addition). (See the cross-references in the parameters FAQ.)

Beyond change-as-reranking, though, OT makes connections with two more specific ideas about diachronic linguistics: the teleological character of language change and diachronic change via synchronic variation. We will look at each briefly.

Kiparsky (1995), harking back to Jakobson (1929), talks about "diachronic 'conspiracies'." Like their synchronic counterparts (§2.1, §3.1.4.3), these con-spiracies show the effect of heterogeneous processes operating over time in support of a particular output target. Kiparsky and others (e.g., Riad 1992) have shown how prosodic targets may function in this way, and the idea works itself out naturally in OT. For example, Green (1997: Chapter 3) shows how a con-straint requiring heavy syllables to be stressed organizes and explains much of the history of prosodic structure in the Goidelic languages Irish, Scots Gaelic, and Manx. Differences in ranking allow this constraint to be satisfied in differ-ent ways: in one language, unstressed heavy syllables become light by vowel shortening; in another, unstressed heavy syllables become stressed, attracting the stress from its preferred initial position. This is homogeneity of target/het-erogeneity of process (§3.1.4.2) – but in diachronic perspective.

Synchronic variation is the source of much diachronic change, at least in phonology (Kiparsky 1995; Labov 1965). According to this view, a sound change begins with a process that is motivated by ease of articulation and that initially is gradient in its effects and variable in its application. Kiparsky argues that learners will favor the variants that conform to universal or language-particular structural principles – that is, OT's markedness constraints. Take this far enough, and the process eventually becomes phonologized, so its effects are categorical and it applies invariantly.

Cho (1998) and Anttila and Cho (1998) argue that this idea can be expressed naturally in OT if constraint reranking is constrained to be a three-stage process, where the ranking is tied at the intermediate step. Initially, two conflicting constraints are in a fixed order [[C1 ≫ C2]], and there is no observed variation with respect to the relevant property. If, say, C2 is a markedness constraint favoring articulatory ease (cf. §4.4), then it may come to assume greater promi-nence as speakers seek to lighten their burden. Then, at the second stage, the two constraints, though conflicting, can be formally tied: [[{C1, C2}]]. At this second stage, variation will be observed, as the [[C1 ≫ C2]] or [[C2 ≫ C1]] order is randomly chosen for each /input/ → [output] mapping. (See §4.6 ¶14 on how learning might proceed in the presence of variation.) Finally, the new ⟦C2 ≫ C1⟧ ranking is regularized.

These few remarks obviously do not begin to plumb the depths of two rich topics, so the references cited in §4.6 ¶15 and ¶16 should be consulted by those interested in going beyond this skeletal summary. For the rest, the main lesson is the wide-ranging implications of factorial typology, as OT's inherently typological character leads naturally to hypotheses about language variation and change.

4.6   For Further Reading

¶1   The Null Parse or Null Output

The null parse is first discussed in Prince and Smolensky (1993: 48ff.). For further development and applications, see Ackema and Neeleman (1998b, 2000), Benua (1997), Cohn and McCarthy (1994/1998), Grimshaw and Samek-Lodovici (1995, 1998), Ito, Kitagawa, and Mester (1996), Kager (2000), McCarthy and Prince (1993b: Chapter 7), and Yip (1998). Orgun and Sprouse (1999) offer a critique and an alternative, and Pesetsky (1997: 151) makes comparisons to Minimalism's approach to absolute ill-formedness.

¶2   Proposals about GEN and the Input in OT Syntax

Almost every paper on OT syntax discusses the GEN and input questions, if only to make the background assumptions clear (e.g., Bresnan 2000, to appear-a, to appear-b; Choi 1996; Grimshaw 1997a, 1997b; Grimshaw and Samek-Lodovici 1995, 1998; Legendre 1996; Legendre, Smolensky, and Wilson 1998; Legendre et al. 1995; Pesetsky 1997, 1998; Samek-Lodovici 1996a; Sells 1998; Woolford to appear).

¶3   Variation in OT: Syntactic Optionality

The optionality issue comes up in nearly every piece of work on OT syntax (e.g., Ackema and Neeleman 1998a; Bakovic and Keer to appear; Broihier 1995; Grimshaw and Samek-Lodovici 1995; Keer and Bakovic 1997; Legendre et al. 2001; Müller 1998, 1999; Pesetsky 1998; Sells, Rickford, and Wasow 1996). (This list is not exhaustive.) Also see ¶15 on phonological variation and ¶14 on learning in the presence of variation.

¶4   Learning as Constraint Demotion

The Recursive Constraint Demotion algorithm and variants were proposed by Bruce Tesar, working in collaboration with Paul Smolensky (Tesar 1995a, 2000; Tesar and Smolensky 1994, 1996, 1998, 2000). For extensions and alternatives, see ¶7.

Cues and *triggers* are two approaches to learning often taken in parametric theories. A cue is a particular kind of linguistic expression whose presence in the ambient language tells the learner to set a specific parameter to a certain value. The cues are part of UG, hardwired to fit individual parameters and avoid ambiguities, and useful only in learning. Dresher and Kaye (1990) implement a cue-based learner tied to the parametric stress theory in Hayes (1980). Dresher (1999) discusses more general properties of cue-based learning, comparing it to alternatives like triggered learning (Gibson and Wexler 1994) or constraint demotion. (In triggered learning, parameter values are switched randomly when the grammar encounters unanalyzable data.) For discussion and further comparison with learning in OT, see Prince and Tesar (1999), Pulleyblank and Turkel (1997), and Tesar and Smolensky (2000: Chapter 6).

¶5 *The Initial State*

The initial ranking $[\![M \gg F]\!]$ is discussed in the context of acquisition data and/or as a solution to the subset problem by Barlow (1997a), Bernhardt and Stemberger (1998), Davidson, Juszcyk, and Smolensky (to appear), Demuth (1995a), Gnanadesikan (1995/to appear), Goad (1997), Hayes (to appear), Levelt (1996), van Oostendorp (1997b), Pater (1997), Pater and Paradis (1996), Smolensky (1996a), Sherer (1994), and Tesar and Smolensky (2000: Chapter 5). (Contrariwise, Hale and Reiss (1998) propose that $[\![F \gg M]\!]$ is the initial state.) Hayes (to appear), Ito and Mester (1999a), McCarthy (1998), Prince and Tesar (1999), and Smith (2000b) show that positing the $[\![M \gg F]\!]$ initial state is insufficient to resolve certain subset problems that arise when there are distributional restrictions (§3.1.3) or output-output faithfulness effects (§3.3.3.5), and so they propose further extensions, including other initial biases or durable but defeasible biases.

¶6 *Extensions of the Constraint Demotion Algorithms*

Tesar has extended the constraint demotion algorithms to the learning of hidden structure in output forms and to include an error-driven learning procedure that finds informative competing candidates (Tesar 1997a, 1997b, 1998a, 1998b, 1999; Tesar and Smolensky 2000: 50f., 53ff.). Tesar and Smolensky (1996, 1998, 2000: 77ff.) address the problem of learning underlying representations in systems with morphophonemic alternations. Samek-Lodovici and Prince (1999) develop a novel formalization of RCD and apply it to the problem of separating winning and losing candidates (§4.3).

¶7 *Alternatives to Constraint Demotion*

Pulleyblank and Turkel have investigated genetic algorithms for learning constraint ranking (Pulleyblank and Turkel 1996, 1997, 1998, 2000; Turkel 1994). The simplest version of the idea starts from a random ranking and then allows it to evolve: add some noise ("mutations") to create several candidate grammars, pick the fittest grammar (the one that yields an output closest to the adult model), and proceed recursively. Boersma and collaborators have developed a Gradual Constraint-Ranking Learning algorithm for numerically weighted constraint rankings (see §4.4.2, §4.5) to accommodate the effect on the developing grammar of variation and frequency in the adult model (Boersma 1998, to appear; Boersma and Hayes 2001, Boersma and Levelt 2000). Hale and Reiss (1997, 1998) present an algorithm intended to learn the ranking and the underlying representations together.

¶8   *Language Acquisition*

Thanks to my colleague Joe Pater, I can provide a nearly comprehensive list of published or otherwise publicly available works on first-language acquisition in OT (Bailey, Plunkett, and Scarpa 1999; Barlow 1996, 1997a, 2000; Barlow and Gierut 1999; Bernhardt and Stemberger 1998; Boersma 1998, 2000; Boersma and Levelt 2000; Davidson, Juszcyk, and Smolensky to appear; Demuth 1995a, 1995b, 1996, 1997a, 1997b; Dinnsen 2001; Dinnsen and Barlow 1998a, 1998b; Dinnsen and McGarrity 1999; Gierut 2001; Gierut and Morrisette 1998; Gierut, Morrisette, and Champion 1999; Gilbers and van der Linde 1999; Gnanadesikan 1995/to appear, 1996; Goad 1996, 1997; Goad and Rose to appear; Grijzenhout and Joppen to appear; Hale and Reiss 1998; Levelt 1995, 1996; Levelt, Schiller, and Levelt 1999; Levelt and van de Vijver to appear; Lleó 1996, to appear; Lleó and Demuth 1999; Massar and Gerken 1998; Menn to appear; O'Connor 1999; Ohala 1996; Ota 1998a, 1998b, 1999; Pater 1997, 1999b, to appear-a; Pater and Paradis 1996; Ramus, Nespor, and Mehler 1999; Roark and Demuth 2000; Stemberger and Bernhardt 1997a, 1997b, 1999b; Stemberger 1996a, 1996b; Velleman and Vihman 1996; Vihman and Velleman 2000, in press, Zonneveld and Nouveau to appear). Hestvik (1999) and Legendre et al. (2001) may be the only widely disseminated works on acquisition of syntax in OT. For additional references on related topics, see ¶4 and ¶5.

¶9   *Second-Language Learning*

The consequences of Natural Phonology for second-language learning are lucidly explained by Nathan (1984). There is a small literature of works applying ideas from OT to second-language learning (Broselow, Chen, and Wang 1998; Goad 1997; Hancin-Bhatt and Bhatt 1997; Hironymous 1999; Lombardi 2000; Wang 1995) or to related issues in loan phonology (Davidson and Noyer 1997; Fukazawa, Kitahara, and Ota 1998; Jacobs and Gussenhoven 2000; Ito and Mester 1999a; Katayama 1995; Shinohara to appear; Yip 1993) or creolization (Alber and Plag 1999).

¶10   *Disordered Development*

There is also a small literature of works applying ideas from OT to the analysis of developmental language disorders (Barlow 1997b, 1999; Barlow and Dinnsen 1998; Barlow and Gierut 1999; Dinnsen and Barlow 1998a; Ueda and Davis 1999; Velleman and Shriberg 1999).

¶11 *Formal Analysis and Computational Modeling*
     In addition to the works cited in the text (Samek-Lodovici and Prince 1999; Tesar 1994, 1995a, 1995b, 1999), the following are relevant to these topics (with some overlap, of course). Eisner (1997), Ellison (1994), Frank and Satta (1998), Gerdemann and van Noord (2000), Wareham (1998), and Wartena (2000), as well as Tesar, analyze the computational complexity of OT under various implementational assumptions. Hammond (1997a), Heiberg (1999), Karttunen (1998), Tesar (1994, 1995a, 1995b), and Walther (1996) investigate techniques for computational modeling of parsing and generation in OT. See also the references to work on harmonic ascent (§3.4 ¶10) and learnability (¶4 in this section).

¶12 *Phonological Naturalness via External Postulates*
     There have been some notable efforts to supply a substantive theory of naturalness to supplement purely formal theories like *SPE* and its successors. Chapter 9 of *SPE* itself is the first; others include Archangeli and Pulleyblank (1994), Chen (1973), and Mohanan (1993). Compare Anderson (1981) and Hale and Reiss (2000).

¶13 *Functionalist Phonology in Optimality Theory*
     This is an area of rapid development with a growing literature (Boersma 1998, to appear; Crosswhite 1999; Flemming 1995; Gafos 1996; Gess 1998c; Gordon 1999; Hayes 1999; Jun 1995a, 1995b; Kaun 1995; Kirchner 1998a, 1998b; MacEachern 1997; Mohanan 1993; Myers 1997a; Ní Chiosáin and Padgett 1997; Padgett 1995a, 1995b; Pater 1999a; Pulleyblank 1997; Silverman 1995; Steriade 1999a, 1999b, 1999c, 2000; Walker 1998).

¶14 *Learning in Functionalist Phonology*
     There is an emerging body of work on learning in functionalist phonology that offers a non-nativist approach to constraints and incorporates variation into the learning procedure (Boersma 1997, 2000, to appear; Boersma and Hayes 2001; Hayes 1999, to appear). Also see Legendre et al. (2001) on variation during the learning process.

¶15 *Language Variation*
     There is a substantial body of work applying the idea of partially ordered or tied constraints to problems of phonological variation (Anttila 1997a, 1997b; Borowsky and Horvath 1997; Hammond 1994; Ito and Mester 1997a; Iverson and Lee 1995; Kiparsky 1993b, 1994; Morris 1998; Nagy and Reynolds 1995; Nevin 1998; Noske 1996; van Oostendorp 1997a; Reynolds and Nagy 1994; Ringen and Heinämäki 1999; Struijke 2000b) and to variation in versification (Hayes and MacEachern 1998). See Guy (1997) and Zubritskaya (1997) for critical responses to the theory of variation described in the text. Also see ¶3 on syntactic optionality and ¶14 on learning.

¶16 *Language Change*

There is a small but rapidly growing literature developing a theory of language change within OT and applying it to diachronic problems. As noted in the text, Cho (1998) and Anttila and Cho (1998) argue that diachronic constraint reranking is a three-stage process, with an intermediate stage where the constraints are unranked and variation is observed. Bermúdez-Otero (1996) argues that this approach is insufficient, Ham (1998) criticizes the overall program of limiting diachronic rerankings, and Zubritskaya (1997) takes issue with the approach to variation in which this model is embedded. Idsardi (1997) offers a general critique of OT on diachronic grounds.

The following attempt at an exhaustive list of other works discussing language change in OT has been compiled with the aid of Gess (1999): Baerman (1998), Bermúdez-Otero (1998, 1999), Bethin (1998), Billings (1996), Blevins (1997), Gess (1996, 1998a, 1998b), Green (1996, 1997), Holt (1996, 1997, 1999), Jacobs (1994, 1995), Kirchner (1998a), Nishiyama (1996), Smith (1997), and Zubritskaya (1995). Relatedly, Alber and Plag (1999) make a proposal about creolization. Also see ¶15 on synchronic variation; there is considerable overlap, with many papers addressing diachronic and synchronic variation together.

Notes

1. There is also a small but growing body of work applying OT in semantics, such as Blutner (2000), Hendricks and de Hoop (2001), de Hoop and de Swart (1999), and de Hoop (to appear).
2. A numeration is like a set, but it allows elements to repeat. Formally, it is a set of ordered pairs (E, n), where E is an element and n is the number of times it occurs.
3. Neglect of this point is the "fallacy of perfection." See the FAQ about unmarked form.
4. Thanks to Jane Grimshaw for discussion of this point.
5. Ackema and Neeleman (1998b: 31–32) suggest that, even if GEN is limited in this way, the null output might be included in the candidate set on the grounds that its interpretation, also null, is nondistinct from the input's.
6. Markedness improvement is the only justification for unfaithfulness in classic OT. See §3.1.4.5.
7. Pesetsky (1998: 345 n. 10) makes this point.
     It is worth noting as a kind of endo-theoretic reason for unrestricted inputs that Moreton's (1996/1999) harmonic ascent theorems (§3.1.4.5) pertain only to those elements of linguistic structure that are homogeneous in the sense that they are permitted in both inputs and outputs. The generality of harmonic ascent, then, depends on making inputs and outputs out of the same stuff.
8. This approach to observational optionality in OT also appears in Grimshaw and Samek-Lodovici (1995) and Legendre (1996).
9. According to Bakovic and Keer (and ultimately Déprez 1994), the decisive markedness constraint in (4d) is T-LEX-GOV, which requires that traces be lexically governed.
10. In a more sophisticated version of RCD, called Multi-Recursive Constraint Demotion (Tesar 1997b), the nascent grammar is used to select *informative* losers – those

that force demotions and so produce learning. It is unnecessary, then, for the learning algorithm to engage all of the losers emitted by GEN.

11. For (5a) specifically, one might object that DEP and its positional counterpart, DEP$_{\text{INIT-}\sigma}$, stand in a fixed universal hierarchy [[DEP$_{\text{INIT-}\sigma}$ ≫ DEP]], as proposed by Beckman (1998). Perhaps, but this does not solve the general problem of which constraint to promote. Look at (5e), where the two winner-favoring constraints are in no special relationship.

12. The constraint *STOP + NASAL is obviously ad hoc. For serious proposals about sonority-distance restrictions in onsets, see Baertsch (1998) and Ito and Mester (1999b).

13. There is, in addition, a small but growing body of research applying OT to second-language learning ▯$_{§4.6¶9}$ and to disordered development. ▯$_{§4.6¶10}$

14. Bernhardt and Stemberger (1998), Goad (1996, 1997), and Pater (1997) discuss consonant harmony from an OT perspective.

15. I am here describing in simplified form the Generalized Template Theory of McCarthy and Prince (1994a et seq.). For further references, see §3.4 ¶20.

16. Additional constraints on the form of feet prevent *spa* from making a foot on its own (FT-BIN – §3.2.1.2) or from being incorporated into the following foot.

17. In parametric theories, the less vigorous effect of PARSE-σ has been obtained by building the priority relationships into the formulation of the constraint itself. See the discussion of Halle and Vergnaud's (1987) Exhaustivity Condition in §1.2.2.

18. Paul de Lacy informs me that Samoan speakers, whose native language has no codas and no voiced obstruents whatsoever, continue to devoice English coda obstruents even after they have learned to produce voiced obstruents in onsets.

19. See Barlow and Gierut (1999) and references there. The examples cited come from Gita (Gnanadesikan 1995/to appear) and Amahl (Smith 1973).

20. Like many children, Gita consistently pronounces *r* as *w* and, as we see, classifies it as a labial.

21. The [k] of *squeeze* is unaspirated after [s], and so it is interpreted as voiced. (Initial voiced obstruents in English are often voiceless unaspirated.)

22. In this context, the terms production and comprehension are being used to describe the grammar as a function from inputs to outputs and the inverse of that function (§1.1.3). No claims about on-line processing are implied.

23. I am greatly indebted to Paul de Lacy for sharing his thoughts on this matter.
    Another way to get functional causality is to deny that the constraints are innate. It may be possible for learners to discover constraints based on their own experience as speakers and hearers. In this way, constraints could be functionally grounded and universal but not innate. ▯$_{§4.6¶14}$

24. Factorial typology is another locus of difference between some phonetically based models and classic OT. Fixed hierarchies containing uncountably many constraints (like LAZY$_n$) yield vast typologies. Alan Prince conjectures that allowing ℵ$_1$ constraints yields ℵ$_2$ possible grammars. The conjecture is based on a generalization of Smolensky's proof sketched in note 15 of Chapter 1, which shows that allowing ℵ$_0$ constraints yields ℵ$_1$ possible grammars. It is not yet clear how further elaborations of the theory, such as additive ranking and the continuous ranking scale, might expand the typology further.

25. The techniques used for obtaining categorical behavior in connectionist or stochastic models – such as taking means of activation values (e.g., Elman 1990: 203ff.) or

using functions that produce sharp discontinuities (e.g., Broe, Frisch, and Pierrehumbert 1995; Frisch 1996, 2000; Frisch, Broe, and Pierrehumbert 1997; Joanisse and Curtin 1999) – are not applicable here because the OT architecture is different.

26. Other work relevant to Dispersion Theory includes Burzio (1999), Ní Chiosáin and Padgett (1997) and Sells (to appear). Burzio and Sells apply it to morphophonology and syntax, respectively.

27. Homophony avoidance as a factor in synchronic grammar seems to be limited to morphology. Identity avoidance in reduplication is one example (Yip 1988); another is obligatory alternation in a paradigm (Alderete 1998, to appear-a; Crosswhite 1997; Kisseberth and Abasheikh 1974). Phenomena like these offer no support for applying MINDIST to individual words rather than to phonological systems. Anti-faithfulness constraints may be more appropriate (§3.4 ¶12).

28. This is what the theory says. In practice, it may not be possible to provide ranking arguments in support of every element of a total ordering (§1.1.2, §4.2.1). A constraint tie, then, is not the same thing as a ranking for which there is no evidence – a tie involves conflicting constraints, so resolving it either way leads to different outcomes.

Epilogue

Nothing we do is complete . . .
No statement says all that could be said . . .
We cannot do everything
and there is a sense of liberation in realizing that.
– Oscar Romero

Throughout this book, I have proceeded in a top-down fashion, starting with the basic premises of OT, deducing various consequences from them, and weighing prediction against observation. This has been possible because of the simplicity and clarity of Prince and Smolensky's basic insights.

We have seen that OT does not have all the answers, but it does have many of them. The idea of comparing output candidates using a hierarchy of ranked, violable constraints really does seem to capture some fundamental truth about human language. The results derived from OT span the traditional linguistic disciplines of phonology, morphology, and syntax. OT has also renewed connections that had been allowed to lapse. For example, in my own field of phonology, language acquisition and, to a lesser extent, language typology seemed always beyond the reach of theoreticians. But because OT is inherently typological and is easily coupled to a plausible learning theory, it has renewed interest in acquisition and typology among those who work in phonological theory.

The insights and the changes of perspective that OT has brought are quite important, but their revolutionary character should not be overestimated. In Chapter 2, I showed how the problems that OT addresses and some of the ideas that it includes have historical continuity with the study of generative grammar dating back to the late 1960s and early 1970s. Notions like conspiracies or mechanisms like surface filters are still important in OT, even if they are apprehended differently.

OT does not have all the answers. When we still know and understand so little about language, no interesting theory could possibly have all the answers.

In Chapters 3 and 4, I highlighted some of the areas where our current under-standing seems incomplete: global or remote interactions, modularity and the role of derivations, the fine structure of acquisition and its relation to learning theory. Throughout, we have also encountered issues that could be loosely char-acterized as questions about the theory of constraints: How do constraint schemata, fixed hierarchies, and local conjunction organize or limit the contents of CON? What are the substantive or formal restrictions on schemata, hierar-chies, and conjunction themselves? What is the relationship between the uni-versal and the language particular (and between the innate and the learned) in the theory of constraints? What is the relationship between properties of the world (such as speech articulation) and the formal constraints? There are also empirical questions that have scarcely been studied in the past because they bear on predictions that OT uniquely makes. The various claims about process coexistence (§3.1.4) fall squarely into this category.

Where do we go from here? Obviously, the outstanding issues just described will supply much stimulus for future research. New findings about the formal properties of OT continue, such as harmonic ascent or Samek-Lodovici and Prince's results described in Chapter 4. Perhaps the most significant and far-reaching question concerns the continuity among phonology, morphology, and syntax in OT. Study of this topic will become more important as a con-sensus emerges about how to analyze the core phenomena in each of these sub-fields. There may perhaps be a return to the representational questions that had previously framed several areas of research. There will surely be a refined understanding of typology as empirical research continues. And even more surely, new problems and new discoveries will emerge that are impossible to anticipate.

Appendix A: Frequently Asked Questions

Certain questions about OT often arise on initial exposure to the theory. Here, I have compiled a list of these frequently asked questions (FAQs). Each question receives a short answer with cross-references to more extensive discussion in the text. Those who are inclined to read desultorily may also find the FAQs useful as a nonlinear guide to the text.

How is it possible for a linguistic expression to be **absolutely ill formed** in an optimizing theory that always manages to find an output?
> The source of absolute ill-formedness is absolute neutralization. If EVAL maps both /A/ and /B/ onto [A], and if EVAL maps nothing else to [B], then [B] is absolutely ill-formed. See §3.1.2.3, §3.4 ¶3, and §4.1.2.

Are the **candidates** the same in all languages?
> Candidate forms may very well be the same in all languages, but the relationship of an individual candidate form to its input (such as a correspondence relation) differs depending on the input. See §1.1.3.

If the **candidate set** is infinite, how is EVAL ever able to find the most harmonic candidate?
> Well-definition of a function and efficient computation of that function are not the same thing (see §1.1.3), and there are both computational and formal techniques for bringing the infinity of candidates under control (see §4.3).

OT analyses sometimes seem much more **complicated** than rule-based accounts of the same phenomena (cf. §3.1.4.1). It can take many constraints to characterize a process that can be expressed with a single rule (see (1) in §3.1.1). So why bother with OT?

Theories as different as OT and rule-based phonology cannot be compared by simply counting analytic constructs – otherwise creationism would be a clear winner over natural selection. (The Evaluation Metric, which is proposed in *SPE* as a way of comparing analyses within a theory (§2.1), has engendered considerable confusion on this point.) Moreover, while a rule-based analysis is, quite literally, an analysis of some phenomenon, an OT analysis brings with it typological commitments that go well beyond that phenomenon. Cross-references are unnecessary; OT's inherently typological character is emphasized on nearly every page of this book.

How is OT different from **connectionism**?
Strict domination is the most important difference. In OT, if A dominates B and C, then no number or combination of B and C violations will be worse than just a single violation of A. Connectionist models assign numerical weights to constraints, permitting them to join forces in various ways. See §2.4 and §4.4.2 and cf. §1.2.3.

What are the **constraints**?
It is too early for this question. If OT is right, then once we know what all the constraints in UG are, we know everything there is to know about human language, putting all linguists out of business. But the general outlines of an answer are becoming clearer – see §1.2 and the answer to the FAQ about constraints on constraints.

It seems as if the theory can do anything, because it is always possible to add another constraint. What are the **constraints on constraints**?
If the constraints are universal and innate, we cannot presuppose that there are "constraints on constraints," except for physical limitations imposed by human biology and genetics. Nevertheless, there has been some success in developing formal and substantive criteria for constraints. See §§1.2, 1.44, 3.1.2.5, 3.1.4.8, 3.1.5.3, 3.2.2.1, and 4.4.2.

Is it a good strategy in OT to posit a violable version of a **constraint** drawn from some other linguistic theory?
No, this comes close to being a category mistake. The constraints of other theories are typically inviolable by design, so simply declaring them to be violable is unlikely to be a productive research strategy. See §1.2.2 and §1.4.4.

Does the Minimalist notion of **Economy** have a counterpart in Optimality Theory?
Not really. Economy in the sense of Chomsky (1995) is understood to require minimal structures, fewer derivational steps, and shorter movements. OT has no analogous principle of such generality but instead approximates

these effects with various constraints operating under EVAL's rubric of minimal violation. See §§1.2.2, 2.3, 3.1.4.3, 3.1.5.2, and 3.2.3.

Do **faithfulness** constraints really make sense as a linguistic principle?

"The existence of phonology in every language shows that Faithfulness is at best an ineffective principle that might well be done without" (Halle 1995: 27). "McCarthy and Prince [(1994a)] propose that 'faithfulness' be restricted to input-output conditions, but what they suggest seems to have no relevance to the standard problems (e.g., 'identity between input and output,' principle that is virtually never satisfied)" (Chomsky 1995: 380 n).

"It is no argument against a theory of constraint violation, to observe that, in it, constraints are violated. More precisely, it is no argument against Optimality Theory to note that the constraints it predicts to be violable are in fact violated, and indeed, if one wishes to look a little further, violated in the way it predicts" (Prince 1996: 24).

Are the **inputs** the same in all languages?

Yes. This is richness of the base, the hypothesis that there are no language-particular restrictions on inputs. (Richness of the base should not be confused with the absurd idea that the vocabulary is the same in all languages.) See §3.1.2.

Without imposing restrictions on inputs, how is it possible to account for **inventories**?

Inventories and distributional restrictions are derived by the grammar from the rich input. Some potential distinctions are merged in the output because the grammar contains $[\![M \gg F]\!]$ rankings. See §3.1.2 and §4.1.2.

Since there are $n!$ ways to permute n constraints, how do **learners** ever find the right grammar in this huge space of hypotheses? (E.g., $27! \approx 10^{28} > 6 * 10^{27} \approx$ mass of the Earth in grams.)

Learners don't search blindly through this huge hypothesis-space. There is a simple strategy that allows them to find a correct grammar much more quickly. See §4.2.1.

What is the initial ranking of constraints and how does it figure in **learning**? Are some rankings preferred or unmarked relative to others?

Current thinking holds that the initial ranking is $[\![M \gg F]\!]$, with all markedness constraints ranked above all faithfulness constraints. This assumption helps to solve subset problems in acquisition and accounts for the observation that children's early productions are typically unmarked relative to adult exemplars. See §§3.1.2.4, 4.2.1, 4.2.2, and §4.6 ¶5.

Does the **lexicon** play a role in accounting for between-language variation?
    No, except in the trivial sense of accounting for differences in vocabulary. Real generalizations about differences between languages never have their source in the lexicon – they all come from the grammar. See §3.1.2.

Not all phonological generalizations are surface true, nor are the conditions for their applicability always apparent at the surface. How is this **opacity** addressed in OT?
    There are various proposals, not easy to summarize here. See §3.3.3.

OT markedness constraints evaluate outputs. Doesn't this make OT a theory of linguistic **performance** rather than competence?
    No. The word "output" is a term of art in OT, referring to the output of the grammar. (It is therefore comparable to expressions like "S-Structure.") The use of this word implies no particular commitment to competence, performance, or anything in between. See the end of §3.1.4.1.

How is constraint ranking different from **parameters**?
    A parameter that is "off" is completely inactive. But a constraint that is crucially dominated can still be active. See §§1.2.1, 3.1.5.2, 3.2.1.3, 3.2.2.2, 3.4, and 4.2.2.

Is the **ranking** of constraints entirely arbitrary?
    It is probably not entirely arbitrary. There is good evidence that UG includes some universally fixed rankings, which are limited to natural linguistic hierarchies like sonority or animacy. See §1.2.3, §3.1.5.4, and §3.4 ¶17.

Is constraint **ranking** a total ordering or a partial ordering? Must all constraints be ranked?
    This can be confusing. In theory, a constraint hierarchy – a grammar – is a total ordering of all the constraints in Con. In practice, though, a partial or stratified ordering is usually all that can be discovered using legitimate ranking arguments. Partially ordered hierarchies are permitted in theory as well as practice in implementations of OT specifically intended to deal with language variation. See §§1.1.2, 3.1.2.2, 3.1.4.3, and 4.5.

How many candidates must be considered in a valid **ranking argument**? How many constraints? What kinds of both?
    A valid ranking argument must contain two candidates, of which one is optimal. It must contain two constraints that conflict on these two candidates. For sufficiency of the argument, other criteria must also be met. See §1.1.1 and §1.4.1.

Does OT demand that linguistic **representations** have certain specific properties? For example, does OT entail a particular representation for epenthetic segments or functional projections?

No. The core assumptions of OT are pretty general, and so they are compatible with a wide range of representational assumptions. See §1.1.3 and
§3.2.1.4.

In what ways do constraint ranking and **rule ordering** resemble each other, and
in what ways do they differ?

Constraint ranking and rule ordering are both ways of establishing precedence relations, but everything else about them is quite different. See
§§3.2.2.3, 3.3.1, 3.3.3.1, and 3.3.3.4. Cf. Speas (1997: 198–99).

OT has only constraints. Why not combine **rules** and constraints?

If a constraints-only theory is workable, then it is preferable, all else being
equal. There are also a number of specific differences between OT and
mixed theories, detailed in §§2.1, 2.5, 3.1.4.3, 3.1.4.6, 3.2.1.4, 3.2.3, and
3.3.2.3.

In a theory where all constraints are violable, how is it possible to account for
truly **universal prohibitions or requirements**?

With factorial typology. If *no* licit permutation of the constraints in UG
yields an output O from any input, then O is universally prohibited.
Likewise, if *all* licit permutations of the constraints in UG yield an output
O, then O is universally required. See §3.1.5.3 for the main discussion of this
point.

Since GEN is the same in every language, isn't it the best place to state
universals?

No. The really interesting results about universals in OT come from factorial typology. See §3.1.5.3 for the main discussion of this point.

Why doesn't every word in every language change into some **unmarked form**,
like *ba* (cf. Chomsky 1995: 380 n).

Since this has been a source of continued misunderstanding, the answer to
this FAQ is longer than the others.

This question either ignores or fundamentally misunderstands the effects
of faithfulness constraints. Since faithfulness constraints are basic to OT and
their overall properties have been reasonably well understood since the
beginning, this is a nonissue, *pace* Uriagereka (1998: 558 n).

More deeply, this question reflects a "fallacy of perfection" (McCarthy
and Prince 1994a): since OT is about finding the optimal form, so the reasoning goes, it must always find the *perfect* form. In reality, though, per-

fection is not to be found: faithfulness constraints conflict with markedness constraints, and markedness constraints may conflict among themselves. Hence, the answer to this question is to be found throughout this book and, indeed, throughout OT.

Another question, different from the one intended, is why there isn't *some* language where all faithfulness constraints are bottom ranked, and so all inputs merge into *ba*. This question is at least nontrivial: according to factorial typology, a grammar where all or most faithfulness constraints are bottom ranked is a possible human language, and one that is actually met with in early acquisition (§4.2). Indeed, all linguistic theories must allow for the formal possibility of a human language with a single lexical item. But the functional considerations militating against such a language are obvious.

It is interesting to note that, in the context of proposing their markedness theory, Chomsky and Halle (1968) show awareness of the *ba* problem. Since having fewer phonemes makes a sound system less marked in their system, why not have a sound system consisting of just two phonemes, such as *b* and *a?* Their answer describes this as an unsolved research problem: "A method must be developed for weighing the extra complexity inherent in a larger inventory of segments against the advantages of having a more nearly optimal lexical system" (Chomsky and Halle 1968: 411). Subsequent work in their framework addresses the matter by simply stipulating a lower bound on the size of the phonemic inventory (Kean 1975: 52f.).

Why doesn't the vocabulary of a language consist of a set of **unmarked words**, like *mama, baba, tata*, etc. "Why should a lexicon ever contain, ahem . . . *emasculate* and other such nightmares?" (This question comes from the dialogist "O" in Uriagereka 1998: 164.)

Faithfulness is, of course, part of the answer, as it is to the previous question. But there is a bit more to be said. Suppose for the sake of argument that *baba* is less marked than *emasculate* according to the markedness constraints as ranked in the grammar of English. (That is, any markedness violation incurred by *baba* is also incurred only by *emasculate* or else is dominated by a markedness violation incurred only by *emasculate*.) It follows, then, from basic premises of OT that *baba* must be a *possible* word because presumptively more marked *emasculate* is an *actual* word (and hence a fortiori a possible word). This prediction, which is a type of harmonic completeness (§3.1.5.4), derives from markedness/faithfulness interaction (with some additional assumptions about the nature of faithfulness constraints; see Prince 1998). The fact that *baba* is not an actual word is irrelevant, since phonology is a theory of possible words, not actual words, just as syntax is a theory of possible sentences rather than those sentences that some syntactician might have heard. (For further discussion, see §3.1.2.2 and §3.1.2.4 on the irrelevance of accidental gaps.)

What ensures that there is only one most harmonic candidate? And what about situations of **variation**, where there is more than one output?

Nothing ensures that there is only one most harmonic candidate. In principle, even a totally ordered constraint hierarchy can emit more than one output, though in practice this is not very important. Observed variation is probably better analyzed in other terms (different inputs, partial orderings, etc.). See §§1.1.2, 4.1.3, and 4.5.

What is the difference between strict domination and numerical **weighting** of constraints?

See the FAQ about connectionism and §2.4.

Appendix B: Symbols and Abbreviations

Standard Symbols

≫   A ≫ B means 'constraint A dominates constraint B'.

>   X ≻ Y means 'the linguistic structure X is more harmonic than structure Y (relative to some shared input and some constraint hierarchy)' (§1.1.2).

>   X > Y means 'the linguistic structure X is more prominent than structure Y' (§1.2.3, §3.1.5.4).

& $[A\&B]_\delta$ is the local conjunction of constraints A and B in domain δ. It is violated if and only if both A and B are violated in some δ (§1.2.3). In local self-conjunction, $[A\&A]_\delta$ is violated if and only if there are two instances of A violation in some δ (§1.5 ¶5).

{ }   {A, B} is the set consisting of A and B. If A and B are constraints, {A, B} appears sometimes in constraint hierarchies to emphasize that the ranking of A with respect to B cannot be determined (or is deliberately tied – §4.5). For example, ⟦{A, B} ≫ C⟧ means 'A and B dominate C', with no ranking specified between A and B.

/ /   Virgules enclose underlying forms (inputs).

[ ]   Brackets surround some surface forms (outputs). Italics are sometimes used instead.

! $n!$ is the product $1*2*\ldots*n - 1*n$. For example, $4! = 1*2*3*4 = 24$. The number of distinct ways to permute n objects is $n!$ (because there are n choices for the first object, $n - 1$ choices for the second, and so on).

λ   LF or Logical Form (only in quotations from Chomsky).

π   PF or Phonological Form (only in quotations from Chomsky).

$\aleph_0$, $\aleph_1$, $\aleph_2$ $\aleph_0$ is the cardinality of the integers or any other denumerable set. $2^{\aleph_0} = \aleph_1$ is the cardinality of the real numbers. $2^{\aleph_1} = \aleph_2$ is the cardinality of the power set (the set of all subsets) of the real numbers.

Other Symbols Used in This Book

§   This symbol is used for cross-references to sections of the book. §*m.n.o* refers to chapter *m*, section *n*, subsection *o*.

📖, ¶   These symbols are used for cross-references to the lists of suggested readings at the end of each chapter. A reference of the form 📖$_{§m.n¶p}$ points to the suggested readings in paragraph *p* of section *n* at the end of chapter *m*.

⟦ ⟧   The brackets ⟦ ⟧ delimit constraint hierarchies when they appear in the midst of text (e.g., ⟦A ≫ B⟧).

⊙   This symbol is introduced in §4.1.2 to stand for the null parse or null output. It is not standard in the OT literature.

Abbreviations

Aspects   *Aspects of the Theory of Syntax* (Chomsky 1965).

C/D Lemma   The Cancellation/Domination Lemma ((15) in §1.3.3).

C_{HL} The computational system for human language (only in quotations from Chomsky).

CON   The universal set of constraints. A grammar of a language is a specific ranking of CON.

ECP   Empty Category Principle (Chomsky 1981). Empty categories must be properly governed.

EVAL   The evaluator. EVAL takes a set of candidates and places them into a partial order according to a language-particular constraint hierarchy.

F   An arbitrary faithfulness constraint or set of faithfulness constraints.

GB   Government-Binding Theory (Chomsky 1981).

GEN   The generator. GEN associates an input with a set of output candidates.

GPSG   Generalized Phrase-Structure Grammar (Gazdar et al. 1985).

H	A language-particular constraint hierarchy. A specific ordering of CON.
IPh	Intonation phrase. A category in the prosodic hierarchy (Selkirk 1980a, 1980b).
LFG	Lexical-Functional Grammar (Bresnan 1982).
LP	Lexical Phonology (Kiparsky 1982b et seq.).
M	An arbitrary markedness constraint or set of markedness constraints.
OT	Optimality Theory (Prince and Smolensky 1993).
OT-LP	A theory that combines OT's constraint-ranking grammars with Lexical Phonology's derivational levels. See §3.3.3.4 for discussion and §3.4 ¶31 for references.
P&P	Principles and Parameters approach (subsuming GB and Minimalism (Chomsky 1995)).
PM	Performance Model (only in quotation from Chomsky).
PPh	Phonological phrase. A category in the prosodic hierarchy (Selkirk 1980a, 1980b).
PS, GRS	Person Scale, Grammatical Relation Scale ((52) in §3.1.5.4).
PWd	Phonological word. A category in the prosodic hierarchy (Selkirk 1980a, 1980b).
RCD	Recursive Constraint Demotion learning algorithm (§4.2.1).
ROTB	Richness of the base. The hypothesis in OT that there are no language-particular restrictions on inputs. See Prince and Smolensky (1993) and §3.1.2.
SPE	*The Sound Pattern of English* (Chomsky and Halle 1968).
TCRS	Theory of Constraints and Repair Strategies (Paradis 1988a, 1988b, et seq.).
TETU	The emergence of the unmarked (§3.2.2).
UG	Universal Grammar.
XP	Any phrasal category.

References

The following common abbreviations are used throughout the bibliography:
CSLI: Center for the Study of Language and Information, Stanford University.
GLSA: Graduate Linguistics Student Association, University of Massachusetts, Amherst.
IULC: Indiana University Linguistics Club.

Abdul-Ghani, Abdul Ghani (1976) Direction and motivation of phonological rules in Palestinian Arabic. In *Papers from the 12th Regional Meeting, Chicago Linguistic Society*, ed. S. S. Mufwene, C. A. Walker, and S. B. Steever, pp. 13–23. Chicago: Chicago Linguistic Society.

Ackema, Peter, and Neeleman, Ad (1998a) Optimal questions. *Natural Language and Linguistic Theory* 16, 443–90.

Ackema, Peter, and Neeleman, Ad (1998b) WHOT? In *Is the Best Good Enough? Optimality and Competition in Syntax*, ed. Pilar Barbosa, Danny Fox, Paul Hagstrom, Martha McGinnis, and David Pesetsky, pp. 15–33. Cambridge, MA: MIT Press.

Ackema, Peter, and Neeleman, Ad (2000) Absolute ungrammaticality. In *Optimality Theory: Phonology, Syntax, and Acquisition*, ed. Joost Dekkers, Frank van der Leeuw, and Jeroen van de Weijer, pp. 279–301. Oxford: Oxford University Press.

Aissen, Judith (1999) Markedness and subject choice in Optimality Theory. *Natural Language and Linguistic Theory* 17, 673–711.

Akinlabi, Akinbiyi (1996) Featural alignment. *Journal of Linguistics* 32, 239–89.

Alber, Birgit (1999) Quantity sensitivity as the result of constraint interaction. Unpublished manuscript. Marburg, Germany: University of Marburg. [Available on Rutgers Optimality Archive.]

Alber, Birgit, and Plag, Ingo (1999) Epenthesis, deletion, and the emergence of the optimal syllable in Creole. Unpublished manuscript. Marburg, Germany: University of Marburg; Hannover, Germany: University of Hannover. [Available on Rutgers Optimality Archive.]

Alcantará, Jonathan B. (1998) *The Architecture of the English Lexicon*. Doctoral dissertation. Ithaca, NY: Cornell University. [Available on Rutgers Optimality Archive.]

Alderete, John (1997) Dissimilation as local conjunction. In *Proceedings of the North East Linguistic Society 27*, ed. Kiyomi Kusumoto, pp. 17–32. Amherst, MA: GLSA.

Alderete, John (1998) *Morphologically-Governed Accent in Optimality Theory*. Doctoral dissertation. Amherst: University of Massachusetts.

Alderete, John (1999) Faithfulness to prosodic heads. In *The Derivational Residue in Phonological Optimality Theory*, ed. Ben Hermans and Marc van Oostendorp, pp. 29–50. Amsterdam: John Benjamins.

Alderete, John (to appear-a) Dominance effects as trans-derivational anti-faithfulness. *Phonology* 18.

Alderete, John (to appear-b) Root-controlled accent in Cupeño. *Natural Language and Linguistic Theory*.

Alderete, John, Beckman, Jill, Benua, Laura, Gnanadesikan, Amalia, McCarthy, John, and Urbanczyk, Suzanne (1999) Reduplication with fixed segmentism. *Linguistic Inquiry* 30, 327–64.

Anderson, John (1986) Suprasegmental dependencies. In *Dependency and Non-Linear Phonology*, ed. Jacques Durand, pp. 55–133. London: Croom Helm.

Anderson, John, and Ewen, Colin (1987) *Principles of Dependency Phonology*. Cambridge: Cambridge University Press.

Anderson, Stephen R. (1974) *The Organization of Phonology*. New York: Academic Press.

Anderson, Stephen R. (1975) On the interaction of phonological rules of various types. *Journal of Linguistics* 11, 39–62.

Anderson, Stephen R. (1979) On the subsequent development of the "Standard Theory" in phonology. In *Current Approaches to Phonological Theory*, ed. Daniel A. Dinnsen, pp. 2–30. Bloomington: Indiana University Press.

Anderson, Stephen R. (1981) Why phonology isn't 'natural'. *Linguistic Inquiry* 12, 493–539.

Anderson, Stephen R. (1985) *Phonology in the Twentieth Century: Theories of Rules and Theories of Representations*. Chicago: University of Chicago Press.

Anderson, Stephen R. (1996a) How to put your clitics in their place or why the best account of second-position phenomena may be something like the optimal one. *The Linguistic Review* 13, 165–91.

Anderson, Stephen R. (1996b) Rules and constraints in describing the morphology of phrases. In *The Parasession on Clitics [Papers from the 31st Regional Meeting of the Chicago Linguistic Society]*, ed. A. Dainora, R. Hemphill, B. Luka, B. Need, and S. Pargman, pp. 15–31. Chicago: Chicago Linguistic Society.

Anderson, Stephen R. (2000) Towards an optimal account of second position phenomena. In *Optimality Theory: Phonology, Syntax, and Acquisition*, ed. Joost Dekkers, Frank van der Leeuw, and Jeroen van de Weijer, pp. 302–33. Oxford: Oxford University Press.

Anderson, Stephen R., and Browne, Wayles (1973) On keeping exchange rules in Czech. *Papers in Linguistics* 6, 445–82.

Angluin, Dana (1980) Inductive inference of formal languages from positive data. *Information and Control* 45, 117–35.

Anttila, Arto (1997a) Deriving variation from grammar. In *Variation, Change, and Phonological Theory*, ed. Frans Hinskens, Roeland van Hout, and W. Leo Wetzels, pp. 35–68. Amsterdam: John Benjamins.

Anttila, Arto (1997b) *Variation in Finnish Phonology and Morphology.* Doctoral dissertation. Stanford, CA: Stanford University.

Anttila, Arto, and Cho, Young-mee Yu (1998) Variation and change in Optimality Theory. *Lingua* 104, 31–56.

Archangeli, Diana (1984) *Underspecification in Yawelmani Phonology and Morphology.* Doctoral dissertation. Cambridge: Massachusetts Institute of Technology. [Published in Outstanding Dissertations in Linguistics Series, Garland Press, New York, 1988.]

Archangeli, Diana, and Langendoen, D. Terence (1997a) Afterword. In *Optimality Theory: An Overview*, ed. Diana Archangeli and D. Terence Langendoen, pp. 200–15. Oxford: Blackwell.

Archangeli, Diana, and Langendoen, D. Terence (eds.) (1997b) *Optimality Theory: An Overview.* Oxford: Blackwell.

Archangeli, Diana, Moll, Laura, and Ohno, Kazutoshi (1998) Why not *NC. In *CLS 34.* Part 1, *The Main Session*, ed. M. Catherine Gruber, Derrick Higgins, Kenneth S. Olson, and Tamra Wysocki, pp. 1–26. Chicago: Chicago Linguistic Society.

Archangeli, Diana, and Pulleyblank, Douglas (1994) *Grounded Phonology.* Cambridge, MA: MIT Press.

Archangeli, Diana, and Suzuki, Keiichiro (1996) Yokuts templates: Correspondence to neither input nor output. In *UCI Working Papers in Linguistics.* Vol. 2, *Proceedings of the South Western Optimality Theory Workshop*, ed. Brian Agbayani and Naomi Harada, pp. 17–28. Irvine, CA: Irvine Linguistics Students Association.

Archangeli, Diana, and Suzuki, Keiichiro (1997) The Yokuts challenge. In *Derivations and Constraints in Phonology*, ed. Iggy Roca, pp. 197–226. New York: Oxford University Press.

Aronoff, Mark (1976) *Word Formation in Generative Grammar.* Cambridge, MA: MIT Press.

Aronoff, Mark, and Sridhar, S. N. (1983) Morphological levels in English and Kannada; or, Atarizing Reagan. In *CLS 19: Parasession on the Interplay of Phonology, Morphology, and Synax*, ed. J. Richardson, M. Marks and A. Chukerman, pp. 16–35. Chicago: Chicago Linguistic Society.

Artstein, Ron (1998) Hierarchies. Unpublished manuscript. New Brunswick, NJ: Rutgers University. [Available for download (6/15/00) at http://www.eden.rutgers.edu/~artstein/hierarchies.pdf.]

Asimov, Isaac (1950) *I, Robot.* New York: Signet.

Avery, Peter, and Rice, Keren (1989) Segmental structure and coronal underspecification. *Phonology* 6, 179–200.

Bach, Emmon, and Wheeler, Deirdre (1981) Montague Phonology: A first approximation. In *University of Massachusetts Occasional Papers in Linguistics 7*, ed. Wynn Chao and Deirdre Wheeler, pp. 27–45. Amherst, MA: GLSA.

Baerman, Matthew (1998) The evolution of prosodic constraints in Macedonian. *Lingua* 104, 57–78.

Baertsch, Karen (1998) Onset sonority distance constraints through local conjunction. In *CLS 34.* Part 2, *The Panels*, ed. M. Catherine Gruber, Derrick Higgins, Kenneth S. Olson, and Tamra Wysocki, pp. 1–15. Chicago: Chicago Linguistic Society.

Bailey, T. M., Plunkett, K., and Scarpa, E. (1999) A cross-linguistic study in learning prosodic rhythms: Rules, constraints, and similarity. *Language and Speech* 42, 1–38.

Baker, C. L. (1979) Syntactic theory and the projection problem. *Linguistic Inquiry* 10, 533–81.

Bakovic, Eric (1996) Foot harmony and quantitative adjustments. Unpublished manuscript. New Brunswick, NJ: Rutgers University.

Bakovic, Eric (1998a) Optimality and inversion in Spanish. In *Is the Best Good Enough? Optimality and Competition in Syntax*, ed. Pilar Barbosa, Danny Fox, Paul Hagstrom, Martha McGinnis, and David Pesetsky, pp. 35–58. Cambridge, MA: MIT Press.

Bakovic, Eric (1998b) Unbounded stress and factorial typology. In *RuLing Papers 1: Working Papers from Rutgers University*, ed. Ron Artstein and Madeleine Holler, pp. 15–28. New Brunswick, NJ: Department of Linguistics, Rutgers University.

Bakovic, Eric (2000) *Harmony, Dominance, and Control*. Doctoral dissertation. New Brunswick, NJ: Rutgers University. [Available on Rutgers Optimality Archive.]

Bakovic, Eric, and Keer, Edward (to appear) Optionality and ineffability. In *OT Syntax*, ed. Géraldine Legendre, Jane Grimshaw, and Sten Vikner. Cambridge, MA: MIT Press.

Bakovic, Eric, and Wilson, Colin (2000) Transparency, strict locality, and targeted constraints. In *Proceedings of the 19th West Coast Conference on Formal Linguistics*, ed. Roger Billerey and Brook Danielle Lillehaugen, pp. 43–56. Somerville, MA: Cascadilla Press. [Available on Rutgers Optimality Archive.]

Barlow, Jessica A. (1996) The development of on-glides in American English. In *Proceedings of the 20th Annual Boston University Conference on Language Development*, ed. A. Stringfellow, D. Cahana-Amitay, E. Hughes, and A. Zukowski, pp. 40–51. Somerville, MA: Cascadilla Press.

Barlow, Jessica A. (1997a) *A Constraint-Based Account of Syllable Onsets: Evidence from Developing Systems*. Doctoral dissertation. Bloomington: Indiana University.

Barlow, Jessica A. (1997b) The representation of on-glides in American English: Evidence from phonologically disordered systems. In *Optimal Viewpoints: In Celebration of the 30th Anniversary of the IULC Publications*, ed. Stuart Davis, pp. 25–44. Bloomington, IN: IULC.

Barlow, Jessica A. (1999) An argument for adjuncts: Evidence from a phonologically disordered system. In *Proceedings of the 23rd Annual Boston University Conference on Language Development*, ed. Annabel Greenhill, Heather Littlefield, and Cheryl Tano, vol. 1, pp. 44–55. Somerville, MA: Cascadilla Press.

Barlow, Jessica A. (2000) A preliminary typology of word-initial clusters with an explanation for asymmetries in acquisition. In *Papers in Experimental and Theoretical Linguistics: Proceedings of the Workshop on the Lexicon in Phonetics and Phonology*, ed. Robert Kirchner, Joe Pater, and Wolf Wikely. Edmonton: Department of Linguistics, University of Alberta.

Barlow, Jessica A., and Dinnsen, Daniel A. (1998) Asymmetrical cluster development in a disordered system. *Language Acquisition* 7, 1–49.

Barlow, Jessica A., and Gierut, Judith A. (1999) Optimality theory in phonological acquisition. *Journal of Speech, Language, and Hearing Research* 42, 1482–98.

Beckman, Jill (1995) Shona height harmony: Markedness and positional identity. In *University of Massachusetts Occasional Papers in Linguistics 18: Papers in Optimality Theory*, ed. Jill Beckman, Suzanne Urbanczyk, and Laura Walsh, pp. 53–75. Amherst, MA: GLSA.

Beckman, Jill (1997) Positional faithfulness, positional neutralization, and Shona vowel harmony. *Phonology* 14, 1–46.

Beckman, Jill (1998) *Positional Faithfulness*. Doctoral dissertation. Amherst: University of Massachusetts. [Available on Rutgers Optimality Archive.]

Beckman, Jill, Walsh Dickey, Laura, and Urbanczyk, Suzanne (eds.) (1995) *Papers in Optimality Theory*. Amherst, MA: GLSA.

Bendor-Samuel, J. (1970) Some problems of segmentation in the phonological analysis of Terena. In *Prosodic Analysis*, ed. F. R. Palmer, pp. 214–21. London: Oxford University Press.

Benua, Laura (1995) Identity effects in morphological truncation. In *Papers in Optimality Theory*, ed. Jill Beckman, Laura Walsh Dickey, and Suzanne Urbanczyk, pp. 77–136. Amherst, MA: GLSA.

Benua, Laura (1997) *Transderivational Identity: Phonological Relations between Words*. Doctoral dissertation. Amherst: University of Massachusetts. [Available on Rutgers Optimality Archive.]

Bermúdez-Otero, Ricardo (1996) Stress and quantity in Old and early Middle English: Evidence for an Optimality-Theoretic model of language change. Unpublished manuscript. Manchester: University of Manchester. [Available on Rutgers Optimality Archive.]

Bermúdez-Otero, Ricardo (1998) Prosodic optimization: The Middle English length adjustment. *English Language and Linguistics* 2, 169–97.

Bermúdez-Otero, Ricardo (1999) *Constraint Interaction in Language Change: Quantity in English and Germanic*. Doctoral dissertation. Manchester, UK: University of Manchester.

Bernhardt, Barbara H., and Stemberger, Joseph P. (1998) *Handbook of Phonological Development from the Perspective of Constraint-Based Nonlinear Phonology*. San Diego, CA: Academic Press.

Bethin, Christina (1998) *Slavic Prosody: Language Change and Phonological Theory*. Cambridge: Cambridge University Press.

Bhat, D. N. S. (1976) Dichotomy in phonological change. *Lingua* 39, 333–51.

Billings, Loren A. (1996) Sandhi phenomena and language change. In *Interfaces in Phonology*, ed. Ursula Kleinhenz, pp. 60–82. Berlin: Akademie Verlag.

Bird, Steven (1990) *Constraint-Based Phonology*. Doctoral dissertation. Edinburgh: University of Edinburgh.

Black, H. Andrew (1993) *Constraint-Ranked Derivation: A Serial Approach to Optimization*. Doctoral dissertation. Santa Cruz: University of California.

Bladon, R. A. W. (1971) Phonotactics in a generative grammar of Old Provençal. *Transactions of the Philological Society* 1970, 91–114.

Blevins, Juliette (1995) The syllable in phonological theory. In *The Handbook of Phonological Theory*, ed. John A. Goldsmith, pp. 206–44. Cambridge, MA: Blackwell.

Blevins, Juliette (1997) Rules in Optimality Theory: Two case studies. In *Derivations and Constraints in Phonology*, ed. Iggy Roca, pp. 227–60. Oxford: Clarendon Press.

Blutner, Reinhard (2000) Some aspects of optimality in natural langue interpretation. Unpublished manuscript. Berlin: Humboldt University. [Available on Rutgers Optimality Archive.]

Boersma, Paul (1997) How we learn variation, optionality, and probability. *Proceedings of the Institute of Phonetic Sciences of the University of Amsterdam* 21, 43–58. [Available on Rutgers Optimality Archive.]

Boersma, Paul (1998) *Functional Phonology: Formalizing the Interaction between Articulatory and Perceptual Drives*. The Hague: Holland Academic Graphics.

Boersma, Paul (2000) Phonology-semantics interaction in OT, and its acquisition. In *Papers in Experimental and Theoretical Linguistics: Proceedings of the Workshop on the Lexicon in Phonetics and Phonology*, ed. Robert Kirchner, Joe Pater, and Wolf Wikely. Edmonton: Department of Linguistics, University of Alberta.

Boersma, Paul (to appear) Typology and acquisition in functional and arbitrary phonology. In *Fixing Priorities: Constraints in Phonological Acquisition*, ed. René Kager, Joe Pater, and Wim Zonneveld. Cambridge: Cambridge University Press.

Boersma, Paul, and Hayes, Bruce (2001) Empirical tests of the gradual learning algorithm. *Linguistic Inquiry* 32, 45–86.

Boersma, Paul, and Levelt, Clara C. (2000) Gradual constraint-ranking learning algorithm predicts acquisition order. In *The Proceedings of the Thirtieth Annual Child Language Research Forum*, ed. Eve V. Clark, pp. 229–37. Stanford, CA: CSLI. [Available on Rutgers Optimality Archive.]

Bonet, M. Eulàlia (1991) *Morphology after Syntax: Pronominal Clitics in Romance*. Doctoral dissertation. Cambridge: Massachusetts Institute of Technology.

Booij, Geert (1988) Morphological and prosodic domains in lexical phonology. In *Certamen Phonologicum*, ed. Pier Marco Bertinetto and M. Loporcaro, pp. 137–56. Turin: Rosenberg and Sellier.

Booij, Geert (1995) *The Phonology of Dutch*. Oxford: Clarendon Press.

Booij, Geert (1996) Lexical phonology and the derivational residue. In *Current Trends in Phonology: Models and Methods*, ed. Jacques Durand and Bernard Laks, pp. 69–96. Salford, Manchester, UK: University of Salford.

Booij, Geert (1997) Non-derivational phonology meets lexical phonology. In *Derivations and Constraints in Phonology*, ed. Iggy Roca, pp. 261–88. New York: Oxford University Press.

Booij, Geert, and Lieber, Rochelle (1993) On the simultaneity of morphological and prosodic structure. In *Studies in Lexical Phonology*, ed. Sharon Hargus and Ellen M. Kaisse, pp. 23–44. San Diego, CA: Academic Press.

Booij, Geert, and Rubach, Jerzy (1984) Morphological and prosodic domains in lexical phonology. *Phonology* 1, 1–27.

Booij, Geert, and Rubach, Jerzy (1987) Postcyclic versus postlexical rules in lexical phonology. *Linguistic Inquiry* 18, 1–44.

Borowsky, Toni (1986) *Topics in the Lexical Phonology of English*. Doctoral dissertation. Amherst: University of Massachusetts.

Borowsky, Toni (1993) On the word level. In *Studies in Lexical Phonology*, ed. Sharon Hargus and Ellen M. Kaisse, pp. 199–234. New York: Academic Press.

Borowsky, Toni, and Horvath, Barbara (1997) L-vocalization in Australian English. In *Variation, Change, and Phonological Theory*, ed. Frans Hinskens, Roeland van Hout, and W. Leo Wetzels, pp. 101–25. Amsterdam: John Benjamins.

Bosch, Anna (1991) *Phonotactics at the Level of the Phonological Word*. Doctoral dissertation. Chicago: University of Chicago.

Breen, Gavan, and Pensalfini, Rob (1999) Arrernte: A language with no syllable onsets. *Linguistic Inquiry* 30, 1–25.

Bresnan, Joan (1971) Sentence stress and syntactic transformations. *Language* 47, 257–81.

Bresnan, Joan (ed.) (1982) *The Mental Representation of Grammatical Relations*. Cambridge, MA: MIT Press.

Bresnan, Joan (2000) Optimal syntax, In *Optimality Theory: Phonology, Syntax, and Acquisition*, ed. Joost Dekkers, Frank van der Leeuw, and Jeroen van de Weijer, pp. 334–85. Oxford: Oxford University Press.

Bresnan, Joan (to appear-a) The emergence of the unmarked pronoun: Chicheŵa pronominals in Optimality Theory. In *OT Syntax*, ed. Géraldine Legendre, Jane Grimshaw, and Sten Vikner. Cambridge, MA: MIT Press.

Bresnan, Joan (to appear-b) Explaining morphosyntactic competition. In *Handbook of Contemporary Syntactic Theory*, ed. Mark Baltin and Chris Collins. Oxford: Blackwell.

Broe, Michael, Frisch, Stefan, and Pierrehumbert, Janet (1995) The role of similarity in phonology: Explaining OCP-Place. In *Proceedings of the 13th International Conference of the Phonetic Sciences*, ed. K. Elenius and P. Branderud, vol. 3, pp. 544–47. Stockholm: Stockholm University.

Broihier, Kevin (1995) Optimality-theoretic rankings with tied constraints: Slavic relatives, resumptive pronouns, and learnability. Unpublished manuscript. Cambridge, MA: Massachusetts Institute of Technology. [Available on Rutgers Optimality Archive.]

Bromberger, Sylvain, and Halle, Morris (1989) Why phonology is different. *Linguistic Inquiry* 20, 51–70.

Bromberger, Sylvain, and Halle, Morris (1997) The contents of phonological signs: A comparison between their use in derivational theories and in optimality theories. In *Derivations and Constraints in Phonology*, ed. Iggy Roca, pp. 93–124. New York: Oxford University Press.

Broselow, Ellen (1976) *The Phonology of Egyptian Arabic*. Doctoral dissertation. Amherst: University of Massachusetts.

Broselow, Ellen (1982) On predicting the interaction of stress and epenthesis. *Glossa* 16, 115–32.

Broselow, Ellen (1992) Parametric variation in Arabic dialect phonology. In *Perspectives on Arabic Linguistics*, ed. Ellen Broselow, Mushira Eid, and John J. McCarthy, pp. 7–45. Amsterdam and Philadelphia: John Benjamins.

Broselow, Ellen, Chen, Su-I, and Huffman, Marie (1997) Syllable weight: Convergence of phonology and phonetics. *Phonology* 14, 47–82.

Broselow, Ellen, Chen, Su-I, and Wang, Chilin (1998) The emergence of the unmarked in second language phonology. *Studies in Second Language Acquisition* 20, 261–80.

Bruck, Anthony, Fox, Robert A., and La Galy, Michael W. (eds.) (1974) *Papers from the Parasession on Natural Phonology*. Chicago: Chicago Linguistic Society.

Buckley, Eugene (1997) Explaining Kashaya infixation. In *Proceedings of the Twenty-third Annual Meeting of the Berkeley Linguistics Society*, ed. Matthew L. Juge and Jeri L. Moxley, pp. 14–25. Berkeley: Berkeley Linguistic Society.

Buckley, Eugene (1998) Iambic lengthening and final vowels. *International Journal of American Linguistics* 64, 179–223.

Burzio, Luigi (1994a) Metrical consistency. In *Language Computations*, ed. Eric Sven Ristad, pp. 93–125. Providence, RI: American Mathematical Society.

Burzio, Luigi (1994b) *Principles of English Stress*. Cambridge: Cambridge University Press.

Burzio, Luigi (1995) The rise of Optimality Theory. *Glot International* 1 (6), 3–7.

Burzio, Luigi (1996) Surface constraints versus underlying representation. In *Current Trends in Phonology: Models and Methods*, ed. Jacques Durand and Bernard Laks, pp. 123–42. Manchester, UK: European Studies Research Institute, University of Salford.

Burzio, Luigi (1997) Italian participial morphology and correspondence theory. In *Proceedings of the First Mediterranean Conference of Morphology (Mytilene, Greece, Sept. 19–21, 1997)*, ed. Geert Booij, Angela Ralli, and Sergio Scalise, pp. 42–53. Patras, Greece: University of Patras.

Burzio, Luigi (1998) Anaphora and soft constraints. In *Is the Best Good Enough? Optimality and Competition in Syntax*, ed. Pilar Barbosa, Danny Fox, Paul Hagstrom, Martha McGinnis, and David Pesetsky, pp. 93–113. Cambridge, MA: MIT Press.

Burzio, Luigi (1999) Surface-to-surface morphology: When your representations turn into constraints. Unpublished manuscript. Baltimore: Johns Hopkins University. [Available on Rutgers Optimality Archive.]

Calabrese, Andrea (1987) The interaction of phonological rules and filters. In *Proceedings of the North East Linguistic Society 17*, ed. Bernadette Plunkett and Joyce McDonough, pp. 79–99. Amherst, MA: GLSA.

Calabrese, Andrea (1988) *Towards a Theory of Phonological Alphabets*. Doctoral dissertation. Cambridge: Massachusetts Institute of Technology.

Calabrese, Andrea (1995) A constraint-based theory of phonological markedness and simplification procedures. *Linguistic Inquiry* 26, 373–463.

Campbell, Lyle (1973) *Extrinsic Order Lives*. Bloomington, IN: IULC.

Carlson, Katy (1998) Reduplication and sonority in Nakanai and Nuxalk. In *Proceedings of the Fourteenth Eastern States Conference on Linguistics '97*, ed. J. Austin and A. Lawson, pp. 23–33. Ithaca, NY: Cornell Linguistics Circle.

Casali, Roderic F. (1996) *Resolving Hiatus*. Doctoral dissertation. Los Angeles: University of California.

Casali, Roderic F. (1997) Vowel elision in hiatus contexts: Which vowel goes? *Language* 73, 493–533.

Causley, Trisha (1997) Identity and featural correspondence: The Athapaskan case. In *Proceedings of the North East Linguistic Society 27*, ed. Kiyomi Kusumoto, pp. 93–105. Amherst, MA: GLSA.

Causley, Trisha (1999a) *Complexity and Markedness in Optimality Theory*. Doctoral dissertation. Toronto: University of Toronto.

Causley, Trisha (1999b) Faithfulness and contrast: The problem of coalescence. In *The Proceedings of the West Coast Conference on Formal Linguistics 17*, ed. Kimary N. Shahin, Susan J. Blake, and Eun-Sook Kim, pp. 117–31. Stanford, CA: CSLI.

Chafe, Wallace (1968) The ordering of phonological rules. *International Journal of American Linguistics* 24, 115–36.

Chao, Yuen-ren (1934) The non-uniqueness of phonemic solutions of phonetic systems. *Academia Sinica (Bulletin of the Institute of History and Philology)* 4 (4), 363–97. [Reprinted in Martin Joos, ed., (1957) *Readings in Linguistics*, vol. 1, pp. 38–54. Washington, DC: American Council of Learned Societies.]

Charette, Monik (1988) *Some Constraints on Governing Relations in Phonology*. Doctoral dissertation. Montreal: McGill University.

Chen, Matthew (1973) On the formal expression of natural rules in phonology. *Journal of Linguistics* 9, 223–49.

Chen, Matthew (1987) The syntax of Xiamen tone sandhi. *Phonology* 4, 109–50.

Cherry, E. Colin, Jakobson, Roman, and Halle, Morris (1952) Toward the logical description of languages in their phonemic aspect. *Language* 29, 34–46.

Cho, Young-mee Yu (1990a) *Parameters of Consonantal Assimilation*. Doctoral dissertation. Stanford, CA: Stanford University.

Cho, Young-mee Yu (1990b) Syntax and phrasing in Korean. In *The Phonology-Syntax Connection*, ed. Sharon Inkelas and Draga Zec, pp. 47–62. Chicago: University of Chicago Press.

Cho, Young-mee Yu (1995) Rule ordering and constraint interaction in OT. In *Proceedings of the Berkeley Linguistics Society 21*, pp. 336–50. Berkeley: Berkeley Linguistics Society.

Cho, Young-mee Yu (1998) Language change as reranking of constraints. In *Historical Linguistics 1995*, vol. 2, ed. Richard M. Hogg and Linda van Bergen, pp. 45–62. Amsterdam and Philadelphia: John Benjamins.

Choi, Hye-Won (1996) *Optimizing Structure in Context: Scrambling and Information Structure*. Doctoral dissertation. Stanford, CA: Stanford University. [Available on Rutgers Optimality Archive.]

Choi, Hye-Won (to appear) Binding and discourse prominence: Reconstruction in "focus" scrambling. In *OT Syntax*, ed. Géraldine Legendre, Jane Grimshaw, and Sten Vikner. Cambridge, MA: MIT Press.

Chomsky, Noam (1951) *Morphophonemics of Modern Hebrew*. MA thesis. Philadelphia: University of Pennsylvania. [Published by Garland Press, New York, 1979.]

Chomsky, Noam (1957) *Syntactic Structures*. The Hague: Mouton.

Chomsky, Noam (1965) *Aspects of the Theory of Syntax*. Cambridge, MA: MIT Press.

Chomsky, Noam (1968) *Language and Mind*. New York: Harcourt Brace Jovanovich.

Chomsky, Noam (1973) Conditions on transformations. In *A Festschrift for Morris Halle*, ed. Stephen R. Anderson and Paul Kiparsky, pp. 232–86. New York: Holt, Rinehart, and Winston.

Chomsky, Noam (1975) *The Logical Structure of Linguistic Theory*. New York: Plenum Press. [Excerpted from 1956 revision of 1955 Harvard/Massachusetts Institute of Technology manuscript.]

Chomsky, Noam (1981) *Lectures on Government and Binding*. Dordrecht: Foris.

Chomsky, Noam (1986) *Barriers*. Cambridge, MA: MIT Press.

Chomsky, Noam (1993) A minimalist program for linguistic theory. In *The View from Building 20: Essays in Linguistics in Honor of Sylvain Bromberger*, ed. Kenneth Hale and Samuel Jay Keyser, pp. 1–52. Cambridge, MA: MIT Press.

Chomsky, Noam (1995) *The Minimalist Program*. Cambridge, MA: MIT Press.

Chomsky, Noam, and Halle, Morris (1968) *The Sound Pattern of English*. New York: Harper & Row.

Chomsky, Noam, and Lasnik, Howard (1977) Filters and control. *Linguistic Inquiry* 8, 425–504.

Chung, Chin Wan (1999) *Reduplication in Korean*. Doctoral dissertation. Bloomington: Indiana University.

Clayton, Mary L. (1976) The redundance of underlying morpheme-structure conditions. *Language* 52, 295–313.

Clements, G. N. (1978) Tone and syntax in Ewe. In *Elements of Tone, Stress, and Intonation*, ed. Donna Jo Napoli, pp. 21–99. Washington, DC: Georgetown University Press.

Clements, G. N. (1986) Syllabification and epenthesis in the Barra dialect of Gaelic. In *The Phonological Representation of Suprasegmentals*, ed. Koen Bogers, Harry van der Hulst, and Maarten Mous, pp. 317–36. Dordrecht: Foris.

Clements, G. N. (1997) Berber syllabification: Derivations or constraints? In *Derivations and Constraints in Phonology*, ed. Iggy Roca, pp. 289–330. New York: Oxford University Press.

Clements, G. N., and Hume, Elizabeth (1995) The internal organization of speech sounds. In *The Handbook of Phonological Theory*, ed. John A. Goldsmith, pp. 245–306. Cambridge, MA: Blackwell.

Clifton, Deborah (1975) Tracing Laffitte's conspiracy or: What went down at Contraband Bayou. In *Papers from the 11th Regional Meeting, Chicago Linguistic Society*, ed. Robin E. Grossman, L. James San, and Timothy J. Vance, pp. 102–11. Chicago: Chicago Linguistic Society.

Cohn, Abigail (1989) Stress in Indonesian and bracketing paradoxes. *Natural Language and Linguistic Theory* 7, 167–216.

Cohn, Abigail (1990) *Phonetic and Phonological Rules of Nasalization*. Doctoral dissertation. Los Angeles: University of California.

Cohn, Abigail, and McCarthy, John J. (1994/1998) Alignment and parallelism in Indonesian phonology. *Working Papers of the Cornell Phonetics Laboratory* 12, 53–137. [Available (1994) on Rutgers Optimality Archive.]

Cole, Jennifer (1995) The cycle in phonology. In *The Handbook of Phonological Theory*, ed. John A. Goldsmith, pp. 70–113. Cambridge, MA: Blackwell.

Cole, Jennifer, and Kisseberth, Charles (1995) Restricting multi-level constraint evaluation: Opaque rule interaction in Yawelmani vowel harmony. Unpublished manuscript. Urbana: University of Illinois. [Available on Rutgers Optimality Archive.]

Coleman, John (1991) *Phonological Representations – Their Names, Forms and Powers*. Doctoral dissertation. University of York, UK.

Coleman, John (1998) *Phonological Representations: Their Names, Forms and Powers*. Cambridge: Cambridge University Press.

Costa, João (1998) *Word Order Variation: A Constraint-Based Approach*. The Hague: Holland Academic Graphics. [Doctoral dissertation, University of Leiden.]

Costa, João (to appear) The emergence of unmarked word order. In *OT Syntax*, ed. Géraldine Legendre, Jane Grimshaw, and Sten Vikner. Cambridge, MA: MIT Press.

Croft, William (1998) What (some) functionalists can learn from (some) formalists. In *Functionalism and Formalism in Linguistics*. Vol. I, *General Papers*, ed. Michael Darnell, Edith Moravcsik, Frederick J. Newmeyer, Michael Noonan, and Kathleen Wheatley, pp. 85–108. Amsterdam: John Benjamins.

Crosswhite, Katherine (1997) Intra-paradigmatic homophony avoidance in two dialects of Slavic. Unpublished manuscript. Los Angeles: University of California. [Available for download (7/23/00) at http://www.humnet.ucla.edu/humnet/linguistics/people/grads/crosswhi/homophon.ps.]

Crosswhite, Katherine (1998) Segmental vs. prosodic correspondence in Chamorro. *Phonology* 15, 281–316.

Crosswhite, Katherine (1999) *Vowel Reduction in Optimality Theory*. Doctoral dissertation. Los Angeles: University of California.

Crowhurst, Megan, and Hewitt, Mark (1994) Directional footing, degeneracy, and alignment. Unpublished manuscript. Chapel Hill, NC: University of North Carolina; Vancouver: University of British Columbia. [Available on Rutgers Optimality Archive.]

Crowhurst, Megan, and Hewitt, Mark (1995) Prosodic overlay and headless feet in Yidiny. *Phonology* 12, 39–84.

Crowhurst, Megan, and Hewitt, Mark (1997) Boolean operations and constraint interactions in Optimality Theory. Unpublished manuscript. Chapel Hill, NC: University of North Carolina; Waltham, MA: Brandeis University. [Available on Rutgers Optimality Archive.]

Csik, Steven, and Papa, Eugene (1979) *Theoretical Issues in Phonology: An Annotated Bibliography*. Bloomington, IN: IULC. [Volumes I and II bound together. Covers 1968–78.]

Dalgish, Gerry (1975) On underlying and superficial constraints in Olutsootso. In *Papers from the 11th Regional Meeting, Chicago Linguistic Society*, ed. Robin Grossman, L. James San, and Timothy Vance, pp. 142–51. Chicago: Chicago Linguistic Society.

Davidson, Lisa, Juszcyk, Peter, and Smolensky, Paul (to appear) The initial state and the final state: Theoretical implications of Richness of the Base and empirical explorations. In *Fixing Priorities: Constraints in Phonological Acquisition*, ed. René Kager, Joe Pater, and Wim Zonneveld. Cambridge: Cambridge University Press.

Davidson, Lisa, and Noyer, Rolf (1997) Loan phonology in Huave: Nativization and the ranking of faithfulness constraints. In *The Proceedings of the West Coast Conference on Formal Linguistics 15*, ed. Brian Agbayani and Sze-Wing Tang, pp. 65–79. Stanford, CA: CSLI.

Davis, Stuart (1995) Emphasis spread in Arabic and Grounded Phonology. *Linguistic Inquiry* 26, 465–98.

Davis, Stuart (1997) A sympathetic account of nasal substitution in Ponapean. In *Phonology at Santa Cruz*, ed. Rachel Walker, Motoko Katayama, and Daniel Karvonen, pp. 15–28. Santa Cruz: Linguistics Research Center, University of California.

Davis, Stuart (1999) The parallel distribution of aspirated stops and /h/ in American English. In *Indiana University Working Papers in Linguistics*, ed. Karen Baertsch and Daniel Dinnsen, pp. 1–10. Bloomington, IN: IULC.

de Lacy, Paul (1998) Sympathetic stress. Unpublished manuscript. Amherst: University of Massachusetts. [Available on Rutgers Optimality Archive.]

de Lacy, Paul (1999) Tone and prominence. Unpublished manuscript. Amherst: University of Massachusetts. [Available on Rutgers Optimality Archive.]

de Lacy, Paul (2000a) Circumscriptive morphemes. In *Proceedings of AFLA VI: The Sixth Meeting of the Austronesian Formal Linguistics Association (Toronto Working Papers in Linguistics)*, ed. Catherine Kitto and Carolyn Smallwood, pp. 107–20. Toronto: Department of Linguistics, University of Toronto.

de Lacy, Paul (2000b) Markedness in prominent positions. In *Proceedings of HUMIT (MIT Working Papers in Linguistics)*, ed. Adam Szcegielniak. Cambridge: Department of Linguistics and Philosophy, Massachusetts Institute of Technology.

de Lacy, Paul (2000c) Prosodic phrasing in Maori. Unpublished manuscript. Amherst: University of Massachusetts. [Available on Rutgers Optimality Archive.]

Dell, François (1973) *Les règles et les sons*. Paris: Hermann, Collection Savoir.

Dell, François (1980) *Generative Phonology and French Phonology*, trans. Catherine Cullen. Cambridge: Cambridge University Press. [An abridged translation appeared as *Generative Phonology* from the same publisher in the same year.]

Demuth, Katherine (1995a) Markedness and the development of prosodic structure. In *Proceedings of the North East Linguistic Society 25*, ed. Jill Beckman, pp. 13–25. Amherst, MA: GLSA.

Demuth, Katherine (1995b) Stages in the acquisition of prosodic structure. In *Proceedings of the 27th Child Language Research Forum*, ed. Eve Clark, pp. 39–48. Stanford, CA: CSLI.

Demuth, Katherine (1996) Alignment, stress and parsing in early phonological words. In *Proceedings of the UBC International Conference on Phonological Acquisition*, ed. Barbara H. Bernhardt, John Gilbert, and David Ingram, pp. 113–24. Somerville, MA: Cascadilla Press.

Demuth, Katherine (1997a) Multiple optimal outputs in acquisition. In *University of Maryland Working Papers in Linguistics 5. Selected Phonology Papers from Hopkins Optimality Theory Workshop 1997/University of Maryland Mayfest 1997*, ed. Viola Miglio and Bruce Morén, pp. 53–71. College Park: Department of Linguistics, University of Maryland.

Demuth, Katherine (1997b) Variation in acquisition: An optimal approach. In *Optimal Viewpoints: In Celebration of the 30th Anniversary of the IULC Publications*, ed. Stuart Davis, pp. 77–88. Bloomington, IN: IULC.

Denton, Jeannette Marshall, Chan, Grace P., and Canakis, Costas P. (eds.) (1993) *Papers from the 28th Regional Meeting of the Chicago Linguistic Society*. Vol. 2, *The Parasession: The Cycle in Linguistic Theory*. Chicago: Chicago Linguistic Society.

Déprez, Viviane (1994) A minimal account of the that-t effect. In *Paths toward Universal Grammar: Studies in Honor of Richard S. Kayne*, ed. Guglielmo Cinque, Jan Koster, J.-Y. Pollock, and R. Zanuttini, pp. 121–35. Washington, DC: Georgetown University Press.

Devine, A. M., and Stephens, Laurence (1974) Phonological rules and structural constraints. *Papers in Linguistics* 7, 51–68.

Dinnsen, Daniel A. (ed.) (1979) *Current Approaches to Phonological Theory*. Bloomington: Indiana University Press.

Dinnsen, Daniel A. (2001) New insights from Optimality Theory for acquisition. *Clinical Linguistics and Phonetics* 15, 15–18.

Dinnsen, Daniel A., and Barlow, Jessica A. (1998a) On the characterization of a chain shift in normal and delayed phonological acquisition. *Journal of Child Language* 25, 61–94.

Dinnsen, Daniel A., and Barlow, Jessica A. (1998b) Root and manner feature faithfulness in acquisition. In *Proceedings of the 22rd Annual Boston University Conference on Language Development*, ed. Annabel Greenhill, Elizabeth Hughes, Heather Littlefield, and H. Walsh, vol. 1, pp. 165–76. Somerville, MA: Cascadilla Press.

Dinnsen, Daniel A., and McGarrity, Laura W. (1999) Variation and emerging faithfulness in phonological acquisition. In *Proceedings of the 23rd Annual Boston University Conference on Language Development*, ed. Annabel Greenhill, Heather Littlefield, and Cheryl Tano, pp. 172–83. Somerville, MA: Cascadilla Press.

Dixon, R. M. W. (1977a) *A Grammar of Yidiny*. Cambridge: Cambridge University Press.

Dixon, R. M. W. (1977b) Some phonological rules of Yidiny. *Linguistic Inquiry* 8, 1–34.

Donegan, Patricia J. (1978) *The Natural Phonology of Vowels*. Doctoral dissertation. Columbus: Ohio State University. [Published by Garland Press, New York, 1985.]

Donegan, Patricia J., and Stampe, David (1979) The study of natural phonology. In *Current Approaches to Phonological Theory*, ed. Daniel A. Dinnsen, pp. 126–73. Bloomington: Indiana University Press.

Downing, Laura (1999) Verbal reduplication in three Bantu languages. In *The Prosody-Morphology Interface*, ed. Rene Kager, Harry van der Hulst, and Wim Zonneveld, pp. 62–89. Cambridge: Cambridge University Press.

Drachman, G., Kager, René, and Drachman, A. (1997) Greek allomorphy: An Optimality account. In *Proceedings of the 2nd International Congress on Greek Linguistics*, pp. 151–60. Salzburg, Austria: University of Salzburg.

Dresher, B. Elan (1983) Postlexical phonology in Tiberian Hebrew. In *The Proceedings of the West Coast Conference on Formal Linguistics 2*, ed. M. Barlow, D. Flickinger, and M. Wescoat, pp. 67–78. Stanford, CA: Stanford Linguistic Association.

Dresher, B. Elan (1993) The chronology and status of Anglian smoothing. In *Studies in Lexical Phonology*, ed. Sharon Hargus and Ellen M. Kaisse, pp. 325–41. San Diego, CA: Academic Press.

Dresher, B. Elan (1999) Charting the learning path: Cues to parameter setting. *Linguistic Inquiry* 30, 27–67.

Dresher, B. Elan, and van der Hulst, Harry (1998) Head-dependent asymmetries in phonology: Complexity and Visibility. *Phonology* 15, 317–52.

Dresher, B. Elan, and Kaye, Jonathan (1990) A computational learning model for metrical phonology. *Cognition* 34, 137–95.

Dressler, Wolfgang (1971) Some constraints on phonological change. In *Papers from the 7th Regional Meeting, Chicago Linguistic Society*, ed. Douglas Adams, Mary Ann Campbell, Victor Cohen, Julie Lovins, Edward Maxwell, Carolyn Nygren, and John Reighard, pp. 340–49. Chicago: Chicago Linguistic Society.

Dressler, Wolfgang (1985) On the predictiveness of natural morphology. *Journal of Linguistics* 21, 321–37.

Durand, Jacques (1986) French liaison, floating segments and other matters in a dependency framework. In *Dependency and Non-Linear Phonology*, ed. Jacques Durand, pp. 161–201. London: Croom Helm.

Eisner, Jason (1997) Efficient generation in Primitive Optimality Theory. Unpublished manuscript. Philadelphia: University of Pennsylvania. [Available on Rutgers Optimality Archive.]

Elenbaas, Nine, and Kager, René (1999) Ternary rhythm and the Lapse constraint. *Phonology* 16, 273–330.

Ellison, T. Mark (1994) Phonological derivation in Optimality Theory. In *Proceedings of the 15th International Conference on Computational Linguistics (COLING)*, pp. 1007–13. Kyoto. [Available on Rutgers Optimality Archive.]

Elman, Jeffrey L. (1990) Finding structure in time. *Cognitive Science* 14, 179–211.

Emonds, Joseph (1970) *Root and Structure-Preserving Transformations*. Doctoral dissertation. Cambridge, MA: Massachusetts Institute of Technology.

Ewen, Colin (1995) Dependency relations in phonology. In *The Handbook of Phonological Theory*, ed. John A. Goldsmith, pp. 570–85. Cambridge, MA: Blackwell.

Farwaneh, Samira (1995) *Directionality Effects in Arabic Dialect Syllable Structure*. Doctoral dissertation. Salt Lake City: University of Utah.

Flemming, Edward S. (1995) *Auditory Representations in Phonology*. Doctoral dissertation. Los Angeles: University of California.

Frank, Robert, and Satta, Giorgio (1998) Optimality Theory and the computational complexity of constraint violability. *Computational Linguistics* 24, 307–15.

Friberg, Timothy, and Friberg, Barbara (1991) Notes on Konjo phonology. In *Studies in Sulawesi Linguistics*, Part 2, ed. J. N. Sneddon. Jakarta, Indonesia: NUSA Linguistic Studies.

Frisch, Stefan (1996) *Similarity and Frequency in Phonology*. Doctoral dissertation. Evanston, IL: Northwestern University. [Available on Rutgers Optimality Archive.]

Frisch, Stefan (2000) Temporally organized lexical representations as phonological units. In *Language Acquisition and the Lexicon: Papers in Laboratory Phonology V*, ed.

Michael Broe and Janet Pierrehumbert, pp. 283–98. Cambridge: Cambridge University Press.

Frisch, Stefan, Broe, Michael, and Pierrehumbert, Janet (1997) Similarity and phonotactics in Arabic. Unpublished manuscript. Evanston, IL: Northwestern University. [Available on Rutgers Optimality Archive.]

Fukazawa, Haruka (1999) *Theoretical Implications of OCP Effects on Features in Optimality Theory*. Doctoral dissertation. College Park: University of Maryland.

Fukazawa, Haruka, Kitahara, Mafuyu, and Ota, Mitsuhiko (1998) Lexical stratification and ranking invariance in constraint-based grammars. In *CLS 32*. Part 2, *The Panels*, ed. M. Catherine Gruber, Derrick Higgins, Kenneth Olson, and Tamra Wysocki, pp. 47–62. Chicago: Chicago Linguistic Society.

Fukazawa, Haruka, and Lombardi, Linda (to appear) To be simple or not to be: Constraints in Optimality Theory. In *Proceedings of the First Tokyo Conference on Psycholinguistics*, ed. Yukio Otsu and Y. Furukawa. Tokyo: Hitsuji-Shobo.

Fukazawa, Haruka, and Miglio, Viola (1998) Restricting conjunction to constraint families. In *Proceedings of the Western Conference on Linguistics 9 (WECOL 96)*, ed. Vida Samiian, pp. 102–17. Fresno: Department of Linguistics, California State University.

Fulmer, S. Lee (1997) *Parallelism and Planes in Optimality Theory*. Doctoral dissertation. Tucson: University of Arizona.

Futagi, Yoko (1998) Root-reduplicant faithfulness. In *The Proceedings of the West Coast Conference on Formal Linguistics 16*, ed. Emily Curtis, James Lyle, and Gabriel Webster, pp. 207–22. Stanford, CA: CSLI.

Gafos, Adamantios (1996) *The Articulatory Basis of Locality in Phonology*. Doctoral dissertation. Baltimore: Johns Hopkins University.

Gafos, Adamantios (1998) A-templatic reduplication. *Linguistic Inquiry* 29, 515–27.

Gafos, Adamantios, and Lombardi, Linda (1999) Consonant transparency and vowel echo. In *Proceedings of the North East Linguistic Society 29*. Vol. 2, *Papers from the Poster Sessions*, ed. Pius N. Tamanji, Mako Hirotani, and Nancy Hall, pp. 81–95. Amherst, MA: GLSA.

Gazdar, Gerald, Klein, Ewan, Pullum, Geoffrey K., and Sag, Ivan A. (1985) *Generalized Phrase Structure Grammar*. Oxford: Blackwell; Cambridge, MA: Harvard University Press.

Gerdemann, Dale, and van Noord, Gertjan (2000) Approximation and Exactness in Finite State Optimality Theory. Unpublished manuscript. Tübingen: University of Tübingen; Groningen: University of Groningen. [Available for download (7/1/00) from http://arXiv.org/find/cs/1/au:+Gerdemann/0/1/0/past,all/0/1/ps/cs.CL/0006038.]

Gerlach, Birgit (1998) Restrictions on Clitic Sequences and Conditions on the Occurrence of Clitics in Romance. Report no. 105. Düsseldorf, Germany: Heinrich-Heine-Universität. [Available on Rutgers Optimality Archive.]

Gess, Randall (1996) *Optimality Theory in the Historical Phonology of French*. Doctoral dissertation. Seattle: University of Washington.

Gess, Randall (1998a) Alignment and sonority in the syllable structure of Late Latin and Gallo-Romance. In *Theoretical Analyses on Romance Languages*, ed. José Lima and Esthela Treviño, pp. 193–204. Amsterdam: John Benjamins.

Gess, Randall (1998b) Old French NoCoda effects from constraint interaction. *Probus* 10, 207–18.

Gess, Randall (1998c) Phonetics versus phonology in sound change: An Optimality-Theoretic perspective. *Texas Linguistic Forum* 41, 71–86.

Gess, Randall (1999) Bibliography: Optimality Theory and language change. Unpublished manuscript. [Available on Rutgers Optimality Archive.]

Gibson, Edward, and Broihier, Kevin (1998) Optimality Theory and human sentence processing. In *Is the Best Good Enough? Optimality and Competition in Syntax*, ed. Pilar Barbosa, Danny Fox, Paul Hagstrom, Martha McGinnis, and David Pesetsky, pp. 157–91. Cambridge, MA: MIT Press.

Gibson, Edward, and Wexler, Kenneth (1994) Triggers. *Linguistic Inquiry* 25, 407–54.

Gierut, Judith A. (2001) A model of lexical diffusion in phonological acquisition. *Clinical Linguistics and Phonetics* 15, 19–22.

Gierut, Judith A., and Morrisette, Michele (1998) Lexical properties in implementation of sound change. In *Proceedings of the 22rd Annual Boston University Conference on Language Development*, ed. Annabel Greenhill, Elizabeth Hughes, Heather Littlefield, and H. Walsh, vol. 1, pp. 257–68. Somerville, MA: Cascadilla Press.

Gierut, Judith A., Morrisette, Michele, and Champion, A. H. (1999) Lexical constraints in phonological acquisition. *Journal of Child Language* 26, 261–94.

Gilbers, D. G., and van der Linde, K. J. (1999) On the acquisition of segments in Optimality Theory: The acquisition of segments as a conflict between correspondence and markedness constraints. In *Phonological Development: Different Perspectives*, ed. M. Beers and S. Peters, pp. 33–68. Antwerp Papers in Linguistics 96. Antwerp: Linguistics Department, University of Antwerp.

Gnanadesikan, Amalia (1995/to appear) Markedness and faithfulness constraints in child phonology. In *Fixing Priorities: Constraints in Phonological Acquisition*, ed. René Kager, Joe Pater, and Wim Zonneveld. Cambridge: Cambridge University Press. [Available (1995) on Rutgers Optimality Archive.]

Gnanadesikan, Amalia (1996) Child phonology in Optimality Theory: Ranking markedness and faithfulness constraints. In *Proceedings of the 20th Annual Boston University Conference on Language Development*, ed. A. Stringfellow, D. Cahana-Amitay, E. Hughes, and A. Zukowski, pp. 237–48. Somerville, MA: Cascadilla Press.

Gnanadesikan, Amalia (1997) *Phonology with Ternary Scales*. Doctoral dissertation. Amherst: University of Massachusetts.

Goad, Heather (1996) Consonant harmony in child language: Evidence against coronal underspecification. In *Proceedings of the UBC International Conference on Phonological Acquisition*, ed. Barbara H. Bernhardt, John Gilbert, and David Ingram, pp. 187–200. Somerville, MA: Cascadilla Press.

Goad, Heather (1997) Consonant harmony in child language: An Optimality-Theoretic account. In *Focus on Phonological Acquisition*, ed. S.-J. Hannahs and Martha Young-Scholten, pp. 113–42. Amsterdam: John Benjamins.

Goad, Heather, and Rose, Yvan (to appear) A structural account of cluster reduction in the acquisition of West Germanic languages. In *Fixing Priorities: Constraints in Phonological Acquisition*, ed. René Kager, Joe Pater, and Wim Zonneveld. Cambridge: Cambridge University Press.

Goldrick, Matthew (2000) Turbid output representations and the unity of opacity. In *Proceedings of the North East Linguistics Society 30*, ed. Masako Hirotani, pp. 231–46. Amherst, MA: GLSA.

Goldsmith, John (1976a) *Autosegmental Phonology*. Doctoral dissertation. Cambridge: Massachusetts Institute of Technology. [Published by Garland Press, New York, 1979.]

Goldsmith, John (1976b) An overview of autosegmental phonology. *Linguistic Analysis* 2, 23–68.

Goldsmith, John (1990) *Autosegmental and Metrical Phonology*. Cambridge, MA: Blackwell.

Goldsmith, John (1991) Phonology as an intelligent system. In *Bridges between Psychology and Linguistics: A Swarthmore Festschrift for Lila Gleitman*, ed. Donna Jo Napoli and Judy Kegl, pp. 247–67. Hillsdale, NJ: Lawrence Erlbaum Associates.

Goldsmith, John (1992) Local modeling in phonology. In *Connectionism: Theory and Practice*, ed. S. Davis, pp. 229–46. New York: Oxford University Press.

Goldsmith, John (1993a) Harmonic phonology. In *The Last Phonological Rule*, ed. John Goldsmith, pp. 21–60. Chicago: University of Chicago Press.

Goldsmith, John (ed.) (1993b) *The Last Phonological Rule: Reflections on Constraints and Derivations*. Chicago: University of Chicago Press.

Goldsmith, John (ed.) (1995) *The Handbook of Phonological Theory*. Oxford: Blackwell.

Goldsmith, John (1996) Tone in Mituku: How a floating tone nailed down an intermediate level. In *Current Trends in Phonology: Models and Methods*, ed. Jacques Durand and Bernard Laks, pp. 267–80. Manchester, UK: European Studies Research Institute, University of Salford.

Goldsmith, John, and Larson, Gary (1990) Local modeling and syllabification. In *Papers from the 26th Regional Meeting of the Chicago Linguistic Society*. Vol. 2, *The Parasession on the Syllable in Phonetics and Phonology*, ed. Michael Ziolkowski, Manuela Noske, and Karen Deaton, pp. 129–42. Chicago: Chicago Linguistic Society.

Golston, Chris (1995) Syntax outranks phonology: Evidence from Ancient Greek. *Phonology* 12, 343–68.

Golston, Chris (1996) Direct OT: Representation as pure markedness. *Language* 72, 713–48.

Gordon, Matthew (1999) *Syllable Weight: Phonetics, Phonology, and Typology*. Doctoral dissertation. Los Angeles: University of California.

Goyvaerts, Didier L., and Pullum, Geoffrey K. (eds.) (1975) *Essays on the Sound Pattern of English*. Ghent, Belgium: E. Story-Scientia.

Green, Antony Dubach (1996) Some effects of the Weight-to-Stress Principle and Grouping Harmony in the Goidelic languages. *Working Papers of the Cornell Phonetics Laboratory* 11, 117–55. [Available on Rutgers Optimality Archive.]

Green, Antony Dubach (1997) *The Prosodic Structure of Irish, Scots Gaelic, and Manx*. Doctoral dissertation. Ithaca, NY: Cornell University. [Available on Rutgers Optimality Archive.]

Green, Tom (1993) The conspiracy of completeness. Unpublished manuscript. Cambridge: Massachusetts Institute of Technology. [Available on Rutgers Optimality Archive.]

Green, Tom, and Kenstowicz, Michael (1995) The Lapse constraint. Unpublished manuscript. Cambridge: Massachusetts Institute of Technology. [Available on Rutgers Optimality Archive.]

Gregersen, Edgar A. (1974) Consonant polarity in Nilotic. In *Third Annual Conference on African Linguistics (1972)*, ed. Erhard Voeltz, pp. 105–9. Bloomington: Indiana University.

Grijzenhout, Janet, and Joppen, Sandra (to appear) First steps in the acquisition of German consonants: Minimal constraint demotion. In *Fixing Priorities: Constraints in Phonological Acquisition*, ed. René Kager, Joe Pater, and Wim Zonneveld. Cambridge: Cambridge University Press.

Grijzenhout, Janet, and Kraemer, Martin (1999) Final devoicing and voicing assimilation in Dutch derivation and cliticization. Unpublished manuscript. Duesseldorf, Germany: University of Duesseldorf. [Available on Rutgers Optimality Archive.]

Grimshaw, Jane (1993) Minimal projection, heads, and optimality. Unpublished manuscript. New Brunswick, NJ: Rutgers University. [Available on Rutgers Optimality Archive.]

Grimshaw, Jane (1994) Minimal projection and clause structure. In *Syntactic Theory and First Language Acquisition: Cross-Linguistic Perspectives*. Vol. I, *Heads, Projections, and Learnability*, ed. Barbara Lust, Margarita Suñer, and John Whitman, pp. 75–83. Hillsdale, NJ: Lawrence Erlbaum.

Grimshaw, Jane (1997a) The best clitic: Constraint conflict in morphosyntax. In *Elements of Grammar*, ed. Liliane Haegeman, pp. 169–96. Dordrecht: Kluwer.

Grimshaw, Jane (1997b) Projection, heads, and optimality. *Linguistic Inquiry* 28, 373–422.

Grimshaw, Jane (to appear) Optimal clitic positions and the lexicon in Romance clitic systems. In *OT Syntax*, ed. Géraldine Legendre, Jane Grimshaw, and Sten Vikner. Cambridge, MA: MIT Press.

Grimshaw, Jane, and Samek-Lodovici, Vieri (1995) Optimal subjects. In *Papers in Optimality Theory*, ed. Jill Beckman, Laura Walsh Dickey, and Suzanne Urbanczyk, pp. 589–606. Amherst, MA: GLSA.

Grimshaw, Jane, and Samek-Lodovici, Vieri (1998) Optimal subjects and subject universals. In *Is the Best Good Enough? Optimality and Competition in Syntax*, ed. Pilar Barbosa, Danny Fox, Paul Hagstrom, Martha McGinnis, and David Pesetsky, pp. 193–219. Cambridge, MA: MIT Press.

Gussenhoven, Carlos, and Jacobs, Haike (1998) *Understanding Phonology*. New York: Oxford University Press.

Guy, Gregory (1997) Competence, performance, and the generative grammar of variation. In *Variation, Change, and Phonological Theory*, ed. Frans Hinskens, Roeland van Hout, and W. Leo Wetzels, pp. 125–43. Amsterdam: John Benjamins.

Haiman, John (1972) Phonological targets and unmarked structures. *Language* 48, 365–77.

Hale, Kenneth (1973) Deep-surface canonical disparities in relation to analysis and change: An Australian example. In *Current Trends in Linguistics*, ed. Thomas Sebeok, pp. 401–58. The Hague: Mouton.

Hale, Kenneth, and Selkirk, Elisabeth (1987) Government and tonal phrasing in Papago. *Phonology Yearbook* 4, 151–83.

Hale, Mark, and Kissock, Madelyn (1998) The phonology-syntax interface in Rotuman. In *Recent Papers in Austronesian Linguistics: Proceedings of the Third and Fourth Meetings of the Austronesian Formal Linguistics Society*, ed. Matthew Pearson, pp. 115–28. UCLA Occasional Papers in Linguistics #21. Los Angeles: UCLA Department of Linguistics.

Hale, Mark, Kissock, Madelyn, and Reiss, Charles (1998) Output-output correspondence in OT. In *The Proceedings of the West Coast Conference on Formal Linguistics 16*, ed. E. Curtis, J. Lyle, and G. Webster, pp. 223–36. Stanford, CA: CSLI.

Hale, Mark, and Reiss, Charles (1997) Grammar optimization: The simultaneous acquisition of constraint ranking and a lexicon. Unpublished manuscript. Montreal: Concordia University. [Available on Rutgers Optimality Archive.]

Hale, Mark, and Reiss, Charles (1998) Formal and empirical arguments concerning phonological acquisition. *Linguistic Inquiry* 29, 656–83.

Hale, Mark, and Reiss, Charles (2000) "Substance abuse" and "dysfunctionalism": Current trends in phonology. *Linguistic Inquiry* 31, 157–69.

Halle, Morris (1962) Phonology in generative grammar. *Word* 18, 54–72.

Halle, Morris (1995) Letter commenting on Burzio's article. *Glot International* 1 (9/10), 27–28.

Halle, Morris, and Idsardi, William (1997) *r*, hypercorrection, and the Elsewhere Condition. In *Derivations and Constraints in Phonology*, ed. Iggy Roca, pp. 331–48. Oxford: Clarendon Press.

Halle, Morris, and Kenstowicz, Michael (1991) The Free Element Condition and cyclic versus noncyclic stress. *Linguistic Inquiry* 22, 457–501.

Halle, Morris, and Mohanan, K. P. (1985) Segmental phonology of Modern English. *Linguistic Inquiry* 16, 57–116.

Halle, Morris, and Vergnaud, Jean-Roger (1987) *An Essay on Stress*. Cambridge, MA: MIT Press.

Ham, William (1998) A new approach to an old problem: Gemination and constraint reranking in West Germanic. *Journal of Comparative Germanic Linguistics* 1, 225–62.

Hammond, Michael (1984) *Constraining Metrical Theory: A Modular Theory of Rhythm and Destressing*. Doctoral dissertation. Los Angeles: University of California. [Published in Outstanding Dissertations in Linguistics Series, Garland Press, New York, 1988.]

Hammond, Michael (1986) The obligatory-branching parameter in metrical theory. *Natural Language and Linguistic Theory* 4, 185–228.

Hammond, Michael (1988) On deriving the Well-formedness Condition. *Linguistic Inquiry* 19, 319–25.

Hammond, Michael (1994) An OT account of variability in Walmatjari stress. Unpublished manuscript. Tucson: University of Arizona. [Available on Rutgers Optimality Archive.]

Hammond, Michael (1995) There is no lexicon! Unpublished manuscript. Tucson: University of Arizona. [Available on Rutgers Optimality Archive.]

Hammond, Michael (1997a) Parsing in OT. Unpublished manuscript. Tucson: University of Arizona. [Available on Rutgers Optimality Archive.]

Hammond, Michael (1997b) Underlying representations in Optimality Theory. In *Derivations and Constraints in Phonology*, ed. Iggy Roca, pp. 349–65. Oxford: Clarendon Press.

Hammond, Michael (2000) The logic of Optimality Theory. Unpublished manuscript. Tucson: University of Arizona. [Available on Rutgers Optimality Archive.]

Hancin-Bhatt, B., and Bhatt, R. M. (1997) Optimal L2 syllables: Interaction of transfer and developmental effects. *Studies in Second Language Acquisition* 19, 331–78.

Hargus, Sharon (1985) *The Lexical Phonology of Sekani*. Doctoral dissertation. Los Angeles: UCLA.

Hargus, Sharon (1995) The first person plural prefix in Babine-Witsuwit'en. Unpublished manuscript. Seattle: University of Washington.

Hargus, Sharon, and Kaisse, Ellen M. (eds.) (1993) *Studies in Lexical Phonology*. San Diego, CA: Academic Press.

Hargus, Sharon, and Tuttle, Siri G. (1997) Augmentation as affixation in Athabaskan languages. *Phonology* 14, 177–220.

Harrikari, Heli (1999) The gradient OCP – Tonal evidence from Swedish. Unpublished manuscript. Helsinki: University of Helsinki. [Available on Rutgers Optimality Archive.]

Harris, James W. (1978) Two theories of non-automatic morphophonological alternation: Evidence from Spanish. *Language* 54, 41–60.

Harris, James W. (1985) Spanish diphthongization and stress: A paradox resolved. *Phonology* 2, 31–45.

Harris, James W., and Kaisse, Ellen M. (1999) Palatal vowels, glides and obstruents in Argentinian Spanish. *Phonology* 16, 117–90.

Harris, John (1990a) Derived phonological contrasts. In *Studies in the Pronunciation of English*, ed. Susan Ramsaran, pp. 87–105. London: Routledge.

Harris, John (1990b) Segmental complexity and phonological government. *Phonology* 7, 255–300.

Harris, John (1994) *English Sound Structure*. Oxford: Blackwell.

Hastings, Ashley (1974) *Stifling*. Bloomington, IN: IULC.

Hayes, Bruce (1980) *A Metrical Theory of Stress Rules*. Doctoral dissertation. Cambridge, MA: Massachusetts Institute of Technology. [Published by Garland Press, New York, 1985.]

Hayes, Bruce (1982) Metrical structure as the organizing principle in Yidiny phonology. In *The Structure of Phonological Representations*, ed. Harry van der Hulst and Norval Smith, pp. 97–110. Dordrecht: Foris.

Hayes, Bruce (1984) The phonology of rhythm in English. *Linguistic Inquiry* 15, 33–74.

Hayes, Bruce (1985) Iambic and trochaic rhythm in stress rules. In *Proceedings of BLS 11: Parasession on Poetics, Metrics, and Prosody*, ed. M. Niepokuj, M. VanClay, V. Nikiforidou, and D. Jeder, pp. 429–46. Berkeley: Berkeley Linguistic Society.

Hayes, Bruce (1986) Assimilation as spreading in Toba Batak. *Linguistic Inquiry* 17, 467–99.

Hayes, Bruce (1987) A revised parametric metrical theory. In *Proceedings of the North East Linguistic Society 17*, ed. J. McDonough and B. Plunkett, pp. 274–89. Amherst: GLSA.

Hayes, Bruce (1989) Compensatory Lengthening in moraic phonology. *Linguistic Inquiry* 20, 253–306.

Hayes, Bruce (1990) Precompiled phrasal phonology. In *The Phonology-Syntax Connection*, ed. Sharon Inkelas and Draga Zec, pp. 85–108. Chicago: University of Chicago Press.

Hayes, Bruce (1995) *Metrical Stress Theory: Principles and Case Studies*. Chicago: University of Chicago Press.

Hayes, Bruce (1997) Four rules of inference for ranking argumentation. Unpublished manuscript. Los Angeles: University of California. [Available for download (7/30/00) from http://www.humnet.ucla.edu/humnet/linguistics/people/hayes/otsoft/.]

Hayes, Bruce (1999) Phonetically driven phonology: The role of Optimality Theory and inductive grounding. In *Functionalism and Formalism in Linguistics*. Vol. I, *General Papers*, ed. Michael Darnell, Frederick J. Newmeyer, Michael Noonan, Edith Moravcsik, and Kathleen Wheatley, pp. 243–85. Amsterdam: John Benjamins.

Hayes, Bruce (to appear) Phonological acquisition in Optimality Theory: The early stages. In *Fixing Priorities: Constraints in Phonological Acquisition*, ed. René Kager, Joe Pater, and Wim Zonneveld. Cambridge: Cambridge University Press. [Available on Rutgers Optimality Archive.]

Hayes, Bruce, and MacEachern, Margaret (1998) Quatrain form in English folk verse. *Language* 64, 473–507. [Available on Rutgers Optimality Archive.]

Heiberg, Andrea (1999) *Features in Optimality Theory: A Computational Model*. Doctoral dissertation. Tucson: University of Arizona. [Available on Rutgers Optimality Archive.]

Hendricks, Petra, and de Hoop, Helen (2001) Optimality Theoretic semantics. *Linguistics and Philosophy* 24, 1–32.

Hendricks, Sean (1999) *Reduplication without Templates: A Study of Bare-Consonant Reduplication*. Doctoral dissertation. Tucson: University of Arizona.

Herbert, R. K. (1986) *Language Universals, Markedness Theory, and Natural Phonetic Processes*. New York: Mouton de Gruyter.

Hermans, Ben, and van Oostendorp, Marc (eds.) (1999) *The Derivational Residue in Phonological Optimality Theory*. Amsterdam: John Benjamins.

Hestvik, Arild (1999) Optimality Theory, child language and logical form. In *New Perspectives on Language Acquisition*, ed. Bartjan Hollebrandse, pp. 155–65. University of Massachusetts Occasional Papers in Linguistics 22. Amherst, MA: GLSA.

Hewitt, Mark (1992) *Vertical Maximization and Metrical Theory*. Doctoral dissertation. Waltham, MA: Brandeis University.

Hewitt, Mark, and Crowhurst, Megan (1996) Conjunctive constraints and templates in Optimality Theory. In *Proceedings of the North East Linguistic Society 26*, ed. Jill Beckman, pp. 101–16. Amherst, MA: GLSA.

Hironymous, Patricia (1999) *Selection of the Optimal Syllable in an Alignment-Based Theory of Sonority*. Doctoral dissertation. College Park: University of Maryland.

Hock, Hans (1975) On the judicious application of rules. In *Papers from the 11th Regional Meeting, Chicago Linguistic Society*, pp. 272–78. Chicago: Chicago Linguistic Society.

Holt, D. Eric (1996) From Latin to Hispano-Romance: A constraint-based approach to vowel nasalization, sonorant simplification, and the Late Spoken Latin open mid vowels. In *Papers from CLS 32*, ed. Lise M. Dobrin, Kora Singer, and Lisa McNair, pp. 111–23. Chicago: Chicago Linguistic Society.

Holt, D. Eric (1997) *The Role of the Listener in the Historical Phonology of Spanish and Portuguese: An Optimality-Theoretic Account*. Doctoral dissertation. Washington, DC: Georgetown University. [Available on Rutgers Optimality Archive.]

Holt, D. Eric (1999) The moraic status of consonants from Latin to Hispano-Romance: The case of obstruents. In *Advances in Hispanic Linguistics: Papers from the Second Hispanic Linguistics Symposium*, ed. Javier Gutiérrez-Rexach and Fernando Martínez-Gil, pp. 166–81. Somerville, MA: Cascadilla Press.

References

de Hoop, Helen (to appear) Optimal scrambling and interpretation. In *Interface Strategies*, ed. Hans Bennis, Martin Everaert, and Eric Reuland. Amsterdam: Koninklijke Nederlandse Akademie van Wetenschappen.

de Hoop, Helen, and de Swart, Henriette (eds.) (1999) *Papers on Optimality Theoretic Semantics*. Utrecht: Utrecht Institute of Linguistics/Onderzoeksinstituut voor Taal en Spraak.

Hooper [Bybee], Joan (1976) *An Introduction to Natural Generative Phonology*. New York: Academic Press.

Hooper [Bybee], Joan (1979) Substantive principles in natural generative phonology. In *Current Approaches to Phonological Theory*, ed. Daniel Dinnsen, pp. 106–25. Bloomington: Indiana University Press.

Horwood, Graham (1999) Anti-faithfulness and subtractive morphology. Unpublished manuscript. New Brunswick, NJ: Rutgers University. [Available for download (9/9/00) from http://www.rci.rutgers.edu/~gvh/%7EF&subtr.pdf.]

Hualde, José (1989) Autosegmental and metrical spreading in the vowel-harmony systems of northwestern Spain. *Linguistics* 27, 773–805.

Hudson, Grover (1974a) The representation of non-productive alternation. In *Historical Linguistics*, ed. J. Anderson and C. Jones, pp. 203–29. Amsterdam: North Holland.

Hudson, Grover (1974b) The role of SPC's in Natural Generative Phonology. In *Papers from the Parasession on Natural Phonology*, ed. Anthony Bruck, Robert A. Fox, and Michael W. LaGaly, pp. 171–83. Chicago: Chicago Linguistic Society.

van der Hulst, Harry (1989) Atoms of segmental structure: Components, gestures and dependency. *Phonology* 6, 253–84.

Hume, Elizabeth (1998) Metathesis in phonological theory: The case of Leti. *Lingua* 104, 147–86.

Hung, Henrietta (1994) *The Rhythmic and Prosodic Organization of Edge Constituents*. Doctoral dissertation. Waltham, MA: Brandeis University.

Hyman, Larry (1975) *Phonology: Theory and Analysis*. New York: Holt, Rinehart and Winston.

Hyman, Larry (1985) Word domains and downstep in Bamileke-Dschang. *Phonology Yearbook* 2, 45–82.

Hyman, Larry, and Inkelas, Sharon (1997) Emergent templates: The unusual case of Tiene. In *University of Maryland Working Papers in Linguistics 5. Selected Phonology Papers from Hopkins Optimality Theory Workshop 1997 / University of Maryland Mayfest 1997*, ed. Viola Miglio and Bruce Morén, pp. 92–116. College Park: Department of Linguistics, University of Maryland. [Available on Rutgers Optimality Archive.]

Idsardi, William (1992) *The Computation of Prosody*. Doctoral dissertation. Cambridge, MA: Massachusetts Institute of Technology.

Idsardi, William (1997) Phonological derivations and historical changes in Hebrew spirantization. In *Derivations and Constraints in Phonology*, ed. Iggy Roca, pp. 367–92. New York: Oxford University Press.

Idsardi, William (1998) Tiberian Hebrew spirantization and phonological derivations. *Linguistic Inquiry* 29, 37–73.

Inkelas, Sharon (1994) The consequences of optimization for underspecification. In *Proceedings of the North East Linguistic Society 25*, ed. Jill Beckman, pp. 287–302. Amherst: GLSA.

Inkelas, Sharon (1999) Exceptional stress-attracting suffixes in Turkish: Representation vs. the grammar. In *The Prosody-Morphology Interface*, ed. René Kager, Harry van der Hulst, and Wim Zonneveld, pp. 134–87. Cambridge: Cambridge University Press.

Inkelas, Sharon, Orgun, Orhan, and Zoll, Cheryl (1997) The implications of lexical exceptions for the nature of grammar. In *Derivations and Constraints in Phonology*, ed. Iggy Roca, pp. 393–418. New York: Oxford University Press.

Inkelas, Sharon, and Zec, Draga (eds.) (1990) *The Phonology-Syntax Connection*. Chicago: University of Chicago Press.

Inkelas, Sharon, and Zec, Draga (1995) Syntax-phonology interface. In *The Handbook of Phonological Theory*, ed. John A. Goldsmith, pp. 535–49. Cambridge, MA: Blackwell.

Ito, Junko (1986) *Syllable Theory in Prosodic Phonology*. Doctoral dissertation. Amherst: University of Massachusetts. [Published in Outstanding Dissertations in Linguistics Series, Garland Press, New York, 1988.]

Ito, Junko (1989) A prosodic theory of epenthesis. *Natural Language and Linguistic Theory* 7, 217–59.

Ito, Junko (1990) Prosodic minimality in Japanese. In *CLS 26: Parasession on the Syllable in Phonetics and Phonology*, ed. K. Deaton, M. Noske, and M. Ziolkowski, pp. 213–39. Chicago: Chicago Linguistic Society.

Ito, Junko, Kitagawa, Yoshihisa, and Mester, Armin (1996) Prosodic faithfulness and correspondence: Evidence from a Japanese argot. *Journal of East Asian Linguistics* 5, 217–94.

Ito, Junko, and Mester, Armin (1995) The core-periphery structure of the lexicon and constraints on reranking. In *Papers in Optimality Theory*, ed. Jill Beckman, Laura Walsh Dickey, and Suzanne Urbanczyk, pp. 181–210. Amherst, MA: GLSA.

Ito, Junko, and Mester, Armin (1997a) Correspondence and compositionality: The ga-gyo variation in Japanese phonology. In *Derivations and Constraints in Phonology*, ed. Iggy Roca, pp. 419–62. New York: Oxford University Press.

Ito, Junko, and Mester, Armin (1997b) Featural sympathy: Feeding and counterfeeding interactions in Japanese. In *Phonology at Santa Cruz*, ed. Rachel Walker, Motoko Katayama, and Daniel Karvonen, pp. 29–36. Santa Cruz: Linguistics Research Center, University of California.

Ito, Junko, and Mester, Armin (1997c) Sympathy theory and German truncations. In *University of Maryland Working Papers in Linguistics 5. Selected Phonology Papers from Hopkins Optimality Theory Workshop 1997 / University of Maryland Mayfest 1997*, ed. Viola Miglio and Bruce Morén, pp. 117–39. [Available on Rutgers Optimality Archive.]

Ito, Junko, and Mester, Armin (1998) Markedness and word structure: OCP effects in Japanese. Unpublished manuscript. Santa Cruz: University of California. [Available on Rutgers Optimality Archive.]

Ito, Junko, and Mester, Armin (1999a) The phonological lexicon. In *The Handbook of Japanese Linguistics*, ed. Natsuko Tsujimura, pp. 62–100. Oxford: Blackwell.

Ito, Junko, and Mester, Armin (1999b) Realignment. In *The Prosody-Morphology Interface*, ed. René Kager, Harry van der Hulst, and Wim Zonneveld, pp. 188–217. Cambridge: Cambridge University Press.

Ito, Junko, and Mester, Armin (to appear) On the sources of opacity in OT: Coda processes in German. In *The Optimal Syllable*, ed. Caroline Féry and Ruben van de Vijver. Cambridge: Cambridge University Press.

Ito, Junko, Mester, Armin, and Padgett, Jaye (1995) Licensing and underspecification in Optimality Theory. *Linguistic Inquiry* 26, 571–614.

Iverson, Gregory (1974) *Ordering Constraints in Phonology*. Doctoral dissertation. Minneapolis: University of Minnesota.

Iverson, Gregory (1995) Rule ordering. In *The Handbook of Phonological Theory*, ed. John A. Goldsmith, pp. 609–14. Cambridge, MA: Blackwell.

Iverson, Gregory, and Lee, Shinsook (1995) Variation as optimality in Korean consonant cluster reduction. In *Proceedings of the Eleventh Eastern States Conference on Linguistics*, ed. J. Fuller, H. Han, and D. Parkinson, pp. 174–85. Ithaca, NY: Department of Modern Languages and Linguistics, Cornell University.

Jacobs, Haike (1994) Lenition and Optimality Theory. In *Aspects of Romance Linguistics: Selected Papers from the Linguistic Symposium on Romance Languages XXIV*, ed. Claudia Parodi, Carlos Quicoli, Mario Saltarelli, and Maria Luisa Zubizarreta, pp. 253–65. Washington, DC: Georgetown University Press. [Available on Rutgers Optimality Archive.]

Jacobs, Haike (1995) Optimality Theory and sound change. In *Proceedings of the North East Linguistic Society 25*, ed. Jill Beckman, pp. 219–32. Amherst, MA: GLSA.

Jacobs, Haike, and Gussenhoven, Carlos (2000) Loan phonology: Perception, salience, the lexicon and OT. In *Optimality Theory: Phonology, Syntax, Acquisition*, ed. Joost Dekkers, Frank van der Leeuw, and Jeroen van de Weijer, pp. 193–210. Oxford: Oxford University Press.

Jakobson, Roman (1929) Remarques sur l'évolution phonologique du russe comparée à celle des autres langues slaves. *Travaux du cercle linguistique de Prague* 2. [Reprinted in *Selected Writings of Roman Jakobson*, Vol. 1 (Berlin: Mouton de Gruyter).]

Jakobson, Roman (1941) *Kindersprache, Aphasie, und allgemeine Lautgesetze*. Uppsala: Almqvist & Wiksell. [1962 reprint in *Selected Writings of Roman Jakobson*, Vol. 1 (Berlin: Mouton de Gruyter); 1969 reprint (Frankfurt am Main: Suhrkamp); 1968 English translation by A. Keiler (The Hague: Mouton).]

Jakobson, Roman (1971) Zur Struktur des russischen Verbums. In *Selected Writings*. Vol. 2, *Word and Language*, pp. 3–16. (Originally published, 1932.) The Hague: Mouton.

Janda, Richard, and Sandoval, Maria (1984) *"Elsewhere" in Morphology*. Bloomington, IN: IULC.

Jensen, John (1995) Constraints and opaque interactions. *Cahiers linguistiques d'Ottawa* 23, 1–9.

Joanisse, Marc, and Curtin, Suzanne (1999) Dutch stress acquisition: OT and connectionist approaches. Unpublished manuscript. Los Angeles: University of Southern California. [Available (6/00) at ftp://siva.usc.edu/pub/coglab/marcj/Joanisse. Curtin.pdf.]

Jun, Jongho (1995a) *Perceptual and Articulatory Factors on Place Assimilation*. Doctoral dissertation. Los Angeles: University of California.

Jun, Jongho (1995b) Place assimilation as the result of conflicting perceptual and articulatory constraints. In *Proceedings of the Fourteenth West Coast Conference on Formal Linguistics*, ed. Jose Camacho, Lina Choueiri, and Maki Watanabe, pp. 221–37. Stanford, CA: CSLI.

Jun, Jongho (1999) Generalized sympathy. In *Proceedings of the North East Linguistic Society 29*, ed. Pius N. Tamanji, Mako Hirotani, and Nancy Hall, pp. 121–35. Amherst, MA: GLSA.

Jun, Sun-Ah (1993) *The Phonetics and Phonology of Korean Prosody*. Doctoral dissertation. Columbus: Ohio State University.

Kager, René (1993) Alternatives to the iambic-trochaic law. *Natural Language and Linguistic Theory* 11, 381–432.

Kager, René (1996) On affix allomorphy and syllable counting. In *Interfaces in phonology*, ed. U. Kleinhenz, pp. 155–71. Berlin: Akademie Verlag. [Available on Rutgers
Optimality Archive.]

Kager, René (1997) Rhythmic vowel deletion in Optimality Theory. In *Derivations and
Constraints in Phonology*, ed. Iggy Roca, pp. 463–99. New York: Oxford University Press.

Kager, René (1999a) *Optimality Theory*. Cambridge: Cambridge University Press.

Kager, René (1999b) Surface opacity of metrical structure in Optimality Theory. In *The
Derivational Residue in Phonological Optimality Theory*, ed. Ben Hermans and
Marc van Oostendorp, pp. 207–45. Amsterdam: John Benjamins.

Kager, René (2000) Stem stress and peak correspondence in Dutch. In *Optimality
Theory: Phonology, Syntax, and Acquisition*, ed. Joost Dekkers, Frank van der
Leeuw, and Jeroen van de Weijer, pp. 121–50. Oxford: Oxford University Press.

Kaisse, Ellen M., and Hargus, Sharon (1993) Introduction. In *Studies in Lexical Phonology*, ed. Sharon Hargus and Ellen M. Kaisse, pp. 1–19. San Diego, CA: Academic
Press.

Kaisse, Ellen M., and Shaw, Patricia (1985) On the theory of lexical phonology. *Phonology* 2, 1–30.

Karttunen, Lauri (1993) Finite-state constraints. In *The Last Phonological Rule: Reflections on Constraints and Derivations*, ed. John Goldsmith, pp. 173–94. Chicago:
University of Chicago Press.

Karttunen, Lauri (1998) The proper treatment of optimality in computational phonology.
In *Finite State Methods in Natural Language Processing*, pp. 1–12. Ankara. [Avail-
able on Rutgers Optimality Archive.]

Karvonen, Daniel, and Sherman [Ussishkin], Adam (1997) Sympathy, opacity, and u-
umlaut in Icelandic. In *Phonology at Santa Cruz*, ed. Rachel Walker, Motoko
Katayama, and Daniel Karvonen, pp. 37–48. Santa Cruz: Linguistics Research
Center, University of California.

Karvonen, Daniel, and Sherman [Ussishkin], Adam (1998) Opacity in Icelandic
revisited: A Sympathy account. In *Proceedings of the North East Linguistic
Society 28*, ed. Pius N. Tamanji and Kiyomi Kusumoto, pp. 189–201. Amherst, MA:
GLSA.

Katayama, Motoko (1995) Loanword accent and minimal reranking in Japanese. In
Phonology at Santa Cruz 6: Papers on Stress, Accent, and Alignment, ed. Rachel
Walker, Ove Lorentz, and Haruo Kubozono, pp. 1–12. Santa Cruz: Linguistics
Research Center, University of California.

Katayama, Motoko (1998) *Optimality Theory and Japanese Loanword Phonology*. Doctoral dissertation. Santa Cruz: University of California.

Katz, Gerrold J., and Postal, Paul (1964) *An Integrated Theory of Linguistic Descriptions*. Cambridge, MA: MIT Press.

Kaun, Abigail (1995) *The Typology of Rounding Harmony: An Optimality Theoretic
Approach*. Doctoral dissertation. Los Angeles: University of California.

Kaye, Jonathan (1974) Morpheme structure constraints live! *Recherches linguistiques à
Montréal* 3, 55–62.

Kaye, Jonathan (1975) Contraintes profondes en phonologie: Les emprunts. *Cahier de linguistique* 5, 87–101.

Kaye, Jonathan (1990) "Coda" licensing. *Phonology* 7, 301–30.

Kaye, Jonathan, and Lowenstamm, Jean (1984) De la syllabicité. In *Forme sonore du language: Structure des représentations en phonologie*, ed. F. Dell, D. Hirst, and J.-R. Vergnaud, pp. 123–59. Paris: Hermann.

Kaye, Jonathan, and Lowenstamm, Jean (1985) A non-linear treatment of Grassmann's law. In *Proceedings of the North East Linguistic Society 15*, pp. 220–33. Amherst, MA: GLSA.

Kaye, Jonathan, Lowenstamm, Jean, and Vergnaud, Jean-Roger (1985) The internal structure of phonological elements: A theory of charm and government. *Phonology* 2, 305–28.

Kean, Mary-Louise (1975) *The Theory of Markedness in Generative Grammar*. Doctoral dissertation. Cambridge: Massachusetts Institute of Technology.

Kean, Mary-Louise (1977) "Natural processes" and "learned rules" in markedness theory. In *Proceedings of the Seventh Annual Meeting of the North Eastern Linguistics Society*, ed. Judy Kegl, David Nash, and Annie Zaenen, pp. 135–46. Cambridge: Department of Linguistics, Massachusetts Institute of Technology.

Kean, Mary-Louise (1992) Markedness: An Overview. In *International Encyclopedia of Linguistics*, ed. William Bright, Vol. 2, pp. 390–91. New York: Oxford University Press.

Keer, Edward (1998) Spirantization and geminate inalterability. In *RuLing Papers 1: Working Papers from Rutgers University*, ed. Ron Artstein and Madeline Holler, pp. 147–68. New Brunswick, NJ: Department of Linguistics, Rutgers University.

Keer, Edward (1999a) *Geminates, the OCP, and Faithfulness*. Doctoral dissertation. New Brunswick, NJ: Rutgers University. [Available on Rutgers Optimality Archive.]

Keer, Edward (1999b) *Som* and Optimality Theory. Unpublished manuscript. Amherst: University of Massachusetts. [Available on Rutgers Optimality Archive.]

Keer, Edward, and Bakovic, Eric (1997) Have FAITH in syntax. In *Proceedings of the Sixteenth West Coast Conference on Formal Linguistics*, ed. Emily Curtis, James Lyle, and Gabriel Webster, pp. 255–69. Stanford, CA: CSLI.

Kenstowicz, Michael (1983) Parametric variation and accent in the Arabic dialects. In *Papers from CLS 19*, ed. A. Chukerman, M. Marks, and J. F. Richardson, pp. 205–13. Chicago: Chicago Linguistic Society.

Kenstowicz, Michael (1994a) *Phonology in Generative Grammar*. Oxford: Blackwell.

Kenstowicz, Michael (1994b) Sonority-driven stress. Unpublished manuscript. Cambridge: Massachusetts Institute of Technology. [Available on Rutgers Optimality Archive.]

Kenstowicz, Michael (1995) Cyclic vs. non-cyclic constraint evaluation. *Phonology* 12, 397–436.

Kenstowicz, Michael (1996) Base-identity and uniform exponence: Alternatives to cyclicity. In *Current Trends in Phonology: Models and Methods*, ed. J. Durand and B. Laks, pp. 363–93. Paris-X and Salford: University of Salford Publications.

Kenstowicz, Michael (1997) Uniform exponence: Exemplification and extension. In *University of Maryland Working Papers in Linguistics 5. Selected Phonology Papers from Hopkins Optimality Theory Workshop 1997 / University of Maryland Mayfest 1997*, ed. Viola Miglio and Bruce Morén, pp. 139–55.

Kenstowicz, Michael, and Kisseberth, Charles (1971) Unmarked bleeding orders. *Studies in the Linguistic Sciences* 1, 8–28.

Kenstowicz, Michael, and Kisseberth, Charles (1977) *Topics in Phonological Theory.* New York: Academic Press.

Kenstowicz, Michael, and Kisseberth, Charles (1979) *Generative Phonology: Description and Theory.* New York: Academic Press.

Kenstowicz, Michael, and Sohn, Hyang-Sook (1997) Phrasing and focus in Northern Kyungsang Korean. In *Certamen Phonologicum III*, ed. Pier Marco Bertinetto, Livio Gaeta, Georgi Jetchev, and David Michaels, pp. 137–56. Turin: Rosenberg and Sellier.

Kikuchi, Seiichiro (1999) Opacity and transparency in Spanish plurals: A sympathetic approach. In *On'in Kenkyu* (Phonological studies), ed. Nihon On'inron Gakkai (The Phonological Society of Japan), pp. 61–68. Tokyo: Kaitakusha.

Kim, Chin-Wu (1972) Two phonological notes: A-sharp and B-flat. In *Contributions to Generative Phonology*, ed. Michael Brame, pp. 155–70. Austin: University of Texas Press.

Kim, No-Ju (1997) *Tone, Segments, and Their Interaction in North Kyungsang Korean: A Correspondence Theoretic Account.* Doctoral dissertation. Columbus: Ohio State University.

Kiparsky, Paul (1965) *Phonological Change.* Doctoral dissertation. Cambridge: Massachusetts Institute of Technology.

Kiparsky, Paul (1968) Linguistic universals and linguistic change. In *Universals in Linguistic Theory*, ed. Emmon Bach and Robert Harms, pp. 170–202. New York: Holt, Rinehart and Winston.

Kiparsky, Paul (1971) Historical linguistics. In *A Survey of Linguistic Science*, ed. W. O. Dingwall, pp. 576–642. College Park: University of Maryland Linguistics Program.

Kiparsky, Paul (1972) Explanation in phonology. In *Goals of Linguistic Theory*, ed. Stanley Peters, pp. 189–227. Englewood Cliffs, NJ: Prentice-Hall.

Kiparsky, Paul (1973a) Abstractness, opacity and global rules. In *Three Dimensions of Linguistic Theory*, ed. O. Fujimura, pp. 57–86. Tokyo: TEC.

Kiparsky, Paul (1973b) "Elsewhere" in phonology. In *A Festschrift for Morris Halle*, ed. Stephen R. Anderson and Paul Kiparsky, pp. 93–106. New York: Holt, Rinehart and Winston.

Kiparsky, Paul (1973c) Phonological representations. In *Three Dimensions of Linguistic Theory*, ed. O. Fujimura, pp. 3–136. Tokyo: TEC.

Kiparsky, Paul (1981) Vowel harmony. Unpublished manuscript. Cambridge: Massachusetts Institute of Technology.

Kiparsky, Paul (1982a) From cyclic phonology to lexical phonology. In *The Structure of Phonological Representations*, ed. Harry van der Hulst and Norval Smith, pp. 131–75. Dordrecht: Foris.

Kiparsky, Paul (1982b) Lexical phonology and morphology. In *Linguistics in the Morning Calm*, ed. I. S. Yang, pp. 3–91. Seoul: Hanshin.

Kiparsky, Paul (1984) On the lexical phonology of Icelandic. In *Nordic Prosody III*, ed. C. C. Elert, I. Johansson, and E. Stangert, pp. 135–64. Umeå, Sweden: University of Umeå.

Kiparsky, Paul (1985) Some consequences of Lexical Phonology. *Phonology* 2, 85–138.

Kiparsky, Paul (1993a) Blocking in non-derived environments. In *Studies in Lexical Phonology*, ed. Sharon Hargus and Ellen Kaisse, pp. 277–313. San Diego, CA: Academic Press.

Kiparsky, Paul (1993b) Variable rules. Handout from Rutgers Optimality Workshop I, October 1993, Rutgers University, New Brunswick, NJ.

Kiparsky, Paul (1994) An OT perspective on phonological variation. Handout from NWAV-23, Stanford University, Stanford, CA.

Kiparsky, Paul (1995) The phonological basis of sound change. In *The Handbook of Phonological Theory*, ed. John A. Goldsmith, pp. 640–70. Cambridge, MA: Blackwell.

Kiparsky, Paul (1997) LP and OT. Handout from LSA Summer Linguistic Institute, Cornell University, Ithaca, NY.

Kiparsky, Paul (to appear-a) *Paradigmatic Effects and Opacity*. Stanford, CA: CSLI.

Kiparsky, Paul (to appear-b) Syllables and moras in Arabic. In *The Optimal Syllable*, ed. Caroline Féry and Ruben van de Vijver. Cambridge: Cambridge University Press.

Kiparsky, Paul, and Menn, Lise (1977) On the acquisition of phonology. In *Language Learning and Thought*, ed. J. Macnamara, pp. 47–78. New York: Academic Press.

Kirchner, Robert (1996) Synchronic chain shifts in Optimality Theory. *Linguistic Inquiry* 27, 341–50.

Kirchner, Robert (1997) Contrastiveness and faithfulness. *Phonology* 14, 83–111.

Kirchner, Robert (1998a) *An Effort-Based Approach to Consonant Lenition*. Doctoral dissertation. Los Angeles: University of California.

Kirchner, Robert (1998b) Preliminary thoughts on "phonologization" within an exemplar-based speech-processing system. Unpublished manuscript. Edmonton: University of Alberta. [Available on Rutgers Optimality Archive.]

Kisseberth, Charles (1970a) On the functional unity of phonological rules. *Linguistic Inquiry* 1, 291–306.

Kisseberth, Charles (1970b) Vowel elision in Tonkawa and derivational constraints. In *Studies Presented to Robert B. Lees by His Students*, ed. Jerrold M. Sadock and Anthony L. Vanek, pp. 109–37. Edmonton, AB: Linguistic Research.

Kisseberth, Charles (1972) On derivative properties of phonological rules. In *Contributions to Generative Phonology*, ed. Michael Brame, pp. 201–28. Austin: University of Texas Press.

Kisseberth, Charles (1973) Is rule ordering necessary in phonology? In *Issues in Linguistics: Papers in Honor of Henry and Renée Kahane*, ed. Braj B. Kachru, Robert B. Lees, Yakov Malkiel, Angelina Pietrangeli, and Sol Saporta, pp. 418–41. Urbana: University of Illinois Press.

Kisseberth, Charles, and Abasheikh, Mohammed (1974) A case of systematic avoidance of homonymy. *Studies in the Linguistic Sciences* 4, 107–24.

Kitto, Catherine, and de Lacy, Paul (2000) Correspondence and epenthetic quality. In *Proceedings of AFLA VI: The Sixth Meeting of the Austronesian Formal Linguistics Association (Toronto Working Papers in Linguistics)*, ed. Catherine Kitto and Carolyn Smallwood, pp. 181–200. Toronto: Department of Linguistics, University of Toronto.

Klausenburger, Jürgen (1974) Rule inversion, opacity, conspiracies: French liaison and elision. *Lingua* 34, 167–79.

Koskenniemi, Kimmo (1983) Two-Level Morphology: A General Computational Model for Word-Form Recognition and Production. Report no. 11. Helsinki: Department of General Linguistics, University of Helsinki.

Koutsoudas, Andreas (ed.) (1976) *The Application and Ordering of Phonological Rules.* The Hague: Mouton.

Koutsoudas, Andreas, Sanders, Gerald, and Noll, Craig (1974) On the application of phonological rules. *Language* 50, 1–28.

Kraska-Szlenk, Iwona (1995) *The Phonology of Stress in Polish.* Doctoral dissertation. Urbana: University of Illinois.

Kučera, Henry (1973) Language variability, rule interdependency, and the grammar of Czech. *Linguistic Inquiry* 4, 499–521.

Labov, William (1965) On the mechanism of linguistic change. *Georgetown University Monographs on Language and Linguistics* 18, 91–114.

Labov, William (1997) Resyllabification. In *Variation, Change, and Phonological Theory*, ed. Frans Hinskens, Roeland van Hout, and W. Leo Wetzels, pp. 145–79. Amsterdam: John Benjamins.

Lakoff, George (1993) Cognitive phonology. In *The Last Phonological Rule: Reflections on Constraints and Derivations*, ed. John Goldsmith, pp. 117–45. Chicago: University of Chicago Press.

Lamontagne, Greg, and Rice, Keren (1995) A correspondence account of coalescence. In *University of Massachusetts Occasional Papers in Linguistics 18*, ed. Jill Beckman, Laura Walsh Dickey, and Suzanne Urbanczyk, pp. 211–24. Amherst, MA: GLSA.

Lapointe, Steven G., and Sells, Peter (1997) Separating syntax and phonology in Optimality Theory: The case of suppletive segment/ø allomorphy. Unpublished manuscript. Davis: University of California; Stanford, CA: Stanford University.

Larson, Gary (1990) Local computational networks and the distribution of segments in the Spanish syllable. In *Papers from the 26th Regional Meeting of the Chicago Linguistic Society.* Vol. 2, *The Parasession on the Syllable in Phonetics and Phonology*, ed. Michael Ziolkowski, Manuela Noske, and Karen Deaton, pp. 257–72. Chicago: Chicago Linguistic Society.

Larson, Gary (1992) *Dynamic Computational Models and the Representation of Phonological Information.* Doctoral dissertation. Chicago: University of Chicago.

Leben, Will (1973) *Suprasegmental Phonology.* Doctoral dissertation. Cambridge: Massachusetts Institute of Technology.

Lee, Hanjung (2000) The emergence of the unmarked order in Hindi. In *Proceedings of the North East Linguistics Society 30*, ed. Masako Hirotani, pp. 469–84. Amherst, MA: GLSA.

Lee, Minkyung (1999) A case of sympathy in Javanese affixation. In *Indiana University Working Papers in Linguistics I*, ed. Karen Baertsch and Daniel A. Dinnsen, pp. 31–36. Bloomington, IN: IULC.

van der Leeuw, Frank (1997) *Clitics: Prosodic Studies.* The Hague: Holland Academic Graphics. [Doctoral dissertation, University of Amsterdam.]

Legendre, Géraldine (1996) Clitics, verb (non-)movement, and optimality in Bulgarian. Report no. JHU_CogSci_96_5. Baltimore: Johns Hopkins University.

Legendre, Géraldine (1998) Second position clitics in a verb-second language: Conflict resolution in Macedonian. In *Proceedings of ESCOL 97*, ed. Jennifer Austin and Aaron Lawson, pp. 139–49. Ithaca, NY: Cornell Linguistics Circle.

Legendre, Géraldine (1999) Morphological and prosodic alignment at work: The case of South Slavic clitics. In *The Proceedings of the West Coast Conference on Formal*

Linguistics 17, ed. Kimary N. Shahin, Susan J. Blake, and Eun-Sook Kim, pp. 436–50. Stanford, CA: CSLI.

Legendre, Géraldine (2000) Morphological and prosodic alignment of Bulgarian clitics. In *Optimality Theory: Phonology, Syntax, and Acquisition*, ed. Joost Dekkers, Frank van der Leeuw, and Jeroen van de Weijer, pp. 423–62. Oxford: Oxford University Press.

Legendre, Géraldine (to appear-a) An introduction to Optimality Theory in syntax. In *OT Syntax*, ed. Géraldine Legendre, Jane Grimshaw, and Sten Vikner. Cambridge, MA: MIT Press.

Legendre, Géraldine (to appear-b) Masked V2 effects and the linearization of functional features. In *OT Syntax*, ed. Géraldine Legendre, Jane Grimshaw, and Sten Vikner. Cambridge, MA: MIT Press.

Legendre, Géraldine, Hagstrom, Paul, Vainikka, Anne, and Todorova, Marina (2001) Evidence for syntactic competition in the acquisition of tense and agreement in child French. In *CLS 36*. Chicago: Chicago Linguistic Society. [Available (6/00) at http://www.cog.jhu.edu/~hagstrom/ling.html.]

Legendre, Géraldine, Miyata, Yoshiro, and Smolensky, Paul (1990a) Can connectionism contribute to syntax? Harmonic Grammar, with an application. In *Proceedings of the 26th Regional Meeting of the Chicago Linguistic Society*, ed. M. Ziolkowski, M. Noske, and K. Deaton, pp. 237–52. Chicago: Chicago Linguistic Society.

Legendre, Géraldine, Miyata, Yoshiro, and Smolensky, Paul (1990b) Harmonic Grammar – A formal multi-level connectionist theory of linguistic well-formedness: An application. In *Proceedings of the Twelfth Annual Conference of the Cognitive Science Society*, pp. 884–91. Mahwah, NJ: Lawrence Erlbaum Associates.

Legendre, Géraldine, Miyata, Yoshiro, and Smolensky, Paul (1990c) Harmonic Grammar – A formal multi-level connectionist theory of linguistic well-formedness: Theoretical foundations. In *Proceedings of the Twelfth Annual Conference of the Cognitive Science Society*, pp. 388–95. Mahwah, NJ: Lawrence Erlbaum Associates.

Legendre, Géraldine, Miyata, Yoshiro, and Smolensky, Paul (1991a) Distributed recursive structure processing. In *Advances in Neural Information Processing Systems 3*, ed. D. S. Touretzky and R. Lippmann, pp. 591–97. San Mateo, CA: Morgan Kaufmann.

Legendre, Géraldine, Miyata, Yoshiro, and Smolensky, Paul (1991b) Integrating semantic and syntactic accounts of unaccusativity: A connectionist approach. In *Proceedings of the Seventeenth Annual Meeting of the Berkeley Linguistics Society*, ed. L. Sutton and C. Johnson, pp. 157–67. Berkeley: Berkeley Linguistics Society.

Legendre, Géraldine, Raymond, William, and Smolensky, Paul (1993) An Optimality-Theoretic typology of case and voice systems. In *Proceedings of the Nineteenth Annual Meeting of the Berkeley Linguistics Society*, ed. Joshua S. Guenter, Barbara A. Kaiser, and Cheryl C. Zoll, pp. 464–78. Berkeley: Berkeley Linguistics Society.

Legendre, Géraldine, Smolensky, Paul, and Wilson, Colin (1998) When is less more? Faithfulness and minimal links in *wh*-chains. In *Is the Best Good Enough? Optimality and Competition in Syntax*, ed. Pilar Barbosa, Danny Fox, Paul Hagstrom, Martha McGinnis, and David Pesetsky, pp. 249–89. Cambridge, MA: MIT Press.

Legendre, Géraldine, Wilson, Colin, Smolensky, Paul, Homer, Kristin, and Raymond, William (1995) Optimality and Wh-extraction. In *Papers in Optimality Theory*, ed. Jill Beckman, Laura Walsh Dickey, and Suzanne Urbanczyk, pp. 607–36. Amherst, MA: GLSA.

Lehman, F. K. (1973) Tibeto-Burman syllable structure, tone and the theory of phono-logical conspiracies. In *Issues in Linguistics: Papers in Honor of Henry and Renée Kahane*, ed. Braj B. Kachru, Robert B. Lees, Yakov Malkiel, Angelina Pietrangeli, and Sol Saporta, pp. 515–47. Urbana: University of Illinois Press.

Levelt, Clara C. (1995) The segmental structure of early words: Articulatory frames or phonological constraints. In *Proceedings of the 27th Child Language Research Forum*, ed. Eve Clark, pp. 19–27. Stanford, CA: CSLI.

Levelt, Clara C. (1996) Consonant-vowel interactions in child language. In *Proceedings of the UBC International Conference on Phonological Acquisition*, ed. Barbara H. Bernhardt, John Gilbert, and David Ingram, pp. 229–39. Somerville, MA: Cascadilla Press.

Levelt, Clara C., Schiller, Niels O., and Levelt, Willem J. M. (1999) A developmental grammar for syllable structure in the production of child langauge. *Brain and Language* 68, 291–99.

Levelt, Clara C., and van de Vijver, Ruben (to appear) Syllable types in cross-linguistic and developmental grammars. In *Fixing Priorities: Constraints in Phonological Acquisition*, ed. René Kager, Joe Pater, and Wim Zonneveld. Cambridge: Cambridge University Press. [Available on Rutgers Optimality Archive.]

Liljencrants, Johan, and Lindblom, Björn (1972) Numerical simulation of vowel quality systems: The role of perceptual contrast. *Language* 48, 839–62.

Lindblom, Björn (1986) Phonetic universals in vowel systems. In *Experimental Phonology*, ed. John J. Ohala and Jeri J. Jaeger, pp. 13–44. Orlando, FL: Academic Press.

Lleó, Conxita (1996) To spread or not to spread: Different styles in the acquisition of Spanish phonology. In *Proceedings of the UBC International Conference on Phono-logical Acquisition*, ed. Barbara H. Bernhardt, John Gilbert, and David Ingram, pp. 215–28. Somerville, MA: Cascadilla Press.

Lleó, Conxita (to appear) The interface of phonology and morphology: The emergence of the article in early acquisition of Spanish and German. In *Approaches to Boot-strapping: Phonological, Syntactic and Neurophysiological Aspects of Early Language Acquisition*, ed. Juergen Weissenborn and B. Hoehle. Amsterdam: John Benjamins.

Lleó, Conxita, and Demuth, Katherine (1999) Prosodic constraints on the emergence of grammatical morphemes: Crosslinguistic evidence from Germanic and Romance languages. In *Proceedings of the 23rd Annual Boston University Conference on Language Development*, ed. Annabel Greenhill, Heather Littlefield, and Cheryl Tano, pp. 407–18. Somerville, MA: Cascadilla Press.

Lombardi, Linda (1999) Positional faithfulness and voicing assimilation in Optimality Theory. *Natural Language and Linguistic Theory* 17, 267–302.

Lombardi, Linda (2000) Second language data and constraints on manner. Unpublished manuscript. College Park: University of Maryland. [Available on Rutgers Optimal-ity Archive.]

Lombardi, Linda (to appear) Why Place and Voice are different: Constraint-specific alternations in Optimality Theory. In *Segmental Phonology in Optimality Theory: Constraints and Representations*, ed. Linda Lombardi. Cambridge: Cambridge Uni-versity Press. [Available on Rutgers Optimality Archive.]

Lovins, Julie (1971) Melodic conspiracies in Lomongo tonology. In *Papers from the 7th Regional Meeting, Chicago Linguistic Society*, ed. Douglas Adams, Mary Ann

Campbell, Victor Cohen, Julie Lovins, Edward Maxwell, Carolyn Nygren, and John Reighard, pp. 469–78. Chicago: Chicago Linguistic Society.

Lovins, Julie (1973) *Loanwords and the Phonological Structure*. Doctoral dissertation. Chicago: University of Chicago. [Distributed by IULC Publications, 1975.]

Lovins, Julie (1974) Why loan phonology is natural phonology. In *Papers from the Parasession on Natural Phonology*, ed. Anthony Bruck, Robert A. Fox, and Michael W. LaGaly, pp. 240–50. Chicago: Chicago Linguistic Society.

Łubowicz, Anna (1999) Derived environment effects in OT. In *The Proceedings of the West Coast Conference on Formal Linguistics 17*, ed. Kimary N. Shahin, Susan J. Blake, and Eun-Sook Kim, pp. 451–65. Stanford, CA: CSLI. [Available on Rutgers Optimality Archive.]

MacEachern, Margaret (1997) *Laryngeal Cooccurrence Restrictions*. Doctoral dissertation. Los Angeles: University of California.

Malone, Joseph (1972) A Hebrew flip-flop rule and its historical origins. *Lingua* 30, 422–48.

Marantz, Alec (1982) Re Reduplication. *Linguistic Inquiry* 13, 483–545.

Marantz, Alec (1995) The Minimalist program. In *Government and Binding Theory and the Minimalist Program*, ed. Gert Webelhuth, pp. 349–82. Cambridge: Blackwell.

Mascaró, Joan (1987) Place and voicing assimilation: A reduction and spreading account. Unpublished manuscript. Barcelona: Universitat Autònoma de Barcelona.

Mascaró, Joan (1996) External allomorphy as emergence of the unmarked. In *Current Trends in Phonology: Models and Methods*, ed. Jacques Durand and Bernard Laks, pp. 473–83. Salford, Manchester, UK: European Studies Research Institute, University of Salford.

Massar, A., and Gerken, L. (1998) Abstract output: An Optimality-Theoretic account of children's omissions from prosodically complex structures. In *Proceedings of the North East Linguistic Society 28*, ed. Pius N. Tamanji and Kiyomi Kusumoto, pp. 253–66. Amherst, MA: GLSA.

McCarthy, John (1986) OCP Effects: Gemination and antigemination. *Linguistic Inquiry* 17, 207–63.

McCarthy, John (1988) Feature geometry and dependency: A review. *Phonetica* 43, 84–108.

McCarthy, John (1995) Extensions of faithfulness: Rotuman revisited. Unpublished manuscript. Amherst: University of Massachusetts. [Available on Rutgers Optimality Archive.]

McCarthy, John (1996) Remarks on phonological opacity in Optimality Theory. In *Studies in Afroasiatic Grammar: Papers from the Second Conference on Afroasiatic Linguistics, Sophia Antipolis, 1994*, ed. Jacqueline Lecarme, Jean Lowenstamm, and Ur Shlonsky, pp. 215–43. The Hague: Holland Academic Graphics.

McCarthy, John (1997) Process-specific constraints in Optimality Theory. *Linguistic Inquiry* 28, 231–51.

McCarthy, John (1998) Morpheme structure constraints and paradigm occultation. In *CLS 32*. Part 2, *The Panels*, ed. M. Catherine Gruber, Derrick Higgins, Kenneth Olson, and Tamra Wysocki, pp. 123–50. Chicago: Chicago Linguistic Society.

McCarthy, John (1999) Sympathy and phonological opacity. *Phonology* 16, 331–99.

McCarthy, John (2000a) Faithfulness and prosodic circumscription. In *Optimality Theory: Phonology, Syntax, and Acquisition*, ed. Joost Dekkers, Frank van der Leeuw, and Jeroen van de Weijer, pp. 151–89. Oxford: Oxford University Press.

McCarthy, John (2000b) Harmonic serialism and parallelism. In *Proceedings of the North East Linguistics Society 30*, ed. Masako Hirotani, pp. 501–24. Amherst, MA: GLSA.

McCarthy, John (2000c) The prosody of phase in Rotuman. *Natural Language and Linguistic Theory* 18, 147–97.

McCarthy, John (to appear) Sympathy, cumulativity, and the Duke-of-York gambit. In *The Optimal Syllable*, ed. Caroline Féry and Ruben van de Vijver. Cambridge: Cambridge University Press.

McCarthy, John, and Prince, Alan (1986/1996) Prosodic morphology 1986. Report no. RuCCS-TR-32. New Brunswick, NJ: Rutgers University Center for Cognitive Science. [Excerpts appear in John Goldsmith, ed., *Essential Readings in Phonology*. Oxford: Blackwell, 1999, pp. 102–36.]

McCarthy, John, and Prince, Alan (1990a) Foot and word in prosodic morphology: The Arabic broken plural. *Natural Language and Linguistic Theory* 8, 209–83.

McCarthy, John, and Prince, Alan (1990b) Prosodic morphology and templatic morphology. In *Perspectives on Arabic Linguistics II: Papers from the Second Annual Symposium on Arabic Linguistics*, ed. Mushira Eid and John J. McCarthy, pp. 1–54. Amsterdam: John Benjamins.

McCarthy, John, and Prince, Alan (1993a) Generalized Alignment. In *Yearbook of Morphology*, ed. Geert Booij and Jaap van Marle, pp. 79–153. Dordrecht: Kluwer. [Excerpts appear in John Goldsmith, ed., *Essential Readings in Phonology*. Oxford: Blackwell, 1999, pp. 102–36.]

McCarthy, John, and Prince, Alan (1993b) Prosodic Morphology I: Constraint Interaction and Satisfaction. Report no. RuCCS-TR-3. New Brunswick, NJ: Rutgers University Center for Cognitive Science.

McCarthy, John, and Prince, Alan (1994a) The emergence of the unmarked: Optimality in prosodic morphology. In *Proceedings of the North East Linguistic Society 24*, ed. Mercè Gonzàlez, pp. 333–79. Amherst, MA: GLSA.

McCarthy, John, and Prince, Alan (1994b) Two lectures on prosodic morphology (Utrecht, 1994). Part I, Template form in prosodic morphology. Part II, Faithfulness and reduplicative identity. Unpublished manuscript. Amherst: University of Massachusetts: New Brunswick, NJ: Rutgers University. [Available on Rutgers Optimality Archive.]

McCarthy, John, and Prince, Alan (1995a) Faithfulness and reduplicative identity. In *University of Massachusetts Occasional Papers in Linguistics 18*, ed. Jill Beckman, Laura Walsh Dickey, and Suzanne Urbanczyk, pp. 249–384. Amherst, MA: GLSA.

McCarthy, John, and Prince, Alan (1995b) Prosodic morphology. In *The Handbook of Phonological Theory*, ed. John A. Goldsmith, pp. 318–66. Cambridge, MA: Blackwell.

McCarthy, John, and Prince, Alan (1999) Faithfulness and identity in Prosodic Morphology. In *The Prosody-Morphology Interface*, ed. René Kager, Harry van der Hulst, and Wim Zonneveld, pp. 218–309. Cambridge: Cambridge University Press.

McCarthy, John, and Taub, Alison (1992) Review of C. Paradis and J.-F. Prunet, eds., *The Special Status of Coronals: Internal and External Evidence*. *Phonology* 9, 363–70.

McCawley, James (1973) On the role of notation in generative phonology. In *The Formal Analysis of Natural Languages: Proceedings of the First International Congress*, ed.

Maurice Gross, Morris Halle, and Marcel-Paul Schützenberger, pp. 51–62. The Hague: Mouton.

McDonough, Joyce (1987) Concerning the nature of certain consonants in Southern Paiute. Unpublished manuscript. Amherst, MA: University of Massachusetts.

McGarrity, Laura Wilbur (1999) A sympathy account of multiple opacity in Wintu. In *Indiana University Working Papers in Linguistics I*, ed. Karen Baertsch and Daniel A. Dinnsen, pp. 93–107. Bloomington, IN: IULC.

Menn, Lise (to appear) Saving the baby: Making sure that old data survive new theories. In *Fixing Priorities: Constraints in Phonological Acquisition*, ed. René Kager, Joe Pater, and Wim Zonneveld. Cambridge: Cambridge University Press.

Merchant, Jason (1997) Sympathetic devoicing and continuancy in Catalan. In *Phonology at Santa Cruz*, ed. Rachel Walker, Motoko Katayama, and Daniel Karvonen, pp. 57–62. Santa Cruz: Linguistics Research Center, University of California.

Mester, Armin (1994) The quantitative trochee in Latin. *Natural Language and Linguistic Theory* 12, 1–61.

Mester, Armin, and Padgett, Jaye (1994) Directional syllabification in Generalized Alignment. In *Phonology at Santa Cruz 3*, ed. Jason Merchant, Jaye Padgett, and Rachel Walker, pp. 79–85. Santa Cruz: University of California.

Mohanan, K. P. (1982) *Lexical Phonology*. Doctoral dissertation. Cambridge: Massachusetts Institute of Technology. [Distributed by IULC Publications.]

Mohanan, K. P. (1986) *The Theory of Lexical Phonology*. Dordrecht: Reidel.

Mohanan, K. P. (1991) On the bases of radical underspecification. *Natural Language and Linguistic Theory* 9, 285–325.

Mohanan, K. P. (1993) Fields of attraction in phonology. In *The Last Phonological Rule: Reflections on Constraints and Derivations*, ed. John Goldsmith, pp. 61–116. Chicago: University of Chicago Press.

Mohanan, K. P. (1995) The organization of the grammar. In *The Handbook of Phonological Theory*, ed. John A. Goldsmith, pp. 24–69. Cambridge, MA: Blackwell.

Moravcsik, Edith (1978) Reduplicative constructions. In *Universals of Human Language*, ed. Joseph Greenberg, vol. 3, pp. 297–334. Stanford: Stanford University Press.

Morelli, Frida (1998) Markedness relations and implicational universals in the factorial typology of onset obstruent clusters. In *Proceedings of the North East Linguistic Society 28*, ed. Pius N. Tamanji and Kiyomi Kusumoto, pp. 107–20. Amherst, MA: GLSA.

Morelli, Frida (to appear) The relative harmony of /s+stop/ onsets: Obstruent clusters and the sonority sequencing principle. In *The Optimal Syllable*, ed. Caroline Féry and Ruben van de Vijver. Cambridge: Cambridge University Press.

Morén, Bruce (1999) *Distinctiveness, Coercion and Sonority: A Unified Theory of Weight*. Doctoral dissertation. College Park: University of Maryland. [Available on Rutgers Optimality Archive.]

Moreton, Elliott (1996/1999) Non-computable functions in Optimality Theory. Unpublished manuscript. Amherst: University of Massachusetts. [Written in 1996; revised and placed on Rutgers Optimality Archive in 1999.]

Moreton, Elliott (2000) Faithfulness and potential. Unpublished manuscript. Amherst: University of Massachusetts.

Morin, Yves-Charles (1976) Phonological tensions in French. In *Current Studies in Romance Linguistics (Proceedings of the Fourth Linguistics Symposium on Romance*

Languages), ed. Marta Luján and Fritz Hensey, pp. 37–49. Washington, DC: Georgetown University Press.

Morris, Richard E. (1998) *Stylistic Variation in Spanish Phonology*. Doctoral dissertation. Columbus: Ohio State University.

Müller, Gereon (1998) Order preservation, parallel movement, and the emergence of the unmarked. Unpublished manuscript. Stuttgart, Germany: University of Stuttgart. [Available on Rutgers Optimality Archive.]

Müller, Gereon (1999) Optimality, markedness, and word order in German. *Linguistics* 37, 777–818.

Mutaka, Ngessimo, and Hyman, Larry (1990) Syllable and morpheme integrity in Kinande reduplication. *Phonology* 7, 73–120.

Myers, James (1994) Rules, constraints, and lexical phonology in Glenoe Scots. Unpublished manuscript. Buffalo: State University of New York. [Available on Rutgers Optimality Archive.]

Myers, Scott (1986) *Tone and the Structure of Words in Shona*. Doctoral dissertation. Amherst: University of Massachusetts.

Myers, Scott (1991) Persistent rules. *Linguistic Inquiry* 22, 315–44.

Myers, Scott (1997a) Expressing phonetic naturalness in phonology. In *Derivations and Constraints in Phonology*, ed. Iggy Roca, pp. 125–52. New York: Oxford University Press.

Myers, Scott (1997b) OCP effects in Optimality Theory. *Natural Language and Linguistic Theory* 15, 847–92.

Myers, Scott (1998) Surface underspecification of tone in Chichewa. *Phonology* 15, 367–91.

Nagy, Naomi, and Reynolds, William T. (1995) Accounting for variable word-final deletion within Optimality Theory. In *Sociolinguistic Variation: Theory, Data, and Analysis*, ed. Jennifer Arnold, R. Blake, B. Davidson, S. Schwenter, and J. Solomon, pp. 151–60. Stanford, CA: CSLI.

Nash, David (1979) Yidiny stress: A metrical account. *CUNY Forum* 7/8, 112–30.

Nathan, Geoffrey S. (1984) Natural phonology and interference in second language acquisition. In *The Uses of Phonology: Proceedings of the First Conference on the Uses of Phonology (Southern Illinois University Occasional Papers in Linguistics 12)*, ed. Geoffrey S. Nathan and Margaret E. Winters, pp. 103–13. Carbondale: Department of Linguistics, Southern Illinois University.

Nelson, Nicole (1998) Right Anchor, Aweigh. Unpublished manuscript. New Brunswick, NJ: Rutgers University.

Nespor, Marina, and Vogel, Irene (1986) *Prosodic Phonology*. Dordrecht: Foris.

Nespor, Marina, and Vogel, Irene (1989) On clashes and lapses. *Phonology* 6, 69–116.

Nessly, Larry (1973) The weakening chain in natural phonology. In *Papers from the 9th Regional Meeting, Chicago Linguistic Society*, ed. Claudia Corum, T. Cedric Smith-Stark, and Ann Weiser, pp. 462–74. Chicago: Chicago Linguistic Society.

Nevin, Bruce E. (1998) *Aspects of Pit River Phonology*. Doctoral dissertation. Philadelphia: University of Pennsylvania.

Newmeyer, Frederick J. (1996) *Generative Linguistics: A Historical Perspective*. London and New York: Routledge.

Newmeyer, Frederick J. (1998) *Language Form and Language Function*. Cambridge, MA: MIT Press.

Ní Chiosáin, Máire, and Padgett, Jaye (1997) Markedness, Segment Realization, and Locality in Spreading. Report no. LRC-97-01. Santa Cruz: Linguistics Research Center, University of California. [Available on Rutgers Optimality Archive.]

Nishiyama, Kunio (1996) Historical change of Japanese verbs and its implications for Optimality Theory. *MIT Working Papers in Linguistics* 29, 155–71.

Noske, Roland (1996) Is French optimal? A question concerning phonological process order. In *Current Trends in Phonology: Models and methods*, ed. J. Durand and B. Laks, pp. 485–507. Paris-X and Salford: University of Salford Publications.

Noyer, Rolf (1993) Mobile affixes in Huave: Optimality and morphological well-formedness. In *The Proceedings of the West Coast Conference on Formal Linguistics 12*, ed. Erin Duncan, Donka Farkas, and Philip Spaelti, pp. 67–82. Stanford, CA: Stanford Linguistics Association.

Noyer, Rolf (1997) Attic Greek accentuation and intermediate derivational representations. In *Derivations and Constraints in Phonology*, ed. Iggy Roca, pp. 501–28. New York: Oxford University Press.

O'Connor, Kathleen M. (1999) On the role of segmental contrasts in the acquisition of clusters. In *Optimal Green Ideas in Phonology: Indiana University Working Papers in Linguistics I*, ed. Daniel Dinnsen and Karen Baertsch, pp. 109–26. Bloomington, IN: IULC.

Odden, David (1986) On the Obligatory Contour Principle. *Language* 62, 353–83.

Odden, David (1994) Adjacency parameters in phonology. *Language* 70, 289–330.

Odden, David, and Odden, Mary (1985) Ordered reduplication in Kihehe. *Linguistic Inquiry* 16, 497–503.

Ohala, Diane (1996) *Cluster Reduction and Constraints in Acquisition*. Doctoral dissertation. Tucson: University of Arizona.

van Oostendorp, Marc (1997a) Style levels in conflict resolution. In *Variation, Change, and Phonological Theory*, ed. Frans Hinskens, Roeland van Hout, and W. Leo Wetzels, pp. 207–29. Amsterdam: John Benjamins.

van Oostendorp, Marc (1997b) *Vowel Quality and Phonological Projection*. Doctoral dissertation: Katolieke Universiteit Brabant.

Orgun, C. Orhan (1994) Monotonic Cyclicity and Optimality Theory. In *Proceedings of the 24st Annual Meeting of the North-East Linguistic Society*, ed. Mercè Gonzàlez, pp. 461–74. Amherst, MA: GLSA.

Orgun, C. Orhan (1996a) Correspondence and identity constraints in two-level Optimality Theory. In *The Proceedings of the West Coast Conference on Formal Linguistics 14*, ed. Jose Camacho, Lina Choueiri, and Maki Watanabe, pp. 399–413. Stanford, CA: CSLI.

Orgun, C. Orhan (1996b) *Sign-based Morphology and Phonology, with Special Attention to Optimality Theory*. Doctoral dissertation. Berkeley: University of California.

Orgun, C. Orhan, and Sprouse, Ronald (1999) From MParse to control: Deriving ungrammaticality. *Phonology* 16, 191–220.

Ota, Mitsuhiko (1998a) The emergence of the unmarked in early prosodic structure. In *Proceedings of the North East Linguistic Society 28*, ed. Pius N. Tamanji and Kiyomi Kusumoto, pp. 321–40. Amherst, MA: GLSA.

Ota, Mitsuhiko (1998b) Phonological constraints and word truncation in early language acquisition. In *Proceedings of the 22rd Annual Boston University Conference on Language Development*, ed. Annabel Greenhill, Elizabeth Hughes, Heather Littlefield, and H. Walsh, pp. 598–609. Somerville, MA: Cascadilla Press.

Ota, Mitsuhiko (1999) *Phonological Theory and the Acquisition of Prosodic Structure: Evidence from Child Japanese.* Doctoral dissertation. Washington, DC: Georgetown University.

Padgett, Jaye (1991) *Stricture in Feature Geometry.* Doctoral dissertation. Amherst: University of Massachusetts.

Padgett, Jaye (1995a) Feature classes. In *University of Massachusetts Occasional Papers in Linguistics 18*, ed. Jill Beckman, Laura Walsh Dickey, and Suzanne Urbanczyk, pp. 385–420. Amherst, MA: GLSA.

Padgett, Jaye (1995b) Partial class behavior and nasal place assimilation. In *Proceedings of the Arizona Phonology Conference: Workshop on Features in Optimality Theory.* [Available on Rutgers Optimality Archive.]

Padgett, Jaye (1995c) *Stricture in Feature Geometry.* Stanford, CA: CSLI.

Paradis, Carole (1988a) On constraints and repair strategies. *The Linguistic Review* 6, 71–97.

Paradis, Carole (1988b) Towards a theory of constraint violations. *McGill Working Papers in Linguistics* 5, 1–43.

Paradis, Carole (1996) The inadequacy of filters and faithfulness in loanword adaptation. In *Current Trends in Phonology: Models and Methods*, ed. Jacques Durand and Bernard Laks, pp. 509–34. Salford, Manchester, UK: University of Salford.

Paradis, Carole (1997) Non-transparent constraint effects in Gere: From cycles to derivations. In *Derivations and Constraints in Phonology*, ed. Iggy Roca, pp. 529–50. New York: Oxford University Press.

Paradis, Carole, and LaCharité, Darlene (eds.) (1993) *Constraint-based Theories in Multilinear Phonology* (Special issue). *Canadian Journal of Linguistics* 39 (2).

Pater, Joe (1997) Minimal Violation and Phonological Development. *Language Acquisition* 6, 201–53.

Pater, Joe (1999a) Austronesian nasal substitution and other NC effects. In *The Prosody-Morphology Interface*, ed. René Kager, Harry van der Hulst, and Wim Zonneveld, pp. 310–43. Cambridge: Cambridge University Press.

Pater, Joe (1999b) Review of Bernhardt and Stemberger (1998) *Handbook of Phonological Development from the Perspective of Constraint-based Nonlinear Phonology. Phonology* 16, 105–14.

Pater, Joe (to appear-a) From phonological typology to the development of receptive and productive phonological competence: Applications of minimal violation. In *Fixing Priorities: Constraints in Phonological Acquisition*, ed. René Kager, Joe Pater, and Wim Zonneveld. Cambridge: Cambridge University Press.

Pater, Joe (to appear-b) Nonuniformity in English secondary stress: The role of ranked and lexically specific constraints. *Phonology.*

Pater, Joe, and Paradis, Johanne (1996) Truncation without templates in child phonology. In *Proceedings of the 20th Annual Boston University Conference on Language Development*, ed. A. Stringfellow, D. Cahana-Amitay, E. Hughes, and A. Zukowski, pp. 540–52. Somerville, MA: Cascadilla Press.

Payne, David L. (1981) *The Phonology and Morphology of Axininca Campa.* Arlington: Summer Institute of Linguistics and University of Texas.

Peperkamp, Sharon (1997) *Prosodic Words.* The Hague: Holland Academic Graphics. [Doctoral dissertation, University of Amsterdam.]

Perlmutter, David (1971) *Deep and Surface Structure Constraints in Syntax.* New York: Holt, Rinehart, and Winston.

Perlmutter, David (1974) Impersonal passives and the unaccusative hypothesis. In *Proceedings of the Fourth Annual Meeting of the Berkeley Linguistics Society*, ed. Jeri J. Jaeger, Anthony C. Woodbury, and Farrel Ackerman, pp. 157–89. Berkeley: Berkeley Linguistics Society.

Perlmutter, David (1998) Interfaces: Explanation of allomorphy and the architecture of grammars. In *Morphology and Its Relation to Phonology and Syntax*, ed. Steven G. Lapointe, Diane K. Brentari, and Patrick M. Farrell, pp. 307–38. Stanford, CA: CSLI.

Pesetsky, David (1997) Optimality Theory and syntax: Movement and pronunciation. In *Optimality Theory: An Overview*, ed. Diana Archangeli and D. Terence Langendoen, pp. 134–70. Oxford: Blackwell.

Pesetsky, David (1998) Some optimality principles of sentence pronunciation. In *Is the Best Good Enough? Optimality and Competition in Syntax*, ed. Pilar Barbosa, Danny Fox, Paul Hagstrom, Martha McGinnis, and David Pesetsky, pp. 337–83. Cambridge, MA: MIT Press.

Pierrehumbert, Janet (1980) *The Phonetics and Phonology of English Intonation*. Doctoral dissertation. Cambridge: Massachusetts Institute of Technology.

Piggott, Glyne (1988) A parametric approach to nasal harmony. In *Features, Segmental Structure and Harmony Processes*, ed. Harry van der Hulst and Norval Smith, pp. 131–67. Dordrecht: Foris.

Polgardi, Krisztina (1998) *Vowel Harmony: An Account in Terms of Government and Optimality*. The Hague: Holland Academic Graphics.

Poole, Geoffrey (1998) Constraints on local economy. In *Is the Best Good Enough? Optimality and Competition in Syntax*, ed. Pilar Barbosa, Danny Fox, Paul Hagstrom, Martha McGinnis, and David Pesetsky, pp. 385–98. Cambridge, MA: MIT Press.

Poser, William (1982) Phonological representations and action-at-a-distance. In *The Structure of Phonological Representations*, ed. Harry van der Hulst and Norval Smith, pp. 121–58. Dordrecht: Foris.

Poser, William (1986) Yidiny stress, metrical structure assignment, and the nature of metrical representation. In *Proceedings of the West Coast Conference on Formal Linguistics 4*, ed. Jeffrey Goldberg, Susannah MacKaye, and Michael T. Wescoat, pp. 178–91. Stanford, CA: Stanford Linguistic Association.

Potter, Brian (1994) Serial optimality in Mohawk prosody. In *Proceedings of the Thirtieth Annual Regional Meeting of the Chicago Linguistics Society*, ed. Katharine Beals, Jeannette Denton, Robert Knippen, Lynette Melmar, Hisami Suzuki, and Erica Zeinfeld, pp. 347–61. Chicago: Chicago Linguistic Society.

Prentice, D. J. (1971) *The Murut Languages of Sabah*. Canberra: Australian National University.

Prince, Alan (1975) McCawley on formalization. *Recherches linguistiques* 3, 194–225.

Prince, Alan (1980) A metrical theory for Estonian quantity. *Linguistic Inquiry* 11, 511–62.

Prince, Alan (1983) Relating to the grid. *Linguistic Inquiry* 14, 19–100.

Prince, Alan (1984) Phonology with tiers. In *Language Sound Structure*, ed. Mark Aronoff and Richard T. Oehrle, pp. 234–44. Cambridge, MA: MIT Press.

Prince, Alan (1990) Quantitative consequences of rhythmic organization. In *Parasession on the Syllable in Phonetics and Phonology*, ed. M. Ziolkowski, M. Noske, and K. Deaton, pp. 355–98. Chicago: Chicago Linguistic Society.

Prince, Alan (1993a) In Defense of the Number *i*: Anatomy of a Linear Dynamical Model of Linguistic Generalizations. Report no. RuCCS TR-1. New Brunswick, NJ: Rutgers University Center for Cognitive Science.

Prince, Alan (1993b) Minimal violation. Handout from Rutgers Optimality Workshop 1 (ROW-1), October 1993, Rutgers University, New Brunswick, NJ.

Prince, Alan (1996) A letter from Alan Prince. *Glot International* 2 (6), 1, 23–24.

Prince, Alan (1997a) Endogenous constraints on Optimality Theory. Handout from Hopkins Optimality Theory Workshop/Maryland Mayfest '97, Baltimore.

Prince, Alan (1997b) Endogenous constraints on Optimality Theory. Handout from course presented at the Linguistic Society of America Summer Institute, Cornell University, Ithaca, NY.

Prince, Alan (1998) Two lectures on Optimality Theory. Handout from Phonology Forum 1998, Kobe University, Kobe, Japan. [Available for download (9/9/00) from http://ling.rutgers.edu/resources/archive/kobe-all.pdf.]

Prince, Alan (2000) Comparative tableaux. Unpublished manuscript. New Brunswick, NJ: Rutgers University. [Available on Rutgers Optimality Archive.]

Prince, Alan, and Smolensky, Paul (1991) Connectionism and Harmony Theory in Linguistics. Report no. CU-CS-533-91: Department of Computer Science, University of Colorado, Boulder.

Prince, Alan, and Smolensky, Paul (1993) Optimality Theory: Constraint Interaction in Generative Grammar. Report no. RuCCS-TR-2. New Brunswick, NJ: Rutgers University Center for Cognitive Science.

Prince, Alan, and Smolensky, Paul (1997) Optimality: From neural networks to universal grammar. *Science* 275, 1604–10.

Prince, Alan, and Tesar, Bruce (1999) Learning Phonotactic Distributions. Report no. RuCCS-TR-54. New Brunswick, NJ: Rutgers University Center for Cognitive Science. [Available on Rutgers Optimality Archive.]

Pulleyblank, Douglas (1986) *Tone in Lexical Phonology*. Dordrecht: D. Reidel.

Pulleyblank, Douglas (1997) Optimality theory and features. In *Optimality Theory: An Overview*, ed. Diana Archangeli and D. Terence Langendoen, pp. 59–101. Oxford: Blackwell.

Pulleyblank, Douglas, and Turkel, William J. (1996) Optimality Theory and learning algorithms: The representation of recurrent featural asymmetries. In *Current Trends in Phonology: Models and Methods*, ed. J. Durand and B. Laks, vol. 2, pp. 653–84. Paris-X and Salford: University of Salford Publications.

Pulleyblank, Douglas, and Turkel, William J. (1997) Gradient retreat. In *Derivations and Constraints in Phonology*, ed. Iggy Roca, pp. 153–93. New York: Oxford University Press.

Pulleyblank, Douglas, and Turkel, William J. (1998) The logical problem of language acquisition in Optimality Theory. In *Is the Best Good Enough? Optimality and Competition in Syntax*, ed. Pilar Barbosa, Danny Fox, Paul Hagstrom, Martha McGinnis, and David Pesetsky, pp. 399–420. Cambridge, MA: MIT Press.

Pulleyblank, Douglas, and Turkel, William J. (2000) Learning phonology: Genetic algorithms and Yoruba tongue root harmony. In *Optimality Theory: Phonology, Syntax, and Acquisition*, ed. Joost Dekkers, Frank van der Leeuw, and Jeroen van de Weijer, pp. 554–91. Oxford: Oxford University Press.

Pullum, Geoffrey (1976) The Duke of York gambit. *Journal of Linguistics* 12, 83–102.

Pyle, Charles (1974) Why a conspiracy? In *Papers from the Parasession on Natural Phonology*, ed. Anthony Bruck, Robert A. Fox, and Michael W. LaGaly, pp. 275–84. Chicago: Chicago Linguistic Society.

Ramus, F., Nespor, Marina, and Mehler, J. (1999) Correlates of linguistic rhythm in the speech signal. *Cognition* 73, 265–92.

Revithiadou, Anthi (1999) *Headmost Accent Wins: Head Dominance and Ideal Prosodic Form in Lexical Accent Systems*. The Hague: Holland Academic Graphics. [Doctoral dissertation, University of Leiden.]

Reynolds, William T., and Nagy, Naomi (1994) Phonological variation in Faetar: An Optimality account. In *Papers from the 30th Regional Meeting of the Chicago Linguistic Society*. Vol. 2, *The Parasession on Variation in Linguistic Theory*, ed. Katharine Beals, Jeannette Denton, Robert Knippen, Lynette Melmar, Hisami Suzuki, and Erica Zeinfeld, pp. 277–92. Chicago: Chicago Linguistic Society.

Riad, Tomas (1992) *Structures in Germanic Prosody: A Diachronic Study with Special Reference to the Nordic Languages*. Doctoral dissertation. Stockholm: Stockholm University.

Rice, Curtis (1992) *Binarity and Ternarity in Metrical Theory: Parametric Extensions*. Doctoral dissertation. Austin: University of Texas.

Rice, Keren (1987) The function of structure preservation: Derived environments. In *Proceedings of the North East Linguistic Society 17*, ed. Bernadette Plunkett and Joyce McDonough, pp. 501–19. Amherst, MA: GLSA.

Ringen, Catherine O., and Heinämäki, Orvokki (1999) Variation in Finnish vowel harmony: An OT account. *Natural Language and Linguistic Theory* 17, 303–37.

Roark, Brian, and Demuth, Katherine (2000) Prosodic constraints and the learner's environment: A corpus study. In *Proceedings of the 24th Annual Boston University Conference on Language Development.*, ed. S. Catherine Howell, Sarah A. Fish, and Thea Keith-Lucas, pp. 597–608. Somerville, MA: Cascadilla Press.

Roberts, Ian (1997) Restructuring, head movement, and locality. *Linguistic Inquiry* 28, 423–60.

Robson, Barbara (1971) Historical notes on the single vowel conspiracy in Turkish. *General Linguistics* 11, 145–50.

Roca, Iggy (ed.) (1997a) *Derivations and Constraints in Phonology*. New York: Oxford University Press.

Roca, Iggy (1997b) Derivations or constraints, or derivations and constraints? In *Derivations and Constraints in Phonology*, ed. Iggy Roca, pp. 3–42. New York: Oxford University Press.

Rosenthall, Sam (1994) *Vowel/Glide Alternation in a Theory of Constraint Interaction*. Doctoral dissertation. Amherst: University of Massachusetts.

Rosenthall, Sam (1997) The distribution of prevocalic vowels. *Natural Language and Linguistic Theory* 15, 139–80.

Rosenthall, Sam, and van der Hulst, Harry (1999) Weight-by-position by position. *Natural Language and Linguistic Theory* 17, 499–540.

Ross, John R. (1973) Leftward, ho. In *A Festschrift for Morris Halle*, ed. Stephen R. Anderson and Paul Kiparsky, pp. 166–73. New York: Holt, Rinehart and Winston.

Rubach, Jerzy (1993) *The Lexical Phonology of Slovak*. Oxford: Oxford University Press.

Rubach, Jerzy (1997) Extrasyllabic consonants in Polish: Derivational Optimality Theory. In *Derivations and Constraints in Phonology*, ed. Iggy Roca, pp. 551–82. New York: Oxford University Press.

Rubach, Jerzy (2000) Glide and glottal stop insertion in Slavic languages: A DOT analysis. *Linguistic Inquiry* 31, 271–317.

Rubach, Jerzy, and Booij, Geert (1990) Edge of constituent effects in Polish. *Natural Language and Linguistic Theory* 7, 121–58.

Russell, Kevin (1995) Morphemes and candidates in Optimality Theory. Unpublished manuscript. Winnipeg: University of Manitoba. [Available on Rutgers Optimality Archive.]

Sagey, Elizabeth (1988) On the ill-formedness of crossing association lines. *Linguistic Inquiry* 19, 109–18.

Samek-Lodovici, Vieri (1992) Universal constraints and morphological gemination: A crosslinguistic study. Unpublished manuscript. Waltham, MA: Brandeis University.

Samek-Lodovici, Vieri (1993) A unified analysis of crosslinguistic morphological gemination. Unpublished manuscript. New Brunswick, NJ: Rutgers University.

Samek-Lodovici, Vieri (1996a) *Constraints on Subjects: An Optimality Theoretic Analysis*. Doctoral dissertation. New Brunswick, NJ: Rutgers University. [Available on Rutgers Optimality Archive.]

Samek-Lodovici, Vieri (1996b) Response by author to dissertation review by Peter Ackema of *Constraints on Subjects: An Optimality-Theoretic Analysis*. *Glot International* 2 (8).

Samek-Lodovici, Vieri (1998) Opposite constraints: Left and right focus-alignment in Kanakuru. *Lingua* 104, 111–30.

Samek-Lodovici, Vieri (to appear) Crosslinguistic Typologies. In *OT Syntax*, ed. Géraldine Legendre, Jane Grimshaw, and Sten Vikner. Cambridge, MA: MIT Press.

Samek-Lodovici, Vieri, and Prince, Alan (1999) Optima. Unpublished manuscript. London: University of London; New Brunswick, NJ: Rutgers University. [Available on Rutgers Optimality Archive.]

Sanders, Gerald (1974) Precedence relations in language. *Foundations of Language* 11, 361–400.

Sanders, Nathan (1997) On sympathetic correspondence. In *Phonology at Santa Cruz*, ed. Rachel Walker, Motoko Katayama, and Daniel Karvonen, pp. 91–102. Santa Cruz: Linguistics Research Center, University of California.

Sapir, Edward (1930) Southern Paiute, a Shoshonean language. *Proceedings of the American Academy of Arts and Sciences* 65 (1–3).

Sapir, Edward, and Swadesh, Morris (1978) *Nootka texts: Tales and Ethnological Narratives, with Grammatical Notes and Lexical Material*. New York: AMS Press.

Schaefer, Ronald P. (1987) *An Initial Orthography and Lexicon for Emai*. Bloomington, IN: IULC.

Schane, Sanford (1973) *Generative phonology*. Englewood Cliffs, NJ: Prentice-Hall.

Schourup, Lawrence (1974) Phonological conspiracies. *Glossa* 8, 198–207.

Scobbie, James (1991) *Attribute Value Phonology*. Doctoral dissertation. Edinburgh: University of Edinburgh.

Scobbie, James (1993) Constraint violation and conflict from the perspective of Declarative Phonology. *Canadian Journal of Linguistics/Revue canadienne de linguistique* 38, 155–67. (Special issue, ed. Darlene LaCharité and Carole Paradis.)

Scott, N. C. (1957) Notes on the pronunciation of Sea Dayak. *Bulletin of the School of Oriental and African Studies* 20, 509–12.

Selkirk, Elisabeth (1972) *The Phrase Phonology of English and French*. Doctoral dissertation. Cambridge, MA: Massachusetts Institute of Technology.

Selkirk, Elisabeth (1978) On prosodic structure and its relation to syntactic structure. In *Nordic Prosody*, ed. T. Fretheim, pp. 111–40. Trondheim: Tapir forlag.

Selkirk, Elisabeth (1980a) Prosodic domains in phonology: Sanskrit revisited. In *Juncture*, ed. Mark Aronoff and M.-L. Kean, pp. 107–29. Saratoga, CA: Anma Libri.

Selkirk, Elisabeth (1980b) The role of prosodic categories in English word stress. *Linguistic Inquiry* 11, 563–605.

Selkirk, Elisabeth (1981) Epenthesis and degenerate syllables in Cairene Arabic. In *Theoretical Issues in the Grammar of the Semitic Languages (MIT Working Papers in Linguistics 3)*, ed. Hagit Borer and Joseph Aoun, pp. 111–40. Cambridge: Department of Linguistics and Philosophy, Massachusetts Institute of Technology.

Selkirk, Elisabeth (1984) *Phonology and Syntax: The Relation between Sound and Structure*. Cambridge, MA: MIT Press.

Selkirk, Elisabeth (1986) On derived domains in sentence phonology. *Phonology* 3, 371–405.

Selkirk, Elisabeth (1995) The prosodic structure of function words. In *Papers in Optimality Theory*, ed. Jill Beckman, Laura Walsh Dickey, and Suzanne Urbanczyk, pp. 439–70. Amherst, MA: GLSA.

Selkirk, Elisabeth (1996) The prosodic structure of function words. In *Signal to Syntax: Bootstrapping from Speech to Grammar in Early Acquisition*, ed. James L. Morgan and Katherine Demuth, pp. 187–214: Lawrence Erlbaum Associates.

Selkirk, Elisabeth, and Shen, Tong (1990) Prosodic domains in Shanghai Chinese. In *The Phonology-Syntax Connection*, ed. Sharon Inkelas and Draga Zec, pp. 313–37. Chicago: University of Chicago Press.

Selkirk, Elisabeth, and Tateishi, Koichi (1988) Constraints on minor phrase formation in Japanese. In *Papers from the 24th Annual Regional Meeting of the Chicago Linguistic Society*, pp. 316–36. Chicago: Chicago Linguistic Society.

Selkirk, Elisabeth, and Tateishi, Koichi (1991) Syntax and downstep in Japanese. In *Interdisciplinary Approaches to Language: Essays in Honor of S.-Y. Kuroda*, ed. C. Georgopoulos and R. Ishihara, pp. 519–44. Dordrecht: Kluwer.

Sells, Peter (1998) Optimality and economy of expression in Japanese and Korean. In *Japanese/Korean Linguistics*, Vol. 7, ed. Noriko Akatsuka, Hajime Hoji, Shoichi Iwasaki, Sung-Ock Sohn, and Susan Strauss, pp. 499–514. Stanford, CA: CSLI. [Available on Rutgers Optimality Archive.]

Sells, Peter (to appear) Form and function in the typology of grammatical voice systems. In *OT Syntax*, ed. Géraldine Legendre, Jane Grimshaw, and Sten Vikner. Cambridge, MA: MIT Press.

Sells, Peter, Rickford, John, and Wasow, Thomas (1996) An Optimality Theoretic approach to variation in negative inversion in AAVE. *Natural Language and Linguistic Theory* 14, 591–627. [Available on Rutgers Optimality Archive.]

Sherer, Tim (1994) *Prosodic Phonotactics*. Doctoral dissertation. Amherst: University of Massachusetts.

Shibatani, Masayoshi (1973) The role of surface phonetic constraints in generative phonology. *Language* 49, 87–106.

Shinohara, Shigeko (1997) *Analyse phonologique de l'adaptation japonaise de mots étrangers*. Doctoral dissertation. Paris: Université de la Sorbonne nouvelle Paris III. [Available on Rutgers Optimality Archive.]

Shinohara, Shigeko (to appear) Emergence of Universal Grammar in foreign word adaptations. In *Fixing Priorities: Constraints in Phonological Acquisition*, ed.

René Kager, Joe Pater, and Wim Zonneveld. Cambridge: Cambridge University Press.

Siegel, Dorothy (1974) *Topics in English Morphology*. Doctoral dissertation. Cambridge, MA: Massachusetts Institute of Technology.

Silverman, Daniel (1995) *Phasing and Recoverability*. Doctoral dissertation. Los Angeles: University of California.

Silverstein, Michael (1976) Hierarchy of features and ergativity. In *Grammatical Categories in Australian Languages*, ed. R. M. W. Dixon, pp. 112–71. Canberra: Australian Institute of Aboriginal Studies.

Singh, Rajendra (1987) Well-formedness conditions and phonological theory. In *Phonologica 1984*, ed. W. Dressler et al., pp. 273–85. Cambridge: Cambridge University Press.

Skousen, Royal (1975) *Substantive Evidence in Phonology: The Evidence from Finnish and French*. The Hague: Mouton.

Smith, Jennifer L. (1998) Noun faithfulness: Evidence from accent in Japanese dialects. In *Japanese/Korean Linguistics*, Vol. 7, ed. Noriko Akatsuka, Hajime Hoji, Shoichi Iwasaki, Sung-Ock Sohn, and Susan Strauss, pp. 611–27. Stanford, CA: CSLI.

Smith, Jennifer L. (2000a) Lexical category and phonological contrast. In *Papers in Experimental and Theoretical Linguistics: Proceedings of the Workshop on the Lexicon in Phonetics and Phonology*, ed. Robert Kirchner, Joe Pater, and Wolf Wikely. Edmonton: Department of Linguistics, University of Alberta.

Smith, Jennifer L. (2000b) Positional faithfulness and learnability in Optimality Theory. In *Proceedings of ESCOL 99*, ed. Rebecca Daly and Anastasia Riehl, pp. 203–14. Ithaca, NY: CLC.

Smith, Jennifer L. (2001) *Phonological Augmentation in Prominent Positions*. Doctoral dissertation. Amherst: University of Massachusetts.

Smith, Neilson V. (1973) *The Acquisition of Phonology: A Case Study*. Cambridge: Cambridge University Press.

Smith, Norval S. H. (1997) Shrinking and hopping vowels in Northern Cape York: Minimally different systems. In *Variation, Change, and Phonological Theory*, ed. Frans Hinskens, Roeland van Hout, and W. Leo Wetzels, pp. 267–302. Amsterdam: John Benjamins.

Smolensky, Paul (1983) Schema selection and stochastic inference in modular environments. In *Proceedings of the National Conference on Artificial Intelligence*, ed. Michael Genesereth, pp. 378–82. Menlo Park, CA: AAAI Press.

Smolensky, Paul (1984a) Harmony Theory: Thermal parallel models in a computational context. In *Harmony Theory: Problem Solving, Parallel Cognitive Models, and Thermal Physics*, ed. Paul Smolensky and Mary S. Riley. (Technical report 8404.) La Jolla: Institute for Cognitive Science, University of California at San Diego.

Smolensky, Paul (1984b) The mathematical role of self-consistency in parallel computation. In *Proceedings of the Sixth Annual Conference of the Cognitive Science Society*, pp. 319–25. Mahwah, NJ: Lawrence Erlbaum Associates.

Smolensky, Paul (1986) Information processing in dynamical systems: Foundations of harmony theory. In *Parallel Distributed Processing: Explorations in the Microstructure of Cognition*, ed. D. Rumelhart, J. McClelland, and the PDP Research Group, pp. 194–281. Cambridge, MA: Bradford Books/MIT Press.

Smolensky, Paul (1988) On the proper treatment of connectionism. *Behavioral and Brain Sciences* 11, 1–74.

Smolensky, Paul (1993) Harmony, markedness, and phonological activity. Handout from Rutgers Optimality Workshop I, New Brunswick, NJ. [Available on Rutgers Optimality Archive.]

Smolensky, Paul (1995a) Constituent structure and explanation in an integrated connectionist/symbolic cognitive architecture. In *Connectionism: Debates on Psychological Explanation*, ed. C. Macdonald and G. Macdonald, vol. 2, pp. 221–90. Oxford: Basil Blackwell.

Smolensky, Paul (1995b) On the internal structure of the constraint component Con of UG. Handout from talk, University of Arizona. [Available on Rutgers Optimality Archive.]

Smolensky, Paul (1996a) The Initial State and "Richness of the Base" in Optimality Theory. Report no. JHU-CogSci-96-4. Baltimore: Department of Cognitive Science, Johns Hopkins University. [Available on Rutgers Optimality Archive.]

Smolensky, Paul (1996b) On the comprehension/production dilemma in child language. *Linguistic Inquiry* 27, 720–31.

Smolensky, Paul (1997) Constraint interaction in generative grammar II: Local conjunction, or random rules in Universal Grammar. Handout from Hopkins Optimality Theory Workshop/Maryland Mayfest '97, Baltimore.

Smolensky, Paul, Legendre, Géraldine, and Miyata, Yoshiro (1992) Principles for an Integrated Connectionist/Symbolic Theory of Higher Cognition. Report no. CU-CS-600-92. Boulder: Department of Computer Science, University of Colorado.

Sommerstein, Alan (1974) On phonotactically motivated rules. *Journal of Linguistics* 10, 71–94.

Spaelti, Philip (1997) *Dimensions of Variation in Multi-Pattern Reduplication*. Doctoral dissertation. Santa Cruz: University of California.

Speas, Margaret (1997) Optimality Theory and syntax: Null pronouns and control. In *Optimality Theory: An Overview*, ed. Diana Archangeli and D. Terence Langendoen, pp. 171–99. Oxford: Blackwell.

Speas, Margaret (to appear) Constraints on null pronouns. In *OT Syntax*, ed. Géraldine Legendre, Jane Grimshaw, and Sten Vikner. Cambridge, MA: MIT Press.

Spencer, Andrew (1991) *Morphological Theory*. Oxford: Basil Blackwell.

Spring, Cari (1990) *Implications of Axininca Campa for Prosodic Morphology and Reduplication*. Doctoral dissertation. Tucson: University of Arizona.

Stampe, David (1969) The acquisition of phonemic representation. In *Papers from CLS 5*, ed. Robert I. Binnick, Alice Davidson, Georgia M. Green, and Jerry L. Morgan, pp. 433–44. Chicago: Chicago Linguistic Society.

Stampe, David (1973a) *A Dissertation on Natural Phonology*. Doctoral dissertation. Chicago: University of Chicago. [Published by Garland Press, New York, 1979.]

Stampe, David (1973b) On chapter nine. In *Issues in Phonological Theory*, ed. Michael J. Kenstowicz and Charles W. Kisseberth, pp. 44–52. The Hague: Mouton.

Stemberger, Joseph (1996a) Optimality theory and phonological development: Basic issues. *Korean Journal of Linguistics* 21, 93–138.

Stemberger, Joseph (1996b) Syllable structure in English, with emphasis on codas. In *Proceedings of the UBC International Conference on Phonological Acquisition*, ed.

Barbara H. Bernhardt, John Gilbert, and David Ingram, pp. 62–75. Somerville, MA: Cascadilla Press.

Stemberger, Joseph, and Bernhardt, Barbara H. (1997a) Optimality Theory. In *The New Phonologies: Developments in Clinical Linguistics*, ed. M. J. Ball and R. D. Kent, pp. 211–45. San Diego, CA: Singular Publishing.

Stemberger, Joseph, and Bernhardt, Barbara H. (1997b) Phonological constraints and morphological development. In *Proceedings of the 21st Annual Boston University Conference on Language Development*, ed. Elizabeth Hughes, Mary Hughes, and Annabel Greenhill, pp. 603–14. Somerville, MA: Cascadilla Press.

Stemberger, Joseph, and Bernhardt, Barbara H. (1999a) Contiguity, metathesis, and infixation. In *The Proceedings of the West Coast Conference on Formal Linguistics 17*, ed. Kimary N. Shahin, Susan J. Blake, and Eun-Sook Kim, pp. 610–24. Stanford, CA: CSLI.

Stemberger, Joseph, and Bernhardt, Barbara H. (1999b) The emergence of faithfulness. In *The Emergence of Language (Carnegie Mellon Symposia on Cognition, 28th)*, ed. Brian MacWhinney, pp. 417–46. Mahwah, NJ: Lawrence Erlbaum Associates.

Steriade, Donca (1982) *Greek Prosodies and the Nature of Syllabification*. Doctoral dissertation. Cambridge, MA: Massachusetts Institute of Technology.

Steriade, Donca (1988) Reduplication and syllable transfer in Sanskrit and elsewhere. *Phonology* 5, 73–155.

Steriade, Donca (1995) Underspecification and markedness. In *Handbook of Phonological Theory*, ed. John Goldsmith, pp. 114–74. Cambridge, MA: Blackwell.

Steriade, Donca (1999a) Alternatives to syllable-based accounts of consonantal phonotactics. In *Proceedings of the 1998 Linguistics and Phonetics Conference*, ed. Osamu Fujimura, Brian Joseph, and B. Palek, pp. 205–42. Prague: Karolinum Press.

Steriade, Donca (1999b) Lexical conservatism in French adjectival liaison. In *Formal Perspectives on Romance Linguistics*, ed. J.-Marc Authier, Barbara Bullock, and Lisa Reid, pp. 243–70. Amsterdam: John Benjamins.

Steriade, Donca (1999c) Phonetics in phonology: The case of laryngeal neutralization. In *Papers in Phonology 3 (UCLA Working Papers in Linguistics 2)*, ed. Matthew Gordon, pp. 25–145. Los Angeles: Department of Linguistics, University of California.

Steriade, Donca (2000) Paradigm uniformity and the phonetics-phonology boundary. In *Acquisition and the Lexicon (Papers in Laboratory Phonology 5)*, ed. Janet Pierrehumbert and Michael Broe, pp. 313–34. Cambridge, MA: Cambridge University Press.

Stevens, Alan M. (1968) *Madurese Phonology and Morphology*. American Oriental Series 52. New Haven, CT: American Oriental Society.

Stockwell, Robert (1975) Problems in the interpretation of the Great English Vowel Shift. In *Essays on the Sound Pattern of English*, ed. Didier L. Goyvaerts and Geoffrey K. Pullum, pp. 330–53. Ghent, Belgium: E. Story-Scientia.

Strauss, Steven (1982) *Lexicalist Phonology of English and German*. Dordrecht: Foris.

Struijke, Caroline (1998) Reduplicant and output TETU in Kwakwala. In *University of Maryland Working Papers 7. Papers in Phonology*, ed. Haruko Fukazawa, Frida Morelli, Caro Struijke, and Y. Su, pp. 150–78. College Park: Department of Linguistics, University of Maryland.

Struijke, Caroline (2000a) *Reduplication, Feature Displacement and Existential Faithfulness*. Doctoral dissertation. College Park: University of Maryland.

Struijke, Caroline (2000b) Why constraint conflict can disappear in reduplication. In *Proceedings of the North East Linguistics Society 30*, ed. Masako Hirotani, pp. 613–26. Amherst, MA: GLSA. [Available on Rutgers Optimality Archive.]

Strunk, William, and White, E. B. (1972) *The Elements of Style*. 2nd ed. New York: Macmillan.

Suzuki, Keiichiro (1998) *A Typological Investigation of Dissimilation*. Doctoral dissertation. Tucson: University of Arizona.

Szpyra, Jolanta (1989) *The Phonology-Morphology Interface: Cycles, Levels and Words*. London: Routledge.

Teoh, Boon Seong (1988) *Aspects of Malay Phonology Revisited – A Non-linear Approach*. Doctoral dissertation. Urbana: University of Illinois.

Tesar, Bruce (1994) Parsing in Optimality Theory: A Dynamic Programming Approach. Report no. CU-CS-714-94. Boulder: Department of Computer Science, University of Colorado.

Tesar, Bruce (1995a) *Computational Optimality Theory*. Doctoral dissertation. Boulder: University of Colorado. [Available on Rutgers Optimality Archive.]

Tesar, Bruce (1995b) Computing Optimal Forms in Optimality Theory: Basic Syllabification. Report no. CU-CS-763-95. Boulder: Department of Computer Science, University of Colorado. [Available on Rutgers Optimality Archive.]

Tesar, Bruce (1997a) An iterative strategy for learning metrical stress in Optimality Theory. In *Proceedings of the 21st Annual Boston University Conference on Language Development*, ed. Elizabeth Hughes, Mary Hughes, and Annabel Greenhill, pp. 615–26. Somerville, MA: Cascadilla Press.

Tesar, Bruce (1997b) Multi-recursive constraint demotion. Unpublished manuscript. New Brunswick, NJ: Rutgers University. [Available on Rutgers Optimality Archive.]

Tesar, Bruce (1998a) Error-driven learning in Optimality Theory via the efficient computation of optimal forms. In *Is the Best Good Enough? Optimality and Competition in Syntax*, ed. Pilar Barbosa, Danny Fox, Paul Hagstrom, Martha McGinnis, and David Pesetsky, pp. 421–35. Cambridge, MA: MIT Press.

Tesar, Bruce (1998b) Using the mutual inconsistency of structural descriptions to overcome ambiguity in language learning. In *Proceedings of the North East Linguistic Society 28*, ed. Pius N. Tamanji and Kiyomi Kusumoto, pp. 469–83. Amherst, MA: GLSA.

Tesar, Bruce (1999) Robust interpretive parsing in metrical stress theory. In *The Proceedings of the West Coast Conference on Formal Linguistics 17*, ed. Kimary N. Shahin, Susan J. Blake, and Eun-Sook Kim. Stanford, CA: CSLI. [Available on Rutgers Optimality Archive.]

Tesar, Bruce (2000) On the roles of Optimality and strict domination in language learning. In *Optimality Theory: Phonology, Syntax, and Acquisition*, ed. Joost Dekkers, Frank van der Leeuw, and Jeroen van de Weijer, pp. 592–620. Oxford: Oxford University Press.

Tesar, Bruce, Grimshaw, Jane, and Prince, Alan (1999) Linguistic and cognitive explanation in Optimality Theory. In *What is Cognitive Science?*, ed. Ernest Lepore and Zenon Pylyshyn, pp. 295–326. Oxford: Blackwell.

Tesar, Bruce, and Smolensky, Paul (1994) The learnability of Optimality Theory. In *Proceedings of the Thirteenth West Coast Conference on Formal Linguistics*, ed. Raul

Aranovich, William Byrne, Susanne Preuss, and Martha Senturia, pp. 122–37. Stanford, CA: CSLI.

Tesar, Bruce, and Smolensky, Paul (1996) Learnability in Optimality Theory (Long Version). Report no. JHU_CogSci_96_3. Baltimore: Johns Hopkins University.

Tesar, Bruce, and Smolensky, Paul (1998) Learnability in Optimality Theory. *Linguistic Inquiry* 29, 229–68.

Tesar, Bruce, and Smolensky, Paul (2000) *Learnability in Optimality Theory*. Cambridge, MA: MIT Press.

Tranel, Bernard (1996a) Exceptionality in Optimality Theory and final consonants in French. In *Grammatical Theory and Romance Languages*, ed. Karen Zagona, pp. 275–91. Amsterdam: John Benjamins.

Tranel, Bernard (1996b) French liaison and elision revisited: A unified account within Optimality Theory. In *Aspects of Romance Linguistics*, ed. Claudia Parodi, Carlos Quicoli, Mario Saltarelli, and Maria Luisa Zubizarreta, pp. 433–55. Washington, DC: Georgetown University Press.

Tranel, Bernard (1998) Suppletion and OT: On the issue of the syntax/phonology interaction. In *Proceedings of the West Coast Conference on Formal Linguistics 16*, ed. E. Curtis, J. Lyle, and G. Webster, pp. 415–29. Stanford, CA: CSLI.

Trubetzkoy, N. S. (1939) *Grundzüge der Phonologie*. Prague: Travaux du cercle linguistique de Prague 7.

Truckenbrodt, Hubert (1995) *Phonological Phrases: Their Relation to Syntax, Focus, and Prominence*. Doctoral dissertation. Cambridge: Massachusetts Institute of Technology.

Truckenbrodt, Hubert (1999) On the relation between syntactic phrases and phonological phrases. *Linguistic Inquiry* 30, 219–56.

Tuller, Laurice (1992) The syntax of postverbal focus constructions in Chadic. *Natural Language and Linguistic Theory* 10, 303–34.

Turkel, William J. (1994) The acquisition of Optimality Theoretic systems. Unpublished manuscript. Vancouver: University of British Columbia. [Available on Rutgers Optimality Archive.]

Ueda, Isao, and Davis, Stuart (1999) Constraint-based analysis of Japanese rhotacism. In *Pathologies of Speech and Language: Advances in Clinical Phonetics and Linguistics*, ed. Ben Maassen and Paul Groenen, pp. 25–33. London: Whurr Publishers.

Urbanczyk, Suzanne (1996) *Patterns of Reduplication in Lushootseed*. Doctoral dissertation. Amherst: University of Massachusetts.

Urbanczyk, Suzanne (1999) A-templatic reduplication in Halq'eméylem'. In *The Proceedings of the West Coast Conference on Formal Linguistics 17*, ed. Kimary N. Shahin, Susan J. Blake, and Eun-Sook Kim, pp. 655–69. Stanford, CA: CSLI.

Uriagereka, Juan (1998) *Rhyme and Reason: An Introduction to Minimalist Syntax*. Cambridge, MA: MIT Press.

Ussishkin, Adam (1999) The inadequacy of the consonantal root: Modern Hebrew denominal verbs and output-output correspondence. *Phonology* 16, 401–42.

Velleman, Shelley L., and Shriberg, L. D. (1999) Metrical analysis of children with Suspected Developmental Apraxia of Speech and inappropriate stress. *Journal of Speech Language and Hearing Research* 42, 1444–60.

Velleman, Shelley L., and Vihman, Marilyn M. (1996) Metathesis highlights feature-by-position constraints. In *Proceedings of the UBC International Conference on Phono-*

logical Acquisition, ed. Barbara H. Bernhardt, John Gilbert, and David Ingram, pp. 173–86. Somerville, MA: Cascadilla Press.

Vennemann, Theo (1974) Words and syllables in natural generative grammar. In *Papers from the Parasession on Natural Phonology*, ed. Anthony Bruck, Robert A. Fox, and Michael W. La Galy, pp. 346–74. Chicago: Chicago Linguistic Society.

Vihman, Marilyn M., and Velleman, Shelley L. (2000) The construction of a first phonology. *Phonetica* 57, 255–66.

Vihman, Marilyn M., and Velleman, Shelley L. (in press) Phonetics and the origins of phonology. In *Conceptual and Empirical Foundations of Phonology*, ed. P. Burton-Roberts, P. Carr, and G. Docherty. Oxford: Oxford University Press.

Walker, Rachel (1996) A third parameter for unbounded stress. In *Proceedings of the North East Linguistic Society 26*, ed. Kiyomi Kusumoto, pp. 441–55. Amherst, MA: GLSA.

Walker, Rachel (1997a) Faith and markedness in Esimbi feature transfer. *Phonology at Santa Cruz* 5, 103–15.

Walker, Rachel (1997b) Prominence-driven stress. Unpublished manuscript. Santa Cruz: University of California. [Available on Rutgers Optimality Archive.]

Walker, Rachel (1998) *Nasalization, Neutral Segments, and Opacity Effects*. Doctoral dissertation. Santa Cruz: University of California.

Walker, Rachel (1999) Reinterpreting transparency in nasal harmony. Unpublished manuscript. Los Angeles: University of Southern California. [Available on Rutgers Optimality Archive.]

Walker, Rachel (2000) Nasal reduplication in Mbe affixation. *Phonology* 17, 65–115.

Walther, Markus (1996) OT-simple: A construction-kit approach to Optimality Theory implementation. Unpublished manuscript, Seminar für Allgemeine Sprachwissenschaft. Düsseldorf, Germany: Heinrich-Heine-Universität. [Available on Rutgers Optimality Archive.]

Wang, Chilin (1995) *The Acquisition of English Word-Final Obstruents by Chinese Speakers*. Doctoral dissertation. Stony Brook: State University of New York.

Wareham, Harold T. (1998) *Systematic Parametrized Complexity Analysis in Computational Phonology*. Doctoral Dissertation. Victoria, BC: University of Victoria. [Available on Rutgers Optimality Archive.]

Wartena, Christian (2000) A note on the complexity of Optimality Systems. Unpublished manuscript. Potsdam, Germany: University of Potsdam. [Available on Rutgers Optimality Archive.]

Wheeler, Deirdre (1981) *Aspects of a Categorial Theory of Phonology*. Doctoral dissertation. Amherst: University of Massachusetts.

Wheeler, Deirdre (1988) Consequences of some categorially motivated phonological assumptions. In *Categorial Grammars and Natural Language Structures*, ed. Richard Oehrle, Emmon Bach, and Deirdre Wheeler, pp. 467–88. Dordrecht: Reidel.

Wheeler, Deirdre, and Touretzky, David (1993) A connectionist implementation of cognitive phonology. In *The Last Phonological Rule: Reflections on Constraints and Derivations*, ed. John Goldsmith, pp. 146–72. Chicago: University of Chicago Press.

Williams, Edwin (1981) On the notions "lexically related" and "head of a word." *Linguistic Inquiry* 12, 245–74.

Wilson, Colin (1999) Consonant cluster neutralization and targeted constraints. Unpublished manuscript. Baltimore: Johns Hopkins University.

Wiltshire, Caroline (1992) *Syllabification and Rule Application in Harmonic Phonology.* Doctoral dissertation. Chicago: University of Chicago.

Wiltshire, Caroline (1998) Extending ALIGN constraints to new domains. *Linguistics* 36, 423–67.

Wolfe, Patricia M. (1970) Some theoretical questions on the historical English vowel shift. *Papers in Linguistics* 3, 221–35.

Wolfe, Patricia M. (1975) On the validity of the Chomsky-Halle analysis of the historical English vowel shift. In *Essays on the Sound Pattern of English*, ed. Didier L. Goyvaerts and Geoffrey K. Pullum, pp. 355–67. Ghent, Belgium: E. Story-Scientia.

Woolford, Ellen (to appear) Case patterns. In *OT Syntax*, ed. Géraldine Legendre, Jane Grimshaw, and Sten Vikner. Cambridge, MA: MIT Press.

Yip, Moira (1988) The Obligatory Contour Principle and phonological rules: A loss of identity. *Linguistic Inquiry* 19, 65–100.

Yip, Moira (1993) Cantonese loanword phonology and Optimality Theory. *Journal of East Asian Linguistics* 2, 261–92.

Yip, Moira (1996) Lexicon optimization in languages without alternations. In *Current Trends in Phonology: Models and Methods*, ed. J. Durand and B. Laks, pp. 757–88. Paris-X and Salford: University of Salford Publications.

Yip, Moira (1998) Identity avoidance in phonology and morphology. In *Morphology and Its Relation to Phonology and Syntax*, ed. Steven G. Lapointe, Diane K. Brentari, and Patrick M. Farrell, pp. 216–46. Stanford, CA: CSLI.

Zec, Draga (1993) Patterns of gemination and consonant loss: Pali, Japanese, and cross-linguistic. Handout from Rutgers Optimality Workshop I, New Brunswick, NJ.

Zoll, Cheryl (1993) Directionless syllabification and ghosts in Yawelmani. Unpublished manuscript. Berkeley: University of California. [Available on Rutgers Optimality Archive.]

Zoll, Cheryl (1996) *Parsing below the Segment in a Constraint-based Framework.* Doctoral dissertation. Berkeley: University of California.

Zoll, Cheryl (1997) Conflicting directionality. *Phonology* 14, 263–86.

Zoll, Cheryl (1998) Positional asymmetries and licensing. Unpublished manuscript. Cambridge: Massachusetts Institute of Technology. [Available on Rutgers Optimality Archive.]

Zonneveld, Wim (1976) A phonological exchange rule in Flemish Brussels. *Linguistic Analysis* 2, 109–14.

Zonneveld, Wim, and Nouveau, Dominique (to appear) Child word stress competence: An empirical approach. In *Fixing Priorities: Constraints in Phonological Acquisition*, ed. René Kager, Joe Pater, and Wim Zonneveld. Cambridge: Cambridge University Press.

Zubritskaya, Katya (1995) Markedness and sound change in OT. In *Proceedings of the North East Linguistic Society 25*, ed. Jill Beckman, pp. 249–64. Amherst, MA: GLSA.

Zubritskaya, Katya (1997) Mechanism of sound change in Optimality Theory. *Language Variation and Change* 9, 121–48.

Index of Names

Hewitt, Mark, 43, 180, 183
Hironymous, Patricia, 232
Hock, Hans, 63
Holt, D. Eric, 186n, 234
Homer, Kristin, 178, 181, 198, 230
de Hoop, Helen, 234n
Hooper [Bybee], Joan, 62, 183
Horvath, Barbara, 233
Horwood, Graham, 180
Hualde, José, 190n
Hudson, Grover, 178, 183
Huffman, Marie, 47n
van der Hulst, Harry, 63, 179–81
Hume, Elizabeth, 43, 167
Hung, Henrietta, 183
Hyman, Larry, 61, 182, 184

Idsardi, William, 44, 184, 234
Inkelas, Sharon, 179, 182, 188n
Ito, Junko, 43, 46n, 53, 64n, 77, 94, 179,
    182, 185, 188n, 190–1n, 230–3,
    235n
Iverson, Gregory, 62, 233

Jacobs, Haike, 62, 232, 234
Jakobson, Roman, 46n, 80, 179, 209, 212,
    216, 220, 229
Janda, Richard, 44
Jensen, John, 184
Joanisse, Marc, 236n
Joppen, Sandra, 232
Jun, Jongho, 185, 233
Jun, Sun-Ah, 185
Juszcyk, Peter, 231–2

Kager, René, 42–3, 183–5, 222, 230
Kaisse, Ellen, M. 185, 185
Karttunen, Lauri, 45n, 62, 185, 233
Katayama, Motoko, 185, 232
Katz, Gerrold, 198
Kaun, Abigail, 233
Kaye, Jonathan, 63, 178, 231
Kean, Mary-Louise, 15, 62, 244
Keer, Edward, 43–4, 178, 181, 186n, 190n,
    201, 230, 234n
Kenstowicz, Michael, 44, 50, 61–2, 178,
    181–5, 189n, 191n, 221
Kikuchi, Seiichiro, 185
Kim, Chin-Wu, 63, 185
Kim, No-Ju, 185
Kiparsky, Paul, 40, 44, 62–3, 64n, 74, 165,
    167, 174, 178, 184–5, 191n, 216,
    227–9, 233
Kirchner, Robert, 43, 47n, 64n, 162, 179,
    181, 222–5, 233–4
Kisseberth, Charles, 50, 53–4, 58, 61–3, 74,
    101, 178, 187n, 191n, 221, 236n
Kissock, Madelyn, 185

Kitagawa, Yoshihisa, 43, 182, 185, 188n,
    230
Kitahara, Mafuyu, 232
Kitto, Catherine, 182
Klausenburger, Jürgen, 63
Koskenniemi, Kimmo, 62, 164
Koutsoudas, Andreas, 44, 62, 169
Kraemer, Martin, 185
Kraska-Szlenk, Iwona, 185
Kučera, Henry, 63

Labov, William, 227, 229
LaCharité, Darlene, 63
Lakoff, George, 62
Lamontagne, Greg, 43
Langendoen, D. Terence, 42, 178, 186n
Lapointe, Steven, 183
Larson, Gary, 64
Lasnik, Howard, 55–7, 64n, 222
Leben, Will, 64n
Lee, Hanjung, 44, 179, 181–2
Lee, Minkyung, 185
Lee, Shinsook, 233
van der Leeuw, Frank, 182, 185
Legendre, Géraldine, 41–3, 59, 61, 64, 124,
    178, 181–2, 188n, 193, 198, 230,
    232–3, 234n
Lehman, F. K., 63
Levelt, Clara, 209–10, 231–2
Levelt, Willem, 232
Lieber, Rochelle, 184
Liljencrants, Johan, 225
Lindblom, Björn, 220, 225
van der Linde, K. J., 232
Lleó, Conxita, 232
Lombardi, Linda, 43–4, 112, 179, 181, 188n,
    232
Lovins, Julie, 62–3
Lowenstamm, Jean, 63
Lubowicz, Anna, 43, 187n

MacEachern, Margaret, 233
Malone, Joseph, 180
Marantz, Alec, 63, 178, 190n
Mascaró, Joan, 153, 167, 183, 190n
Massar, A., 232
McCarthy, John, 16, 36, 43, 46–7n, 52, 63,
    121, 128, 178–85, 186–91n, 216,
    230–1, 235n, 241, 243
McCawley, James, 62
McGarrity, Laura, 185, 216, 232
Mehler, Jacques, 232
Menn, Lise, 216, 232
Merchant, Jason, 185
Mester, Armin, 43, 63, 64n, 77, 94, 179,
    181–3, 185, 188n, 191n, 230–3, 235n
Miglio, Viola, 43
Miyata, Yoshiro, 61, 64

Mohanan, K. P., 128, 174, 177, 185, 233
Moll, Laura, 187n
Moravcsik, Edith, 178
Morelli, Frida, 44, 181
Morén, Bruce, 181
Moreton, Elliott, 24, 45n, 101–2, 180, 184,
  187n, 190n, 216, 218, 234n
Morin, Yves-Charles, 63
Morris, Richard, 233
Morrisette, Michele, 232
Müller, Gereon, 182, 230
Mutaka, Ngessimo, 184
Myers, James, 191n
Myers, Scott, 63, 64n, 145, 157, 178–9,
  189n, 233

Nagy, Naomi, 233
Nash, David, 183
Nathan, Geoffrey, 62, 232
Neeleman, Ad, 178, 185, 199, 230, 234n
Nelson, Nicole, 181
Nespor, Marina, 64n, 183, 189n, 232
Nessly, Larry, 63
Nevin, Bruce, 233
Newmeyer, Frederick, 47n, 63, 64n, 93, 179
Ní Chiosáin, Máire, 233, 236n
Nishiyama, Kunio, 234
Noll, Craig, 44, 62, 169
van Noord, Gertjan, 233
Noske, Roland, 233
Nouveau, Dominique, 232
Noyer, Rolf, 181, 184, 232

O'Connor, Kathleen, 232
Odden, David, 64n, 184, 189n
Odden, Mary, 184
Ohala, Diane, 232
Ohala, John, 220
Ohno, Kazutoshi, 187n
van Oostendorp, Marc, 184–5, 231, 233
Orgun, C. Orhan, 43, 162, 178–9, 184–5,
  230
Ota, Mitsuhiko, 232

Padgett, Jaye, 64n, 77, 94, 128, 179, 190n,
  233, 236n
Paradis, Carole, 63, 137, 145, 180, 184
Paradis, Johanne, 231, 232
Pater, Joe, 62, 179, 182, 187n, 210, 216,
  231–3, 235n
Payne, David, 47n, 191n
Pensalfini, Rob, 46n
Peperkamp, Sharon, 182, 185
Perlmutter, David, 55, 64n, 183
Pesetsky, David, 47n, 63, 178, 230, 234n
Pierrehumbert, Janet, 64, 189n, 236n
Piggott, Glyne, 189n
Plag, Ingo, 179, 232, 234

Plunkett, K., 232
Polgardi, Krisztina, 63
Poole, Geoffrey, 16
Poser, William, 167, 183
Postal, Paul, 198
Potter, Brian, 185
Prentice, D. J., 188–9n
Prince, Alan, 1–3, 6, 7, 11–12, 21–2, 28, 32,
  36, 42–4, 46n, 47n, 54–6, 61–4, 77, 80,
  114, 121, 128, 131, 152, 167, 178–85,
  186–91n, 197, 218–20, 230–1, 233,
  235n, 237–8, 241, 243–4
Pulleyblank, Douglas, 52, 63–4, 185, 189n,
  222, 231, 233
Pullum, Geoffrey, 62, 189n
Pyle, Charles, 63

Ramus, F., 232
Raymond, William, 178, 181, 188n, 198,
  230
Reiss, Charles, 185, 186n, 216, 231–3
Revithiadou, Anthi, 179, 180
Reynolds, William, 233
Riad, Tomas, 229
Rice, Curtis, 189n
Rice, Keren, 40, 43, 63
Rickford, John, 230
Ringen, Catherine, 233
Roark, Brian, 232
Roberts, Ian, 16
Robson, Barbara, 63
Roca, Iggy, 178, 184, 185
Rose, Yvan, 232
Rosenthall, Sam, 46n, 180–1, 187n
Ross, John, 63
Rubach, Jerzy, 177, 184–5
Russell, Kevin, 178, 183

Sagey, Elizabeth, 53
Samek-Lodovici, Vieri, 7, 43–4, 45n, 63,
  107, 109–10, 126–7, 178–81, 188–9n,
  218–19, 230–1, 233, 234n, 238
Sanders, Gerald, 44, 62, 169, 185
Sandoval, Maria, 44
Sapir, Edward, 182, 189n
Satta, Giorgio, 233
Scarpa, E., 232
Schaefer, Ronald, 187n
Schane, Sanford, 61
Schiller, Niels, 232
Schourup, Lawrence, 63
Scobbie, James, 62
Scott, N. C., 191n
Selkirk, Elisabeth, 13, 43, 64n, 125, 127,
  137, 148, 174, 183–5, 188–9n
Sells, Peter, 183, 230, 236n
Shaw, Patricia, 185
Shen, Tong, 185

Index of Constraints

305

Index of Languages

Index of Topics

Page numbers in bold indicate the primary discussion of a topic. Small capitals are used for constraint names, which appear in the index of constraints.

ba pseudo-problem, 243–4
blocking (of a process), **26–8**, 53, 68, 74–5, 92, 95, 100–1, 122, 188n, 214, *see also* triggering
  process-specific constraint, 103–6
  in rule-based theory, 53–4, 58
  by syntactic filter, 56–9

Cancellation/Domination Lemma (C/D Lemma), **28–9**, 33, 37, 44n, 68, 195, 202–5
candidate comparison, **3–6**, 30, 32–3, 76, *see also* tableau
  importance in allomorphy, 152–6
  inherent to OT, 3, 33
  not by constraints, 40–1
  in other theories, 16, 137–8
  role of EVAL, 6–8, 109, 218–20, *see also* EVAL
candidate set, **3**, 143, 159, 166–9, *see also* GEN
  fully faithful candidate, 35, 77, 101, 110, 195
  includes null output, *see* null output
  infinite size, 64n, 216–21
  interface conditions, 194
  perpetual losers, 218–21, *see also* harmonic bounding
  relation to input, 9, 199–200, 239
  selecting informative candidates, 34–6
  in syntax, 194–6, 198–9, 200–1
case marking, 29, 81, 126–7, 199, *see also* CASE-ADJ
chain shift
  approaches in OT, 43, 161–2
  circular, 102–3
  in harmonic serialism, 160–1
  opacity of, 176–7
chicken-egg effect (of parallelism), 143–6
clash (stress), 52, 64n, 152, 183, *see also* metrical phonology
clitic, 26, 81, 93, 123–4, 125, 147–9, 182
comprehension/production dilemma, 214–15
computation
  complexity of OT, 233
  distinct from grammar, 9–10, 217
  infinity of candidates, 9–10, 64n, 216–18, 239
  model for OT, 216–18, 233
CON, **11–12**, 17–22, 102, 119–20, 187n, 218–21, *see also* constraint; edge Alignment; fixed hierarchy; local conjunction
  arguing against a constraint, 38–9, 74, 158, 199–200
  arguing for a constraint, 36–8, 103, 161–2
  constraint typology, 13–22
  implicational universals, 15, 117–20

introducing new constraints, 16, 36–8, 39–42
specific theory important, 17, 38, 107–8, 112–17, 119–20, 197
universality of, 11–12, 18–19, 120, 130–1, 208, 213
conflict, constraint, **4–5**, 12, 15–16, 109, 121, 145, 200, 227, 229, 242, *see also* constraint ranking; ranking argument
connectionism, 4, 18, 59–61, 65, 223–4, 235–6n, 240
conspiracy, **53–5**, 63, 71, **95–101**, 168, *see also* Duplication Problem; homogeneity of target/heterogeneity of process
  acquisition, 214
  diachronic, 229
  genesis of OT, 54–5
  not explained by filters, 58–9, 100
constraint, *see also* CON; edge Alignment; faithfulness; markedness
  active, **12**, 26–30, 53, 109–10, 120, 127–8, 164, 174, 242, *see also* emergence of the unmarked
  arguing for/against, 36–9, 74, 103, 158, 161–2, 199–200
  inviolable (in other theories), *see* principles
  language-particular, 18–19, 43, 47n, 233, 235n
  opposite constraints, 127–8, 140–2
  process-specific, 103–6
  schema for, 17–19, 186n, *see also* edge Alignment; local conjunction
  stringency relation, *see* stringency
  theory of constraints, *see* CON
  triggering specific repair, 106–7
  types, **13–15**, 46n, 101–3
  weighted, *see* weighted constraints
constraint alignment, *see* harmonic alignment
constraint and repair theory, *see* rule-and-constraint-based theory
constraint conjunction, *see* local conjunction
constraint hierarchy, 3, **7**, 10, 73, 92, 103–8, 202–5, 227, 242, 245, *see also* constraint ranking; factorial typology; fixed hierarchy; globality; modularity; power hierarchy; variation
constraint ranking, **3–8**, *see also* factorial typology; fixed hierarchy; ranking argument; strictness of strict domination
  in acquisition, 208–10, *see also* Recursive Constraint Demotion
  additive, 224
  compared to parameters, *see* parameter
  continuous scale, 228
  diachronic re-ranking, 229–30, 234
  diagram for, 73

initial state, *see* initial state
irrelevant to losers, 218–20
tied, *see* optionality; partial ordering of
   constraints; tied candidates; variation
transitivity, 6, 36, 105
constraint violability, **3–4**, 15–16, 23, 26, 67,
   120, 240–1, 234, *see also* constraint
   violation; economy; emergence of the
   unmarked; extremism; non-uniformity
   in acquisition, 208, 210–12
   relation to universality, **11**, 58
constraint violation, **4–5**, 20, 23, 40, 241, *see
   also* constraint violability; minimal
   violation
   gradient, *see* edge Alignment
   multiple, 5–6, **135–6**, *see also* mark
      cancellation
contrast, *see also* distribution; faithfulness
   in Dispersion Theory, 225–7
   exemplifying non-uniformity, 124, 182
   from grammar not lexicon, *see* richness of
      the base
   in Natural Phonology, 50–1
   neutralization, 87–8, 179, 201
   role of faithfulness, 74, 84, 91, 179, 201,
      see also faithfulness
control (of *Pro*), 41
convergence
   in harmonic serialism, 11, 159–61, 166–9,
      184
   in Minimalism, 134, 164
correspondence theory, *see* faithfulness
cycle
   in OT, 170–2, 184
   in phonology and morphology, 49, 172,
      177, 184
   Strict Cycle, 43, 146

Declarative Phonology, 49, 56, 62, 164
default
   and emergence of the unmarked, 130
   and language typology, 130, 148–9, 156
   in Minimalism, 133–4
   in phonology, 86, 150–1
   in syntax, 90–1, 156
   in underspecification theory, 132–4
deletion
   in acquisition, 213–14
   in computation, 217
   in phonology, 13, 25–9, 35, 54, 58, 89,
      93–4, 95–100, 102, 106–7, 111,
      112–13, 137, 165–7, 167–70, 174–5,
      187n, 190n
   in syntax, 89, 91, 95, 123, 199–200,
      201
disordered language, 232
Dispersion Theory, 225–8, 236n, *see also*
   contrast

dissimilation, 18, 43, 93, 214
distribution, 82–91, 178–9, 241
   complementary, 84–7
   contextual neutralization, 87–9
   and emergence of the unmarked, 130
   non-uniform, 121, 124
   and optionality, 200
   overlapping, 84
   in syntax, 42, 89–91, 118–19, 156
do-support, 89–91, 121, 195–8
domination relation, *see* constraint ranking;
   EVAL; strictness of strict domination
Duplication Problem, 71–5, 178, *see also*
   conspiracy; richness of the base

economy
   in constraint and repair theory, 54, 100,
      137–8
   localistic approach, 137–8
   in OT, 23–4, 111, 134–8
   OT compared to Minimalism, 14, 137–8,
      240–1
edge Alignment, **17–18**, 43, 181–2, 184–5,
   see also ALIGN, COINCIDE, HEAD-
   LEFT/RIGHT, SPEC-LEFT
   of affixes, *see* infixation
   of clitics, *see* clitic
   compared to cyclicity, 170–2
   compared to parameters, 127–8
   focus, *see* focus
   gradient/minimal evaluation, 18, 114–15,
      123–4, 130–1, 135–6, 189n
   of heads, *see* ALIGN: ALIGN-L(Ft, Hd(Ft));
      HEAD-LEFT/RIGHT; IDENT:
      IDENT$_\sigma$(nasal)
   of metrical constituents, *see* metrical
      phonology
   non-uniformity in, 123–4
   opposite constraints, *see* constraint
   phrasing, *see* sentence phonology
   relation to ANCHOR, 46n
   relation to edge-based theory, 127–8,
      184–5
   universality of, 18–19
effort minimization
   and additive ranking, 224
   in functionalist phonology, 222–3
   and minimalist Economy, 14
   in Natural Phonology, 50–1
   need for abstraction, 224–5
Elsewhere Condition, 44, 149, 174, 189n
emergence of the unmarked (TETU),
   129–34, 153–6, 182, *see also*
   constraint: active
   in acquisition, 208, 212–13, 214
   compared to parameters, 110, 131–2
   connection to typology, 130, *see also*
      factorial typology

without parallelism, 158–9, 169–70,
170–2, *see also* harmonic serialism
Government-Binding Theory (GB), 55–8,
63, 163
gradient evaluation, *see* edge Alignment;
EVAL; extremism; minimal violation

harmonic alignment, **21–2**, 44, 117–19, *see
also* fixed hierarchy
harmonic ascent, **101–3**, 108, 142, 163,
169–70, 180, 190n, 218, 234n
harmonic bounding, **23–4**, 44, 151, 154
choosing informative candidates, 35
collective, 218–19
role in universals, 39, 110–11, 112–14
harmonic completeness, 117, 119, 188n, *see
also* inventory
harmonic serialism, 11, 159–63, *see also*
serial derivation
limited (LHS), 167–70
harmony (phonological process), 83–7, 104,
198–9, 210, 235n, *see also* assimilation
Harmony Theory, 59–61, 64
harmony threshold, 198–9, *see also* null
output
heads, constraints on, *see* *NUCLEUS/LIQUID;
*NUCLEUS/VOWEL; ALIGN: ALIGN-
L(Ft, Hd(Ft)); HEAD-LEFT/RIGHT;
IDENT: IDENT$_\sigma$(nasal)
hierarchy, linguistic, *see* scale
historical change, 49, 186n, 228–9, 234
homogeneity of target/heterogeneity of
process, **25–6**, 51, 68, 93–101, 146,
154, 179
in acquisition, 208, 213–14
diachronic, 229
homophony, avoidance of, 226, 236n, *see
also* contrast; Dispersion Theory

implicational universals, *see* CON; fixed
hierarchy; scale; universals
inclusivity, *see* freedom of analysis
infixation
and edge Alignment, 19, 181
exemplifies emergence of the unmarked,
130–1
exemplifies extremism, 136
exemplifies minimal violation, 130–1
factorial typology and CON, 114–17
initial state, 80, 206–13, 215, 231, *see also*
acquisition; learnability
input, 3, 10–11, **13–14**, 42, 67–8, 69–70,
73–4, 101–2, 110–11, 138–9, 153, *see
also* faithfulness; harmonic serialism;
learnability; Lexical Phonology; lexicon
optimization; richness of the base
in early acquisition, 208–9
and GEN, 8–9

in (morpho)syntax, 81, 119, 193–6,
199–200, 201, 230
insertion
and infinity of candidates, 9, 216–18
lexical, *see* allomorphy
in phonology (epenthesis), 13, 23–4,
26–8, 33, 54, 58, 89, 91, 93, 95, 102,
135–7, 157–8, 170, 171, 182, 187n,
243, *see also* DEP
in syntax, 89–91, 199, 201, *see also*
FULL-INT
integrality (of OT grammar), *see* globality
interaction, **22–30**, 44, *see also* blocking;
triggering
"as little/much as possible," *see* economy;
extremism
"except when," **27**, 121
"only when needed," 24, 54, 84, 86,
89–91, 100, 130, 147, 156, 196
special case/default case, *see* default
"worst of the worst," *see* local
conjunction
interface
morphology/syntax, 123–4, *see also*
ALIGN: ALIGN-L(Clitic, S), ALIGN-
L/R(Focus, VP); allomorphy
phonology/morphology, 19, 124, 181, *see
also* ALIGN: ALIGN-L/R(Lex, PWd),
ALIGN-L/R(XP, PPh), ALIGN-PFX;
EXH(PPh); MORPH-REAL
phonology/syntax, 19, 43, 125, 127–8, *see
also* PWDCON; allomorphy; infixation;
reduplication; sentence phonology
inventory, 20, 29, 57, **68–71**, 244
derived from constraint interaction, 70,
71–6, 76–7, 81–2, 91, 194, *see also*
absolute ill-formedness; distribution;
richness of the base
learning, 205–6
non-uniformity effects, 124

last resort, *see* default
learnability, 44, 202–7, 218, 227, 230–2,
241, *see also* acquisition
constraint demotion, 203–5, 219, 230
of constraints, 19, 47n, 233, 235n
with inconsistent data, 233
initial state, *see* initial state
in Natural Phonology, *see* Natural
Phonology
parameters, 55, 131–2, 180–1, 211–12
of rules, 48–9, 170–1, 209, 212–13
subset problem, *see* subset problem
of underlying representations, 78–80,
214–16, *see also* lexicon optimization
lenition, 222–4
Lexical-Functional Grammar (LFG), 55, 93,
164